Modelling and Analysis in Arms Control

NATO ASI Series

Advanced Science Institutes Series

A series presenting the results of activities sponsored by the NATO Science Committee, which aims at the dissemination of advanced scientific and technological knowledge, with a view to strengthening links between scientific communities.

The Series is published by an international board of publishers in conjunction with the NATO Scientific Affairs Division

A Life Sciences **B Physics**	Plenum Publishing Corporation London and New York
C Mathematical and Physical Sciences	D. Reidel Publishing Company Dordrecht, Boston, Lancaster and Tokyo
D Behavioural and Social Sciences **E Applied Sciences**	Martinus Nijhoff Publishers Boston, The Hague, Dordrecht and Lancaster
F Computer and Systems Sciences **G Ecological Sciences** **H Cell Biology**	Springer-Verlag Berlin Heidelberg New York London Paris Tokyo

Series F: Computer and Systems Sciences Vol. 26

Modelling and Analysis in Arms Control

Edited by

Rudolf Avenhaus
Reiner K. Huber

Federal Armed Forces University Munich
Werner-Heisenberg-Weg 39, 8014 Neubiberg/FRG

John D. Kettelle

Ketron, Inc., Rosslyn Center, 1700 N. Moore Street
Arlington, VA 22209/USA

Springer-Verlag
Berlin Heidelberg New York London Paris Tokyo
Published in cooperation with NATO Scientific Affairs Divison

Proceedings of the NATO Advanced Research Workshop on Modelling and Analysis of Arms Control Problems held in Spitzingsee/FRG, October 20–25, 1985

Co-sponsored by the VW Foundation

ISBN-13:978-3-642-82945-1 e-ISBN-13:978-3-642-82943-7
DOI: 10.1007/978-3-642-82943-7

Library of Congress Cataloging in Publication Data. NATO Advanced Research Workshop on Modelling and Analysis of Arms Control Problems (1985 : Spitzingsee, Germany) Modelling and analysis in arms control. (NATO ASI series. Series F, Computer and systems sciences ; vol. 26) "Published in cooperation with NATO Scientific Affairs Division." Includes index. 1. Arms control—Research—Congresses. 2. Arms control—Mathematical models—Congresses. 3. Arms control—Decision making—Congresses. I. Avenhaus, Rudolf. II. Huber, Reiner K. III. Kettelle, John D. IV. Title. V. Series: NATO ASI series. Series F, Computer and system sciences ; no. 26. JX1974.N395 1985 327.1'74 86-29658
ISBN-13:978-3-642-82945-1 (U.S.)

Softcover reprint of the hardcover 1st edition 1986

2145/3140-543210

EDITORS' PREFACE

This book presents the results of an international workshop on Modelling and Analysis of Arms Control Problems held in Spitzingsee near Munich in October 1985 under the joint sponsorship of NATO's Scientific Affairs Division and the Volkswagen Foundation.

The idea for this workshop evolved in 1983, as a consequence of discussions in the annual Systems Science Seminar at the Computer Science Department of the Federal Armed Forces University Munich on the topic of Quantitative Assessment in Arms Control[1]. There was wide agreement among the contributors to that seminar and its participants that those efforts to assess the potential contributions of systems and decision sciences, as well as systems analysis and mathematical modelling, to arms control issues should be expanded and a forum should be provided for this activity. It was further agreed that such a forum should include political scientists and policy analysts working in the area of arms control.

The ensuing activities were greatly facilitated by the Scientific Affairs Division of NATO which provided funds for an organizing committee to convene and work out a proposal for a meeting to be supported by the NATO Science Committee's Advanced Research Workshop (ARW) program. Prof. Yves Jeanclos of the University of Strasbourg joined these editors in the organizing committee. His role in getting French scientists involved in the workshop is highly appreciated. In addition to the ARW grant, substantial financial assistance was also provided by the Volkswagen Foundation. We wish to express our gratitude to these two institutions and their representatives, in particular to Prof. John A. Buzacott of the ARW Panel, Dr. Mario Di Lullo of NATO's Scientific Affairs Division, and Dr. Alfred Schmidt of the Volkswagen Foundation.

Thanks are also extended to Dr. John Fichtner, who assisted in organizing the scientific program and the related correspondence, and to Mrs. Carin Jones, who carried the brunt of administrative and clerical work throughout the

---

[1] The proceedings were published in 1984 under the same title by Plenum Press (Avenhaus and Huber, Eds.).

planning and operation of the workshop and the preparation of the manuscript for this book. Thirty-nine scientists and analysts from ten countries participated in the workshop. Their competence and dedicated involvement as presenters of position papers, discussants, panelists, rapporteurs and working group chairmen made the workshop a productive and enjoyable event. We are particularly indebted to Secretary of State Dr. Lothar Rühl of the German Ministry of Defence for his interesting opening statement and analysis of some recent arms control proposals with respect to their implications for crisis and arms race stability, to Prof. Paul Bracken of the Yale University for his stimulating keynote address outlining some key arms control issues and strategic trends that bear on those, and to Dr. Gwyn Prins of the University of Cambridge for his acuminous, albeit not uncontroversial, historical analysis of arms control and its lessons.

Last but not least, the editors want to thank the contributors to these proceedings for their patience and diligence in preparing the papers and providing inputs to the working group reports compiled by Dr. Sydell P. Gold, Dr. Ernest Gilman and Prof. Derry W. Jones to all of whom we are deeply indebted.

It is noteworthy that several papers in this book had not been contributed to the workshop originally. Rather, they address aspects that surfaced as a result of the discussions and interactions throughout the workshop. The views expressed by the authors are strictly personal ones and do not necessarily represent those of the institutions of their affiliation.

Thanks also go to Mr. Julyan Watts and to Springer-Verlag for their technical assistance in preparing the manuscript of this book.

Neubiberg and Arlington, June 1986

Rudolf Avenhaus | Reiner K. Huber | John D. Kettelle

CONTENTS

Part III

Negotiations

Part IV

Verification and Post-Agreements Assessments

INTRODUCTION: SYSTEMS ANALYSIS AND MODELLING IN ARMS CONTROL[1)]

Rudolf Avenhaus and Reiner K. Huber
Institut für Angewandte Systemforschung und Operations Research
Fakultät für Informatik
Universität der Bundeswehr München
D-8014 Neubiberg, FRG

1. BACKGROUND AND RATIONALE

Even though desires for limiting, if not eliminating, weapons and armies seem to be almost as old as human society[2)], not until the invention and accumulation of nuclear weapons, with their potential of endangering the very survival of mankind, have these desires been transmuted into internationally accepted imperatives. Since the late 1950's, the superpowers have been engaged in a series of bilateral negotitations on the limitation of strategic nuclear weapons, which resulted in several agreements in the 1960's and 1970's[3)].

However, perhaps except for the Anti-Ballistic Missile (ABM) Treaty of 1972, these agreements have done little to curb the growth of nuclear arsenals. On the contrary, despite the continual bilateral and multilateral negotiations, the last 15 years have witnessed a rather significant build-up of nuclear and conventional capabilities by the Soviet Union. This and the ensuing Western reactions contribute to the widely held perception of

---

[1)] Sections of this contribution are contained in a joint paper with John D. Kettelle published in the Journal of the German Society of Operations Research (DGOR) "OR Spectrum" 3/86. The authors thank its publishers for the permission of reproducing the respective parts.

[2)] See, e.g. ISAIAH 2,4: "And he shall judge among the nations, and shall rebuke many people: and they shall beat their swords into plowshares, and their spears into pruning hooks: nation shall not lift up sword against nation, neither shall they learn war anymore". The Holy Bible, King James Version, p. 554

[3)] E.g., Antarctic Treaty (1959), Partial Test Ban Treaty (1963), Outer Space Treaty (1967), Establishment of a direct communication link (1967), Non-Proliferation Treaty (1968), ABM-Treaty (1972), SALT I (1972), Threshold Test Ban Treaty (1974), SALT II (1979, not ratified). See also Goldblat (1982).

NATO ASI Series, Vol. F 26
Modelling and Analysis in Arms Control
Edited by R. Avenhaus et al.

an unprecedented arms race. Many have even raised serious doubts whether the nationalized structure of today's civilization is in fact capable of making and adhering to effective arms control agreements (see, e.g., J. SCHELL (1982)). Indeed, the very perception of that incapability seems to have been one of the motivations for the Strategic Defense Initiative (SDI) because it might offer the chance for unilaterally channelling the arms race into a less dangerous and potentially more stable direction.

Admittedly simple mathematical models of battle interactions lend support to the basic idea underlying SDI of a *defense emphasis strategy*. For example, AVENHAUS et al. (1983) have shown that there exists no stable equilibrium for antagonistic conventional forces which are equally capable of offensive and defensive operations. For such forces, the mutual desire to have sufficiently large armaments for a successful defense leads to an arms race. However, this dilemma may be alleviated by force structures which specialize in defensive at the expense of offensive capabilities. HUBER and HOFMANN (1984) point out that there would be a compelling military and economic rationale for adopting such structures if the *defense efficiency hypothesis* could be verified, i.e., if forces specialized in defense operations could be more efficient in exploiting the basic defense advantage than multipurpose forces. The strategic nuclear equivalent of this conventional force hypothesis would imply a higher cost-effectiveness for defensive than for offensive strategic systems.

The proponents of SDI must eventually base their case on the satisfaction of this hypothesis. In fact, the initial (research and development) phase of SDI is inescapably only a feasibility study. If incremental defense proves more expensive than incremental offense, implementation of SDI would be self-defeating. But even if the cost-effectiveness can be established, there are obvious instability hazards to be encountered during the transition from an offense-offense posture (such as today's Mutually Assured Destruction) to a defense-defense one (of Mutually Assured Survival). In the conventional arena, similar arguments are voiced against a transition from today's all-purpose force structures to ones in which the offensive and defensive capabilities are decoupled and defense is emphasized. However, from a theoretical standpoint it seems somewhat paradoxial that those who most vehemently oppose SDI in the Federal Republic of Germany simultaneously endorse conventional "*defensive defense*" and vice versa (see, e.g., von MÜLLER and DÜRR (1983), DÜRR (1985), and SCHULTE (1985) and (1986)). This may reflect a fundamental lack of understanding the dynamics of today's security systems, an area that by its nature is largely and fortunately devoid of empirical validation. Thus, what little chance there may be for a rational resolution of arms contol and security issues, one of its essential prerequisites seems to be a structured holistic approach that considers the interdependencies and interactions of arms control, weapon systems and force planning and acquisition, economic interest and many others. Today, there is little interdisciplinary discussion of such matters. Weapon system planners are mainly concerned with the cost-effectiveness of specific systems and force planners with the military effectiveness of force structures, both disregarding arms control implications in most cases. Even the academic debate of security issues is frequently still devoid of an interdisciplinary analytical approach[4].

Against this background, these authors have attempted an international mobilization of the capabilities of the analytic community relevant to arms control. Thanks to the generous sponsorship by the NATO Science Committee and the Volkswagen Foundation they succeeded in organizing a one-week international expert workshop in October 1985 some of the findings of which are summarized below.

2. THE THREE PRINCIPAL PROBLEM AREAS

In his foreword to Francis P. HOEBER's book "How Little is Enough?" (1981), Elmo ZUMWALDT deplores the fact that many participants in the U.S. public debate consider the pursuit of nuclear arms reduction as an end in itself rather than as an integral part of policies designed to enhance national security. One must agree with ZUMWALDT at least insofar as the disappointing results of arms control in the 1970's seem to indicate that reduction of weapons and constraints of their build-up - the principal theme pursued by the U.S. in the SALT negotiations - should not be considered an objective but rather a long-term result of arms control. But does enhancement of national security incorporate a viable goal? It appears that this is

[4] For example, in a recent (29-30 May 1986) conference on "Alternative Military Concepts for NATO" at Harvard University the implications of alternatives were discussed almost exclusively with regard to their military operational effectiveness and in qualitative terms only. In addition, the main ingredient of operational effectiveness was considered to be flexibility, a notion that may be quite incompatible, not only with arms control objectives but also with regard to resource constraints.

exactly what the Soviets have consistently pursued in their own approach to arms control which - in combination with their somewhat paranoid threat perception - has lead to today's rather dismal situation. Thus, enhancing national security as an objective for arms control implies that it can be accomplished without deference to the reciprocal goal of the antagonist and, just as bad, one's allies perceiving the result as an impairment of their respective securities. This suggests that *nonimpairment of mutual security* might be a more reasonable goal or, more accurately, a boundary condition for arms control. Whether it is a practical guideline for negotiations will depend largely on the acceptance of the assessment tools available to the negotiators[5].

Another aspect that is frequently overlooked in the public debate relates to the fact that arms control is embedded in an enduring competition between societal systems the fundamental goals of which are historically diverse. This a priori divergence of goals limits mutual trust and makes the verifiability of agreements an essential component of real progress in arms control.

Furthermore, the arms control negotiation process involves much more than the bilateral bargaining at the conference table which, superficially, might be considered to resemble a two-person game. Statements at or off the negotiation table frequently seem to be aimed more at third parties, or at home constituencies, than at the opponent's negotiation team. In fact, Uwe NERLICH (1985) observes that in many Western democracies arms control may have become more of a domestic gambit than part of a rational security policy. In his contribution to this book Gwyn PRINS maintains that, being a form of *implicit negotiation*, independent actions engendering appropriate reciprocal actions may often be the superior choice over formal negotiations. Thus, arms control negotiations must address some of the problems implicit in multi-person, n-staged games that present a challenging field of unsolved methodological problems.

---

[5] A logical consequence of the goal of *mutual national security* and *international stability* would seem to be a mutual acceptance of the present international (and internal) status quo. There are many indications that neither side has such an acceptance. This essential complication must be confronted internally by the antagonists if they are to come to the negotiation table with a readiness for workable trade-offs.

Based on such considerations, the workshop was organized around three principal problem areas which were treated in parallel working groups on

- Pre-Arms Control Assessment focussing on criteria and methods for the evaluation of the military-strategic situation and force equilibria;
- Negotiations including negotiation strategies and information management;
- Verification emphasizing its decision-theoretical aspects.

2.1 Pre-Arms Control Assessment

Based on a review of the past fifteen years of arms control negotiations, the working group identified, among others, deficiencies in the assessment of the stability and robustness of force structures, force posture asymmetries, the linkage between strategic and theater capabilities, and the verifiability and negotiability of arms control proposals and their economic effects. The emphasis of the discussions was on the aspects related to the military-strategic situation and to force equilibria.

2.1.1 Definitions

Stability: The foremost goal of arms control is considered to be, for the near term, the achievement and enforcement of *crisis stability* and, in the longer term, the dampening and eventually curtailment of the arms build-up (*arms race stability*) in such a way as to preclude the development of crisis-unstable postures.

Arms Race: In the context of two countries, the process behind an arms race resembles an action-reaction mechanism in which a real or perceived change Δx_i in the military power X of one country causes the other country to implement a counter-vailing change Δy_i in its military power Y. This in turn leads to a further reaction Δx_{i+1} of the former country followed by a reaction Δy_{i+1} by the latter, and so on (see Fig. 1).

Arms Race Stability: At a given military capability arms race stability is assumed to exist if, beginning with step i_0, the magnitude of the military power reaction is always less than the magnitude of the military power action, i.e.,

$$\Delta x_i < \Delta y_i < \Delta x_{i+1}, \; i=i_o, \; i_o+1, \ldots \tag{1a}$$

such that

$$\sum_i \Delta x_i < \infty, \; \sum_i \Delta y_i < \infty . \tag{1b}$$

If this condition is satisfied, the arms race will come to a halt at finite capability levels. Otherwise it continues, theoretically ad infinitum.

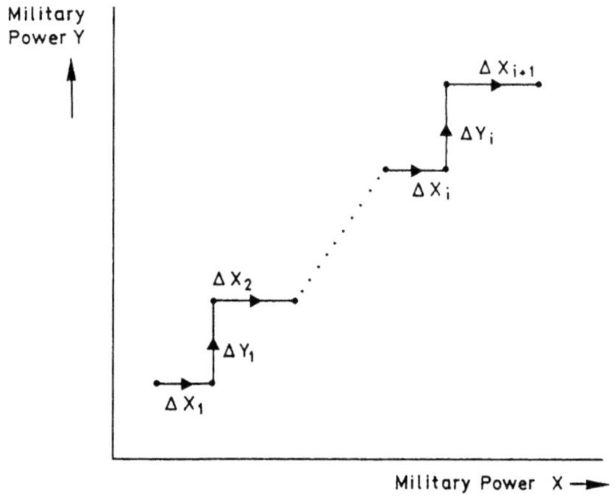

Fig.1: The Arms Race Mechanism

Crisis Stability: At given military capabilities for both sides crisis stability is assumed to exist if, in a given crisis, neither side perceives an advantage from attacking first or, vice versa, both sides consider it advantageous to strike second. An advantage might imply that the perceived relative military capability of the attacker improves as a result of attacking first. This is depicted in Fig. 2 where the index 0 holds for the initial state and E for the final state at the end of the respective military operation. Thus, crisis stability can be assumed to exist if

$$\frac{y_E}{x_E} \begin{cases} > \dfrac{y_o}{x_o}, & \text{if X attacks first,} \\[2ex] < \dfrac{y_o}{x_o}, & \text{if Y attacks first.} \end{cases} \tag{2}$$

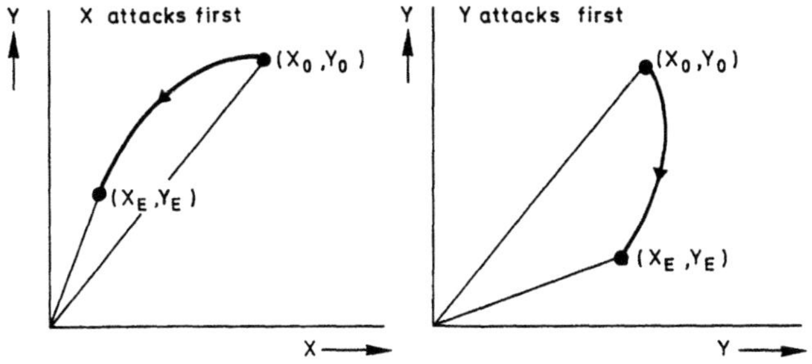

Fig. 2: Crisis - stable State Trajectories of Antagonistic Military Forces

Of course, in reality the capability perceptions are subject to limited intelligence and communication errors and delays, which cause the instantaneous states of the opposed military forces to be known only within certain confidence limits. In addition, due to the stochastic nature of military operations and their tactical variability, the state trajectories may vary considerably. Thus, depending upon the confidence requirements, the outcomes (x_E, y_E) of an attack must be expected within a more or less extended region (see Fig. 3).

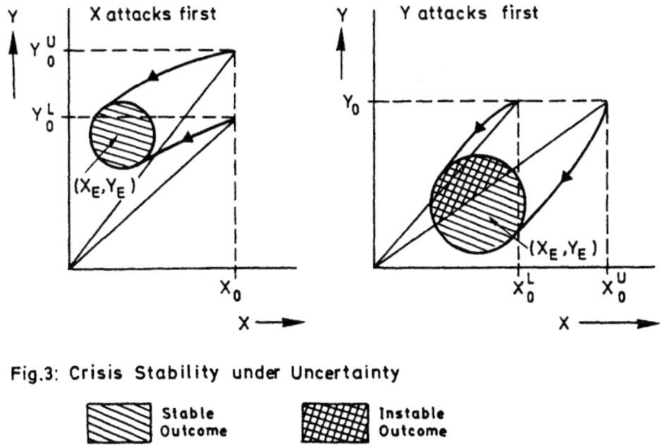

Fig.3: Crisis Stability under Uncertainty

There is no question as to the crisis stability as long as the region of outcome uncertainties falls well outside the cone that characterizes the uncertainty about the opponent's initial state. However, if they overlap there is always a certain probability that an attack would result in an improvement of the force capability ratio. In this case, crisis stability depends largely on the risk attitude of the potential first attacker.

Equilibrium: An equilibrium situation is considered to exist if the conditions for both, arms race and crisis stability, hold. Arms control should aim at attaining an equilibrium state and bringing about the conditions necessary to remain at that state.

Robustness: Arms control agreements need to be sufficiently robust and flexible to be able to adjust to future environments and changes in force posture of both sides. Robustness of an equilibrium point measures the relative amount of change in the opponents' military power for which the system remains in equilibrium.

Asymmetries: With a view to differences in geography, proximity to threats, culture, history, and technology, to name just a few, crisis stability requires that arms control agreements allow for asymmetries in the force posture of the opponents.

Linkages: There are links between the security of the major powers and the security of their alliance partners and of neutral third parties. A stabilization of the strategic security relationship between the major powers does not necessarily imply regional stabilization. For example, the adoption of an effective strategic defense for the territories of the United States and the Soviet Union may well lead to a decrease in European crisis stability unless accompanied by major force posture changes in that region. It is for such reasons that arms control proposals must be evaluated in a holistic manner that accounts for the tightly woven fabric of global and regional military capabilities, arms control, and international policy.

2.1.2 Assessment Tools

The methodological approaches that may be employed to support the assessment of the strategic balance are of either one of two basic forms: *static* or *dynamic analyses*. The former array, mostly by means of some additive value functions on both sides, indices which reflect the respective force capabilities. The latter employ models of the dynamic interactions of the opposed forces in war to provide estimates of conflict outcomes.

Today, the most prevalent form of analysis in arms control seems to be of the static type[6]. However, static analysis results imply, among others, a more or less symmetric situation on both sides, especially with regard to the opponents' geographic conditions. This clearly is not a very realistic prerequisite in the context of NATO versus the Warsaw Pact. In addition, static analysis techniques are by their nature incapable of addressing questions related to the stability of force balances. The main reason for their rather widespread use inspite of such shortcomings appears to be their inherent simplicity. The results are simple sums of numbers of items weighted by their marginal capability indices, the underlying assumptions of which are supposedly easy to check, at least in a formal sense. This is certainly not the case for the assumptions underlying most of the richer dynamic analysis models, in which items interact in more or less complex ways. Thus, for every analysis problem there is a trade-off between the adequacy and the communicability of the model being used and its results.

Depending upon the solution procedures and the representation of stochastic events, there are essentially four fundamental classes of dynamic analysis tools:

- Deterministic Analytical Models (DAM)
- Stochastic Analytical Models (SAM)
- Deterministic Simulation Models (DSM)
- Stochastic Simulation Models (SSM).

Models of the DSM and SSM varieties provide time histories of the simulated conflicts or battles in terms of average outcomes $\bar{x}(t)$ and $\bar{y}(t)$ in the former, and of frequency distributions $f_X(x(t))$ and $f_Y(y(t))$ of possible outcomes $x(t)$ and $y(t)$ in the latter case. Except for rather simple cases such as, for example, described by the original arms race model of

---

[6] Alfred LIEBERMAN provides a comprehensive summary of the indices developed for the static assessment of nuclear force capabilities. An example of a static analysis of the conventional force balance is presented by Lucas FISHER (1976).

RICHARDSON (1939)[7] or the battle models of LANCHESTER (1914), DAM and SAM-type models are usually restricted to providing the outcomes - average or probability distributions thereof - but no time histories.

With regard to the relevance of these analysis techniques to the main force balance issues, there seems to be general agreement that analytical models represent a viable methodology to assess the *strategic nuclear force balance* and its stability. This is well illustrated by Werner GÜTH's deterrence analysis using 2x2 bimatrix games with incomplete information and by the nuclear exchange models presented by Alfred LIEBERMAN and Jerome BRACKEN in this volume. LIEBERMAN's paper also suggests that deterministic models are quite suitable for the parametric assessment of variations of the mutual force postures or brought about by the uncertainties of future developments. A similar conclusion was reached with regard to *conventional force balance* assessments by a group of systems analysts reviewing the state of the art of combat modelling at a scientific symposium in 1982[8]. They recommend that, in order to better account for uncertainty, "... more uses be made of systematic variations in the course of deterministic analyses rather than designing probability distributions (describing input uncertainties) into the models" (see BONDER (1984)).

However, contrary to the strategic nuclear case where force structures are rather homogeneous and synergistic effects of comparatively little importance, conventional force balance analyses require simulation rather than analytical models. This is due to the heterogeneous structure and the synergistic (combined arms) design of conventional forces which do not permit closed form solutions of their mathematical battle models (see also TAYLOR (1979)). An-

---

7) An interesting RICHARDSON-type model is discussed in this book by PASTIJN and STRUYS which describes the dynamics of the defense expenditures between NATO and the Warsaw Pact based on historical data for the period of 1965 to 1981. Accordingly, the Warsaw Pact seems to behave "abnormally" with regard to the assumptions underlying the original RICHARDSON model: Its defense expenditure level 1) stimulates its own expenditure growth rate and 2) recedes when threatened by a high level of defense expenditures by NATO.

8) Symposium on *"Modelling and Analysis of Defence Processes"* in Brussels, July 1982, directed by R.K. HUBER, sponsored by the Panel VII (on Defence Applications of Operations Research) of the Defence Research Group of NATO (see HUBER (1984)).

other reason for using simulation models is that they generate time histories of conflicts. These permit to estimate *rates of change* in the force state parameters which represent indispensable information for the assessment of conventional force capabilities, especially in the context of NATO's flexible response strategy. HUBER (1980) argues that NATO's conventional defense capabilities would be sufficient if they warrant a high chance of denying the Warsaw Pact a quick accomplishment of its objectives. GIBSON (1984) expresses a similar view by stating that "... NATO will deter agressions by possessing a demonstrable (conventional) capability for response, such that the Soviet perception of the odds of achieving an objective, within a short period of time, would be insufficiently high".

Considering the stochastic versus the deterministic models it must be kept in mind that the results of the latter represent expected ("average") values only. Thus, from a DAM or a DSM one merely knows that in reality there is an equal chance for the outcomes to the better or worse than the model results. However, nothing is known on how much better or worse these results must be expected to be and what the associated probabilities are. In order to illustrate the significance of information on the probability or frequency distribution of outcomes for force balance assessments, the reader is referred to Fig. 4 in which the distribution functions F(z) of a state variable Z are given for two different force structure proposals D and E. Assuming that the force balance improves as z increases, case E is undoubtedly preferable to case D based on a comparison of average outcomes $\bar{z}_E$ and $\bar{z}_D$.

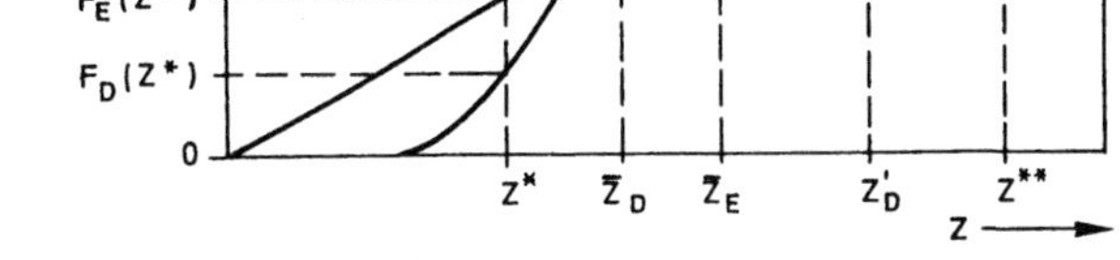

Fig. 4: Distribution Functions of State Parameter Z for Force Structures D and E

However, if z^* were a critical value below which, for example, crisis stability would be rather shaky, then case D should be preferable since $F_D(z^*) < F_E(z^*)$, i.e., in case D the probability that $z \leq z^*$ is only about one third of that probability in case E. But in case E there is a not insignificant chance of $1-F_E(z'_D)$ of achieving results that exceed the upper limit z_D that is achievable in case D. There is no simple answer as to which of the two cases, D or E, is preferable. It depends, among others, on how one values the chance of eventual disaster ($z \leq z^*$) versus the chance of being secure, say, for $z > z^{**}$. Thus, the choice depends essentially on the *risk attitude* of the decision maker. Being cautious and risk-averse he would prefer D over E, even though E holds the potential for a more stable situation.

In summary, the following observations can be made with regard to the suitability of systems modelling and analysis techniques for the assessment of the military strategic situation and its stability (see Table 1): Being of limited value for nuclear force balance assessments and incapable of shedding light on the stability of force equilibria, static analysis is nevertheless regarded as a valuable preprocessor for the development of data bases and the set of likely scenarios to be considered in the subsequent dynamic analysis. For the latter, the use of analytical models of the deterministic (DAM) and to a lesser extent, the stochastic (SAM)-type is usually of the deterministic variety. Conventional force balance assessment

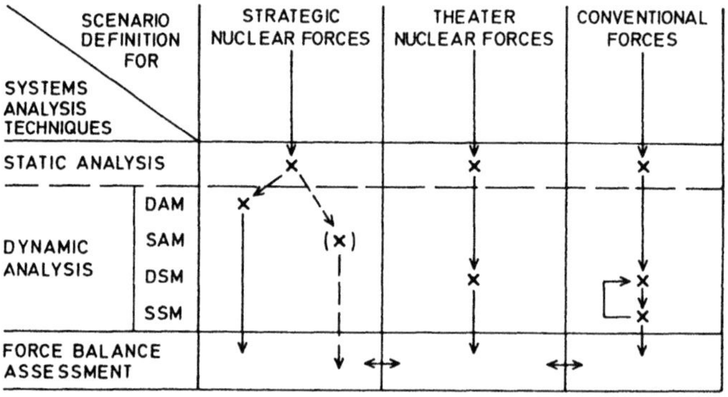

Table 1: Systems Modelling Techniques for Force Balance Assessment

is best supported by using deterministic and stochastic simulation models iteratively. The interactions and interdependencies of the three principal force categories must be considered with respect to both, the scenario definition for the quantitative analysis as well as the final assessment of its results.

2.2 Negotiations

The working group identified aspects of arms control negotiations to which the analytic community might be able to make helpful contributions. Of these, those related to the linkage of issues in negotiations, the management of information, and the implicit negotiation through sequential unilateral moves shall be briefly discussed here.

2.2.1 Linkage

Any treatise on negotiation theory quickly establishes the advantage of widening the issues that are to be put on the negotiating table. In fact, that is the grist for the "yes-yes" results that third-party negotiators relish modifications that benefit both sides. A simple case: a buyer and seller argue over the price of a house. The negotiator finds the seller wants to brag that he got a high price. He then introduces a new issue - asking the seller in effect to provide the mortgage. By structuring the mortgage at a low interest rate, the theoretical price can be high even though the actual payments are low. Both sides win. More generally, the possible results of any multi-issue negotiations can be plotted as shown in Fig. 5 where V_X is the value of a deal to side X, V_Y is the value of a deal to side Y, and $V_Y = G(V_X)$ is the convex hull of all possible deals. G is called the Pareto frontier.

For any deal on the frontier, side Y is getting the maximum value consistent with the value realized by side X. Putting it another way, for any deal *not* on the frontier, there will be a deal on the frontier (or weighted average of two such deals) that is better for both sides.

The cooperative forces associated with this search for efficient deals are always theoretically enhanced by increasing the scope of the negotiation. All issues thereby put on the same table are *ipso facto* "linked". There are of course contrary forces that counter-indicate linkage. The simplest is that linkage complicates the negotiations. If the theoretical advantage

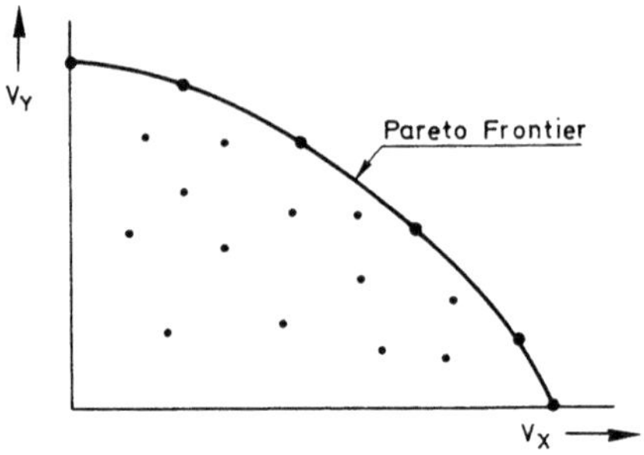

Fig. 5: Values V_Y and V_X of Agreements perceived by the Negotiation Parties Y and X

(always present) is in fact sufficiently compelling, the "complication" will be justified. A more compelling deterrent is that one side (or both) may have some reason not to let an issue on the table, in spite of its logical relevance. Often the problem is associated with the publicity that unfortunately accompanies such negotiations. This problem may be addressed by some of the ideas presented below in the section on information management.

Even at best, one must concede that there are prices for adding issues to the table. So how to economize on issues? A natural analytical approach is to partition the negotiations into *goal-oriented* groups. This means putting onto one table all issues that are centrally relevant to one goal. Present partitions are typically by weapon types, or by geography. Although these tend to separate by goals, the exceptions are too obvious to belabor. Possible examples of such goal-oriented groups are:

- Maximize times of flight for weapons directed at critical targets within the US or the USSR. Consequently put on the same table restrictions on nuclear missiles in European countries that can reach Moscow, and restrictions on Soviet submarines off the coast of the US.

- Minimize threat of "Blitzkrieg" incursions into Western Europe, or into Eastern Europe. Consequently explore ways to deploy existing mechanized and artillery forces as far back from the present "boundary" as possible - in the Soviet case well east of Moscow.

- Maximize warning times of both sides with respect to first strikes. Consequently include on the same table agreements about locations of deployed weapons and locations of warning devices. Perhaps even cooperate by furnishing platform locations to facilitate each other's warning abilities.

2.2.2 Information Management

A particular difficulty with arms control negotiations (as opposed, for example, to trade negotiations) is the background of sensitive military secrets that presumably underlie the logic each side must apply to the assessment of potential agreements. Just as centrally, *any* negotiation typically suffers if the adversary knows one's bargaining position: the values put on the various components of a possible deal, and the limits to which one is prepared to go. The search for efficient treaties - the ones on the Pareto frontier - is thus complicated by the nonavailability of information about the desires of *both* sides. In other contexts this dilemma is often addressed by using a "trustworthy" third party - trustworthy in the sense that each side can tell him its value functions, and depend on his not relaying them directly to the opponent.

The possibility of the superpowers entrusting their secrets to such a third party is too remote even to consider. Even if there were someone (or some agency) they both considered sufficiently neutral, the possibility of inadvertant compromise of the necessary sensitive information would be unacceptable.

One solution to this problem might result from designing a system that could serve as a computerized third party (CTP; see also KETTELLE (1984)). The CTP would have to be demonstrably (to both sides) inaccessible except by mutual agreement. Each side would need confidence that its inputs could not be ascertained by the other. Only questions mutually agreed to could be asked of the CTP. At any stage, a central such question would be: Given the limits both sides have stated, is there room for an agreement? There is a rich variety of issues regarding a CTP such as:

- Is it technically feasible, given its confidentiality requirements?
- How could dimensions of arms control agreements be structured to lend themselves to efficient valuations to be put on the results?
- What negotiating strategies, other than straightforward input of sincere values and limits, should be used with a CTP?

- To what extent is it necessary or useful for each side to present the CTP with its own highly classified models of strategic warfare, that reflect its calculation of the impact of arms limitations?

2.2.3 Sequential Unilateral Moves

A remarkable part of the arms control negotiations process has not been in the form of explicit treaties or even agreements, but rather a sequence of unilateral moves, or non-moves. A current (March 1986) example, is the Soviet announcement of its cessation of underground testing, and the US decision to nevertheless proceed with its planned tests. Which was the move and which the non-move is an interesting question. Even within the context of explicit agreements, there has been a long history of such unilateral moves. Some of these are near what might be called the boundaries of the agreements. An obvious example would be the Soviet encoding of missile telemetry data. Others involve actions not subject to agreements, but which are clearly relevant to arms control. Here continuing examples are annual defense expenditures of NATO on the one hand and the Warsaw Pact countries on the other.

What can be said about this form of defacto negotiations? Recent work in game theory has addressed what seems to be a similar problem, namely repeated plays of the *Prisoner's Dilemma* game. The result seems to be a consensus that the best strategy (or at least a robust and effective one) is "*tit-for-tat*": if the other player double-crosses you on one play, you double-cross him on the next; conversely, if he makes a cooperative move you make one in the next play. Although this seems to be suggestive for the case of sequential unilateral moves, it is irrelevant when viewed by strict logic. With tit-for-tat, a positive move on one side would lead to a reciprocal positive move on the other, which would lead to another positive move by the first and so on indefinitely; conversely, for a single negative move. Although the analytic community does not seem to have any ready-made theoretical contribution to the process of unilateral moves, there seem to be at least several problems to work on, for example:

- What have been the historic sequences of such moves, and their responses? To what extent have these moves been communicative, such as invitations to cooperate, or such as reprimands for precedent moves which were viewed as hostile? To what extent, on the other hand, were they dictated by internal (in a sense exogenous) considerations?

- How effective have various sequences of unilateral moves been, as a form of communication, or as an influence on the other side's behavior?
- What can be learned about the tactics of such moves? Are many small ones more effective than a single large one (equal to the sum of the small ones)? Is a large positive move enhanced if it is preceded by a small hostile move?
- What time constants, or delays are to be expected for responses to positive moves? To negative moves?
- What are effective combinations of actions and words? When should words precede, accompany, or follow actions?
- Can you make a case that the essential nature of relations between superpowers is in fact *only* unilateral actions? If not, to what extent are treaties useful (as opposed to action patterns, accompanied by appropriate "words"). To the extent treaties are useful, how can unilateral actions expedite the formation of treaties?

2.2.4 Multi-lateral Negotiations

One result of the multi-lateral constituency of the workshop itself was the concern with the treatment of multilateral aspects of arms control negotiations. Simply put, an efficient treaty of NATO as a whole may have very inefficient implications, or very uncomfortable disparities, for individual countries within NATO[9] with regard to economic and political concerns as well as military. For example, the "military-industrial complex" of the United States has its counterparts in the other members of the Western alliance. The economic benefits (and sometimes hardships) of arms control agreements can parse themselves out in ways that make various members very nervous[10].

The Pershing deployments have been a recent example of the impact of arms control agreements (or sequences of unilateral actions) on internal politics

[9] Although one might regard the countries within the Warsaw Pact as less autonomous, it would be simplistic to assume that some version of this problem does not bedevil the Soviets.

[10] The analyses of PASTIJN and STRUYS (see also footnote 7)) suggest that analogous considerations may apply to the Eastern counterpart of the Western "military-industrial complex", the Soviet "military-industrial bureaucracy".

of member countries. Even if regimes, or administrations currently in power, ratify NATO decisions regarding arms control, one should anticipate the political consequences within each member nation - consequences that may not accrue until subsequent elections.

Multi-lateral negotiations can of course be conducted simultaneously or sequentially - in this arena there are at least a few techniques that operations analysts and negotiation theorists have thought about. For arms control one natural procedure would be first to get agreements among component members of one side, and then negotiate with the opposing side. An essential complication of this natural procedure is secrecy - not just "military" secrets, but negotiating policy secrets such as reserve prices and tradeoff values. An elegant solution to this problem might be a variant of the computerized third party (CTP) discussed above. A less elegant (but perhaps likely) approach is exemplified by the workshop itself. Although the workshop was partially sponsord by NATO, it had no official status with respect to the component members. Conceivably similar "workshops" could sharpen the issues of concern to member countries - with clearly no official implications, but with the benefit of well-informed and well-structured analysis. Subsequently a group that must be small in order to be secret can exploit the thinking of this broader community.

2.3 Verification

GILMAN and JONES point out that, in the context of arms control and disarmament, verification in its general sense involves "... the authentication of truth or accuracy by such means as facts, statements, measurements ..." (WEBSTER (1966)) or, as accepted by Canada which has taken a lead in these issues during the last years, "establishment of the truth, by examination or demonstration" (OXFORD (1983)). The truth or reality to be ascertained by verification may be defined as "the process of determining the degree to which parties to an agreement are complying with the provisions of the agreement" (ACDA (1976)). Another definition describes verification as an "adequate system of safeguards which, by including an agreed system of international supervision, will ensure the observance of treaty provisions by all parties thereto" (CCA (1956)). KARKOSZKA (1977) generalizes these definitions in that he considers verification as "a process specifically established or approved by a disarmament agreement, carried out by individual state parties to the agreement, either reciprocally or not, or by an international body established or empowered to carry out the process, by personnel or by technical means, in order to determine the degree to which the parties to the agreement have implemented its provisions and thereby observed or discharged their obligations under the treaty."

2.3.1 Technical Means and Procedures

With regard to the means and procedures for the verification of arms control or disarmament agreements Canada, in 1978, developed a programme to study these questions conceptually to see what had actually been proposed and why, with the objective of developing a common perspective and verification typology. Table 2 summarizes some of the results presented by CLEMINSON and GILMAN in 1984. Accordingly, the verification process can be broadly categorized into a three-tier matrix:

(1) *Verification Regimes* (level of confidence required): The major determining factor would be the application of political judgement influenced by deployment practices, developed and agreed cooperative measures and security perceptions;

(2) *Verification Methods* (concepts of inspection and detection methodology): The major determining factors would be the technological level of monitoring systems and the capability of existing and projected analytical techniques;

(3) *Verification Systems* (existing and projected national and international systems available): Systems would include the physical hardware developed nationally and internationally to accomplish the monitoring, synthesis, analytical and dissemination tasks.

Verification technology, particularly in the area of remote sensing, has advanced dramatically as a result of the vast amount of financial and material resources poured into the improvement of *National Technical Means* (NTM) of verification by the superpowers. Satellite reconnaissance and surveillance platforms, electronic intelligence collection systems and seismic detection methods form a sophisticated package of high technology verification techniques. To the extent that bilateral agreements based on NTM between the superpowers are perceived as contributing to international stability, new technology can be said to have made an impact in this area already. As the multi-lateral aspects of arms control negotiations become significant, however, international verification methods will have to be developed.

REGIMES	METHODS	SYSTEMS
1 ABSOLUTE VERIFICATION	1 GENERAL ON-SITE INSPECTION	1 PHOTO RECONNAISSANCE SATELLITE
2 ADEQUATE VERIFICATION	2 SELECTIVE ON-SITE INSPECTION	2 "FERRET" SATELLITE
3 LIMITED VERIFICATION	3 CHALLENGE ON-SITE INSPECTION	3 NUCLEAR RADIATION DETECTION SATELLITE
4 TOKEN VERIFICATION	4 CONTROL POSTS/OBSERVER/ LIAISON MISSIONS	4 SPACECRAFT LABORATORY
5 NO VERIFICATION	5 REMOTE SENSING IN-SITU	5 SEISMIC SENSORS
	6 REMOTE SENSING-NATIONAL TECHNICAL MEANS	6 CONTROL POSTS
	7 COMPLAINTS/CONSULATION	7 REMOTE SENSING POSTS
	8 COLLATERAL ANALYSIS	8 PEACE KEEPING/OBSERVE MISSION
		9 LITERATUR SURVEY
		10 INTERNATIONAL INFORMATION EXCHANGE
		ETCETERA ETCETERA

Table 2: Verification Matrix (CLEMINSON and GILMAN (1984))

2.3.2 Decision Theoretical Analysis

With regard to modelling in support of arms control verification, R. CLEMINSON observed in the final panel discussion of the workshop: "... So if I were looking at something to do research on, I would look at *Game Theory*. Does it have an application to verification? Should the theorists be in front of the negotiator, or in behind in a support role? And if that is a support role, is he an innovator or is he an individual who is assessing what is going on and determining that what is being proposed by a negotiator, is in fact the logical line from which one is going to gain?"

It has been pointed out by BRAMS (1985) and by BRAMS and KILGOUR in this book that game theoretical approaches towards rational solutions of conflicts between antagonistic states might provide a valuable theoretical foundation for policy formulation. Whereas the analyses of BRAMS and KILGOUR are based on the so-called *Nash-Equilibrium* as a solution concept - unilateral deviation from this equilibrium by one party is to the disadvantage of that party - FICHTNER (1986) applies the well-known *Stackelberg* or *Price-Leadership Concept*, whereby maximum payoff is achieved by a rational inspector announcing his detection strategy.

Given the payoffs of the two 'players' (Inspector, Inspectee)

Inspector \ Inspectee	Illegal Behavior	Legal Behavior
Alarm	(-a,-b)	(-e,-f)
No alarm	(-c,d)	(0,0)

where $(a,b,c,d,e,f)>(0,\ldots,0), e<a<c, b>f$. Now let us assume that the inspector uses a detection mechanism with the help of which he detects an illegal action with probability $1-\beta(\alpha)$, where α is the false alarm probability the value of which he can fix. Then the expected payoffs to the two players are

$$\begin{matrix} (-a+(a-c)\cdot\beta, -b+(b+d)\cdot\beta) & & \text{illegal} & \\ & \text{in case of} & & \text{behavior .} \\ (-e\cdot\alpha, -f\cdot\alpha) & & \text{legal} & \end{matrix}$$

Rational behavior provided, the inspectee will behave legally if his gain in this case is larger than his gain in case of illegal behavior, i.e., if

$$-b+(b+d)\cdot\beta(\alpha)<-f\cdot\alpha.$$

Since the gain of the inspector in case of legal behavior of the inspectee is $-e\cdot\alpha$, according to this leadership concept the inspector will minimize α, subject to this condition, and announce this strategy to the inspectee.

If both players have more strategies than those given above, e.g., if the inspector has the set X_ε of strategies for spending his inspection effort ε, and the inspectee the set Y_μ to achieve the illegal goal μ, then it has been shown by FICHTNER (1985) that one has to solve the following optimization problem

$$\underset{x\in X_\varepsilon}{\text{minimize}} \quad \max_{y\in Y_\mu} \beta(x,y;\alpha) =: \beta(\alpha)$$

and proceed as described above. This formalism may serve as the basis for statistical analyses of verification problems where random errors - whether due to inaccurate measurement and/or random sampling cannot be avoided.

2.3.3 IAEA Safeguards

FICHTNER's program has been worked out for the case of international safeguards in partial fulfillment of the Non-Proliferation Treaty (NPT). This treaty poses difficult problems to sovereign states and may be regarded as "unfair" in at least two respects: Firstly, the rules apply only to those states which have ratified the treaty and not, of course, to non-signatories. Consequently, it is arguable that restrictions should not be too severe. Secondly, the treaty discriminates between non-weapons-states for which controls are mandatory, and weapons-states for which they are optional. For the weapons-states the treaty aimed at the reduction of their nuclear potentials - this was explicitly recalled and called for in each of the review conferences (WILKIE (1985), STEIN (1986)) forseen by the treaty. But even this implied promise does not remove the imbalance of the treaty but is accepted in the higher interest of reducing the risk of nuclear war.

IAEA safeguards are based on the principle of nuclear material accountancy: The plant operators report to the IAEA all the data needed to establish the material balances via their national or regional authorities. Since these data might be falsified, IAEA inspectors verify these data by making independent measurements on a random sampling basis. By means of statistical tests, it is decided whether or not the difference between reported and independently generated data can be explained by measurement errors, and furthermore, whether or not the material balances indicate any anomaly.

By application of non-constant-sum game theory - neither side presumably favors a false alarm, therefore the sum of the payoffs to both players cannot be zero - the capability of the system, defined as the guaranteed probability of detecting a diversion of nuclear materials, can be determined (AVENHAUS (1986)). If, however, the *timely* detection of diversions becomes an additional criterion, then considerable statistical complexities arise.

It has been discussed at various occasions whether or not the NPT verification procedures of the IAEA could be used also for other arms control agreements than the NPT (FISHER (1982)). Especially, some effort has been spent to analyse the applicability of these procedures to an eventually concluded verification agreement for an MBFR treaty for Central Europe (HÄFELE (1980), WITTEKINDT (1984)).

2.3.4 Example: Data Verification

Let us assume that the inspectee has reported the set of data x_{ij}, $i=1...K$, $j=1...N_i$ to an inspectorate, and that the inspectorate verifies these data with the help of independent measurements y_{ij}, $i=1...K$, $j=1...n_i$, $n_i \leq N_i$. Since the inspectorate is not interested in the true values but only in the differences $z_{ij}=x_{ij}-y_{ij}$, $i=1...K$, $j=1...n_i$, a statistical test is performed for the two hypotheses

$$H_0: E(Z_{ij})=0 \;;\quad H_1: E(Z_{ij})=\mu_i,\quad i=1...K,\ j=1...n_i.$$

(For a more detailed discussion of these assumption see AVENHAUS (1986)).

According to the *Neyman-Pearson-Lemma*, the best test for this problem leads to the probability of detection

$$1-\beta_{NP} = \Phi\left(\sqrt{\underline{\mu}'\cdot\Sigma^{-1}\cdot\underline{\mu}} - U(1-\alpha)\right),$$

where $\underline{\mu}'=(\mu_1...\mu_K)$, $\underline{\underline{\Sigma}}$ the covariance matrix of the Z_{ij}, Φ the normal distribution and U its inverse. If one now assumes that the inspectee will falsify all data by the total amount

$$\mu = \sum_{i=1}^{K} \mu_i\cdot N_i \,,$$

and that the total inspection effort is

$$\varepsilon = \sum_{i=1}^{K} \varepsilon_i\cdot n_i \,,$$

where ε_i is the effort to verify one datum in the i-th class, then the solution of the optimization problem given above leads to the guaranteed probability of detection

$$1-\beta^*_{NP} = \Phi\left(\frac{\mu}{\sigma} - U(1-\alpha)\right); \quad \sigma = \frac{1}{\sqrt{\varepsilon}} \cdot \sum_{i=1}^{K} N_i \cdot \sigma_i \cdot \sqrt{\varepsilon_i}; \quad \sigma_i^2 = \mathrm{var}(Z_{ij}) \ ,$$

and the optimal strategies of both players are

$$\mu_i^* = \frac{\mu}{\sigma^2} \cdot \frac{\sum_k N_k \sigma_k \sqrt{\varepsilon_k}}{\varepsilon} \cdot \sigma_i \cdot \sqrt{\varepsilon_i},$$

$$n_i^* = \frac{\varepsilon}{\sum_k N_k \sigma_k \sqrt{\varepsilon_k}} \cdot \frac{N_i \sigma_i}{\sqrt{\varepsilon_i}} \ , \quad i=1\ldots K \ .$$

Thus, one sees that the optimal class sample sizes $n_i^*, i=1\ldots K$, are the larger, the larger the number of data, the larger the measurement uncertainty and the smaller the verification effort for one datum of that class.

It should be mentioned that the test statistic which corresponds to the guaranteed probability of detection, is the so-called D-statistic

$$D = \sum_{i=1}^{K} \frac{N_i}{n_i^*} \cdot \sum_{j=1}^{n_i^*} Z_{ij}$$

which was proposed by K.B. STEWART (1970) in this context who justified it that time with heuristic arguments.

Models of this type which, in addition, take into account systematic errors, more complicated alternative hypotheses and others, have been applied to inventory verification problems in IAEA safeguards as well as in proposals for MBFR verification schemes (WITTEKINDT (1984)).

3. CONCLUSION

In summarizing the foregoing discussion one must conclude that the present state of the art of systems analysis and mathematical modelling with regard to arms control is at best spotty. It is rather safe to say that, except for some isolated studies on specific issues, a more or less comprehensive analysis of arms control problems has not yet been attempted, not even on a conceptual level. This is in stark constrast to the public attention arms control gets, at least in the open societies of the Western countries. Historical evidence suggests that arms control is a little understood process of quite some complexity, one that is embedded in an international environment of wide socio-economic, technological and cultural diversity and ongoing East-West competititon characterized by largely incompatible value systems. Indeed, oversimplified, if not faulty, conceptual models frequently seem to be responsible for counter-productive arms control proposals and agreements. Thus, an interdisciplinary research effort aimed at the development of adequate conceptual, and later also mathematical, models of the dynamics of international security systems is considered to be of utmost importance. Such models must account not only for the linkages between strategic and theater force capabilities, various weapon categories, and geographic, technological and doctrinal asymmetries. They also need to consider the asymmetries with regard to the political systems of the negotiation parties. The latter aspect may be illustrated by taking a look at the verification problem as it relates to the extent of changes in the military status quo involved in a given arms control proposal and to its negotiability.

For example, it appears plausible to assume that the verification requirements become more demanding as the extent of the change of the status quo increases. Similarly, the negotiability[11] of proposals might increase exponentially as the verifiability grows. This said, the linkages between negotiability, verifiability and extent of status quo change might be described in terms of a surface as depicted by the shaded area in Fig. 6.

However, it is well known that according to the Soviet position it only makes sense to talk about verification after an agreement in substance has been reached. Thus, this position might be characterized by the straight line ($N=1$, $V=0$, $0 \le E \le 1$). And the West's answer - which has been given in many similar situations (Krass (1985)) - is that it makes no sense to have a nice agreement and subsequently find out that it cannot be verified. Thus, depending upon the prevalent risk attitude, the Western position may be located anywhere on the shaded surface, at its extreme on the line ($N=1$, $V=1$, $0 \le E \le 1$).

Of course, the fundamental reason for this incompatibility of positions is to be found in the information asymmetry between the open Western societies and the closely guarded Soviet society. Thus, assuming that Fig. 6 depicts

---

11) The term 'negotiability' is meant to indicate the degree of suitability of an arms control proposal for a workable agreement, assuming that that's what negotiations are lastly entered in for.

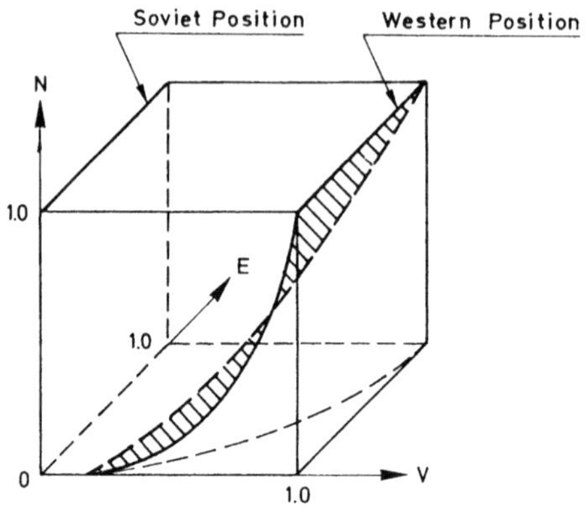

Fig. 6: Conceptualization of Linkage between Verifiability V, Negotiability N, and Extent E of Status-Quo Changes of Arms Control Proposals

a viable model, then it should be quite clear that workable status quo changes which can be brought about through arms control are largely limited by the performance level of the Western national technical means (NTM) of verification and their invulnerability. Therefore, one near-term objective for further research is considered to be the determination of the efficiency of verification measures and means with a view to all possible acts of non-compliance. Here, the work done in support of the IAEA within the framework of the Non-Proliferation Treaty (NPT) seems like a logical point of departure considering, however, that contrary to the NPT-situation, the inspector-inspectee relationship is a symmetrical one in the military strategic arena, at least as long as there is no supranational agency monitoring compliance.

Crisis and arms race stability and their interrelationship are considered another area for priority research. As a minimum, they represent boundary conditions for the negotiability of proposals and the associated extent of status quo changes. This is because, if anything, arms control agreements certainly should not impair whatever prior stability may exist. However, the respective methodological problems awaiting solution are regarded as quite demanding, as are those related to eventually obtaining mutual and multi-lateral acceptance of the evolving analysis tools.

The issue of model acceptance may be greatly alleviated by the availability of a computerized third party (CTP) to which the negotiation parties present their assessment models. Indeed, a CTP-type device might be a prerequisite to the mission-oriented approach to arms control proposed by BERTRAM (1978). Its crucial element is the idea of "*justification by challenge*" which implies that, when challenged, each party must demonstrate why the introduction of new systems does not violate certain (negotiated) mission capability limitations.

References

ACDA (1976): Verification: The Crucial Element in Arms Control. Publication No. 85, U.S. Arms Control and Disarmament Agency, Washington, D.C.

Avenhaus, R., Fichtner, J., Huber, R.K. (1984): Conventional Force Equilibria - Some Arms Control Implications of Analytical Combat Models. In: Supplemental Ways for Improving International Stability (Chestnut, Genser, Kopacek, Wierzbicki, Eds.), Oxford, pp. 201-211

Avenhaus, R. (1986): Safeguards Systems Analysis. New York

Bertram, Ch. (1978): The Future of Arms Control: Part II, Arms Control and Technological Change: Elements of a New Approach. Adelphi Paper No. 145, IISS, London

Bonder, S. (1984): Findings of Workshop A. In: Systems Analysis and Modelling in Defense (Huber, Ed.), New York, pp. 37-54

Brams, S.J. (1985): Superpower Games. New Haven

CCA (1956): Resolution of the Commission for Conventional Armaments, Proposals of 12th August 1948. In: Documents on Disarmaments, 1945-1959, Vol. I, 1945-1956, p. 175

Dürr, H.P. (1985): Der Himmel wird zum Vorhof der Hölle. Der Spiegel, Nr. 29, 1985, pp. 28-42

Fichtner, J. (1985): Statistische Tests zur Abschreckung von Fehlverhalten - Eine mathematische Analyse von Überwachungssystemen mit Anwendungen. Dissertation, Universität der Bundeswehr München

Fisher, D.A.V. 1982: Safeguards - A Model for General Arms Control? IAEA Bulletin, Vol. 24, No. 2, pp. 45-49

Fischer, R.L. (1976): Defending the Central Front: The Balance of Forces. Adelphi Paper No. 127, IISS, London

Gibson, J.E. (1984): Some Important Issues in Allied Command Europe to which Analysis Could Contribute. In: Systems Analysis and Modelling in Defence (Huber, Ed.), New York 1984, pp. 3-10

Goldblat, J. (1982): Agreements for Arms Control: A Critical Survey. SIPRI Publication. London

Häfele, W. (1980): Verifikationssysteme bei einer ausgewogenen Verminderung von Streitkräften in Mitteleuropa. Europa Archiv, Folge 6, pp. 189-200

Hoeber, F.P. (1981): How Little is Enough? SALT und Security in the Long Run. New York

Huber, R.K. (1980): Die Systemanalyse in der Verteidigungsplanung - Eine Kritik und ein Vorschlag aus systemanalytischer Sicht. Wehrwissenschaftliche Rundschau No. 5, 1980, pp. 133-143

Huber, R.K. (Ed.): Systems Analysis and Modelling in Defense. New York

Huber, R.K., Hofmann, H.W. (1984): Gradual Defensivity - An Approach to a Stable Conventional Force Equilibrium in Europe? Operational Research '84 (J.P. Brans, Ed.), Amsterdam-New York-Oxford, pp. 197-211

IAEA (1971): The Structure and Content of Agreements between the Agency and States Required in Connection with the Treaty on the Non-Proliferation of Nuclear Weapons. INFCIRC/153, International Atomic Energy Agency, Wien

Karkoszka, A. (1977): Strategic Disarmament, Verification and National Security, Chapter 2. London

Kettelle, J.D. (1985): Information Management in Arms Control Negotiations. In: Quantitative Assessment in Arms Control (Avenhaus and Huber, Eds.), New York and London, pp. 445-461

Krass, A.S. (1985): The Soviet View of Verification. In: Verification and Arms Control (W.C. Potter, Ed.), Lexington, Mass.

Lanchester, F.W. (1914): Aircraft in Warfare: The Dawn of the Fourth Arm - No. V, The Principle of Concentration. Engineering 98 (1914), pp. 422-423

Müller, A.C. (1983): Grundzüge einer europäischen Sicherheitspolitik für die 80er und 90er Jahre mit einem Vorwort von Prof. H.P. Dürr. Max-Planck-Institut für Physik und Astrophysik, Arbeitsgruppe Gottstein. München

Nerlich, U. (1985): Rüstungskontrolle oder über den politischen Umgang mit der Notwendigkeit nuklearer Abschreckung. In: Weltpolitik: Strukturen - Akteure - Perspektiven. (Kaiser und Schwarz, Eds.), Stuttgart, pp. 153 -168

Oxford (1983): Concise Oxford English Dictionary, 7th Edition (J.B. Sykes, Ed.). Oxford

Richardson, L.F. (1939): Generalized Foreign Politics. British Journal of Psychology, Monograph Supplement No. 23

Schell, J. (1982): The Fate of Earth, New York

Schulte, L. (1985): Das Schlagwort von der "defensiven Umrüstung". Europäische Wehrkunde/WWR 9, 1985, pp. 474-479

Schulte, L. (1986): Die Strategie der Verweigerung. Truppenpraxis 2/1986, pp. 4-18

Stein, G. (1986): Die Nichtverbreitung in der Überprüfung. Atomwirtschaft - Atomtechnik, Vol. 31, pp. 70-73

Stewart, K.B. (1970): A Cost-Effectiveness Approach to Inventory Verification. Proceedings of the IAEA Symposium Safeguards Techniques in Karlsruhe, Vol. II, Vienna, pp. 387-409

Taylor, J.G. (1979): Attrition Modelling. In: Operational Research Games for Defense (Huber et al., Eds.). München-Wien, pp. 139-189

Webster (1966): 3rd International Dictionary. Merriam, Springfield, Mass.

Wilkie, T. (1985): New Scientist, 3rd October 1985, p. 26

Wittekindt, R. (1984): Verification of MBFR-Agreements - A Systems Analysis. In: Quantitative Assessments in Arms Control (Avenhaus and Huber, Eds.), New York, pp. 383-411

PART I
HISTORY, LESSONS, ISSUES

ARMS CONTROL AND STRATEGIC MILITARY STABILITY

Lothar Rühl
Secretary of State
Ministry of Defence Bonn

At the beginning of the Advanced Research Workshop, I would like to speak to you about the key issue of arms control: It is the relationship with strategic and generally military stability. We must discuss this complex relationship in practical terms.

There is the stability of arms control and there is the crisis stability of a given force relationship, the balance of military options or, generally, a crisis stability of deterrence. Both need not mean the same and can even be mutually exclusive. Hence, there always is the requirement for harmonizing arms control objectives and methods with strategy and military criteria for defence and stability of given relationships.

Let me quote one of the chief negotiators in arms control in recent years, Ambassador Paul Nitze, on this point. He says, 'consistent with the objectives of promoting stability and rough equality - he is, of course, talking about the SALT experience - arms control should aim to achieve sharp reductions in the levels or armaments. Reductions per se may not always be good. For example, reductions in the number of launchers can be destabilizing if they increase the ratio of warheads to vulnerable launchers. But well-conceived proposals embodying reductions which bring about improvements in the proper indices can do much to enhance stability'.

Let me take up perhaps the most recent example of what Paul Nitze had in mind when he traced his experience; that is the Gorbachev proposal on reduction in strategic delivery vehicles and nuclear force buildings and in strategic systems of the three component categories included in the definition of the strategic force relationship. Gorbachev has proposed, as you know, the reduction of strategic delivery vehicles by 50% and a definite ceiling on warheads on such strategic delivery vehicles at 6000 and a definite limitation of each component SLBM, ICBM and aircraft to carry only 60% of the overall, meaning 3600 warheads.

NATO ASI Series, Vol. F 26
Modelling and Analysis in Arms Control
Edited by R. Avenhaus et al.

The first question one has to ask is how are strategic delivery vehicles defined? Which are the criteria? And here we are presented with a re-definition of the agreed terms under the SALT-Agreements which define the strategic systems in a pragmatic, technical way: In one case with the criterion of a minimal geographical distance between two landmasses and that means roughly 5500 km for land-based missile systems. And another, a very technical criterion, concerning nuclear powered submarines carrying modern sea-launched ballistic missiles, has been introduced in 1964. So, these are the criteria for the definition of strategic arms under the 1972 SALT I-Agreement and these criteria definitions have been written into the Vienna SALT Treaty and are still valid, at least until the end of this year unless the two partners agreed to further observe the stipulations of the treaty beyond the end of 1985.

The Gorbachev proposal as it has been of late explained by the Soviet Delegation in Geneva attempts at a comprehensive re-definition of strategic systems, a definition that is not consistent with SALT, but would translate the Soviet forward-based systems claim on American delivery vehicles, launchers and aircraft outside the territory of the United States according to the Soviet criteria of 'all systems are strategic if and when they can reach the territory of the other side". The Soviets have tried to include this definition into the SALT-Agreements since 1969 and they have not succeeded in doing this.

However, in the Vladivostoc Guideline of 1974 when the forward-based systems issue was again laid aside, an understanding was reached that in the next negotiation, in SALT III, as it was called then, the forward-based systems issue would be taken up and come under negotiations. And that was the final understanding when the Vienna Agreement was signed so that in 1979 it was understood by both sides that, once the SALT process would be continued by a third comprehensive negotiation, all the matters settled in the protocol and the Soviet forward-based systems claim would come under review and eventually become subject of the negotiation.

When the START negotiation began in 1981 the Russians introduced the forward-based system theme as a subject for the negotiation. Between 1981 and 1983, both sides tabled proposals. The issue how to count or whether to count so-called forward-based systems in comprehensive strategic arms reductions was not substantially discussed since.

In the parallel INF Limitation Negotiation, the forward-based systems issue was central to the subject. So there remained an ambivalence about both the Soviet intentions of how to bring this issue under negotiation and the American disposition not to negotiate on that issue at all. Since in the INF Limitation Negotiation the Russians proposed an agreement centered around and limited to European maritime regions, the forward-based systems issue that the Soviet Union brought up in the context of that negotiation was also limited to Europe and therefore no comprehensive globally valid criteria of definitions were advanced by the Soviet Union, but just the general criterion of systems that can reach Soviet territory with nuclear arms from their starting points. The Soviet Union counted 723 nuclear-capable aircraft for the United States as being forward-based systems in Europe or in European waters. And when they broke down this number of 723, it became clear that what they had in mind was the crisis-alert deployment of American nuclear-capable, but mostly conventional aircraft not only in Europe and in the Mediterranean but also in the Atlantic, and even those deployed in the United States but designed to be forward-deployed eventually to Europe. With this quantity of more than 700 so-called forward-based strategic systems, it became evident that no parity level for INF, for long-range INF limitations between the two SALT-partners, could be established since the Soviet nuclear aircraft and Soviet missile launchers, all of them mobile, in the European Soviet Union and Eastern Central Europe that can reach Western European NATO territory, would not be included in the negotiation.

The Soviet argument derived from the SALT criteria, that strategic systems are systems that can reach the other side's territory, was then no longer applied with rigorous logical consequences since Brezhnev in November 1981 extended the Soviet definition to all the countries of the Warsaw Pact in Eastern Europe. So now, forward-based systems were systems that could either reach Soviet territory or the territory of the Eastern European countries allied to the Soviet Union. This logical departure from the original FBS definition by the Soviet negotiators was confirmed by Andropov when he was Secretary General. And that meant a completely symmetrical definition for relevant subjects under negotiation in the INF negotiation. All American nuclear-capable aircraft or aircraft that were considered to be nuclear-capable in Western Europe, in the Mediterranean, and at least in the Eastern Atlantic, but also deployed in the Western Atlantic and ashore in North America, but designed to go to Europe eventually, were counted in on the grounds that they could reach either Soviet territory or Eastern European territory, while still none of the Soviet nuclear-capable aircraft or missile launchers, either in the Western Soviet Union or Eastern Europe, capable of reaching the territory of the European allies of the United States were counted in.

The Soviet definition of intermediate range nuclear-capable systems for the INF Limitation Negotiation was repeated concerning French and British strategic systems. While, under the rules of the SALT logic, a particular missile system or a particular category of strategic systems are to be considered strategic and subject to SALT in either Soviet or American forces, they immediately cease to be considered strategic if transferred to a third country which has produced the peculiar consequence that the American Polaris A-3 missile system, when in a United States SLBM-submarine, is a strategic system to be counted against the SALT-ceiling, while the same missile taken out of an American submarine and put into a British submarine ceases to be a strategic system. And the same goes for the TRIDENT SLBM.

This was the agreed criteria and the Russians then broke the logic of that agreement by claiming that the British Polaris SLBMs be counted against the American INF-ceiling. They insisted, during the INF negotiation, that weapon systems which were clearly outside the SALT context be considered INF-relevant weapon systems and included in the INF negotiation while they based the INF negotiation on the agreed SALT criteria. The entire definition was illogical and lopsided and, of course, - this is why I said in my first remarks: you have to look at these objects in a practical way - it was chosen in order to serve Soviet strategic interest in designing an arms control agreement in such a way that it would give the Soviet Union a numerical advantage that former parity would cover a substantive disparity to Soviet advantage and because the Soviet Union tried, and still tries, to hammer out a European arms control structure as a framework for a European strategic structure between the Soviet Union and several of America's European allies meaning France and Britain and possibly Western Germany.

Gorbachev has simplified all this by re-defining as strategic delivery vehicles all such systems that can reach the other side's territory. Since this is a global proposal, the Soviet Union counts 940 such systems and they also count about 200 deployed INF systems (missile systems) into that category of strategic delivery vehicles which adds up to 1140 such systems that have to be counted on the American side.

Let's have a look at what this means. The present approximate balance in strategic systems according to the SALT definition is about 2000 for the United States and 2500 for the Soviet Union which means that a 50% reduction would leave the Americans with 1000 such systems and the Soviet Union with 1250. But counting in these about 1140 systems, you come up with roughly 3300 including a different count in Soviet heavy bombers. There have always been quarrels between the United States and the Soviet Union about the exact number of nuclear-capable heavy bombers, but the exact number of heavy bombers had been stipulated at Geneva and, on the basis of these exchanged data - by no means agreed data, but exchanged data - the quarrel was provisionally settled. Backfire, by the way, was not counted in because it was not stipulated. So, by the Soviet count, you have about 3300 American strategic delivery vehicles against 2500 on the Soviet side. That means that the United States would have to de-commission exactly 1650 systems. The Soviet proposal with these counting rules leads to a choice on the American side, if an agreement were concluded on that basis, and the choice is connected with the 60% of 6000 warheads-rule. The United States has about 10.800 strategic warheads according to the SALT definition on their strategic delivery systems and will have to demolish 4800 of them if they accepted the 6000-rule. But 5200 of these warheads are on SLBMs. As you know, the American strategic force structure has been developed to what it is now for various reasons. The most important one, as far as SLBMs is concerned, is embedded in the conviction that ocean-going sea-stationed submarines are practically invulnerable and that their second strike capability could not be annihilated by a pre-emptive action or even neutralized for a critical time in an exchange and that therefore strategic stability lies, to a large degree with an ocean-going SLBM force.

As I said, there are 5200 strategic warheads and SLBMs and, in order to make the distribution between the various categories of the warheads under the 60%-rule, the United States would have to reduce this warhead number to 3600. One would assume that the United States would then at least wish to maintain these 3600 warheads. If we put these aside and say that is the minimum deterrence investment that is going to be secure against any Soviet pre-emptive strike, then the rest of the free choice of the United States in re-structuring the forces according to the Gorbachev rules would mean that they would either have to abandon practically the entire air force assets in Europe - because they are all of the type of aircraft that can be nuclear-capable - and in Korea and Japan and on the aircraft carriers, or that they would have to reduce their remaining strategic systems if they kept the SLBM force at a level that would give them 3600 warheads in that component. They would have to reduce their ICBM force and the heavy bomber force to 530 systems against 1250 Soviet strategic systems under the old SALT Agreement. And here we come to what Nitze says: Reductions per se may not always be good. For example, reductions in the number of launchers can be destabilizing if they increase the ratio of warheads to vulnerable launchers, and that would be precisely be the effect. The ratio of warheads to launcher would then be raised from 6:1 in favour of the Soviet warheads to 9:1 in favour of the Soviet warheads. Now, the question has to be asked if this kind of arms control - and I admit that this is an extreme example because it is the Gorbachev proposal as it stands now and it is all designed to unilateral Soviet advantage - if this kind of arms control can serve strategic stability.

As a second example, we take a look at MBFR. As you know the Western and Eastern countries in Europe have negotiated since 1973 on mutually balanced force reductions in Central Europe and have agreed that the level to which one would reduce the size of the forces would be 700.000 men on either side for the land forces and 900.000 for the personnel of land and air forces, naval forces and amphibious forces being excluded. This criterion of definition is active military personnel in uniform. This might strike the mind as being a rather peculiar way of defining soldiers, but here it is: it has been chosen because it is irrespective of equipment, training and readiness. It is designed to exclude the reservists while they are out of the force but, it does include them, while they are doing their reserve duty, active military personnel in uniform.

The Western goal in this negotiation has always been first to reduce the active forces of the Warsaw Pact and NATO in Central Europe to that 700.000 men-level. Secondly, to reduce in particular the Soviet armoured offensive capability in Central Europe by removing one Soviet tank army from Central Europe back into the Soviet Union. Later, this plan was reduced somewhat to the equivalent of the armour holdings of the divisions forming such an army, which means that the whole army equipment and tanks, artillery, missiles of all kinds would remain. The third goal was to change and reduce the size of the composition of the forward deployed offensive structure of the Warsaw

Pact forces by the reduction of the personnel in the armies and, of course, of all the Warsaw Pact forces in Central Europe.

It is irrelevant, how this could be brought about, irrelevant to the subject I deal with here, however, I assume this goal could be achieved by the kinds of reductions that the West has proposed and is trying to negotiate for an MBFR agreement. But since there has been no progress and since in particular no exchange of relevant military data for verification purposes has as yet been agreed upon in the negotiation while other things have been partially agreed upon, the West has made, on American insistence, in 1984 a new proposal. The proposal is, on the basis of a prior data exchange and adequate verification to be agreed upon, that, in the first phase of bilateral US/Soviet reductions both sides should reduce combat and combat support forces only. And here, we are confronted with about the worst business proposition the American arms control shop could have invented in order to upgrade Soviet interest in MBFR results on the side - we have in vain insisted for one year on the US administration to abandon this approach - but in concluding my talk, I am going to deal with this subject because it shows how arms control can defeat its own purpose and how it can defeat military stability and particular crisis stability of a given geographical military situation and the balance in forces.

In 1973, it was clear for the NATO countries that MBFR must enhance the military stability in Central Europe, that reductions must not lead to a loss of military security. And this principle had been selected as the main, the central guideline because it was clear, from the very beginning, that if you reduce Warsaw Pact forces and NATO forces to a common ceiling you might do this or you might end up with cutting much deeper into the muscle of the NATO forces than you would on the other side cut into the muscle of the Warsaw Pact forces. Therefore, the central guideline had been selected as the governing rule of Western MBFR strategy. For this reason NATO did not commit itself in 11 years of negotiation to proposing to reduce in specific types of forces or by specific force measurements such as batallions, regiments, brigades and so on. The Soviet Union on the other hand insisted that all the reductions be done in specific kinds of forces and in specific kinds of units, asking again and again for force reductions in organic units with their armaments, equipments and what they call, combat technique. You have to keep in mind that, for the reductions of indigenous forces, the general rule that has been brought forward by the Warsaw Pact is that these reductions result in definite reductions from the national forces while Soviet and American reduction contingents, and also British reduction contingents, would be brought home, would leave Central Europe. Dutch, Belgian and German reductions would have to be made from the forces definitely. And the same on the other side: Polish, Czechoslovac and East German reductions would be reductions from the indigenous forces definitely, while Soviet reductions would just be moved back behind the Soviet frontier.

As long as the Western position was that reductions will be made as the participants will choose, may be in units or by just thinning out personnel, the reduction method could be designed in such a way as to leave intact the structures of the armed forces in Central Europe. Although one has to admit that, if the German land forces must reduce between 40 and 60.000 men according to the various proposals, this cannot be achieved by just thinning out personnel. Organic units would have to be stripped down and the size of the land forces would have to shrink to a volume compatible with this kind of reduction. So, any MBFR result would cut into the fighting strength and into the structure of the German land forces. It also would do this to the Dutch and the Belgian forces, but to a much lesser degree. It would do this to the British forces, but again to a much lesser degree, and then the forces could be brought back to Britain and could be maintained there. So, NATO had closed itself into a box already with the MBFR proposal as it stood. But to propose that reductions for verification reasons should be centered on and limited to combat and combat support forces, and that 90% of the reductions be done in organic units and only 10% by thinning out personnel, and in offering, as a non-circumventing measure, as the West has done last year, that none of the other forces may be equipped and trained as combat or combat support forces, that means we are not only going to disorganize the German active army but also the territorial army if this proposal, that in the American/Western proposition only stands for the first phase of bilateral American/Soviet reductions, ever were to be applied to the indigenous forces as well.

As you know the Russians have rejected this Western offer of 1984. But then they have made themselves a counter-offer, and in this counter-offer - as anybody could have forecast - they proposed what they always have proposed, but now in Western language, that the reductions be done in combat and combat support forces which means that, if we applied it on the basis of the data that have been tabled by NATO and, if there is an agreement along those lines, that we would pay for the removal of one Soviet tank army and further reductions in other Soviet forces to be made, with a reduction in the number of brigades of the German field army and with a definite shrinking of the German land forces, an interdiction to the Federal Republic of training personnel in similar military functions than those used in and for combat and combat support forces.

For now time is lacking, but it is worthwhile to do an analysis of what the combat forces and combat support forces are in NATO. As you all know combat support forces are artillery, combat engineers, for example, and this means that the entire German territorial army then would have to be watered down to soldiers standing watch in front of barracks' gates, and patrolling the streets with an individual rifle or a light machine gun, that already the training of a machine gun crew might be in violation of the rules offered by the Western MBFR negotiators. I have made this point to show how arms control can be detrimental to military stability. There are many other examples, and one example is the reinforcement capability and the mobilization capability. So, what arms control must respect in pursuing its own goal of the stability of an arms control agreement and the optimal way of verifying such an agreement is the factual capability of the remaining forces to fulfill their purpose. In essence, it is a mutual assured defence capability and a general balance in the composition and structure of opposing forces that are to be made the subject of mutual arms control. And in doing this right, one must relate this to the current doctrine and military art and what the Russians call 'operational style' of the forces under consideration. That means that arms control just centered on weapons systems will not be able to serve stability and to achieve its own major purpose, that is to enhance the security of the countries that conclude an arms control agreement.

ARMS CONTROL FOR THE LONG TERM

Keynote Address

Paul Bracken
Yale University, New Haven, Connecticut 06520

Thank you very much for inviting me to this important meeting. What I would like to do in the time we have is to discuss what I think are some key arms control issues and some key strategic trends that bear on these.

What I have done is to divide up my discussion into five different areas. These are categories under which many broader strategic trends come as well.

I will go through them to try to give a sense of my overall theme, so that we don't confuse the forest with the trees. The first is the possible shift to a *defense emphasis strategy* and ways to think about the Strategic Defense Initiative proposed by the Reagan administration in the United States. The second is *US coupling to Europe*, third is *confidence-building measures* and their role in arms control. The fourth, I'm going to call "education", particularly of the Soviets, and finally there is *crisis management.*

The possibility of a Strategic Defense Initiative leads to the idea of having a defensive rather than an offensive arms race with the Soviet Union. The logic is as follows. Defensive systems that destroy attacking missiles could be accompanied by negotiated arms control agreements to *reduce* the number of offensive missiles each side could deploy. As defensive systems increase, and as offensive numbers decrease, a transition point is reached when each state can no longer destroy the other's society by nuclear attack. The purpose of a *defense emphasis* strategy is to disengage security policy from the threat of killing millions of innocent people - a threat judged as immoral by a great many strategists. The idea has been around since the early 1960's, I believe it was first promulgated by Donald Brennan of the Hudson Institute, who died in 1981. In many ways it is a shame that Brennan is no longer with us, because if one wants to go back and do the best case analysis of why one would have a *defense emphasis,* I think Don's writings in the Sixties and Seventies, are really among the best. This is a subject which inspires a great deal of extreme opinion on both sides of the debate - but what I think is most relevant for our purposes here with the defense emphasis, the Strategic Defense Initiative, are really two things:

NATO ASI Series, Vol. F 26
Modelling and Analysis in Arms Control
Edited by R. Avenhaus et al.

one, that it focuses attention on *long-term issues* rather than what our negotiating tactics will be next month in Geneva. Proponents of the Strategic Defense Initiative, I think, have a very good point when they ask the rest of us "Do you have any better ideas for getting out of the current situation over many, many years or even many, many decades?", "Do you think that there is any real possibility of deep reductions in strategic nuclear warheads, by 1995 or the year 2000, without some driving device like the Strategic Defense Initiative?".

I think a realistic answer to these questions is "No". Although the Strategic Defense Initiative makes the search for long-term solutions more compelling it doesn't lead one necessarily to an acceptance of defense emphasis. But the SDI really does get at the question of the longterm effects of new technology on the old political order. Most poeple, I think, do not believe that the probability of war has increased; it seems to me that it has decreased, if anything, over, say the past 10 or 15 years. But, if you ask whether this state of affairs can continue forever, one notes that "forever" is a long time. Is it really possible to maintain the security of the United States and the Western World on this threat of apocalyptic destruction, and have that system work forever, for centuries into the future?

Proponents of the Strategic Defense Initiative say that they do not feel that it will work forever, and there is a replacement: getting into a defensive arms race with the Soviet Union rather than an offensive arms race.

The second point that can be made about defense emphasis is that it is an area which has made some strange bedfellows. Not only did Ronald Reagan propose it in March 1983, but Jonathan Schell, an eloquent spokesman of major disarmament, has also proposed the defense emphasis in a book he wrote called *The Abolition*. His proposal, not surprisingly, was a bit different from Mr. Reagan's. He wanted a complete nuclear disarmament first, then reliance on defensive systems. The logic in both proposals is the same however. If disaster were to strike, instead of having today's huge arsenals exchanging salvos back and forth, we would have large arsenals which were shooting down the small arsenals of offensive forces. This is the logic which has driven the defense emphasis strategy from the early 1960s. The implications are clear for what we are trying to do here - look at the long-term rather than the short-term. Having been in the arms control business for a number of years, it has struck me the extent to which people in government are driven by the question "What should our negotiating posture be next month?", or "How many GLCMs equal a SLCM?", and all the sort of counting rules that Mr. Rühl discussed this morning. While governments have to make proposals on these issues, it is useful not to lose sight of the longterm trends in the arms race, and how to break away from them, if one feels as I do that the current situation cannot continue forever.

The second area I would like to discuss is *US coupling to Europe*, a subject Mr. Rühl dealt with at the end of his talk. When we think about the tremendous difference that nuclear weapons have made, one way to characterize it is that for centuries the risk of war between any two countries was determined by their respective foreign policies. Since 1945 we had a major reversal of this. What we have now is the *risk of war shaping foreign policies*. The consequences of major levels of destruction are apparent to one and all concerned, on both sides, East and West. And a good part of NATO-policy itself, and I think also of Soviet policy, is driven by avoiding nuclear war, even avoiding situations where a crisis could escalate into a nuclear war.

I believe this also leads to another change in our fundamental conceptions, that the balance of power that people have been talking about here in Europe since Napoleonic times, is increasingly replaced by a *balance of interests*. A balance of power loses a lot of its meaning if a state can introduce nuclear weapons into a situation. It is very hard to conceive of a foreign policy goal of the United States that would justify a major nuclear exchange. That is why, when both sides get into a crisis in some part of the world or in Europe, what they have to do is assess their interests in pursuing the contest further in that region. With nuclear missiles and with modern developments in conventional force mobility, each nation can escalate if it wants to do so in a local theater. The question then becomes one of risks and benefits, rather than one of capabilities.

What does this have to do with European arms control and coupling? It recognizes that there are very strong super-power codes of behavior that have developed outside of any official arms control agreements. One of which, for example, is "don't rock the boat too much" - and, I think, this is the strongest security relationship between the United States and the Soviet Union. A second is, if you are going to rock the boat, do it in

El Salvador or Afghanistan, but for God's sake, do not do it in Central Europe because it is entirely too dangerous there. What all of this means for coupling is that there should be harmony between strategy and arms control. What NATO is trying to do is really not to deter attack on Western Europe, because attack is outside of the rules of the game that have been built up. What NATO is trying to do instead is to deter conventional *reinforcement* from the western military districts of the Soviet Union into Eastern Europe. If NATO were to deter reinforcement, it would be able to manage the conventional threat of the 19 Soviet divisions in East Germany, plus possibly a few more, without using nuclear weapons. And, I think, here is the critical threshold which we could build our European arms control policy on. Just ask the question: What can NATO do to deter the Soviet Union in a crisis from reinforcing its garrisons in Eastern Europe from the western military districts? I think the answer has a lot of implications for NATO strategy, such as the kind of nuclear posture that is deployed, the amount of U.S. reinforcement needed, and the political resolve to modernize NATO's conventional forces.

Confidence-building measures are the third broad area of arms control that has received attention over the past several years. It is one that needs to be conceptualized much more thoroughly than it has been to date. Arms control throughout the 1970s, it seems to me, was dominated by what could be called "SALT-type" of counting agreements. Each side would count certain things and array them out in vectors to see who was ahead, and then run it through computer simulations to look at the outcomes. There was not enough emphasis put on constraining the military *operations* of the two sides. There is a new attraction to *operational arms control*, partly, out of exasperation over major arms control breakthroughs of the counting variety after the demise of SALT II and the lack of progress in the START talks.

An example of operational arms control: Secretary Weinberger in April 1983, issued a very interesting and comprehensive report on this subject, proposing to the Soviet Union a whole menu of things which they have mainly ignored but in ome cases have rejected outright or accepted: giving advanced notification of bomber take-offs above a certain number, and of submarines leaving port. One other item proposed was an expansion of the Soviet/American "Hot"-line - something the Soviets have agreed to.

It is useful to remember when arms control strategy started back in the late 1950s and early 1960s, it was always premissed on two parts:

one, constrain the arsenal of each side; second, control their operations in peace and war, so that if a war or crisis would break out the damage or escalation that followed would not be as great as would otherwise be the case. In the 1970s, we forgot the operational arms control side, a question that is now coming back.

Operational arms control is difficult to conceptualize because it mixes apples and oranges together. It includes items such as stand-off zones for submarines so that the Soviet submarines off the Atlantic coast of the United States would not be able to attack Washington, D.C., with flight times on the order of ten minutes, thereby threatening American national command and control. It also deals with softer issues, such as thinking through the declaratory policy that one side makes about nuclear doctrine. I was in the Soviet Union last year and we got into a discussion with some of their scholars. They were very upset about the issue of Presidential Directive 59 in 1980 which they took as an open declaration by the United States that we were going to attack their political control system. I am not saying that is what Presidential Directive 59 stated, but rather that was the way it was perceived in Moscow. They pointed out that, at the same time in summer of 1980, the U.S. was going ahead with the Pershing II missile. The point they made was an interesting one. In the summer of 1980, the U.S. was declaring to attack their political command and control system on the one hand, and was taking actions to deploy a weapon which can actually carry out that strategy, namely the Pershing II with its short flight time to the Soviet command targets. I assured them that I had never found one single person in the Pentagon who saw a relationship between Presidential Directive 59 and the Pershing II missile in 1980. But sitting in Moscow it looked like there was a very careful orchestration of the two developments. On this, the Soviets do have a point. Really, it is hard for them to believe what, I think, if you work in Washington, is only too easy to believe that the right hand does not know what the left hand is doing. And if one is going to make open threats to attack the enemy's command system, and if weapons are being built which have that capability, then, I think, you owe it to yourself to ask about the perceptions generated.

One possible consequence of the above perceptions could be to drive the Soviets to greater use of predelegated launch authority given to the military. There will almost surely be more studies inside the Soviet Strategic Rocket Forces organization on devolution of command authority, and probably more careful thought devoted to execution of launch under attack.

This gets into the fourth area which I would like to emphasize, and that is the educational value of arms control. Here is an area where I think there has been some progress.

The Soviet Union, by the nature of its bureaucratic society, is more secretive and compartmentalized than is the case in the United States. Herman Kahn was once in Moscow, and the Russians were claiming to him that the Americans were rigid in their arms control proposals. His response was: "We may be rigid, but you are *transcendentally* rigid". The Soviets carry rigidity to such an extreme level that the 1985-1986 arms control proposals made by Mr. Gorbachev are remarkable, because they a) were made at all, which is unusual for the past 15 years and b) they were complex and must have required the military and the politicians to talk with one another to a greater extent than was the case in the past.

There is a story told about the SALT I-talks, that the Soviet chief negotiator reproached Gerard Smith, the American negotiator of the time, after he put up a chart with the levels of Soviet armaments displayed on it. The Soviet asked Gerard Smith to take the chart down because the other Soviet negotiators at the table did not have the necessary security clearances to know that information! That was back in the early 1970s, and I think it is essentially impossible for this to happen today. There is a much greater exchange of information back and forth within the Soviet security bureaucracy today that is all to the good because one of the things which has troubled people is that the Soviets, because of their over bureaucratized system may be creating a situation where they take dangerous actions in a crisis, unaware of their political implications.

The final area where arms control could make a contribution is *crisis management*. The guiding imperative in crisis management is that politicians should have a great deal of control over military operations. Flexibility is a good thing, but in real world military operations there are often major gaps in information about the state of affairs, gaps that remove the possibility of flexibility. The Korean airliner incident revealed two relevant aspects of crisis operations. One, that that airliner seems to have been brought down on the decision of the local air defense commander in the Far East without political authorization; Second that no one in Moscow in the political high command knew that that was happening until after the fact. There may be a technical ability of high level leaders in government to monitor military operations, but it seems to me that the ability to actually carry out those detailed levels of control is problematic. The question is this: Can senior political authorities in each government control their military forces if those military forces are locked in combat at least for some period of time?

I fear that political leaders on each side do not have control of military operations to the extent they need to, and that the leaders do not realize the implications in certain circumstances of military actions. This is all compounded in the current day and age because we may be in a unique time in history in that political leaders may know less about military operations today than almost at any time in world history. If you look back to 1914, at the outbreak of World War I, it was considered an honorable and respectable thing for the heads of state to know about the mobilization plans of their armies and how those armies would be used. Today, there is overwhelming and almost exclusive attention on actions that occur *before* a crisis or *before* war, such as weapon acquisition programs. There is such focus on the apocalyptic consequences of nuclear war, that it tends to drive politicians out of considering some of the things that they can do, and must or must not do in the middle of a crisis.

I have never in my life seen a study of terminating a nuclear war in Europe, for example. This deficiency is astonishing. One would think that somebody would look at this. But this is not looked at because most of the focus in Europe is on deterrence and arms control. A lot of effort could be put into crisis management, to give political leaders greater transparency about military operation, so they could see the consequences of their actions.

What is needed is some method for political decision makers to assess the consequences of putting forces on alert, or operating them in particular ways. The military establishments of the two sides can not usefully be modeled as a two-player-game, because they are really a set of n-player-games, where a hierarchy of n-players on each side, namely the military forces, often have their own objectives and pay-off functions which can be different from those of the political leaders. Witness again the Korean airliner incident which lead to widespread condemnation of the Soviet Union. It is hard to believe that the resulting political ramifications were an issue for the air defense commander who ordered the aircraft brought down.

In conclusion, I would say that arms control has not been the disaster that some people feel it has been, either harming U.S. security or inducing large opportunity costs. I believe that the greatest arms control success of the the past 40 years has not been on things like the SALT process, but in the fact that we have not had accidental nuclear war. Both the U.S. and the Soviet Union in the 1950s had forces which were, to put it mildly, tricky to manage in crisis and when placed on alert. And they both have made major investments in putting locks on nuclear weapons, and other safeguards to make sure that some bomber pilot with a hydrogen bomb does not fly over enemy airspace accidentally in peacetime. We have done a very good job at that, it is not recognized that accidental war is under control only because a lot of attention and investment were paid to the problem. It did not come automatically.

The second thing, I think, that arms control has done is that it really has bought time. Arms control has helped us buy time in the sense that deterrence has, broadly speaking, worked. We have not had a nuclear war, nor conventional war with the Soviet Union. One is on thin ice when one says "deterrence has worked" because you are not sure that a war would not have broken out had there been a lack of arms control or deterrent policies. But it seems to me that not only has it worked here in Central Europe but also that the probability of war in Europe is today judged to be very low. So it has bought time, but I get back to the first point that I made: "Bought time for what?" How have we used the time purchased for getting out of a reliance on these deadly weapons? And here, I think, we have not done as nearly as well as we might. Arms control has bought time, but I do not believe that it has done anything but postpone some very difficult decisions, probably because governments are not good at these long-term conceptual problems, and governments, by and large, are in charge of the arms control agreements and the arms control process. So, although it is pessimistic that we have not used the time as effectively as might have used it, it still is optimistic to know that large scale war, major nuclear conflict, has been avoided.

ARMS CONTROL: LESSONS LEARNED AND THE FUTURE

Gwyn Prins
Emmanuel College, University of Cambridge, United Kingdom

1. SOME HISTORICAL OBSERVATIONS

In a fairly regular cycle over the last fifteen years the western public has been offered a standard view of arms control by western politicians, amplified by the western press typically in breathless reportage of arms control negotiations. This view is that the nuclear arms race is not nice, that somehow it should be halted and that whatever particular set-piece of summitry or further episode of complicated Geneva negotiation is imminent is the last, best hope of humanity to achieve that halt. The Reagan administration signalled public endorsement of this goal for arms control when it changed SALT to START: Limitation to Reduction. Is this view correct, either as an historical statement of past arms control or as a realistic prescription for arms control in the future? A picture, they say, is worth a thousand words.

NATO ASI Series, Vol. F 26
Modelling and Analysis in Arms Control
Edited by R. Avenhaus et al.

So if the goal of arms control has been arms reduction, as the public has been taught to believe, it has manifestly failed.

Arms control in the nuclear age moved to the centre of public attention with the agreement of the Partial Test Ban Treaty in 1963 (I deliberately exclude the Acheson-Lilienthal Report and Bernard Baruch's bowdlerized version of it from the dawn of the nuclear age in 1945-46, since these were attempts at nuclear *disarmament*, not arms control, and it is important to maintain the difference between these goals and processes clearly in mind). The PTBT was to be, said President Kennedy in presenting it to the American public, the first step in a journey of a thousand miles. It certainly opened a twenty year period during which nuclear arms control measures of one sort or another were a constant feature of superpower diplomacy and on a couple of occasions, notably the years of effort which lead to the Non-Proliferation Treaty, arms control engaged a much wider active constituency.

However, these same twenty years witnessed the implementation of the momentous American decision made in March 1961, within months of the Kennedy administration taking office, to authorise the strategic missile programme (Ball (1980))[1]. This, with the initial Soviet responses to it over the next nine years (the accelerated deployment of SS-9s and 11s), propelled a quantitative escalation of launchers and later of warheads. The systems called forth on both sides by the 1961-64 decision period had no sooner been deployed (topping out 1967-70) when a qualitative arms race grew out of them. This was not terribly surprising. From 1961, Robert McNamara had seen increased operational flexibility as a latent potential in the new ICBM force. But it was only upon emergence from its Southeast Asian defeat, that the American strategic mind turned back to the nuclear arena with growing enthusiasm for the idea of "increasing options". In practical terms, it was not really a new departure. Curtis LeMay's Strategic Air Command had done its bit in the 1950s to keep alive the vision of the militarily usable bomb (Rosenberg (1981), Bracken (1983), pp. 81-84). But the new situation called for the presence of a comprehensive counterforce capability

---

1) Subsequent to the publication of Ball's book, Mr. McNamara has expanded upon the implication of the fact that there were voices within the USAF advocating the acquisition of a first-strike capability. This he had rejected at the time, but stresses the likely effect upon Soviet thinking of hearing such rumours. Interview with R. Sheer in The Los Angeles Times, 12 April 1982. The salient passages are reproduced in Prins (1983), pp. 92-93.

in a nuclear rocket force, not just in bombers, and associated, tighter-coupled command, control, communication and intelligence systems (Bracken (1983), p. 54). MIRVs and micro-processors were there to make it possible. This produced a partially analogous Soviet response, notably in the fourth generation SS-18 and 19 replacements for, respectively, the third generation SS-9 and 11. But it was not a mirror response because by the 1970s the Soviets had almost certainly effected a fundamental change in their nuclear strategy at both the military-political and military-technical level, emanating from decisions taken in December 1966 which had been in turn part of the final response to the American Minuteman and Polaris surge. In consequence, the already different views of nuclear strategy and its technical requirements held by each superpower were now markedly more divergent (MccGwire (1986)). With the sole major exception of the drop in deployment rate of fourth generation Soviet ICBMs in the years following the conclusion of SALT II in 1979, which appears to have been in part in order to keep the SALT limits, it is difficult to see any concrete evidence that the twenty years of arms control materially limited the parallel process of spiralling build-up.

The arms control measures that were agreed between 1963 and 1983 came in two groups[2]. There were the various peripheral treaties, mostly from the first decade, and the SALT process which dominated the second. The peripheral treaties fell into two categories. First were *agreements not to do things which it was unlikely that anyone would want to do*. This included those restraining nuclear activities in certain environments, like the Seabed and Antarctic treaties (Goldblat (1983), pp. 56-73). Then there were agreements *not to do what could not be done* at the time that the treaty was made. The major example of this was the Outer Space Treaty of 1967. But there has been little compunction about breaking these treaties as soon as they conflict with what a state perceives as a higher interest. Senior members of the Reagan administration like Mr. Perle have made it perfectly clear that neither the Outer Space Treaty - nor any other treaty - will stand in the way of the "Strategic Defense Initiative". Indeed, it is difficult to see how the Partial Test Ban Treaty will survive if the United States begins

---

[2] A fuller version of the argument of this paragraph and the next is given in Prins (1983), pp. 117-132.

to test in space the nuclear-pumped X-Ray lasers which are, if funding patterns are any indication, the favoured instrument for Star Wars (Allen and Dombey (1985)). Of the peripheral treaties, the Non-Proliferation treaty stands in a category of its own, and has a special importance, to which I shall return later in this paper.

But it has been the SALT process which since 1969 has carried most hopes of curbing or stopping the nuclear arms race. SALT I was concluded in autumn 1973 with the ABM Treaty and an interim agreement limiting numbers of launchers and delivery systems to those currently deployed, the intention being to move to a comprehensive treaty on offense weapons at SALT II (Goldblat (1983), pp. 169-175). The ABM Treaty was in one sense like the Seabed Treaty, being a treaty to prevent something which, for very different reasons, neither side wanted to do; in another, it was like the Outer Space Treaty, for the experience of the Grand Forks ABM in North Dakota and of the Galosh ABM around Moscow had convinced both the Americans and probably the Soviets also that their respective first generation ABM technologies would not work to acceptable criteria (although Galosh remained formally deployed). The ABM Treaty was felt by the arms controllers to be especially valuable because it was the first to ban an entire "mission". Today its nakedness is concealed only by a tissue-thin distinction between "research" and "testing and deployment" and by a change of acronym from ABM to BMD. There is little doubt that it has been broken in spirit by both superpowers (Polanyi (1984)). But the problem with the SALT process was that each of the two negotiations failed to control the really pressing technological threat of the day. Writing of SALT I, George Smith, the chief American negotiator, observed that "In retrospect, the weak effort to ban MIRVs was a key aspect of SALT. It was considered by some knowledgeable people as the leading lost opportunity of the negotiation" (Smith (1980)). Speaking the day after the Senate confirmed his appointment as chief negotiator for SALT II in 1977, Paul Warnke cautioned that the lesson of the failure to ban MIRV must be learned and that in SALT II, the next dangerous technology - cruise missiles - should be confronted head-on (quoted in Talbott (1979)). In the event it was not. Warnke returned to his law practice before the negotiation ended. It is true that land- and sea-launched cruise missiles were prohibited in the protocol to SALT II; but this had in any case expired before deployments began; and of greater consequence was that Richard Perle had successfully frustrated the attempt of Mr. Nitze and the INF delegation to discuss a blanket ban on cruise missiles in the subsequent negotiations. Part of the problem was that to give such a ban verifiability, the potential use of cruise missiles for conventional payloads would have to be foregone; and while the Joint Chiefs were prepared to certify that they perceived no operational role for conventionally armed ground-launched cruise missiles, Mr. Perle's determination to retain the possibility of a future development won the day (Talbott (1984)). The SALT II ceiling fixed for air-launched cruise missiles was quite congenial to currently planned US deployments (the cruise missile load per bomber was fixed at the maximum possible for a B-52) and from the American point of view, similarly painless ceilings were set for other categories of weapons. But even this deal Congress could not be persuaded to ratify, even coupled to what a senior member of the arms control community has described as the "immutable logic of arms control": that no correlation of forces occurring as a natural product of unrestrained competition can plausibly be imagined that would be preferable to one arrived at by agreement (Kincade (1981)).

The Congressional refusal was in part the product of a resourceful campaign by the Reagan administration-in-waiting constitued as the Committee on the Present Danger; but more importantly, both decision and lobbying reflected a profound change in American public opinion. Two rounds of oil price shocks coming on the heels of the defeat in Vietnam had prepared the ground. The frustration aroused by the extended display of powerlessness in the Iran hostage crisis catalysed deeper, less coherent feelings of resentment about an outside world that seemed no longer to sit up and pay attention when Number One told it to. Mr. Reagan's two election successes were not a conspiratorial hoodwinking of the electorate. Reagan's style chimed exactly with the introspective, self-pitying and belligerent xenophobia of much of Middle America. Tee-shirts carried slogans like "Nuke 'em till they glow!", not "Remember the past experience of arms control".

Of all the people who needed to be brought into line, thought the neo-conservatives, none needed it more than the Soviets. The wily s-o-b's had preyed on American good nature. While the United States practiced unilateral nuclear disarmament during the 1970s (and this precise description is that given by Mr. Edwin Meese III during a visit to Cambridge in 1983), the Soviets had engaged in a massive, coordinated, comprehensive arms build-up. So the first years of the Reagan presidency witnessed a succession of blood-curdling anti-Soviet pronouncements making this case. The Soviets bore the attacks with immense public patience. They did not react until September 1983, immediately after the still murky episode of the Korean airliner which by coincidence or design (we still do not know) had given the Americans a further and undeniably conveniently timed opportunity to attack the Soviet Union in the blackest terms shortly before the emplacement of the first Euromissiles in the teeth of widespread European public resistance. The vigour and scope of that opposition was also in no small part a product of the early Reagan rhetoric which well before 1983 had scared the pants off substantial parts of the European public. The patience of the Soviets under the provocations of the first Reagan administration was later described by Alexander Haig as "mind-boggling" (MccGwire (in press), Ch. 12). But it did not last forever. However it did last through the period of the most recent episodes of set-piece arms control, the START and INF negotiations which must be judged to have been failures in terms of their formal goals. What happened when the Soviets' patience ended I shall take up in the next section.

2. FIVE EXPLANATIONS OF ARMS CONTROL OBJECTIVES

So what was this sinuous history of arms control all about? The formal goal of arms reduction carries no more conviction than the pious reiteration of an eventual goal of general and complete disarmament, included in the preamble of arms control treaties. Given therefore that we are all against sin in the long term, what are we for in the short term? I see five different explanations of the objectives of arms control currently offered. They are not individually exclusive, but for clarity, I shall discuss them separately.

2.1 *Arms control is a narcotic*

Arms control is especially a narcotic administered by the superpowers to the rest of the international community, to stop them interfering in their symbiotic hegemony over their respective blocs.

This argument is most powerfully made by the former Swedish Minister of Disarmament Alva Myrdal. It is derived in part from her own intimate knowledge of the fruitless Geneva negotiations for a Comprehensive Test Ban which preceded the realisation of the Partial Test Ban in 1963. Non-aligned countries like Sweden played an important role in pressing for the CTB. Suddenly, she recalls, the two superpowers (and not forgetting Britain, which likes not to be forgotten) took themselves off to Moscow and within a fortnight had produced a treaty which was presented with a fulsome preamble speaking of the desirability of proceeding to a comprehensive ban. But no timetable was mentioned. The Geneva negotiators, who had wrestled with the nuclear powers' changing demands on verification, who had finally striven to bridge the gap between the two or three on-site seismic stations which the USSR offered and the seven which the US demanded, and whose position was undermined by the Partial Test Ban, at first accepted the superpowers' assurance that they had merely made a temporary concession to political expediency. But, argued Myrdal bitterly with hindsight, the moment had passed irretrievably. The waves of public anxiety which had been generated by the atmospheric testing and which had contributed to the political pressure which brought the nuclear powers to Geneva subsided, in the belief that indeed the journey of a thousand miles had begun. Meanwhile, the nuclear powers continued testing but now did their testing underground (Myrdal (1976)). CTB demands have continued to be made by the non-nuclear nations, and until the US broke off negotiations in 1982 the issue remained alive between the superpowers. The Third Review Conference of the Non-Proliferation Treaty in Geneva in 1985 has seen the demand return with renewed strength, especially since the Soviet offer of a CTB lies untested on the table and the verification objections raised by the US (and the British too - don't forget the British) have no serious scientific credence[3]. The NPT Review ended with a sharp demand from the non-nuclear countries for the nuclear states to produce a CTB within a year as minimum evidence of adherence to Article VI of the NPT. When the Soviets compounded the discomforture of the USA and UK by adroitly linking a test moratorium to continued restraint by the western powers, the USA decided to cut its diplomatic losses by asserting directly that it intended to continue to test and by then doing so in March 1986. As this essay goes to press, the Soviets have not let the Americans off the hook by recommencing testing themselves.

---

[3] Prof. L.R. Sykes (Higgins Professor of Geological Sciences, the Lamont-Doherty Geological Observatory, Columbia University), "Verification of Nuclear Test Ban Treaties". Testimony before the Subcommittee on Arms Control, International Security and Science, Committee on Foreign Affairs, United States House of Representatives, 8 May 1985, Washington, D.C.

2.2 *Arms control is about establishing "rules of the road"*

Arms control cannot end an arms race. It must not be pushed further than it may reasonably go. It can regulate an arms race and reduce crisis instability. That is worth doing. Half a loaf is better than no bread.

This view commonly heard in the western arms control community. It recognises that politicians and the press have tended to over-sell arms control and fears that thereby, the whole process will fall into discredit for failing to deliver what it never can deliver. What it can best deliver, it is suggested, are agreements on bi-lateral communication such as the original 1963 Hot Line agreement, the 1971 modernisation agreement and the 1973 agreement to reduce the risk of war by avoiding provocative acts (Goldblat (1983), pp. 73-75, 80, 163). However, opinion then sharply divides if it is suggested that one proceed beyond the general to the particular. The current debate over the desirability of a No First Use declaration by the West is the best illustration of the depth of the division, exacerbated by the eminence of the Gang of Four who proposed it. In a celebrated speech given preemptively, shortly before the No First Use article was to be published, Secretary of State Haig suggested that adoption of such a policy would call for a *tripling* of the US armed forces, the return of the draft and placing the economy on a "wartime footing". Since then, more mature reflection has tended broadly to support the Gang of Four's original contention (Bundy et al. (1982), Haig (1982), Steinbrunner et al. (1983)).

But the main example adduced by western arms controllers of arms control serving to civilise the arms race is the SALT process. The case put has three underlying assumptions. The first is that arms races cannot be stopped. This point was made in a memorable analogy by Professor Michael Howard[4). Arms racing is like adolescent sexuality. You cannot stop it; but what you can do is to channel it so that its exuberance does not do damage until the individual is mature enough to put his or her sexuality to responsible, productive use. The second assumption Professor Howard made strongly also. Arms racing is not dangerous so long as it is stable. This means that the maintenance of balance is more important than the absolute level at which the balance is held. It might be desirable to return to lower numbers, but

4) In a paper to the British Pugwash seminar, Kings' College, London, 6 February 1985.

the numbers are of secondary importance. This is a comprehensively contentious view, of course, starting from the relevance of "balance" as a concept in the nuclear age and ending with its implication that some day, somehow, arms control may turn into disarmament. But it is an assumption axiomatic to the SALT process. Thus the argument goes that the fact that SALT compelled both sides (which really means the secretive Soviets, since we publish everything) to table data about their strategic forces and to agree concepts of "balance" and ceilings of any sort derived from those agreed concepts, even if the ceilings were no more than what might have been done anyway without agreement, it meant *de facto* "rules" for admissible and inadmissible behaviour were established.

There is something very odd about this form of reasoning beyond the metaphysical problem with "balance" just mentioned. The cause of this oddness will be one of my main concerns in the next section, but in passing its product must be noted. It is that it only holds good if predicted upon the third assumption. This is of an otherwise limitless Soviet desire to conduct an arms race. By making this assumption, western arms control is thereby absolved from the necessity to look at the action/reaction dynamic of arms racing - which means the role of American catalysis - still less to search for and seek to understanding any autonomous Soviet logic in its approach to the arms control process. Should it be that in fact there *is* an autonomous Soviet logic which fits arms control into a wider political objective which is not one of limitless expansionism, one which actually gave the Soviets good reasons of self-interest to change the size and composition of the Strategic Rocket Force in ways favoured by western arms controllers, we would then have a difficult task of separating coincidence and cause, in which the causal role of the SALT process may be overestimated (which is *not* to say that it was irrelevant (MccGwire (in press) Ch. 10).

However, there is another type of "rule of the road" which combines the communicative quality of the diplomatic treaties with the precision of the operational proposals like NFU, although it is not as dramatic as that. Concluding his study of how a major, unintended consequence of the incremental complication of the command, control and communication systems of nuclear forces, especially during the last decade, has been to make a "nuclear Sarajevo" a much greater probability than the "nuclear Munich" which preoccupies most western public strategic thinking, Paul Bracken suggested ways in which arms control might serve to lessen that risk. The "rules of the road" to which he ascribed urgency are far more detailed than NFU: they are to do with sharing information about operating patterns to control the most dangerous points of contact between American and Soviet nuclear forces, with an object of improving "command stability" (Bracken (1983), pp. 243-247)[4]. This is therefore part of that same broader awareness of the importance of crisis stability which was one of the lessons of Cuba. There, it was the corollary of the Kennedy crisis team's realisation of the insignificance of nuclear superiority (Bundy (1984)). It has taken some time for that message to percolate more widely. The new literature on command and control came at a time when that hitherto hidden dimension was rather suddenly striking public consciousness. Thus his sort of "rule of the road" may prove to be a more elegant way to put classical arms control back on the tracks than a renewed concern with missiles, always assuming that we want to see it re-railed.

2.3 *Arms control is not first and foremost about arms control*

Arms control's value is principally in keeping the superpowers talking to each other. It happens to be about missiles. It could just as well be about sardines.

This is the view typically found among diplomats, especially thoughtful ones. It has the benefit of history to support it. In sixty-nine years of relationship between the capitalist nations and the Soviet Union, barely ten have been years of cooperation, including the years of the World War. The rest have been years of confrontation, each breakdown usually triggered by the west[5]. From the time of the wars of intervention to *Defense Guidance 1984-88*

---

[4] A similar conclusion is reached by B. Blair (1985).

[5] Historically the most important was the break at the end of the World War. By the summer of 1946, well before the Truman Declaration, in response to a request from President Truman's special counsel, Clark Clifford, memoranda from senior officials across the Administration revealed a virtual consensus that America was "in effect, at war with the Soviet Union..." (Yergin (1980)). That this fixed attitude precluded recognition of the potential for a different outcome to the superpower confrontation of these years is stressed by Yergin (notably in relation to the Czechoslovakian elections) and by Alperovitz (1985)). Others felt this well before 1946. For example, Professor Joseph Rotblat recalls how, when working on the Manhatten Project in 1944, General Leslie Groves told him that the atomic bomb was, of course, really to deal with the Russians, not the Germans or Japanese.

and beyond there runs a long trail of mistrust[6). While the USA and USSR have remarkably little in dispute between each other in terms of those old-fashioned, material clashes of interest that used to lead to war (no territorial dispute, no competition for markets or raw materials etc.) there is a profound ideological confrontation. The history of religious wars shows how vital it is in such situations to shatter the stereotypes which the potential antagonists have of each other and, argues the diplomat, it means that keeping open communication in as many ways as possible is supremely important. Arms control offers one constantly legitimate channel, which was the added benefit of being about something more important than sardines. Thus in this view, the worst eventuality is for talks to cease.

This view holds in common with the preceding one the first two, rather pessimistic assumptions about what arms control may achieve within its formal brief but may not hold the third assumption, about Soviet aggressiveness, as strongly. For this reason, today it tends to be a European establishment view, rather than an American one. In the 1960s it was much more equally trans-atlantic, during the period when that visceral anti-Sovietism which is always present in the American political system was more muted than it had been before, in the McCarthy period, or has become again since. It is a rather detached and cynical view, which does not recommend it to idealists of any persuasion. There is also considerable evidence that in the importance which they attached to the *process* of arms control as a means of avoiding world war, the Soviets during the years of *detente* subscribed to this view also.

2.4 *Arms control is a complex diplomatic game in which the object is to checkmate your rival*

This is a Machiavellian view also, but rather more assertive than Number Three. It has been routinely practiced by both superpowers at a superficial level, but with special concentration during the later stages of the SALT/INF process, once on the one hand Carter's inability to obtain Congressional ratification of SALT II was clear and on the other that arms control was again a principal object of wide public concern in the west. The aim was to win a chess. This meant planning to win the endgame from the outset. To do this, a bundle of proposals would be tabled, most of which were sweet

[6] For amplification, see Ch. 2 "The Trail of Mistrust, 1914-73" in Prins (1983), pp. 36-59.

and reasonable, but one or two of which could, with confidence, be expected to be unacceptable to the other side, upon whom blame could then be heaped for the eventual breakdown when it came. The Soviets did it by making doctrinal undertakings, such as of No First Use, or respect of Nuclear Free Zones, and most recently the unilateral moratorium on nuclear testing. If the west agreed to any of these, it was, from a Soviet perspective, a net gain (although Soviet military-technical reasons, relating to their operational plans for war in their Western TVD, for wishing NATO to adopt No First Use are rather different from those of the Gang of Four or the western peace movements). But they didn't expect agreement, so made propaganda of the American and NATO refusal to follow suit. The Americans did it by smuggling assumptions, for example that "zero" means zero in the INF negotiation, and then excoriating the Soviets for refusing to accept their definition.

Of course, sometimes things could go wrong. In the summer of 1955 the *coup de grace* was delivered to the ten years post-war quest for nuclear disarmament apparently following an episode of miscalculation. American objection to the UN disarmament package which had been laboriously assembled over the preceding two years was centred on verification. Under Eisenhower's "Open Skies" scheme, verification would be from the air. The Soviets favoured land-based control posts. In Geneva negotiations which prefigured the wrangles over test ban verification in 1962/63 and 1985, suddenly the American negotiator, Harold Stassen, announced a veto. America "placed a reservation on all its pre-Geneva substantive positions". Philip Noel-Baker, the veteran British diplomat concluded at the time, rather as Alva Myrdal was to conclude later with regard to the Test Ban, that the Americans got out because it looked as if the negotiations might succeed (Prins (1983) and references given there).

However, there is a deeper level at which arms control has been used as an integrated instrument of policy. The most accomplished exponents have been the Soviets during the years of *detente* between the 1966/67 and 1982/84 decision periods. MccGwire argues in common with many other Sovietologists that the intellectual framework of Soviet ideology and the nature of the bureaucratic structures which it inhabits, compounded by the searing shared experiences which first decimated and then recreated the leadership cohorts in the 1930s and 40s, militate towards a policy formulation process that is rather self-conscious. For analysts, this is an extrinsic virtue in that it is expressed in identifiable codes which clearly mark the documentary portions of the total empirical spectrum from which the broad trends of Soviet policy are identified and periodised[7]. One of the intrinsic virtues of such a method of expressing policy is that it maintains distinct the ranking of first order and lesser order priorities. First order national objectives remain constant: to promote the well-being of the Soviet State and to preserve its capacity for independent action. These lead to a third: to avoid world war. Obviously, this objective may at times be in tension with the second. But in the event that war becomes inescapable, a second order (military) priority becomes elevated: not to lose. The calculation of arms control's costs and benefits are always subordinate to and thus informed by these goals.

At the heart of MccGwire's argument is the identification of a critically important secular change in the principles of Soviet policy. It emanated from certain operational decisions taken in December 1966 when it was decided that whereas hitherto it had appeared inevitable that the Soviet homeland would be devastated in a world war, there was now a chance (not a certainty, only a chance) that Russia could be preserved by intra-war deterrence of the American strategic missile force at the time that NATO Europe was going down to defeat in a conventional blitzkrieg.

This change of operational assessment had far-reaching ramifications throughout the Soviet force structure. The rocket force had to be reshaped from the original SRF mission of the blanket and hopefully preemptive devastation of the USA to the immensely demanding task of intra-war deterrence. The non-nuclear forces in the western TVD had to be reshaped and enlarged for the task of kicking the Americans out of Europe within a fortnight of the outbreak of hostilities and without the use of nuclear weapons. These restructurings took about ten years to accomplish.

The implications for arms control were equally vast, although unlikely to have been the dominant factor in causing the Soviets to give a positive response to the first American overtures for SALT in 1966. Then a higher order national rather than military objective was engaged, for if the

---

7) I can offer here no more than this skeletal indication of the powerful methodology which MccGwire has developed in order to track Soviet policy historically. Early expositions are to be found in his essays in the Praeger series on Soviet naval policy which he co-edited in the 1970s, notably in MccGwire et al. (1975). Fearing to do it injustice, I would only reiterate my recommendation to read this book the instant that it is published. The following argument is mainly taken from Ch. 10.

Americans would enter constructive negotiations on strategic arms, this could help the objective of avoiding world war. They might even be brought to agree to the doctrine of "peaceful coexistence". But with the changed military objectives, the balance of cost and benefit changed dramatically.

Basically, the new military requirements for intra-war strategic deterrence meant that the political and economic benefits of the SALT process could be taken also. The post 66 mission demanded a much smaller rocket force than the 1959-66 mission of strategic preemption but increased the importance of being able to launch under attack. That called for hardened silos and/or mobility. The original plan was for a solid-fuel land-mobile ICBM. But the SS-13 did not work and so as a second expedient, the Soviets put their insurance force to sea, hurriedly modifying the "Yankee" SSBN hull into the distinctive hump-backed Delta I SSBN to carry the longer range and one third longer SS-N-8 (MccGwire (in press), Appendix B). This shift to sea-basing happened to be favoured by western arms-controllers because submarines are less prone to preemption and land-mobile missiles were disliked because of the verification problems which they posed. So fortuitously, the Soviets made decisions for their own, very different reasons which chimed with the SALT agenda. And if the arms control process could as well as aiding *detente* and facilitating sorely needed economic relief from arms construction also curb the growth of the American arsenal, all the better. In order to achieve such an abmitious and delicate complex of objectives, the Soviets have used a wide repertoire of techniques. Three episodes serve to illustrate the range.

Brezhnev had invested much political capital in the thesis that *detente* was an irreversible process. When the evidence began to accumulate from the Reaganauts before and then in office that this was not so, the Soviets made considerable efforts to resuscitate the SALT process. So when START began, they signalled a willingness to stick to the "Basic Guidelines for Subsequent Negotiations" signed by Carter and Brezhnev, offering significant reductions on the SALT II central strategic system ceilings (from 2,250 to 1,800, limits on MIRVed ICBMs from 820 to 680 and 400 MIRVed SLBMs). No doubt this was partly because their force structure was moving in this direction anyway. Intra-war deterrence requires flexible retargeting for which, given the lower technical level of Soviet computer technology as well as recollection of the Clausewitzian concept of "friction" in war, MIRVed weapons are not as suitable as single warhead rockets. But it is equally important to note that while the Soviets might be able to "afford" to make such an offer, they also managed to accommodate US plans: 680 MIRVed ICBMs would allow for 550 Minuteman IIIs plus 100 MXs leaving 430 for submarines. This would permit the construction of 18 Trident SSBNs at a cost of reducing the ICBM force by only two missiles. That suggests that they regarded MX and Trident as normal upgrading programmes, but by the same token, their vigorous attempt to obtain a ban on all land and sea-launched cruise missiles suggests where they saw the major new technological threat. That they failed is not the point. The way that they worked is.

This example must not be thought to be representative. No example is representative. In contrast, Soviet conduct at the Mutual and Balanced Force Reduction talks in Vienna illustrates well the coordination of arms control with other priorities. Following the 1966 decision, a fundamental restructuring of Soviet land and air forces in Europe was undertaken. When NATO first suggested mutual force reductions in Europe in 1968, the restructuring had hardly begun and so the political benefit of entering negotiation was outweighed by the military requirement. The Soviets stonewalled. By the early 1970s, the reforms were well in hand, so in 1973 MBFR began but with no serious negotiation until 1976. Only when the restructuring of Soviet forces was complete in 1979 did the Soviet position begin to become really flexible.

The last example underscores the point of the second, but adds another and very worrying dimension. The Soviet response to President Reagan's Star Wars ABM project reveals a degree of inflexibility which there is good reason to believe is not bluff. One lower order reason is military, another is political. The military reason is that if successful, a space-based ABM would threaten the primary mission of the Soviet strategic rocket force, namely intra-war deterrence. This in turn would threaten the objective "do not lose" in the event of war. The political reason is that Star Wars threatens an immediate and intense new arms race; indeed *Defense Guidance 1984-88* promises it. It is another piece of evidence to support the view that the US is seeking to overturn the existing "correlation of forces" and to regain the military superiority which it had until 1970. This means a challenge to the national objective of a "capacity for independent action", which in turn threatens the first order objective to "avoid world war". But there is a further significant and ominous difference from the position in the first example, at the beginning of START. We are now on the other side of what was probably a further, major reassessment of the principles of Soviet policy.

The Andropov Declaration of 28 September 1983 seems to have marked a further, fundamental shift in Soviet thinking. It signalled that after considerable thought, the leadership had concluded that pursuit of the *detente* policy with which Brezhnev was so closely associated was no longer possible. There is evidence that the most intransigent position which the USSR might have adopted has not been adopted. This would have involved three things: operational changes in the peacetime Soviet military structure to embed wartime C^3I in the TVDs, adoption of a much more assertive Third World military posture and a diplomatic offensive involving comprehensive withdrawal from bi-lateral US/USSR negotiations. The operational changes appear to be in train, but so far a root and branch disownment of the arms control process has not occurred. The three General Secretaries since Brezhnev, and Gromyko, all appear to believe that there may be still some juice in the orange.

The shift was in response to the deterioration in US/Soviet relations the genesis of which occurred around 1973. It became explicit by 1976 and became dangerously corrosive under Reagan. In an ominous sense, it looks like a repeat of 1947, following Truman's Declaration, with Andropov echoing Zhdanov's "two camps doctrine" in his view that the United States had again launched a crusade against the Soviet Union, that there was no way in which the US administration would change its ways and that the USSR would therefore respond as necessary to frustrate the American drive to attain again military supremacy.

Knowledge of the leaked *Defense Guidance 1984-88*, made public in May 1982, is thought to have been a significant consideration. Even taking account of the usual goal inflation of American political in-fighting and the expansiveness of American rhetoric, it is not hard to understand why this might have been so. The document calls for explicit plans to put strain on the Soviet economy especially by choosing for development weapons that would be costly for the USSR to replicate or counter like the "prototype development of space-based weapons systems", to foment irredentist movements in the Soviet's East European and Asian buffer states and to prepare, should the Soviet state not be destroyed in this way, to wage war at every level from guerrilla insurgency in third countries to general, prolonged nuclear war (Halloran (1982)).

So the signs are that the consequences of the September 1983 Andropov Declaration will include a return to many of the views held in the years immediately after the destruction of the wartime alliance. That suggests a reversal of the cost/benefit calculations which gave arms control its prominence in Soviet policy during the years of *detente* and may mean a shift in future Soviet arms control dealings closer to the final explanation of arms control currently to be seen.

2.5 *Arms control is a way of opening the war by other means*

Arms control is a way to attack your enemy's nuclear forces without using your own.

In retrospect, the American arms control community was guilty of complacency, dismissing Senator Jackson's aide and those who thought like him as a wild fringe of largely East European and often also Jewish emigrees whose good judgement had been affected by their intense, personal hatred of the Russians. What was not foreseen was the success with which this group would take over the terms within which arms control is currently defined by the American administration. But it would probably be a mistake to personalise responsibility to the extent that Talbott does in *Deadly Gambits*. Mr. Perle's coup was in part no more than the elevation of a theme that had been constant if mostly concealed in the American approach to arms control. First, let us be clear about the nature of his coup.

In Geneva in June 1985 I asked Mr. Perle in open forum to confirm or deny that those portions of *Defense Guidance 1984-88* which are in the public domain represent his Administration's policy. This he declined to do. But he has given his answer clearly in other ways; for if we are to believe Talbott's minutely detailed narrative of the arms control policy of the first Reagan administration then in the spectral battle of Perle versus Burt over how that policy should be shaped and conducted, Perle won and the terms of definition changed accordingly: Arms control as practised since the early 1960s was to be killed. It was appeasement of the Soviets. This time, there would be no bargaining, no polite diplomacy. Arms control would be the handmaiden of rearmament or it would be nothing. That meant that its role was to attack the Soviet missile force diplomatically. So we see Perle successfully blackmailing the Joint Chiefs of Staff into support of his "Zero Option" for the INF negotiation and we are forced to adjust our ornithological vocabulary. Those like Paul Nitze the INF chief negotiator, member of the Committee of the Present Danger, author of NSC-68 in 1950, that axiomatic statement of the Manichaean Cold War vision of the world (Freedman (1981)), Nitze who was a hawk in any former classification was now, while certainly not a dove, a lesser bird of prey: a kestrel perhaps? Hawks were something else, with Perle as the best example. Talbott structured his book around the view that this "revolution in arms control" failed and that in his view, the second Reagan administration would be compelled by circumstance to return from its apocalyptic idealism to a more constrained pragmatism. As we approach the November summit, all I can say is that I have seen no sign that Mr. Perle is not still riding the wind. Two earlier historical moments may serve to show that the route to this position was not wholly new.

Gerard Smith's account of SALT I contains a gripping passage in which he describes President Nixon's reaction to mounting domestic pressure to include a MIRV ban in the negotation: "Any, repeat any, individual who gives any, repeat any, encouragement to this kind of speculation should be first reprimanded and then discharged" (Smith (1980), pp. 162-163).

SALT I was at least ratified, but neither the subsequent Nuclear Threshold Test Ban (signed by Nixon in 1974), nor the Peaceful Nuclear Explosions treaty (signed by Ford in 1976) were, and in July 1982 the Reagan administration sought to renegotiate both. And then there was SALT II, negotiated under three Presidents, signed by two, it was condemned as "fatally flawed" by Reagan. Despite being unratified, adherence to its terms was used as a test of Soviet behaviour while the USA declined to say whether it would be bound or not until, at the very moment that the commissioning of a new Trident submarine threatened to breach the SALT ceiling, an older vessel was withdrawn.

So on top of this record, the American starting positions for START and INF, while more extreme, fitted an established pattern. The START position would have permitted the US to modernise its strategic forces according to plan while demanding that the Soviets reduce their ICBM warheads by 60%, which would have involved dismantling almost 70% of their most modern MIRVed missiles. That, in Alexander Haig's view, offered no basis for negotiation. And that was the point. Mr. Perle wanted no negotiation, for he saw negotiation as a sure route to conceding something. The contrast between the intellectual crudity and diplomatic gaucheness of this position and the Soviet one examined above is striking. One task in the next two sections of this paper is to probe more deeply the reasons for it. But the sombre note on which to end this section is to repeat how indeed Mr. Perle may have his way by helping to trigger a fundamental reassessment in Soviet thinking which will cause them to come to his conclusion, but for very different reasons.

3. PROBLEMS WITH THE MEDIUM AND THE MESSAGE

At a press conference in Geneva shortly before the Third Non-Proliferation Treaty review, Ambassador Lewis Dunn of ACDA stressed one of what he regards as the most telling reasons why the current American Administration refuses to agree to a Comprehensive Test Ban: To do so would deflect peoples attention away from the highest priority, which is to achieve radical reductions in the existing nuclear arsenals; and both superpowers are committed to 50% reductions in offensive missiles although not agreeing upon how that should be calculated (Groupe de Bellerive (1985)). So here we find Ambassador Dunn of the United States standing in the same city and metaphorically joining across twenty years with the Swedish Minister of Disarmament Alva Myrdal, offering the same basic analysis of the dangers of narcotic arms control and yet plainly holding radically different views about most aspects of the arms control process. What does this mean? It suggests that there may be problems with both the medium and the message.

The problem with the message is clear from the evidence adduced in the previous section: The western definition of arms control as classically expressed in the SALT process, which has been the ruling definition in that the Soviets have publicly been prepared to speak and deal within it, is framed overwhelmingly in technical terms. A currency of the numbers and characteristics of nuclear weapons has been used despite the fact that both are strictly meaningless in terms of that "existential deterrence" which, McGeorge Bundy has carefully argued, is the only linkage between nuclear weapons and international relations since 1945 which will stand rigorous historical examination (Bundy (1984), New York Review of Books (1983)). Maintenance in the nuclear context of the pre-nuclear military concept of a balance of power is one of the most dangerous consequences of the normal operation in human history of cultural lag in the matching of concepts to reality. In this, since both superpowers hold for different reasons to operational doctrines that envisage nuclear war-fighting, responsibility is shared.

Ambassador Dunn and Minister Myrdal's critique is apposite here, for undue concentration on questions of nuclear missiles obscures the fact that these are only secondary symptoms of the primary illness, which is the failure to establish after nearly seventy years a *modus vivendi* between Russia and America. For this the blame is shared also, but differently. For our present concerns, the West's current failure has two parts. On the one side of the Atlantic an American obsession with a technical and militarised presentation of a clash of Titans, on the other, a European failure to present an alternative strategic analysis, but instead a misguided preparedness to follow tamely in American footsteps in the name of preserving Alliance cohesion. The Soviets carry blame for failing to explain more clearly and consistently what in fact they understand rather better than us: that the problem is neither primarily technical nor military. But they have chosen secrecy and as a consequence, they have suffered from their failure just as we have from ours.

In fact, the history of arms control has, with one notable and revealing exception, been marked by more failures than any explanation linked to open (or hidden) agenda, such as the first four reviewed in the previous section, might lead us to expect. So perhaps there is something wrong with the internal dynamics of the process itself?

The ruling paradigm for arms control is linear. That means that progress is presumed to come step by step in round after round of patient negotiation. The favourite image used for this is of a game of chess. This is interesting, for chess is a game which institutionalises total mistrust and extreme intellectual aggression. But I think that a more accurate image is that of the Prisoner's Dilemma. Each prisoner must choose independently how to act. For each individual, defection always has a higher pay-off than cooperation; but if both defect, both do worse than if both had cooperated.

The Prisoner's Dilemma

		Column Player	
		Cooperate	Defect
Row Player	Cooperate	**$R=3$, $R=3$** Reward for mutual cooperation	**$S=0$, $T=5$** Sucker's payoff, and temptation to defect
	Defect	**$T=5$, $S=0$** Temptation to defect and sucker's payoff	**$P=1$, $P=1$** Punishment for mutual defection

NOTE: The payoffs to the row chooser are listed first.

The reason that this matches arms control better than chess is that chess has no space for trust, whereas beneficial solutions to the Prisoner's Dilemma do. Officially it was by hard-headed negotiation that the range of measures covered by the peripheral treaties and the SALT process was eventually agreed. However, during the years of *detente*, a fund of personal relationships developed between Soviet and American negotiators. It facilitated the complex interplay between formal "front door" and informal "back channel" negotiations which the detailed accounts of the negotiations by participating arms controllers argue to have been of considerable importance and to which Mr Perle took such strong exception, blaming it for the selling out of what he conceived to be American interests.

There is a paradox here. Adherence to a linear mode of procedure in arms control is strengthened by awareness that human behaviour, like the behaviour of other animals, is typically not linear. In a game of chess, the endgame will often witness a rapid and comprehensive deterioration of the loser's position. By refusing to make or to respond to "extravagant" gestures such as Soviet offers to freeze, it seemed to negotiators that they were maximising the chances of a successful outcome and minimising those of falling into a Soviet trap in the endgame. But adherence to this linear mode helps ensure that the highest formal objectives of arms control (transformation into arms reduction) cannot occur, because that requires large movements and mutual cooperation which the linear mode cannot accommodate.

What is the evidence for the artificiality of a linear model of behaviour, beyond an analogy with chess? The diagram illustrates from ethology a typical procedure for the non-fatal resolution of a conflict over a scarce resource (Krebs et al. (1978))[8]. It shows clearly how the two stags progressively escalate the competition, each roaring defiance thereby signalling his strength implicitly through his conspicuous waste of energy. (The human equivalent was seen in the *potlach* ceremonies of the Kwakiutl Indians of the Pacific North West who engaged in competitive destruction of wealth as a way of gaining prestige by showing how much they could afford to de-

[8] I am endebted to Professor Patrick Bateson and Dr. Paul Martin of the Sub-Department of Animal Behaviour, University of Cambridge, for their guidance in the field of ethology, while absolving them absolutely from responsibility for anything which I say about it here.

stroy (Benedict (1943)). Eventually, rather suddenly, one stag decides to give up and the other wins.

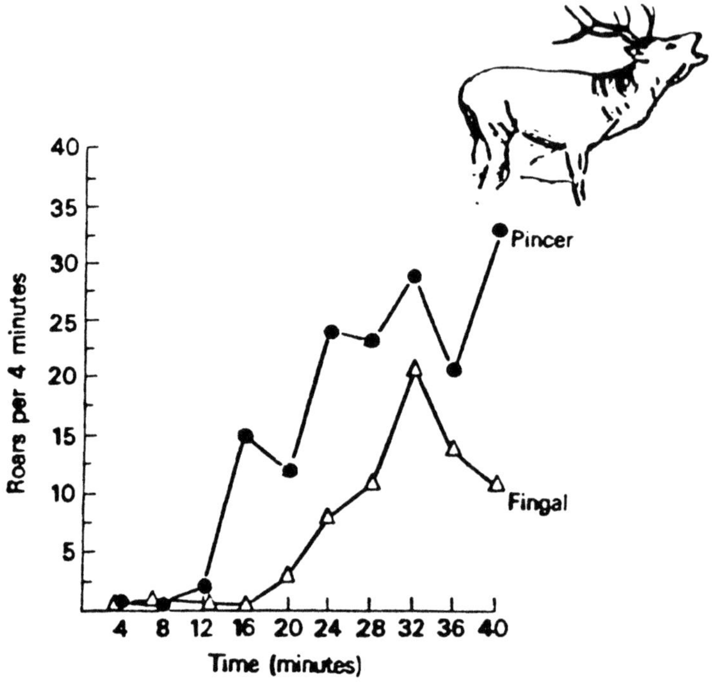

Roaring as a means of assessment in red deer stags. This graph shows a contest between two stags called Pincer and Fingal. As the contest proceeds, both stags roar at a progressively faster rate until one (Fingal) appears to 'give up'. His roaring rate drops off sharply while Pincer's continues to rise. Pincer won the contest which was over a harem. (Clutton Brock in prep.)

What does this example show? One popular reading is that it demonstrates that those who argue that toughness always pays in the end have Nature on their side. It shows the survival of the fittest. But this, argues Patrick Bateson, is a fundamental misreading of Darwin, occasioned by treating differential survival as if it were equivalent to social conflict. The stag fight type of example is also taken as evidence of the importance of concealing one's true intentions for as long as possible. This is certainly the case. But the stag fight example is not the only form of animal interaction, as the popular view assumes. In fact the animal world is full of examples of cooperation between animals and for cooperation to succeed, honest signalling is crucial. While it is true that in some situations animals dissemble, in others they signal honestly (Bateson (1985)).

This point deserves amplification. What the stag fight also shows is that animal behaviour, like human behaviour, is deeply affected by *context*. In a vicious escalating competition the objective is to manipulate the behaviour of the other party to one's advantage. It is a "zero-sum game". The circumstance causes the stags to engage in dishonest signalling, and this continues for most of their competition. But eventually there will come a moment of decision: to fight or to flee. At that moment, to avoid injury, the submitter's signals have suddenly to be changed and become very honest indeed. It means that the moment of decision will come in a split second. In other words, the process is highly unstable, despite the plateau of seeming stability which marks the long build-up; and if the two opponents are equally matched in strength this actually increases the unpredictability of the onset of breakdown. This new emphasis on the individual in ethology, compared to the classical concern with the abstract interests of the species, thus stresses that for vicious escalating conflicts it is the ability to dissemble and to resist false signals which is central, and that these qualities are engaged in an evolutionary arms race (Dawkin et al. (1975)). The corollary also holds: that for success in a virtuous escalating competition, honest signalling is axiomatic.

This is of special interest for arms control, because it is here that negotiation occurs; and the point which is relevant from the example of the stags' competition is that the stability of that process is deceptive and most dangerous in consequence. It appears to enhance the prospects of compromise, but in fact it is a slippery terrain where false or misunderstood signalling may unintentionally and catastrophically tip both parties over the edge. The emerging interpretation of the implication of the Andropov Declaration of September 1983 triggered by the first Reagan administration's conduct is a case in point.

But conversely there is one major example of the results which may be achieved if the superpowers can engage in a virtuous rather than a vicious competition. This was the successful negotiation of the Partial Test Ban Treaty in 1963. We must therefore examine it again, but this time not to consider its relative merits as a treaty but to recall the process of the negotiation.

The story is well known and has recently been narrated in detail by one of the actors in the piece (Prins (1983), pp. 118-124; Seaborg (1981)). The experience of the Cuban missile crisis helped to convince President Kennedy that substantial movement toward nuclear disarmament should be sought strenuously. A combination of the deadlock at Geneva and what he perceived to be a receptive public mood at home in the late spring of 1963 convinced him to attempt to obtain that movement by a breathtaking gesture to the Soviets[9]. This he made on 10 June in a speech at the American University in Washington, D.C.

He first defined the nature of the peace which he sought: *"What kind of peace do I mean? What kind of peace do we seek? Not a Pax Americana, enforced on the world by American weapons of war. Not the peace of the grave or the security of the slave. I am talking about genuine peace, the kind of peace that makes life on earth worth living, the kind that enables men and nations to grow and to hope and to build a better life for their children. I speak of peace because of the new face of war ... . I speak of peace, therefore, as the necessary rational end of rational men."*

Then he called for Americans to reexamine their attitudes. He challenged the idea that peace was unattainable. ("... *a dangerous, defeatist idea* ..."). He called for a reexamination of American attitudes towards the Soviets and towards the Cold War. In the process he offered a striking portrayal of the scale of Soviet suffering during the World War while at the same time scolding Soviet propaganda for its caricature of the USA. This he offered as a warning to Americans not to fall into the same trap of seeing *"only a distorted and desperate view of the other side"*. He made plain a size of the differences which divided the values and social systems of the two countries. *"but"*, he added, *"no government or social system is so evil that its people must be considered as lacking in virtue ..."*. *"So let us not be blind to our differences"*, he concluded, *"but let us also direct attention to our common interests and to the means by which those differences can be resolved ... . For in the final analysis, our most basic common link is that we all inhabit this small planet. We all breath the same air. We all cherish our children's future . And we are all mortal"*. The speech then conveyed two concrete pieces information: that high-level discussions would shortly begin in Moscow towards a comprehensive (*sic*) test ban and that the United States would uni-

---

[9] The term used by Norman Cousin in a telephone conversation with Kennedy which he reported to Seaborg and which Seaborg believes may have been the first spark of the idea for the speech (Seaborg (1981), p. 212 and MccGwire (in press), p. 308).

laterally observe a ban on atmospheric testing forthwith so long as other states did so also (U.S.G.P.O. (1964), Prins (1983), pp. 121-123).

While receiving little attention in the West (where the media were preoccupied with a sex scandal in the then British cabinet), the effect of the speech on the Soviet leadership was profound. VOA transmission of it in Russian to the USSR was not jammed and it was widely disseminated by the Russian media. It began a virtuous circle of events which, despite some retrogression in which Kennedy's hope for a comprehensive ban was dashed, ended with the formal signature of the Partial Test Ban in Moscow on 5 August, almost eighteen years to the hour from the birth of the nuclear age at Hiroshima.

The point to stress is that the American University speech was precisely the sort of initiative that classical arms control would shun. It was a quantum leap; it demonstrated the President's high investment of personal political capital and was therefore visibly both a risk and an act of trust; it was wise: a judicious mixture of disapproval and understanding of the other side's position and finally and vitally, it announced an independent, sovereign initiative without strings attached - the moratorium - which invited reciprocity and defied rupture (as the Americans have found in 1985/6 when the Soviets used exactly Kennedy's tactic on them).

It was therefore a very clear piece of signalling, carefully situated within a context designed for virtuous, not vicious escalation. It was undoubtedly one of the great documents of American statesmenship and (as he himself regarded it in the last months of his life) the most important speech of Kennedy's Presidency[10]. But the PTBT story has another lesson for the present if we look at it in terms of solving a series of rounds of the Prisoner's Dilemma.

There exists a substantial body of game theoretical writing as applied to the problem of superpower arms control negotiations. I am not a mathematician. I am wholly incompetent to discuss the inner workings of such procedures. But as an historian and anthropologist, I take an extreme interest in their defining and underlying assumptions. In this regard, the most important book that I have encountered recently is Robert Axelrod's report of the computer tournament which he ran to discover the best solution to the Prisoner's Dilemma (Axelrod (1984)).

---

10) I owe this insight to McGeorge Bundy.

The winner in both rounds was the simplest program. It was called TIT FOR TAT and was submitted by Professor Rapoport of the University of Toronto. It has two steps:

1) Cooperate on the first move.

2) Thereafter, do what the other prisoner did on the previous move.

Axelrod argues that what explained the success of TIT FOR TAT was not its simplicity or its length but the fact that it possessed four particular qualities: that it was *nice* (his term ..) in that it was never the first to defect; that it was *retaliatory* in that a defection was immediately punished by a defection, which discouraged persistent defection; that it was *forgiving* in that conversely, cooperation would immediately elicit cooperation, and finally that it was *clear*, which made it non-exploitable. Niceness and clarity were the qualities which gave TIT FOR TAT success over the most successful of the "non-nice", exploitative entries to the second tournament. (Interestingly, 14 of the top 15 programs were "nice" (Axelrod (1984), pp. 50-54)).

If we examine the process of the PTBT negotiation as an attempt to solve the Prisoner's Dilemma, the fit to TIT FOR TAT is close. Most striking in this regard is the long sequence of reciprocal deterioration broken by Kennedy's decision during the morning of 28 October 1962 to allow Khrushchev an escape route from the Cuban impasse by acceding to the Soviet demand for an American guarantee never to try and invade Cuba again, as in the Bay of Pigs operation. This fits the learning procedure of the program. Thereafter, the striking feature is how swiftly after the American University speech of 10 June 1963 "niceness" (and I do hope that Axelrod can think of a better term for it ..) sets in and how handsomely it paid off. The best example of this was when, upon arrival in Moscow on 15 July 1963 to conduct the negotiation, Averill Harriman was asked how long he expected to be in the USSR. He replied that if Mr. Khrushchev was as eager for a Test Ban as President Kennedy, he would be out within a fortnight: This the Soviets appear to have taken as a challenge, for he left twelve days later.

Secondly, it shows that throughout, the independent decisions of both leaders to stake substantial personal political capital in the process was vital in overwhelming the bureaucratic opposition entrenched on both sides. (As Air Force Chief of Staff Curtis LeMay was to testify at the Senate hearings on ratification, up to the time of Harriman's appointment, the Air Force had not realised how serious the Administration was in its pursuit of the treaty and so was caught a little by surprise (Seaborg (1981), p. 220).)

Thirdly, that means that this was an occasion and a structured situation in which Great Men could Make History. My capitalisation is intended to indicate how unusual I believe such events to be. Even then, as Alva Myrdal and others including Glenn Seaborg have observed, in the final analysis, the relative success of the PTBT must always be measured against the absolute failure to obtain what was really needed - a Comprehensive Ban. When contrasted with the years that followed, it is plain that the success in this episode was aberrant and that the failure to achieve a CTB was normal. My final analytic task in this paper is therefore to suggest that there is a sobering reason for this which lies at a level deeper than is accessible to any explanation posited in terms of game theory.

4. ON THE FALLACY OF NUCLEAR DETERRENCE

The total American military death toll in the World War was 405,000, about 1/325th of the 1940 population of the United States. Civilian casualties in the United States were zero. In Great Britain, the 398,000 battle casualties represented 1/150th of the 1940 population. In addition, the Blitz created some civilian casualties. 2,850,000 German soldiers died: 1/25th of the 1940 population. But there were substantial civilian casualties in Germany also from the area bombing campaigns of the RAF and USAAF as well as during the final assault on Germany in 1944-45. The Red Army sustained 7,500,000 deaths, being 1/22nd of the Russian population of 1940 (Prins (1983), Table 1, p. 50. Sources cited in fn 3, p. 352). "No nation in the history of battle suffered more than the Soviet Union suffered in the course of the Second World War", President Kennedy pointed out in the American University speech. For the battle casualties were only a fraction of the totality of destruction. "At least 20 million lost their lives. Countless millions of homes and farms were sacked and burned. A third of the nation's territory, including two third of its industrial base, was turned into a wasteland - a loss equivalent to the devastation of this country east of Chicago". It is no disrespect to the war dead of the other nations to dwell upon what that means, because for most Americans, it is quite beyond imagining. For the British also. For continental Europeans, those who suffered from battle, Nazi occupation and their genocidal War against the Jews and other *untermenschen*, there is the personal horror of the fractured families, the lost generations, that make real across a society the memory of war. The further east you go, the worse the experience and the stronger the memory (Erickson (1979,1983), Dawidowicz (1975), Fleming (1982)).

What possible relevance has this dragging up of the past to our present purposes? Professor Pipes once argued notoriously that we should remember this Soviet experience because it meant that having once suffered so appallingly, they would contemplate the potential casualties of a nuclear war with less concern than the more fortunate United States. I draw a different message, with exactly the reverse emphasis and informing a totally different issue: It is not that Americans are as Pipes portrayed the Soviets with such stunning insolence and inhumanity. It is the western strategic mind is much less good at thinking about the relationship between war and society and in consequence about the dynamics of what causes war, than is the Soviet strategic mind[11]. This applies crucially to the challege of the nuclear weapon. And the historical source of these intellectual differences rises directly from the starkly different national experiences of war in the twentieth century.

For the west, the nuclear age arrived with the shock of the new. The destructiveness which it portended, of which a sample was displayed in Japan, was quite beyond the repertoire of popular experience. So this strange, unearthly creature of western society's creativity needed a new frame of reference to accommodate it. This emerged from the seed of Bernard Brodie's work to grow in America in the 1950s into a special theory of "nuclear deterrence"[12]. In contrast, to Soviet eyes, this promised destructiveness was not so strange, being not so far distant from widespread popular experience. Therefore it did not require a radically new conceptual frame.

"Nuclear deterrence" deserves its inverted commas in order to distinguish

---

11) With one or two scholars as notable exceptions, e.g. M. Howard (1983).

12) In the following pages, I draw upon my earlier writing on deterrence in "Defended to Death" especially pp. 131-140, pp. 182-184, but much amplified by the ideas in M. MccGwire (1984), pp. 75-97 and his further development of that essay (1985). My debt to Professor MccGwire's thinking and generous sharing of his thought will be readily apparent.

it at the outset from two other concepts. The first is deterrence, an inescapable feature of human relationships, especially between groups, from earliest times in Man's history as a social being. The second is Bundy's "existential deterrence", already mentioned above. Existential deterrence is like nuclear deterrence in that it also describes the political effect of nuclear weapons. But it is fundamentally different in that it describes an automatic historical effect, independent of conscious strategy, whereas nuclear deterrence describes and prescribes a phenomenon which is the product of explicit and conscious intention. Its conclusions, both descriptive and prescriptive, are thus so comprehensively distant from those of nuclear deterrence that it merits conceptual severance. Existantial deterrence has very little intellectual common ground with the precepts of nuclear deterrence. Accordingly, it follows that it is in similar proportion less touched by the dissection which follows.

It is commonly asserted by advocates of nuclear deterrence that it has kept the peace since the end of the World War. But the more thoughtful of them, as also the more thoughtful of their critics, concede that this remarkably strong historical judgement can be neither proven nor disproven on direct evidence. That being so, a fall-back position is occupied: Prudence suggests that it is better to be over-insured rather than at risk, and even if we have been over-insured, we have only wasted some resources. It hasn't actually done us any harm.

It is this fall-back position which I wish to attack from several directions - nine, in fact - at once, for I see nine reasons to believe that this view is profoundly mistaken. It is indeed the heart of the argument of this paper that the deepest reasons why arms control has failed in the past and will fail again in the future if attempted without radical reconstruction, flow from the baleful intellectual hegemony of nuclear deterrence in the west's practice of international relations over nearly forty years. I shall number the objections for clarity.

1) Nuclear deterrence is simple. It promises that aggression will be met with sure retaliation. In the 1950s, the retaliation was sure, massive and indiscriminate; later, as technology permitted the strategic refinement, it could be threatened as sure, measured and precise. But it is predicated upon a smuggled assumption that the threat of aggression is real and in its own way as apocalyptic as the retaliation threatened.

The British physicist P.M.S. Blackett pointed out in the late 1940s that possession of an absolute weapon created a psychological necessity to conjure up an absolute enemy to deserve the punishment threatened. This nuclear deterrence does, and given that nuclear deterrence theory is mainly preoccupied with the intellectual problem of how to organise the nuclear weapons so as to pose the threat credibly and thus "to deter the Russians", the prior assumption is taken as given. The first mortar bomb to be lobbed into the dug-out of nuclear deterrence is therefore the charge that it addresses the central problem of international relations at too low a level. The problem is not "how do we deter the Russians/Americans/Ruritanians" but "how do we avoid a world war?". This the Soviets understand very well. We in the West would be well advised to copy them in this respect.

2) Given that nuclear deterrence identifies the problem as it does, it is not surprising that it offers overwhelmingly technical solutions to what are in fact political problems. The assumptions of classical arms control are, as we have seen above, a vivid example of this tendency. Given that the solutions are seen in technical terms, it is not surprising that nuclear deterrence employs an appropriate logic of analysis. This is the "worst-case assumption", the indispensable tool of any colonel worth his salt as he plans to commit his men to battle. If his intelligence is good, he knows the enemy's capabilities. But if he is wise, he assumes the worst. He assumes that the enemy will in fact present in greater number, and with faultless operational skill, with ample logistical supply, without breakdowns of men or machines, and with maximum aggressiveness. Capabilities equal intentions (Garthoff (1984)).

The error is as tragic as it is great. George Kennan has eloquently warned how the relations between great states are militarised in this fashion to our great peril (Kennan (1982)). Foreign Ministers should not analyse evidence in a way appropriate to a colonel in battle. Ministers are obliged to consider two other aspects in the policies of other powers, and to proceed from capabilities to intentions by a lengthier route:

```
CAPABILITIES * * * * * * * * REQUIREMENTS
                                   *
                                   *
                                   *
                                   *
 INTENTIONS * * * * * * * * * INTERESTS
```

A minister who acts as if he were a colonel is as derelict in his duty as a colonel who acts as if he were a minister. Both would deserve dismissal. While the latter is the exception, the former is the rule. Yet dismissal of ministers for employing the (for them) colonel's fallacy has not occurred to date in western countries.

In armies, worst-case analysis is not positioned at the colonel's level without good reason. Generals were once colonels, but what should distinguish them, theoretically, from junior officers is their ability and duty to combine the military and political forms of analysis. Quoting the ancient Chinese strategist Sun Tzu, one of this century's most successful exponents of generalship, Mao Tse Tung put it crisply: "Know the enemy and know yourself; in a hundred battles you will never be in peril". But nuclear deterrence places such distorting lenses before the eyes of those who use it that they are condemned never to be able to see their opponent clearly, to hold always that "distorted and desperate view of the other side" against which one President once warned.

Being free of the notion that nuclear deterrence prevents war, Soviet strategic thinking does not make this mistake. It may hold caricature views of the capitalist world for other reasons, but not for this one. A clear distinction is maintained between politico-military and military-technical issues. The result is that the Soviets possess a much more robust and realistic way of assessing their threat environment and of deriving from that analysis guidelines for political and military action than does the west. Again, we would be well advised to copy them.

3) The need to maintain the image of the Great Enemy to warrant the making of the Great Threat of nuclear deterrence has had dreadful effects upon the domestic western, especially American, image of the outside world. First of all, it has meant that a generation of Americans have been socialised with a ghastly, ogrelike image of the Soviet Union as an unremarkable part of their normal intellectual furniture. The image is highly resistant to change, being hard-shelled, like the beliefs of most primitive religions. It resists falsification in just the ways that Sir Edward Tylor, one of the nineteenth century fathers of modern anthropology, suggested that a witchdoctor protected his beliefs from falsification in the face of empirical evidence of their incorrectness

(Tylor (1873)). One of the commonest is to represent any deviation from the extreme as being an assertion of the opposite extreme. The reader may test this in him or herself by asking whether the account of arms control given earlier in the paper elicited at all the reaction that since it was in places strongly critical of the United States, the author must therefore be "pro-Soviet". The pendulum reaction indicates that the image is brittle as well as hard-shelled. This is frequently the case in fundamentalist religions with elaborate dogmas. So there is a hopeful possibility that one day Humpty Dumpty may be pushed off the wall, in which case all the President's men will not be able to put him back together again.

Nuclear deterrence has had two other specific effects on American views of the world in general and the Soviets in particular. Once the assumption of the Great Enemy is accepted, it brings with it, as a costless extra, a feeling of moral virtue. For if one is restraining a potential aggressor, with some justice, one can feel that one is the good guy. The parable of the mote in your neighbour's eye and the beam in your own is of relevance here.

Secondly, like a Bach fugue, the simple basic theme of nuclear deterrence has been intricately elaborated into many complicated variations. This has been the achievement of that strange pseudo-discipline of "strategic studies". It prided itself on its successful incorporation of mathematics into political science whereas it was, in fact, a lobotomised sub-discipline of history. The product of a very particular time and place (the United States in the early 1950s), strategic studies successful depersonalised its subject matter by cutting out its historical identity. It necessarily dealt in abstract players, whereas the real problem in the real world concerned real Americans and real Russians living in real, historically rooted societies. As well as legitimising the operationalisation of nuclear deterrence, the example of the procedures of strategic studies helped the general public, already propagandised with the image of the Great Enemy, to feel that it was probably intellectually and morally respectible to depersonalise the enemy to the extent that it has been done. And of course, thinking your enemy to death is an essential preparative to actually committing the act.

4) Nuclear deterrence has a grandeur to match the terrible latent power of the nuclear weapon. King Charles I, a seventeenth century English king who subscribed to the doctrine of the Divine Right of Kings, refused to recognise the right of mere men in Parliament assembled to try him for his life. In the same way, nuclear deterrence tolerates ill the suggestion that it be tried in the court of history. It is above history. It fitted the world of its birth at the beginning of the first Cold War. It cannot escape from what Daniel Yergin called the "Riga Axioms": the alarmist view of Russia first given discrete expression by the group of American Sovietologists gathered at Riga in the 1930s and given formidable political momentum by George Kennan's famous Long Telegram of Spring 1946 (Yergin (1980), pp. 168-171). For nuclear deterrence, the logically possible policy towards the Soviet Union is one of containment. Since nuclear deterrence cannot accommodate change, change must accommodate nuclear deterrence. It must stop, or at least be said to have stopped. So a further damaging effect has been to trap the axioms of American foreign policy as if in amber, unable to reorientate to a multi-polar world in which America no longer possesses the economic or political dominance which it had at the end of the World War. This has been extremely dangerous, because the continuing dominance of the bipolar, Manichaean analysis in American foreign policy makes the Soviet Union the automatic scapegoat for any and all of the wholly expected deviation from this norm which is anchored so irrationally and immoveably in the late 1940s. It means that the issue of possible long-term cooperation between the USA and the USSR for anything other than cosmetic purposes does not appear - cannot appear - on an American political agenda that could command majority electoral support. This stag cannot see itself in anything other than a vicious escalating competition with one other, while in fact, behind its back, other stags in the western herd (known technically in the ethological literature as "sneaky fuckers") have been having their way with the harem. That has made the American stag angry, but unlike the real stag, it has eccentrically preferred to blame its chosen competitor for putting the sneaky fuckers up to it!

However, within this gloomy panorama, two sparks of light may be seen. One is that in the PTBT episode, we have one example, faint and guttering though it may be, of a few months when the dynamism of one President succeeded in pulling American policy out of this pattern of behaviour.

It was ironic that the same President was also responsible for the strategic missile decision which we can only now begin to see in its fullest ramifications and thus understand to have been that which more than any other launched the main upward spiral of the nuclear arms race to date. The other spark of light is the recollection that Charles I of England lost his head.

5) Nuclear deterrence theory helped to justify the Minuteman and Polaris decision. It was in this way that unintentionally, nuclear deterrence has fuelled the arms race. It has done it paradoxically, through its pursuit of stability. It was argued that deterrence would be more stable at higher numbers of missiles, for at lower numbers, there was always the chance of an enemy "break-out", which could threaten the credibility of the Great Threat. But a build-up was not perceived as a peaceful gesture by the Soviets. It engendered an action/reaction response. So the sought-for stability was found to have evaporated at the 1,000 missile level, like a crock of fairy's gold. Therefore in the interest of renewing the now eroded credibility, nuclear deterrence demanded further build-up, and so we have gone on in a stately dance towards the abyss.

The point is that "stable nuclear deterrence" *is* a crock of fairy's gold. It cannot be kept, it can only be sought. Because it believes that it is stable, nuclear deterrence is the more perniciously degenerative. It is a wasting condition. But, recollecting the first charge levelled above, proponents of nuclear deterrence are prevented from seeing this obvious and empirically undeniable point because they cannot recognise this as a possible route to war.

6) It is said with good reason that generals are always preparing to fight the last war. This is true of politicians also. It is true today. For conservative western politicians in the age-range Reagan to Thatcher, a political rule-of-thumb is taken from a common mis-recollection of the history of the 1930s. Why did the World War happen? Because of Munich. What was Munich? Appeasement of Hitler. What is the lesson? Better to deter than to appease. Forgotten are the facts that appeasement was originally a conservative policy (with which, to be sure, many mainstream

European socialists (i.e. not those who fought for the Spanish Republic against Franco) agreed), that it was overwhelmingly supported by the French and British public, that early rearmament was not economically feasible, and that the policy was not without logic (Taylor (1964), Kennedy (1981), Howard (1978)). Furthermore it is forgotten that there was a deterrent in the 1930s, and it did not prevent war. The exaggerated expectation of the performance of the heavy bomber had caused the air-power theorists of the 1930s to believe that in it they possessed an absolute weapon. (Indeed, in their work on deterrence are to be found the roots of nuclear deterrence (Paskins at al. (1979), pp. 3-48). The myth works better for present purposes than the awkward lumpiness of the reality.

This casting backwards onto the mythic account of the 1930s of the web of ideas which intertwine nuclear weapons and Russia has captured and dragged to prominence an idea which obscures more than it reveals. It is use of the shorthand of "Munich" to stand for the danger of international blackmail, which means in present terms, nuclear blackmail of the west by Hitler's successor in conservative eyes, the Soviet Union. It is a sleight of hand. "Munich" (whatever that event actually was) was actually quite important in the march to war. By association, nuclear blackmail is assumed to be a threat worth taking seriously also, to which possession of an equivalent threat is suggested as the only possible response. The potential threat of Soviet nuclear blackmail is frequently invoked by the western nuclear powers to justify their own nuclear programmes (McMahan (1983))[13]. Yet when subject to historical examination nuclear blackmail is found to be as chimeric as the stability of nuclear deterrence, because it is so easy to defy. When attempted, it has been largely unsuccessful, and therefore is not now attempted, either between nuclear powers or, of more interest for the popular application of "Munich", by nuclear of non-nuclear powers. If it were the threat that it is represented to be, I submit that forty years of history should be if not littered with examples, at least able to provide a number of con-

---

13) McMahan also gives a useful sharp discussion of the similarities and differences between nuclear deterrence and nuclear blackmail. pp. 84-87.

vincing cases, which it cannot. In the real world, nuclear blackmail is a non-issue (Bundy (1984), p. 71, Prins (1983), pp. 285-286).

What the preoccupation with nuclear blackmail really shows is the effect of those variations on the theme of nuclear deterrence upon the western strategic mind. They caused it to boggle at abstract, chess-like solutions to remote and highly speculative possibilities, solutions which were Platonic in their assumption of tranquil and constant rationality in the players and of clear and honest signalling between them. In consequence, it failed to notice that it was looking at the wrong war for historical insight.

From time to time, agents of the German General Staff slipped into Russia. As they waited for their trains, increasingly worried men paced the platforms of stations the length and breadth of western Russia. The result of their pacings created alarm in Berlin. It became evident that Russia had instigated a platform lengthening construction programme. To the General Staff which had developed the comprehensive integration of railways and telegraphs into operational planning from Moltke's embryo of the 1866 Königgratz campaign (Creveld (1985)) to Schlieffen's maturity, the sign was ominous indeed: for the time it took to entrain or detrain a given unit was directly proportionate to the available length of railway platform. Scaled up, this could have a significant effect on the potential speed of Russian mobilisation. If that happened, and worst-case assumptions suggested that it would be prudent to assume that it would, Germany's "window of opportunity" would narrow considerably (Fischer (1984)). In fact, the Russian Imperial Staff were anything but confident of their ability to mobilise at a fraction of the rate which worst-case assumptions caused the Germans to presume. On the contrary, the outcome of their worst-case thinking was to believe that the Russian Army had dangerously little leeway if called to mobilise.

Thus, when the Tsar wanted a partial mobilisation as a response to the Serbian crisis, he was advised that his only options were total mobilisation or none; and from that action sprang like a coiled spring the reaction of German mobilisation. Men in 1914 had provided the material means which took up, cruelly twisted and took control of the hankering for war which the Germans certainly had. But they didn't mean the war to be like it was or when it was, nor did they intend its result. "Sarajevo", if carefully examined, is the historical shorthand to which we should attend, not "Munich".

7) Those best equipped to learn the lessons of Sarajevo and to warn of their dangers are the military. Yet a further paradox of nuclear deterrence is that this militarised world-view has driven the military from the strategic debate. One example is painful enough to be sufficient. The adoption of "flexible response" and "extended deterrence" by NATO may have been consistent with the doctrine of nuclear deterrence, but they bore no relation to sensible military strategy. Extended deterrence is a contorted nonsense (Gayler (1984)); flexible response is a recipe for disaster if ever called upon to defend western Europe (Collins (1984)). What it actually did, as we saw earlier, was to offer the Soviets a strategic opportunity in their planning for the second-order objective "do not lose" which helped justify a radical restructuring of Soviet forces and the introduction of new operational concepts (MccGwire (in press), Chs 2 & 3). It is high time to bring the military back into the strategic debate, for real military insight is important in planning real defence.

8) Military men know war. Civilians in the fortunate English speaking countries generally do not. What do the military know? They know that "War is Hell". This is not just a description, it is a doctrine. For General Sherman was explaining that the horror of war is limitless. In replying to the protest of the Confederate General Hood at his order to evacuate and burn Atlanta, Sherman observed that "War is cruelty and you cannot refine it", and therefore, he concluded, "those who brought war into our country deserve all the curses and maledictions a people can pour out", (Walzer (1980)). He refused to accept any moral blame for the acts which the tyranny of a war not of his making obliged him, the more swiftly to end it, the more terribly to undertake. The Means are both justified and purged of moral taint by the Ends.

Sherman's doctrine has become a commonplace since the World War. For in defeat of an evil as palpable as that of the Third Reich, its logic seemed undeniable. But there had been those in Britain like George Bell, the Bishop of Chichester, who maintained that the obligation of the Christian doctrine of the Just War to fight cleanly, in due proportion to the injury suffered and with discrimination between combatants and civilians could not be escaped, even in the war against Hitler. Accordingly the ethical status of the terror bombing campaign of "Bomber" Harris's Bomber Command looked to him to be profoundly dubious. It was specifically to prevent Bell and other troubled religious leaders from making public condemnation of the bombing offensive had they known its true purpose that the Secretary of State routinely misrepresented the reason for each raid as he reported it to the House of Commons, stating it to have had a military purpose, achieved or not as the case might be, with regrettable collateral damage. The Air Ministry feared that such condemnation might affect the morale of bomber crews (Paskins et al. (1979), p. 42)). The ambivalence was obviously deeper, for Harris was the last of the British wartime commanders to be honoured, and that not until late in his life.

Nuclear deterrence is truculently amoral and therefore claims the blanket absolution of Sherman's doctrine. Yet its proponents, like their wartime bomber predecessors, lack the full courage of their convictions. Whether this is for genuine personal reasons, or, as in wartime Britain, for a felt need of political expediency, is of no consequence for our purposes. When Robert McNamara announced counterforce nuclear targeting to the public in his Ann Arbor speech, he justified it on practical grounds. But by the time of the first Reagan Administration it was being argued that it was more moral than Shermanite counter-city targeting. The *locus classicus* came in President Reagan's Star Wars speech, which asserted clearly the long-term moral impossibility of accommodating nuclear deterrence within the ethical and legal values which the west cherishes.

This was a huge leap forward. Nuclear deterrence is wicked. Indeed it cannot be squared in any way with the Christian tradition, as the former Chief of Chaplains of the United States Army has recently concluded (Johnson (1984)). It corrodes the very fibres of those ethical and legal virtues which in the west we so jealously and rightly guard. It is impossible to construct a defence upon a strategy that destroys, before the war begins, the very thing that you wish to defend; that beckons on the war and in it will destroy the possibility of ever learning from the mistake.

9) Why has it taken so long for any and all of the eight charges lobbed into the bastion of nuclear deterrence to begin to explode? Because nuclear deterrence has made people complacent. The prison in which their minds have been trapped is a silken cage, its bars unnoticed in daily life. It has given the false impression that the conjoined problems of nuclear weapons and the Russians have been solved. No illusion could be more dangerous. It has permitted, actually encouraged, self-indulgent and sloppy thinking. So this, the last charge to be considered, is the one which as it explodes, fires all the rest.

5. LESSONS LEARNED

If the intellectual thralldom of nuclear deterrence is the root cause of our inability to control our nuclear environment, and if the prisoners are now to escape from their thralldom, what do we put in its place? Nothing. This is obvious to any prisoner. You do not choose to exchange one prison for another. George Kennan used a slightly different analogy, comparing the grip of the nuclear delusion to an evil spell (Kennan (1984)). The central problem is a political problem of the Soviet-American relationship. This can only be addressed in old-fashioned, historically conscious, politically sensitive, nuanced, diplomatic terms. The removal of nuclear deterrence from the western body politic is like the removal of a malignant tumor. One does not ask in the case of cancer "what will you put in its place?".

Of course, there are obvious practical questions which arise as a consequence. There remains the fact that the USSR possesses formidable armed might in eastern Europe, sufficient to launch a devastating non-nuclear attack should it so wish. Here old-fashioned deterrence is the guide, for neither "existential deterrence" nor "deterrence" were present in the bunker of nuclear deterrence just demolished. It is certainly not beyond the wit or resources of the NATO nations to construct a proper military (i.e. non-nuclear) defence of western Europe. To do so will, in military-technical terms, be construed as a threat by the USSR, for it will frustrate their plans for a swift non-nuclear victory in western Europe during the first phase of a world war.

Their military will doubtless wish to counter-optimise. But this is a game in which the west will always win, if it plays its cards right. Playing its cards right means constructing a prudent and clever defence while avoiding a conventional arms race; and that means paying as much attention to the politico-military significance of such operational changes as the Soviets will do. For a western abandonment of nuclear deterrence and reversion to old-fashioned deterrence and diplomacy would be rightly perceived in Moscow as a move which lessened the risk of world war. The minute hand of the famous clock of the Bulletin of the Atomic Scientists could be moved back farther from fatal midnight than ever before. Before the September 1983 decision-point, we might have confidently expected the Soviet leadership to conclude that the politico-military gain for a first-order national objective ("avoid world war") outweighed the loss for a second-order military objective ("do not lose"). Now we cannot be so sure. But it is lesser risk that the threat to our first-order national and Alliance objective ("avoid world war") posed by continuing as we are now going.

What, finally, is the implication for arms control? We may now see clearly why arms control has failed to deliver. Classical nuclear arms control was the child of nuclear deterrence. It had no autonomous intellectual basis. The test of parentage is simple. Nuclear deterrence asserts that the relationship between nuclear weapons and security is a rising, positive correlation: More nuclear weapons, more security. Arms control holds a modified form of that view: a balance of nuclear weapons, more security. Nuclear disarmaments stands on a wholly different premise. It sees the relationship between nuclear weapons and security to be an inverse correlation: Increasing nuclear weapons, decreasing security. Classical arms control could not hop across the gulf between the contradictory positions and so, at the first serious challenge, it failed. The child would not attack the parent.

That challenge and failure, it must be remembered, was its inability to obtain Congressional ratification of SALT II, not to come to some sort of agreement with the Soviets. Since then, its position, crippled by its genes, has been steadily weakened further as treaty after treaty signed when it cost nothing to do so, has been scorned to suit the convenience of some other now more fashionable goal. And we must also remember that there is not one lesson from the history of arms control. The halcyon years of nuclear arms control coincided with the post December 1966 to September 1983 period in Soviet politico-military thinking, which was, for its own reasons, favourably inclined to the expressed goals of western arms control. It was during *that* period that the failure occurred. It seems likely that we are now, in no small part thanks to our efforts, back in a period when Soviet attitudes to arms control will be much less attractive to western ways of thinking. What, in such a grim situation, is to be done?

Lenin asked himself that same question in another context, probably in the winter of 1901, as he wondered how to speed the revolution (Lenin (1970)). His reply was unequivocal: to bring what he believed would be a better future for Russia, he had to destroy the liberalised *ancien regime* created by Stolypin and the Duma. One does not have to be quite as fiery as pre-revolutionary Lenin to recognise that it is common sense that an understanding of past weaknesses is an essential preparative for the successful reconstruction of virtually anything, no less of arms control.

What has this investigation revealed? First, some salutary lessons: That classical nuclear arms control was crippled from birth by its nuclear deterrence genes and that nuclear deterrence is at the root of the problem, having done us grave, demonstrable damage on nine counts in return for one highly speculative benefit (stopping the Russians from invading western Europe since 1945), a claim which is, on the best circumstantial historical evidence, more likely to be coincidental than causal. Even the more moderate claim, that it has been at best helpful, at worst irrelevant - that it has been at least not malign - may not be true at all. For ironically, by heightening the risk of a Sarajevo slide to war, nuclear deterrence may, in fact, have made the absolute chance of a Soviet invasion of western Europe, which would be their highest military objective once the world war had begun, more likely than it would have been under a different, more realistic system of international relations. It is also salutary to see how unrealistic is the western assumption of linearity in escalation of nuclear deterrent threat or arms control.

This pointed to a second, more hopeful group of insights arising from the observation that in human affairs as in the animal kingdom, things move not in smooth linearity but in sudden leaps. It was seen how much the choice of behaviour is conditioned by the framing circumstance, and of considerable interest was the finding, counter-intuitive to the popular mis-reading of Darwin, that hard-headed, selfishly motivated co-operation was the best solution to the Prisoner's Dilemma. It was hopeful to note that in one episode of arms control, that of the Partial Test Ban in 1963, there was some modest indication that selfish co-operation had worked. There is evidence that the Soviets have understood these qualities of behaviour well for longer than we have, and that at both the politico-military and military-technical level, this knowledge has informed their political and military dispositions and plans.

Finally, as a consequence of removing the distorting lenses placed over our eyes by nuclear deterrence, and running through the paper, has been the urgent need to clarify our understanding of why, from a Soviet point of view, the Soviets have done what they have done in the field of nuclear weapons and nuclear arms control. Assisted by Professor MccGwire's generous sharing of the manuscript of his forthcoming book on Soviet military objectives, a book which is in my opinion without question one of the two or three most important on East/West relations of this generation, we may begin that fascinating and vital task.

References

Allen, L. and Dombey, N. (1985): X-Ray Lasers to Shoot Holes in the Test Ban Treaty? New Scientist, 19 Sept. 1985, pp. 30-33

Alperovitz, G. (1985): Atomic Diplomacy: Hiroshima and Potsdam, Appendix IV. London, pp. 328-338.

Axelrod, R. (1984): The Evolution of Cooperation. New York

Ball, D. (1980): Politics and Force Levels: The Strategic Missile Program of the Kennedy Administration. California

Bateson, P. (1985): The Recovery of Trust. Medicine and War, 1, pp. 169-176

Benedict, R. (1943): Patterns of Culture. Boston, pp. 184-186

Blair, B. (1985): Strategic Command and Control: Redefining the Nuclear Threat. Washington, D.C., pp. 286-287

Bracken, P. (1983): The Command and Control of Nuclear Forces. New Haven

Bundy, McGeorge, Kennan, G., McNamara R. and Smith, G. (1982): Nuclear Weapons and the Atlantic Alliance. Foreign Affairs, 60, Spring 1982

Bundy, McGeorge (1984): The Unimpressive Record of Atomic Diplomacy. In: The Choice (Prins, Ed.), p. 50

Collins, A.S. (1984): Current NATO Strategy: A Recipe for Disaster. In: The Choice (Prins, Ed.)

Creveld, M. van (1985): Command in War. Cambridge, Mass., Ch. 4

Dawidowicz, L. (1975): The War against the Jews, 1933-45. London

Dawkin, R. and Krebs, R. (1975): Animal Signals: Information or Manipulation? In: Behavioral Ecology (Krebs and Davies, Ed.). Oxford

Erickson, J. (1979): The Road to Stalingrad: Stalin's War with Germany. Vol. I. London

Erickson, J. (1983): The Road to Stalingrad: Stalin's War with Germany. Vol. II. London

Fischer, F. (1972): Germany's Aims in the First World War. London

Fleming, G. (1982): Hitler and the Final Solution. California

Freedman, L. (1981): The Evolution of Nuclear Strategy. London, p. 69

Garthoff, R.L. (1984): Worst-case assumptions: uses, abuses and consequences. In: The Choice (Prins, Ed.), pp. 98-108

Gayler, N. (1984): A Commander-in-Chief's Perspective on Nuclear Weapons. In: The Choice (Prins, Ed.)

Goldblat, J. (1983): Arms Control Agreements: A Handbook. London

Groupe de Bellerive colloquium "Nuclear War, Nuclear Proliferation and their Consequences", Press Conference 29 June 1985; L. Dunn, "The Non-Proliferation Treaty Review: An American Perspective" typscr. paper presented at Colloquium, p.11

Haig, A. (1983): Peace and Deterrence. Speech at Georgetown University, Washington, D.C., 6 April 1982, Bureau of Current Affairs, Current Policy Document no. 383

Halloran, R. (1982): Pentagon draws up first strategy for fighting a long nuclear war. New York Times, 29 May 1982

Howard, M. (1983): The Relevance of Traditional Strategy. The Forgotten Dimensions of Strategy. In: The Causes of Wars (Howard). London

Howard, M. (1978): War and the Liberal Conscience. Oxford, pp. 73-115

Johnson, K.D. (1984): The Morality of Nuclear Deterrence. In: The Choice (Prins, Ed.)

Joll, J. (1984): The Origins of the First World War. London, p. 1-8

Kennan, G. (1982): The Nuclear Delusion: Soviet-American Relations in the Atomic Age. New York

Kennan, G. (1984): The State of US-Soviet Relations: Breaking the Spell. In: The Choice (Prins, Ed.)

Kennedy, P. (1981): The Realities behind Diplomacy: Background Influences on British External Policy, 1865-1980, Pt. III. The Politics of Appeasement, 1919-39. London

Kinkade, W.M. (1981): Arms Control: Negotiated Solutions. In: Cruise Missiles: Technology, Strategy and Politics (Betts, Ed.), Washington, D.C., p. 326

Krebs, J.R. and Davies, N.B. (1975): Behavioral Ecology: An Evolutionary Approach. Oxford, p. 295

Lenin, V.I. (1970): What is to be Done? Burning Questions of our Movement. Lenin, Selected Works, Vol. I. Moscow, p. 264

MccGwire, M., Booth, K., McDonnell, J. (1975): Soviet Strategic Weapons Policy 1955-70. New York, pp. 468-502

MccGwire, M. (1983): The Dilemmas and Delusions of Deterrence. In: Defended to Death (Prins, Ed.), London, pp. 75-79

MccGwire, M. (1985): Deterrence: The Problem Not the Solution. SAIS Review, 5, ii, Summer/Fall 1985, pp. 105-124

MccGwire, M. (in press): Soviet Military Objectives. Appendix A: Development of the Strategic Rocket Forces. Washington, D.C.

McMahan, J. (1983): Nuclear Blackmail. In: Dangers of Deterrence: Philosophers on Nuclear Strategy (Blake and Pole, Eds.). London, p. 84

Myrdal, A. (1976): The Game of Disarmament: How the United States and Russia Run the Arms Race. New York, pp. 85-88

New York Review of Books (1983): The Bishops and the Bomb. New York, pp. 3-8

Paskins, B. and Dockrill, M. (1979): The Ethics of War. London

Polanyi, J.C. (1984): We must avoid an arms race in space. In: The Choice: Nuclear Weapons versus Security (Prins, Ed.). London. Also under a different title (The Nuclear Crisis Reader), New York, 1984, pp. 65-68

Prins, G., Ed. (1983): Defended to Death: A Study of the Nuclear Arms Race. London

Rosenberg, D.A. (1981): A Smoking Radiation Ruin at the End of Two Hours: Documents on American Plans for Nuclear War with the Soviet Union, 1954-55. International Security. Winter 1981-82, pp. 3-38

Seaborg, G.T. (1981): Kennedy, Khrushchev and the Test Ban. California

Smith, G. (1980): Doubletalk: The Story of the First Strategic Arms Limitation Talks. London, p. 154

Steinbrunner, J.D. and Sigal, L.V., Eds. (1983): Alliance Security: NATO and the No-First-Use Question. Washington, D.C.

Talbott, S. (1979): Endgame: the Inside Story of SALT II. New York, p. 57

Talbott, S. (1984): Deadly Gambits: The Reagan Administration and the Stalemate in Nuclear Arms Control. New York, pp. 99-100

Taylor, A.J.P. (1964): The Origins of the Second World War. London, pp. 25-27

Tylor, E.B. (1873): Primitive Culture Vol.I. London, p. 134

U.S.G.P.O. (1964): Commencement Address at American University in Washington, D.C., 10 June 1963. Public Papers of the Presidents of the United States. J.F. Kennedy 1963. Washington, D.C., pp. 459-464

Walzer, M. (1980): Just and Unjust Wars: A Moral Argument with Historical Illustrations. London

Yergin, D. (1980): Shattered Peace: The Origins of the Cold War and the National Security State. London, p. 242

ARMS CONTROL FRUSTRATION – UNDERSTANDING THE IMPASSE AND HOW TO BREAK IT

John R. Bode and Stephan E. Schoderbek
The BDM Corporation
Albuquerque, NM 87106

1. INTRODUCTION

During the past few years a sense of disenchantment with arms control has been growing in the United States. Colin GRAY (1982) stated: "*Today it is acknowledged that there is a general crises of arms control. The more liberal side of the defense policy debate is concerned because arms control agreements seem merely to record and endorse the arms competition as usual, while defense-minded conservative analysts tend to believe that an on-going arms control process unsettles rational defense planning.*" (p.165).

More recently, Kenneth ADELMAN (1984) presented a similar view: "*Of all emotions arising from strategic arms control today, the most profound is disappointment. In this, as in little else in the vast realm of arms control, conservatives and liberals concur--conservatives for the failure of arms control to diminish the evermore ominous Soviet strategic build-up, liberals for its failure to diminish the evermore wasteful strategic 'arms race'.*" (p.240).

Yet, despite widespread frustration with the lack of progress to date, arms control retains a high level of political interest. It is probably safe to say that the United States is neither satisfied with the progress of arms control negotiations nor willing to abandon the process. Nor is the interest limited to the American public. In addition to pressure from a broad constituency at home, our NATO partners demand continued negotiation as a partial price for deployments of Pershing weapons and cruise missiles, and participation in the Strategic Defense Initiative (SDI).

Are we misleading ourselves by continuing to seek arms control in spite of the dismal record of the past? Is it likely that our expectations are incompatible with the limited potentials available in the process? Or are we approaching the whole problem in an inappropriate way? Answers to these questions are fundamental to breaking the current impasse.

NATO ASI Series, Vol. F 26
Modelling and Analysis in Arms Control
Edited by R. Avenhaus et al.

We begin by reviewing United States and Soviet stated positions and past actions to infer whether goal compatibility is sufficient to underwrite real agreement.

2. STATEMENT OF BROAD GOALS

Many Americans believe that the Soviet Union has the same objectives or goals in arms control negotiations as the United States. These Americans support arms control negotiations with the Soviet Union because they believe that the Soviet Union, like the United States, will negotiate in good faith. They further believe that the Soviet Union, like the United States, will accept reasonable mutual concessions on arms reduction as a necessary risk to avert war. This confidence among many Americans that the Soviet Union shares our goals in arms control negotiations and will accept the attendant risks is based, in large part, upon official Soviet declarations to this effect. But are American and Soviet objectives in arms control really the same? Do official American and Soviet statements regarding arms control reflect policy or propaganda? The following discussion seeks to answer these questions by comparing present American and Soviet attitudes towards arms control negotiations.

To most Americans, our own goals in arms control are clear and straightforward. Secretary of State Charles SHULTZ, in a May 1984 public address, set out the U.S. objectives for negotiations for START (Strategic Arms Reduction Talks), INF (Intermediate Nuclear Force), Non-Proliferation, MBFR (Mutual Balanced Force Reductions), and Chemical Weapons. He made it clear that "*... a responsible national security policy must include both a strong deterrence and an active pursuit of arms control to restrain competition and make the world safer*" (C. SHULTZ (1984), p.1). He spoke about American general goals in past negotiations: "*... to be able to shift resources to other more productive uses, and to add a measure of restraint, predictability, and safety to a world of political rivalries*" (see also BROWN and DAVIS (1985)). And on the limitations of arms control he stated: "*... By itself it cannot deliver security and prevent war, and we should not impose on the fragile process of arms control burdens it cannot carry and expectations it cannot fulfill.*" (p.2, see also BURT (1978 and 1981)). Further, he recognized that "*... Success or failure in achieving objectives depends on more than the technical feasibility of the proposals or the skills of the negotiators*" (p.4).

The Secretary cited four prerequisites for progress: 1) Maintenance of a credible deterrent, 2) unity within the Western alliance, 3) low levels of international tension, and 4) recognition of the common interest in reducing the risk of war.

For all arms control efforts today, Secretary SHULTZ established four basic objectives: reductions, equality, stability, and verifiability. In the matter of reductions, it is clear that our position will involve *'substantial'* changes in the level of forces, but these reductions must leave both nations with roughly equivalent forces. *"An agreement that legitimizes an unequal balance of forces creates instability and may increase the risk of eventual conflict"* (p.5). The goal of stability has been the foundation of US national policy since the concept of mutual assured destruction was enunciated in 1954. Finally, the U.S. holds that arms control agreements cannot be effective agents of disarmament without the absolute assurance of compliance verifiability.

Ambassador Paul H. NITZE, Special Advisor on Arms Control Matters, repeated these same attitudes in a speech in March 1985 *"... Arms control should be viewed as one element of our security policy. It complements the measures that we must take unilaterally such as maintaining weapons and forces necessary for an adequate deterrent... Arms control is not a substitute or replacement for adequate deterrence... Consistent with the objectives of promoting stability and rough equality, arms control should aim to achieve sharp reductions in the level of armaments... Moreover, we should have confidence in our ability to verify adherence to an agreement's provisions"* (pp.1-7).

President REAGAN'S statements are equally direct and lucid. In reporting to Congress in February 1986, specifically on Soviet noncompliance with arms control, he stated: *"... In order for arms control to have meaning and credibly contribute to national security and to global and regional stability, it is essential that all parties to agreements fully comply with them. Soviet compliance with all provisions of arms control agreements is fundamental... Soviet noncompliance is a serious matter. It calls into question important security benefits for arms control, and could create new security risks"* (p.1).

The public, official goal of the United States in arms control is clear, straightforward, and unchanging. Behavior has been consistent with stated policy; there is no hidden agenda.

What of Soviet goals in arms control? Are policies clear, straightforward, and consistent? Does behavior underwrite stated policy? On January 15, 1986, IZVESTIA reported a statement by M. S. GORBACHEV, General Secretary of the Communist Party of the Soviet Union, in which he spoke of fundamental arms control actions: *"Their point is to promote to the maximum extent the improvement of the international situation. They are dictated by the need to overcome the negative and confrontational tendencies that have built up in recent years and clear the way for the curtailing of the nuclear arms race on earth and its prevention in space, a general reduction in the war danger, and an establishment of trust as an unalienable component of relations between states"* (p.1).

This clearly echoes SHULTZ'S speech of May 1984 wherein he set out American goals in arms control. Gorbachev went on to speak of *"new bold approaches; new political thinking...time to abandon stone age ways of thinking, when the main preoccupation was to provide oneself with a bigger club or a heavier rock."* Do these statements really represent the vision of a new type of Soviet leader, truly interested in breaking out of the mold of innuendoes and deception?

A way to check for historical consistency in Soviet objectives in arms control is to look at what the Soviets say to themselves and about themselves, in their professional publications. Samuel B. PAYNE Jr. (1980) does this in an intriguing short book *'The Soviet Union and Salt'* filled with 500 references to Soviet publications. In reference to SALT I, his sources imply that the Soviet goals are aimed at *"... preventing a new round in the arms race without harming the security of the country, and releasing significant resources for creative objectives"* (pp.75-76). In reference to SALT II, BRESHNEV described his goal in the follow-on efforts as: *"... Finding a way to turn the temporary agreement [an offensive missile limitation] into a permanent one...[and] to consider how to proceed from the limitation of weapons to their gradual reduction, and also the establishment of some limit to their qualitative improvement"* (from PAYNE (1980), p.84).

On the face value of these statements it would be fair to say that the Soviet Union and the United States share the broad goals of reducing the risk of war and limiting the destructive power of nuclear weaponry. However, when Soviet and American behaviors are viewed critically, as proposed by W. WOLFE (1979), through four aspects of national policy--national security, political, technological, and doctrinal--very different arms control strategies become apparent.

3. STRATEGIES AND BEHAVIOR

In terms of national security, WOLFE believes it is patently clear from all negotiations that the Soviets are determined to protect their strategic gains and improve their future competitive position (see p.248). Rebecca V. STRODE (1984) supports this view by stating that *"... The USSR had a massive missile and submarine building program underway during the course of the SALT I talks... Negotiations did not even begin until the Soviet Union had obtained parity with the United States in the number of ICBMs. Agreement did not come until May 1972, when the USSR had virtually closed the gap in SLBMs as well"* (p.122).

PAYNE (1980) notes: *"... The leitmotif of Soviet attitudes toward international relations is an obsession with power. The Soviets believe that the Soviet Union's ability to achieve any objective is determined by its power relative to that of other countries"* (p.106, see also PIPES (1977)).

Referring to the more recent past, SHULTZ states: *"Throughout the negotiations of 1982 and 1983, however, the Soviets seemed determined to hang on to the great advantage in destructive power of their missiles"* (p.3). In contrast, the U.S. stance has been one to concede to the Soviets on this objective. STRODE (1984) notes that, from the signing of the SALT I accords in 1972 to the conclusion of the SALT II agreement in 1979, 1) the Soviet Union deployed three new ICBM systems, while the United States parried with the MX missile (not yet deployed as of Spring 1986); 2) the Soviet Union deployed two new SLBM systems while the United States deployed none; and 3) the Soviet Union continued production of the Backfire bomber while the United States cancelled the B-1 programme (pp. 122-123). This is not to imply that the United States did nothing to improve their strategic forces--technical improvements were introduced in both the ICBM and SLBM forces.

From the political standpoint, WOLFE (1979) comments that the Soviet Union intends to preserve its superpower status and do all it can to weaken the Western alliance (p.248). PAYNE supports this view with remarks that during the SALT negotiations Soviet proposals were *"... primarily designed to increase the Soviet Union's power by weakening NATO and reducing or eliminating the American presence in Europe"* (p.79). Uwe NERLICH (1980) contends that Soviet demands for inclusion of American nuclear-strike forces based in Europe as an element in any negotiable SALT proposals were a concerted effort to fragment the alliance. In relation to U.S. intentions, WOLFE (1979) asserts that the United States has fully validated the Soviet claim as a superpower (p.254). PAYNE (1980) confirms this assertion: "... *By the SALT I agreements, the United States officially and publicly accepted the strategic parity of the Soviet Union*" (p.67). NITZE (1985) also recognizes this validation: "... *Once the Soviets judged the military correlation of forces had become favorable, they were adamant in refusing to consider any agreement which would result in rough equality or which would improve crises stability*" (p.5).

In the technology area, the Soviets used the ABM treaty as a means to prevent the United States from deploying a system they could not then match. As WOLFE (1979) stresses, in this way they attempted to prevent the impact of U.S. technological potential from ever being realized (p.248). In comparison to past administrations which delayed or cancelled state-of-the-art weapon systems, the present American administration has been insistent on forging ahead with high-technology based programs--the MX missile, B-1 and Stealth bombers, Trident II, and especially, SDI, where ultrahigh technology will be the crux of success. The present action of the Soviets to block the continuation of the Strategic Defense Initiative research program is believed by SDI supporters to be another attempt to blunt the technological advantage of the United States. (More specifically, they probably want to interdict U.S. military dominance in space). In a doctrinaire sense, WOLFE (1979) insists that the Soviets do not believe in mutual assured destruction as a foundation of deterrence. The salient prescription for deterrence in Soviet strategic thinking has been that the better the armed forces are prepared to fight and win a nuclear war, and the society to survive its effects, the more effectively a political adversary will be deterred (p.249, see also Department of State (1978), ERICKSON (1971), HOLLOWAY (1971)). Richard PIPES (1977) sustains this view: "... *The strategic doctrine adapted by the USSR over the past two decades calls for a policy diametrically opposite to that adapted in the United States...not deterrence but victory, not suffiency in weapons but superiority* (p.27).

Compared to this determined Soviet attitude, American policy has oscillated between 1) the maintenance of a minimum deterrence force sufficient to prevent war, coercion, and blackmail (as in the Carter administration when the need for controlling arms was seen as overriding that of continued acquisition and upgrading of the strategic forces) and 2) a force limited only by the money available (as in the Reagan administration where DOD outlays have doubled since 1980).

We conclude that these analyses of behavior show that there are sharp contrasts in the U.S. and Soviet strategies for arms control. In an overall sense, we should understand that Soviet arms control strategy is aggressive, or using WOLFE'S word, "tenacious". Edward LUTTWACK (1982/83) states: *"Soviet negotiators invariably seek to make each bargain as specific as possible, and far from trying to create a good "negotiating climate", will sometimes deliberately stage episodes of uncivil conduct as a bargaining tactic, to intimidate the other side..."Soviet policy constantly probes such arms agreements as there are to exploit any gaps in American vigilance."* Foy D. KOHLER (1979) describes their action as *"... they have increasingly staked out extreme demands, stuck doggedly to them, and waited for the United States to decide upon the consessions necessary for a breakthrough"* (p.17).

In contrast, the U.S. strategy might best be described, using WOLFE'S words, as "accommodating" -- adjusting to Soviet preferences -- overly concerned about detente, peaceful coexistence, fairness, and equality. (p.31, see also SYMMS and SULLIVAN (1984), p.447). KOHLER (1979) contends: *"[we have] adapted our negotiation position...giving, as it were, Moscow control of the game before it even started.... The U.S. response has been to constantly shift positions in attempts to accomodate to Soviet intransigence"* (p.17-18).

Coupled with this tenacious Soviet strategy has been their deliberate and continual open assault upon the legal obligations under, or political commitments to, the arms control agreements they have negotiated. The presidential Report of December 1985 on Soviet noncompliance with arms control agreements cites nine clear violations - five of which relate to strategic matters under SALT. The Report notes a "pattern of Soviet noncompliance" and further, that "through its noncompliance, the Soviet Union has made military gains in the areas of strategic offensive arms (pp.1-3).

4. THE FUNDAMENTAL INCOMPATIBILITY

The evidence shows that the U.S. and Soviets share common goals in one broad sense: reduction of the risk of war. But the goals diverge in the strategies for achieving this end point. The Soviets want dominance as opposed to the U.S. perception of a rough equivalence that is supposed to lead to stability. Rather than adopt the Western view that arms control is concerned primarily with reducing nuclear weapons and enhancing crises stability, Soviet strategy uses arms control, in conjunction with their overall force design and political actions, to constrain U.S. forces in a manner favorable to Soviet interests. This incompatibility, in our judgment, is the source of western frustration with arms control. Since the Soviets are unlikely to change, the U.S. has only the choice of muddling along as in the past or accepting the dichotomous nature of our strategies and subgoals and making some adjustments in approach and expectations.

5. AN HOLISTIC U.S. STRATEGY

The opportunity for creative U.S. initiative is at hand. Our ultimate objectives for stability and reduction of weapons are clearly stated and acceptable to the broad American constituency. Over the years we have come to know our protagonist well. We know what he wants to accomplish and how he will go about it. Most importantly, we know what he values and we understand his needs, even his weaknesses. History shows that he will react in his own best interest according to his own value sets and perceptions. It is up to us to formulate an approach that will provide an incentive for the Soviets to move in directions acceptable to us. Specific proposals are beyond the scope of this paper, but the general guidelines are clear. Specific strategies must recognize the following facts:

(1) Power is what really matters.

(2) The Soviets will give us nothing. Any adjustment or concession will be based on their perception of their best interests, in their value space.

(3) They will not trade, in the Western sense. One of their goals is to deny benefits to the U.S., while achieving benefits for themselves. This is not bargaining as understood in Western cultures.

(4) U.S. positions/propositions must be integrated within (and underwritten by) a total framework of national policies and forces.

As a first step in formulating this new approach, we must develop an effective synthesis of political, military, economic, and ideological beliefs and requirements with an arms control policy which constrains Soviet forces in a manner favorable to American and Western interests. Such an achievement on our part requires careful and continuing considerations to the compatibility of the political ends sought and the strategic doctrines and forces involved, both existing and in development. This demands new thinking, new examination of the fundamentals of policy content and strategic premises--the value of arms control processes; the relevance of deterrence theory and policy, particularly extended deterrence to allies; the forces and processes that produce particular arms programs; the dynamics of arms competition; the utility of American limited-war theory; defense policy-making process in Moscow; the strategic beliefs and attitudes towards negotiations of their leadership; and most importantly, the political realities of the budget cycle, of legislative interests and pressures, and of domestic other foreign political problems (see also GRAY (1982), pp.185-195).

The time is ripe for a major new western thrust integrated over these policy, military and economic dimensions. Mr. Gorbachev seems to recognize that unbridled military expenditures are undesirable. He clearly has economic incentives for turning national resources toward more productive pursuits than arms production. The U.S. is on the verge of major strategic force modernization, with a likely attendant adjustment in the Soviets' perception of the power relationship. SDI clearly highlights U.S. technological strengths, and is obviously much feared by the Soviets. President Reagan (1984) says "the U.S. is on the move". We should take advantage of this momentum by taking the high ground on arms control.

6. REFERENCES

Adelman, K.L. (1984): Arms Control With and Without Agreement. Foreign Affairs, Winter 1984

Brown, H. and L.E. Davis (1985): Nuclear Arms Control: Where Do We Stand? In: The Nuclear Controversy (Bundy, W.P., Ed.), New York 1985, pp.227-228

Burt, R. (1978): Arms Control and Soviet Strategic Forces: The Risks of Asking SALT To Do Too Much. The Washington Review 1/1978, pp.19-33

Burt, R. (1981): The Relevance of Arms Control in the 1980s. Daedalus 110, 159-177

Department of State (1978): Special Report 'Soviet Civil Defense', No. 47

Erickson, J. (1971): Soviet Power. RUSI London, pp.8-11

Gorbachev, M.S. (1986): Statement on Arms Control. Izvestia, Jan.16, p.1

Gray, C.S. (1982): Strategic Studies and Public Policy. Lexington, KY

Holloway, D. (1971): Strategic Concepts and Soviet Policy. Survival, p. 365

Kohler, F.D. (1979): SALT - How not to Negotiate with the Russians. Advanced International Studies Institute, Miami, FL

Luttwack, E.N. (1982/83): Why Arms Control Has Failed. In: Military Strategy: Theory and Applications, U.S. Army War College, pp.13-15

Nerlich, U.(1980): Nuclear Weapons and East-West Negotiations. In: Arms Control and Military Force (Bertram, C., Ed.), Hampshire, pp.31-32

Nitze, P. (1985): The Objectives of Arms Control. In: Current Policy 677 (U.S. Department of State), Washington, D.C., pp.1-7

Payne Jr., S.B. (1980): The Soviet Union and SALT. Cambridge, MS

Pipes, R. (1977): Why the Soviet Union Thinks it could Fight and Win a Nuclear War. Commentary Vol.63, No.7, pp.21-34

Reagan, R. (1984): The President's Unclassified Report on Soviet Noncompliance With Arms Control Agreements, Washington D.C., 23. Dec. 1984

Schultz, J.: Realism and Responsibility: The U.S. Approach to Arms Control. In: Current Policy No. 577 (U.S. Department of State), Washington, D.C.

Strode, R.V. (1984): Soviet Policy Toward the Freeze in Historical Perspective. In: The Nuclear Freeze Controversy (Payne, K.B. and Gray, S., Eds.), New York

Symms, S. and Sullivan, D. (1984): Soviet Violations of Existing Arms Control Treaties May Make Future Treaties Ineffective. In: Quantitative Assessment in Arms Control (Avenhaus, R. and Huber, R.K., Eds.), New York-London, pp. 413-444

DEFENSE OUTLAYS AND ARMS CONTROL IN THE ELECTION CYCLE

Wulf Albers and Gisela Albers
University of Bielefeld, FRG

SUMMARY

The function of the US military defense outlays after World War II can by and large be presented as a piecewise linear continuous function. A new linear piece with a new degree of increase or decrease is initiated when the president changes, when a war starts, or when the de-escalation phase after a war is ended. The only phase with nonlinear defense outlays was the time of Carter, when the sum of the Warsaw Pact defense outlays reached that of the NATO countries. This caused a constant acceleration of the outlays. It could be shown that for the phases after elections the increase of the pieces is negatively related to the economic activity of the election year. A system of three rules is given which explains at what times arms control agreements can be signed. This system is again closely related to the election cycle. It predicts arms control agreements mainly for the two last years of the election periods. Both approaches indicate that the influence of the US public opinion on the policy more or less concentrates on the years of the election.

1. PHASES OF UNIFORM OUTLAYS POLICY

The shape of empirical outlays functions of ressorts or subressorts of the federal household suggests a subdivision of the time axis into phases of uniform motivation of the decision makers. Accordingly, it is assumed that the decision maker changes the strategic parameters predefining his behavior for the following phase only in the breakpoint between these phases.

As a typical example we give the function presenting the budget authority of the US Department of Defense for military outlays between 1948 and 1984 (see Figure 1).

Within each interval corresponding to a uniform phase of policy the function can be modelled as

NATO ASI Series, Vol. F 26
Modelling and Analysis in Arms Control
Edited by R. Avenhaus et al.

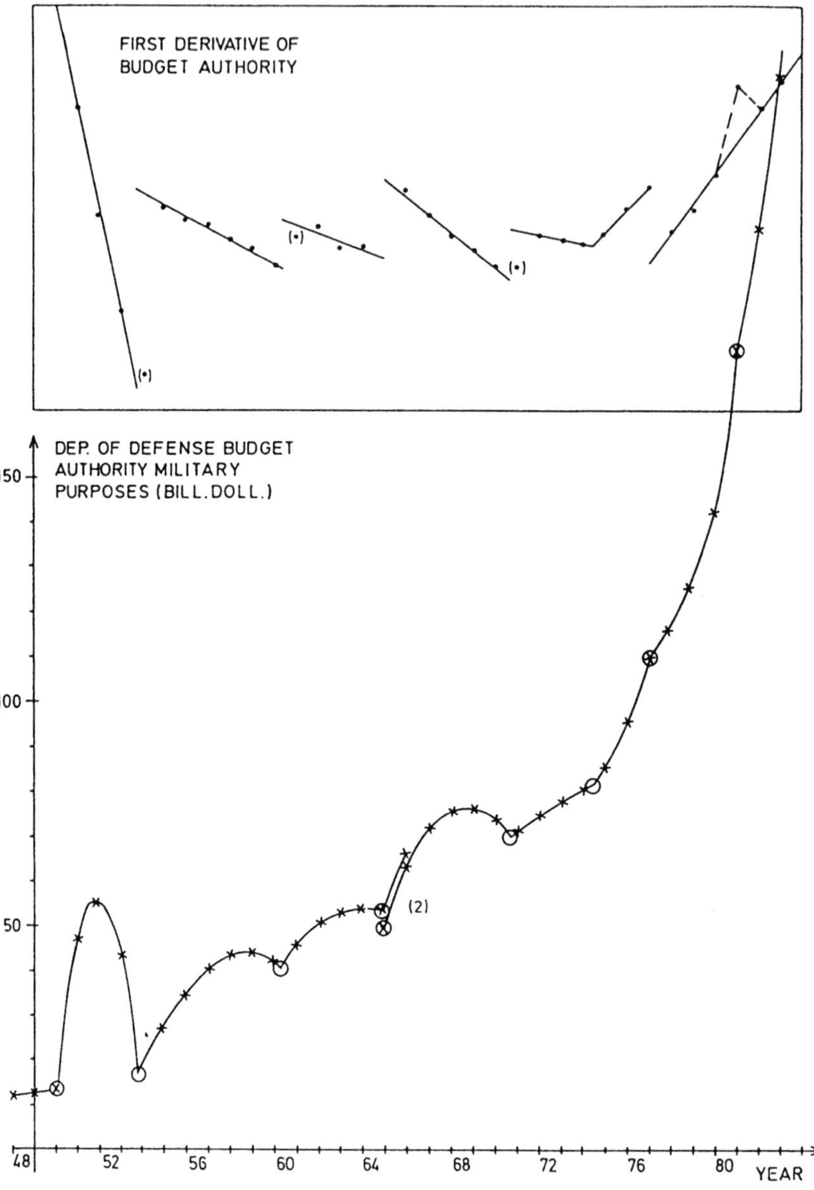

Fig. 1: Budget Authority of the US Department of Defense for Military Purposes - An Example of a Piecewise Quadratic Outlays Function[1].

[1] Source: Budget authority data from: US Office of Management and Budget, The Annual Budget of the United States Government.

[2] The jump follows from different values in different sources.

[3] The piecewise linear shape of the derivative demonstrates the piecewise quadratic character of the original function.

$$x = x_o + v_o \cdot (t-t_o) + 1/2 \cdot a_o \cdot (t-t_o)^2 \quad (1)$$

where x_o gives the value of the variable x at time t_o; $v_o \cdot (t-t_o)$ describes a linear increase or decrease of x where v_o is the velocity with which x changes at time t_o; and $1/2 \cdot a_o \cdot (t-t_o)^2$ can be interpreted as the additional movement caused by a constant acceleration a_o.

It is well known that the first derivative

$$v = x' = \frac{dx}{dt} = v_o + a_o \cdot (t-t_o) \quad (2)$$

gives the velocity with which x changes, and that the second derivative

$$a = x'' = \frac{d^2x}{dt^2} = \frac{dv}{dt} = a_o \quad (3)$$

gives the acceleration of x, which is constant in this model. The acceleration is the velocity with which the velocity changes.

Within this model the defense outlays function of a homogenous phase of policy is fully described by the corresponding parameters x_o, v_o, and a_o, i.e. amount, velocity, and acceleration of x at time t_o. Without loss of generality it can be assumed that t_o is the initial point of the phase, so that the initial parameters x_o, v_o, and t_o completely determine the outlays during the whole phase.

Corresponding to equation (1) the value of x is given by three terms, namely the initial value x_o, the term $v_o \cdot (t-t_o)$ representing a constant movement initiated by an impuls at time t_o, and the term $1/2 \cdot a_o \cdot (t-t_o)^2$ giving the influences of a constant acceleration which may be thought as the effect of a constant force.

This model is analogous to that of mass point mechanics. There the movement with constant velocity is the most natural behavior. This can be influenced by impulses, which change direction and amount of velocity at a point of time, and by permanent forces. A special case of a permanent force is a constant force which causes a uniformly accelerated movement.

It seems that also in the case of outlays policies the movement with constant velocity v_0 is the natural movement, and that a nonlinear shape of the function (i.e. $a_0 \neq 0$) indicates the action of an additional force. It is surprising that in those cases, when an additional force acts, this force is more or less constant during the whole phase.

The observations of empirical data indicate that outlays functions of specific ressorts or subressorts can be modelled as continuous functions, so that the initial point x_0 of a new phase is given by the end point of the preceding interval. Therefore the only strategic parameters of a politician at time t_0 are speed v_0 and acceleration a_0 for the next phase.

Our impression is that for a specific budget an acceleration a_0 different from zero is only selected when the actual situation enforces a speed v_0 which is presently necessary but not adequate for the farther future. So an acceleration $a_0 \neq 0$ indicates that the corresponding decision has been essentially influenced by short run aspects which were not adequate from a long run point of view.

2. THE DEFENSE OUTLAYS FUNCTION

Throughout the next two paragraphs we consider the function of the federal budget outlays for national defense functions[1] (see Figure 2).

This function can be split up into time intervals or phases of uniform policies as described in the preceding section. The function is continuous (i.e. the end points of the preceding phases determine the initial points of the respective following phases).

Although the outlays function of the subressorts generally involve acceleration terms (i.e. the shape of the function is curved), the total sum of outlays can normally be presented as a more or less linear function involving no acceleration terms.

Slight deviations from this linear shape in one or another direction can be

---

[1] Source: Office of Management and Budget, The Annual Budget of the United States Government.

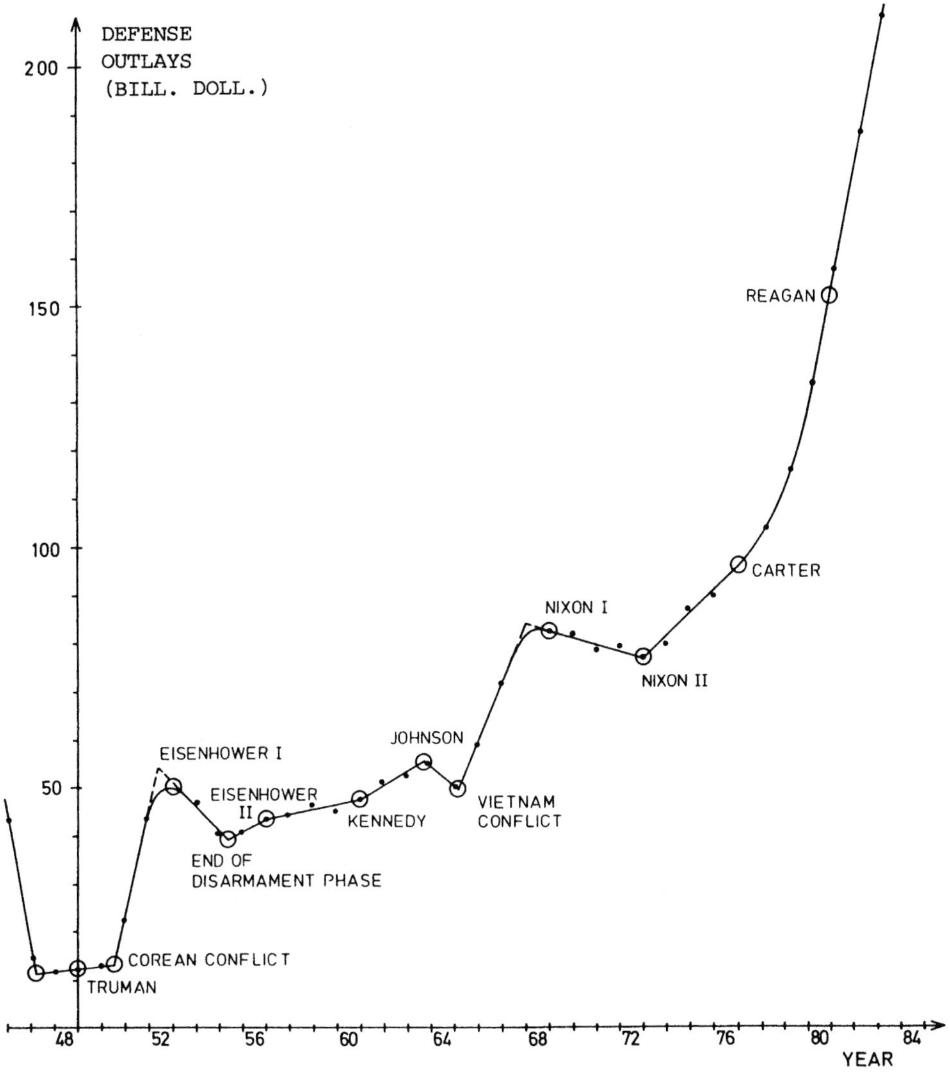

Fig. 2: National Defense Outlays as a Piecewise Linear Function[1),2)].

1) During the Carter era the shape is quadratic.

2) The circles mark the end points of the linear pieces.

explained by political events. As for instance the effect of the Quemoy/ Matsu-crisis (1958) or of Camp David (1959).

Both effects are, however, comparably low and did only cause marginal adjustments of the general defense outlays policies of the corresponding period.

There are two points of time and one period where the defense outlays function cannot be presented as piecewise linear.

The two points are the culmination points of the Korean and the Vietnam Wars. In these points the shape of the defense outlays function is rounded and not angle-shaped. This result follows from the fact that the outlays functions of the subressorts as "procurement" and "operation and maintenance" have to be modelled with constant acceleration during the whole conflict with the same acceleration parameter a_0 for the escalation and the de-escalation phase. So these subressorts give quadratic outlays functions with smooth maxima. Since there were no reasons for additional outlays in the culmination point, the sum of the defense outlays also gives a rounded shape of the maximum.

There is only one time period with a permanent acceleration of the defense outlays function, namely the Carter period. At that time the sum of the defense outlays of the Warsaw Pact countries reached the sum of the NATO countries (see Figure 3). In our opinion central questions of this time were firstly, if it would be possible to coordinate the defense outlays policies of both blocs in such a way that from then on the defense outlays of the blocs developed equally, and secondly, at which rate of increase this would happen - at the lower rate of the NATO countries or at the higher rate of the Warsaw Pact countries. In this situation it seems reasonable that Carter tried to reach the lower rate of increase, and therefore increased the defense outlays hesitatingly. The effect was that in this time period the defense outlays developed with constant acceleration.

Overall it does not surprise that the defense outlays function cannot be presented as piecewise linear everywhere. On the contrary, it does surprise

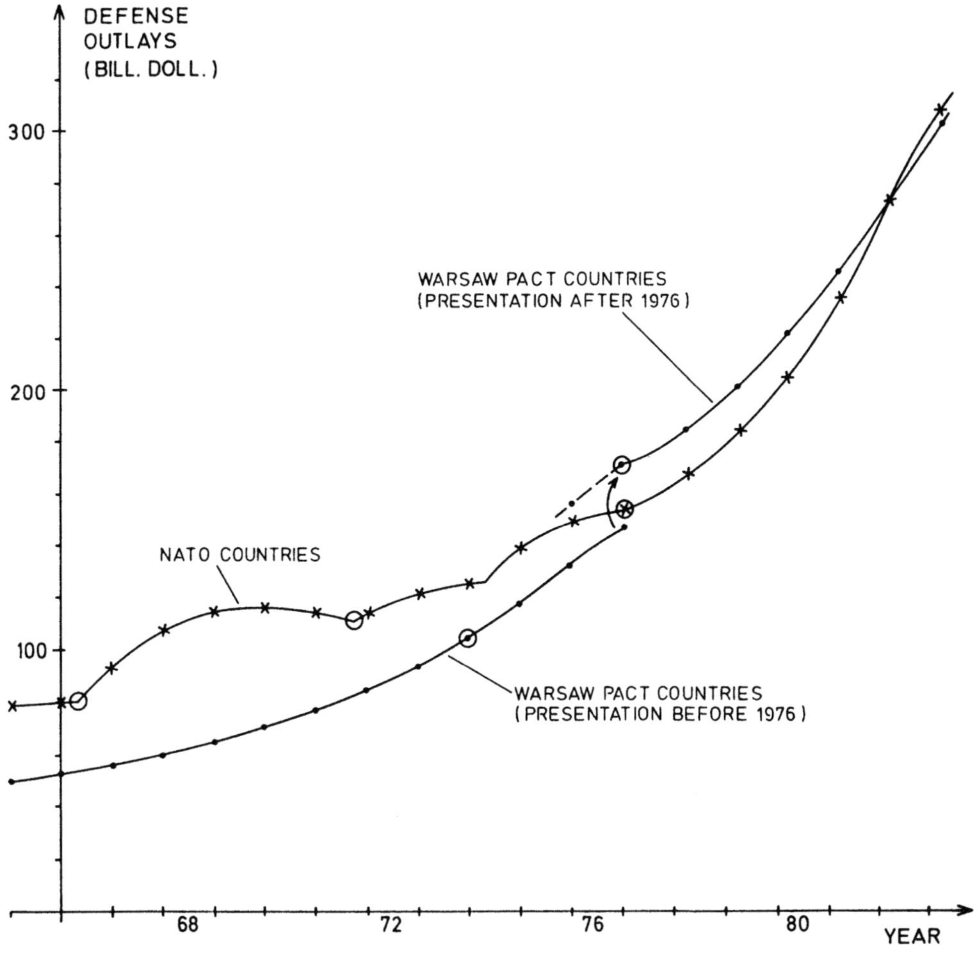

Fig. 3: Defense Outlays of NATO and Warsaw Pact Countries 1964-1984[1].

[1] Source: US Arms Control and Disarmament Agency, World Military Expenditures and Arms Transfers.

that it can be modelled as piecewise linear to such an extent.

Except for starting points of wars and points of disarmament phases after wars the phases of uniform defense outlays policies are closely related to the presidents' election periods (see Figure 2): The phases start more or less exactly at the time when the election period starts, or when the president changes.

Summing up, we get the following phenomena:

New phases of defense outlays policies are initiated

(a) when a war starts,
(b) when the disarmament phase after a war is ended,
(c) when the president changes or when the president enters a new election period.

The shape of the defense outlays function during these phases is basically linear, except for

(a) culmination points of wars; in these points the function is rounded,
(b) the time when the defense outlays of the Warsaw Pact countries reached the NATO outlays; during that time the acceleration parameter was constant and positive.

From these observations follows that the basic parameters of the aggregated defense outlays function are constant for each phase and given more or less exactly in the beginning of the phase. From this point of view it seems reasonable to assume that defense outlays can be influenced by public opinion mainly during the time when the general outlines of the policy are made, i.e. during the election year.

3. DEFENSE OUTLAYS IN THE ECONOMIC CYCLE

It seems reasonable to assume that it is difficult to reduce the defense outlays in times of declining economic activity since this might increase unemployment. Accordingly, the resistance against a reduction of defense outlays will be lower in times of increasing economic activity.

A corresponding hypothesis cannot be verified on the basis of annual data. But this is not surprising in the context of the result of the preceding paragraph, that the basic parameters of the defense outlays policy of a government can be influenced by public opinion only during the time when the corresponding policy is made up, i.e. during the election year.

Accordingly, it must be expected that it is mainly the economic activity of the election year which determines the annual increase of the defense outlays policies of the subsequent period.

To verify this hypothesis we consider the following variables:

- the economic activity of the respective election years (measured by the increase of the gross national product per annum), and
- the tendency to increase armament (measured by the mean increase of the proportion of the defense outlays as part of the federal outlays during the respective next election period)[2].

The correlation of the two variables is $r = .89$, which is significant on the .01 level (see Figure 4).

An interesting result in this context is, that the values of the post-war phases 1952 and 1968 are comparably low. This indicates that in addition to the "natural" arms reduction according to the economic activity a further reduction of armament was intended.

On the other hand, in 1976 the pressure of the increasing defense outlays of the Warsaw Pact countries which reached the outlays of the NATO countries caused an increase of armament which was essentially higher than the "natural" increase corresponding to the increase of the economic activity.

---

[2] For the phase of Carter with nonlinear increase of the defense outlays we only considered the first two years.

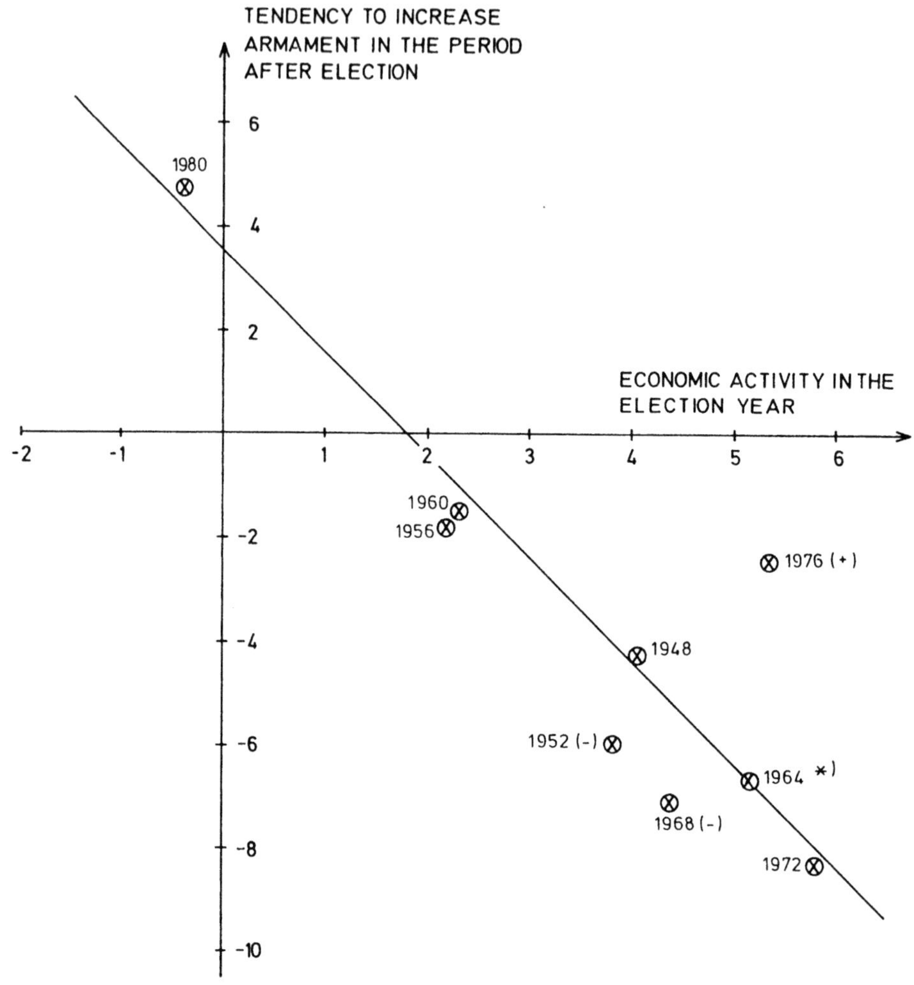

Fig. 4: Relation of the Economic Activity in the Election Year and the Tendency to Increase Armament in the Period Afterwards.

*) Since in the phase after 1964 the armament increased for extern reasons (escalation of the Vietnam War), we took the increase during 1964 as a predictor for the increase Johnson would have selected in case the conflict had not escalated. - This seems reasonable since Johnson could (and did) arrange the defense outlays policy in 1964 independent from the preceding rate of increase.

4. ARMS CONTROL AGREEMENTS IN THE ELECTION CYCLE

We now consider the major arms control agreements after World War II in which the US has participated[3].

The first observation is that no agreements have been signed within this time before 1956. The other observations are based on a definition of a "phase of policy", which can be defined in this context by the following condition:

DEFINITION: A *new phase of policy* is initiated

- by the election of a new president (in the US),
- by the election of a new general secretary (in the SU),
- by an important political event.

There are four conditions which restrict the possibility to sign treaties within these phases of policy, namely

(A) No agreement can be signed during the first two years of a phase, except for treaties according to rule (B). The two years time can be reduced to one and a half year, if the next president continues the policy of his predecessor with the same foreign minister.

(B) Prepared agreements can be taken over from a preceding phase of policy, if the text of the agreement has been adopted in a preceding phase. (In this case the treaty is signed during the first year of the new phase.)

(C) Except from events which coincided with the change of presidents, the Soviet invasion in Afghanistan was the only important political event which initiated a new phase of policy.

These rules completely describe the times during which arms control treaties have not been signed after World War II. Moreover - except from the first phases during which only one treaty was signed (in 1959) - *at least one*

---

[3] We refer to the selection of the US ACDA, listed in Table 1.

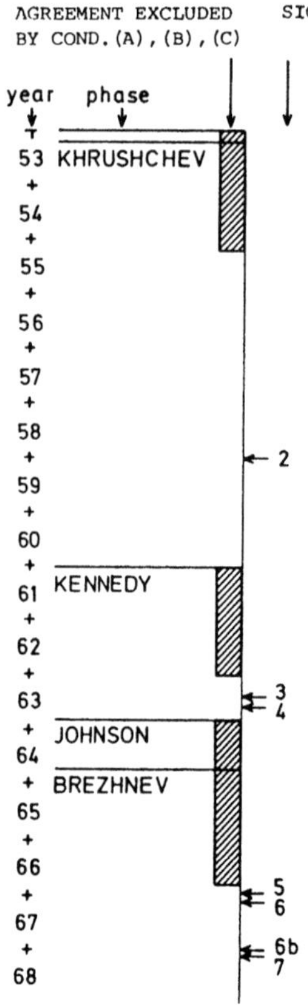

No	Treaty	Complexity by: No of Articles (No of Breaks)	Signed[3]	Ratificat Advised b Senat[3]
1	Geneva Protocol	1 (10)	6/17/25(3)	12/16/74(
2	Antactic Treaty	14 (58)	12/1/59 (1)	8/10/60(
3	Hot Line Agreement	1 (3)	6/20/63(1)	----
	- Annex	7 (19)	----	----
4	Limited Test Ban Treaty	5 (19)	8/5/63 (1)	9/24/63(
5	Outer Space Treaty	17 (40)	1/27/67(1)	4/25/67(
6	Prohibition of Nuclear Weapons in Latin America	32(130)	2/14/67(1)	----
	- Additional Protocol I	3 (8)	5/26/77(3)	11/13/81(
	- Additional Protocol II	5 (10)	4/1/68(0)	4/19/71(
	- Proclamation by Nixon	3 (12)	5/12/71(1)	----
7	Non-Proliferation Treaty	11 (37)	7/1/68(0)	3/13/69(
8	Seabed Arms Control Treaty	11 (30)	2/11/71(1)	2/15/72(
9	Measures of Risk of Nuclear War	9 (15)	9/30/71(1)	----
10	Hot Line Modernization	5 (12)	9/30/71(1)	----
	- Annex	3 (21)	----	----
11	Biological Weapons Convention	15 (37)	4/10/72(0)	12/16/74(
12	SALT I, ABM Treaty	16 (52)	5/26/72(0)	8/3/72((
	- Agreed Statements	3 (25)	5/26/72(0)	----
13	SALT I, Interim Agreement	8 (17)	5/26/72(0)	[9/30/72(
	- Protocol	1 (8)	5/26/72(0)	----
	- Agreed Statements	3 (25)	5/26/72(0)	----
14	Prevention of Nuclear War Agreement	8 (17)	6/22/73(3)	----
15	SALT I, ABM Protocol	4 (13)	7/3/74(2)	11/10/75(

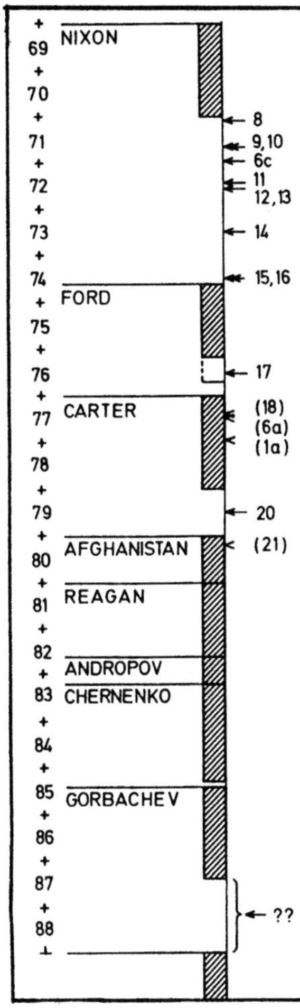

16	Threshold Test Ban Treaty	5 (17)	7/3/74(2)	[7/29/76(0
	- Protocol	3 (13)	7/3/74(2)	----
17	Peaceful Nuclear Explosions Treaty	8 (44)	5/28/76(0)	[7/29/76(0
	- Protocol	10(140)	5/28/76(0)	----
	- Agreed Statement	1 (3)	5/13/76(0)	----
18	Environmental Modification Convention	10 (34)	5/18/77(1)	11/28/79(3)
	- Annex	5 (5)	----	----
	- Understandings	4 (10)	----	----
19	US-IAEA Safeguards Agreement	90(293)	11/18/77(3)	7/2/80(0)
	- Protocol	28 (73)	11/18/77(3)	----
20	SALT II	19(248)	6/18/79(1)	----
	- Protocol	4 (18)	6/18/79(1)	----
	- Memorandum	1 (3)	6/18/79(1)	----
	- Statements of Data	1 (2)	6/18/79(1)	----
	- Joint Statements for Subsequent Negotiations	1 (13)	6/18/79(1)	----
21	Nuclear Material Convention	23 (96)	3/3/80(0)	7/30/81(3)
	- Annex I	2 (8)	3/3/80(0)	----
	- Annex II	1 (10)	----	----

[1] As selected by the US ACDA

[2] The entries refer to the order number. Numbers in parentheses refer to treaties which had been completed by a preceding president.

[3] The numbers in parentheses give the number of years before the next elections.

[4] SALT I, Interim Agreement has been ratified by the House of Representati

[5] Ratification failed.

Table 1: Arms Control Agreements

treaty has been signed in every year after 1960 which is not ruled out by conditions (A), (B), and (C).

We now discuss the effects of rules (A) and (B) in detail:

Rule (A): It seems reasonable that negotiations with a new general secretary or a new president need some time before a treaty can be signed. Our result is that this time is normally at least two years. This condition is not violated by the treaties of Kennedy, Johnson, Nixon, and Reagan. None of them signed treaties during the first two years of his presidentship. Corresponding results hold for the changes of the general secretaries: The change of October 1964 (Brezhnev) excluded agreements until October 1966 (the next agreement was made in January 1967). The changes in November 1982 (Andropov), February 1983 (Chernenko), and March 1985 (Gorbachev) excluded (and will exclude) agreements between 1982 and March 1987. This explains why Reagan did not reach an agreement until now (1986).

Rule (A), reduced time: Ford who continued the foreign policy of Johnson with the same foreign minister (Kissinger) reached his first arms control agreement (the Threshold Test Ban Treaty, signed in May 1976) already after 19 months of presidentship, according to rule (A). It may be that this treaty could be signed after such a short time of presidentship, because the first half of the treaty (the Peaceful Underground Nuclear Explosions (PNE) Treaty, signed by Nixon in 1974) had already been prepared by the same foreign minister, and/or because the second half had been announced in the PNE Treaty for March 1976.

Rule B: The other two treaties prepared by Ford could not be signed in time before the next elections. However, the main parts of both treaties including the complete texts have been arranged in 1976[4]. According to rule (B) Carter signed the treaties in 1977. He also decided to sign the additional protocol I of the treaty for the prohibition of nuclear weapons

---

4) The text of the Environmental Modification Convention was agreed upon by the Conference of the Committee on Disarmament (CCD) in summer 1976. The UN adopted the resolution in December 1976. The completion of the Verification Agreement by the nonnuclear states of the European Community was reached in September 1976.

in Latin America which had been signed by the United Kingdom already in 1967 and by the Netherlands in 1968. This also happened in 1977 according to rule (B).

Condition (C): Within Carter's election period the Soviet invasion in Afghanistan (December 1979) initiated a new phase of policy, so that no new contracts could be negotiated successfully. Only the Nuclear Material Convention, which had been adopted in October 1979, was signed in March 1980 according to rule (B).

A general impression is that after 1956 all presidents were interested to arrange arms control agreements, and that they tried to complete the treaties in time before the respective next elections. It seems that the successful arrangement of arms control treaties supports the chance of a president to be reelected and/or improves his image in the view of history.

From this point of view each president should try to arrange his arms control treaties just before the elections, since the influence on the election is higher when the agreement is new. On the other hand a late agreement increases the pressure to reach a result and thereby weakens the position of the US. It may be that this is the reason why about half of the treaties have been signed during the third year of the election period of a president.

It must, however, be remarked that the Soviet Union also has reasons to arrange arms control agreements in time. Assuming permanent arms control negotiations between the US and the Soviet Union, it makes sense to fix up some of the obtained results in order to guarantee the continuity of the process and to prevent that the discussions are thrown back with every change of a president. Of course, it may be an advantage of the longer time perspective of the Soviet Union that it can select those positions to be fixed up in which the respective president is less tough.

5. CONCLUDING REMARK

The result of this analysis is that the US election cycle significantly influences the two aspects of policy considered here, namely the defense outlays policy and the arms control negotiations.

Concerning arms control agreements this influence does not only hold for bilateral agreements with the Soviet Union, but also for multi-lateral contracts. This shows the strong influence of the US on international arms control negotiations.

A surprising result concerning the defense outlays is the low short run influence of events such as the Soviet invasion of Hungary, the Cuban Crisis, or the Suez Crisis. The defense outlays policies of the presidents have only been reflected in context of elections, and generally followed the principle of *linear* increase (or decrease). It seems that even the escalation of the Vietnam War followed this rule, so that the condition of linear increase of the total defense outlays may have determined the possible military actions.

REFERENCES

US Department of Commerce, Bureau of Census (Annually): Statistical Abstract of the United States. Washington, D.C.

US Department of Commerce, Bureau of Economic Analysis (1977): The National Income and Product Accounts of the United States, 1929-74, Statistical Tables. United States Government Printing Office, Washington, D.C.

Prepared for the Joint Economic Committee by the Council of Economic Advisors: (Quarterly), Economic Indicators, United States Government Printing Office, Washington, D.C.

US Arms Control and Disarmament Agreements (1982): Texts and Histories of Negotiations. United States Government Printing Office, Washington, D.C.

PART II

PRE-ARMS CONTROL ASSESSMENT OF OPTIONS AND OBJECTIVES

WORKING GROUP MEMBERS:

GOLD, Sydell P. (Chairwoman)

BODE, John R.
BRACKEN, Jerome
BRACKEN, Paul
BUZACOTT, John A.
GIBSON, John W.
GÜTH, Werner
HUBER, Reiner K.
JENKINS, Frank
KIRCHHOFER, Elmar
LIEBERMAN, Alfred
MACHADO-JORGE, Henrique
PALDY, Lester G.
PASTIJN, Hugo
SAATY, Thomas L.
STRUYS, Wally
WITTMANN, Stefan

REPORT OF THE CHAIRMAN: WHAT ROLE CAN ANALYSIS PLAY IN ILLUMINATING ARMS CONTROL OBJECTIVES AND OPTIONS?

Sydell P. Gold
Department of Defense, Washington, D.C.

1. BACKGROUND

Although titled Report of the Chairman, this paper is truly the collaborative product of the Pre-Arms Control Assessment Working Group members. The views expressed are not those of any one individual or organization, nor are they necessarily a consensus view. We have, rather, tried to present a sampling of ideas. Although we have various professional backgrounds and nationalities, we had the common goal of working cooperatively, intensely and enthusiastically to better understand, and perhaps contribute to, issues in the arms control arena.

Our motivation, in developing the skeleton of this paper during the conference, was to force rigorous thinking about arms control and to lay an analytical foundation upon which to build. Arms control is an area rich in opportunities for interaction between policy makers and analysts since the arms control process is primarily political, but produces treaties that are in the broadest sense technical. The information that should be communicated includes not only the numerics that result from quantitative analysis, but also insight into the process by developing the quantization and the relationship of the numerical measure to the political objectives.

In order to communicate clearly, we recognized that the most basic arms control vocabulary, including words such as arms race and stability, needed to be defined with sufficient precision to make them useful analytical building blocks. Our foray into mathematically conceptualizing some arms control terminology is contained in section 2.1.1 of the workshop directors' *Introduction* which summarizes a selection of the findings of the three working groups. In particular, this working group was of the opinion that stability is a notion that should be further explored analytically. In his paper presented below LIEBERMAN points out, the U.S. and the Soviets approach strategic analysis differently and use different measures to assess strategic forces. These various mathematical measures can contribute to different notions of stability and lead to differing assessments of

NATO ASI Series, Vol. F 26
Modelling and Analysis in Arms Control
Edited by R. Avenhaus et al.

the existence of stability in the force structures of the U.S. and U.S.S.R. We feel that additional effort, directed towards clarifying the notion of stability, will prove to be quite fruitful.

2. OBJECTIVES AND CONCERNS OF ARMS CONTROL

While arms control has been a part of the security strategy of the U.S. and NATO Allies for several decades, there is a pervasive feeling that it has not contributed as successfully as was hoped. Kenneth ADELMAN, the current director of the U.S. Arms Control & Disarmament Agency, expressed this sentiment by stating that "...*Of all the emotions arising from strategic arms control today, the most profound is disappointment. In this, as in little else in the vast realm of arms control, conservatives and liberals concur-conservatives for the failure of arms control to diminish the ever-more ominous Soviet strategic buildup, liberals for its failure to diminish the evermore wasteful strategic 'arms race'*." (ADELMAN 1984, p.240).

One need not conclude from this gloomy assessment that arms control should be abandoned. Rather, it is instructive to examine the past and current goals of arms control and determine which are appropriate arms control objectives. After briefly examining these objectives, we will discuss the role that analysis can play in helping to achieve them.

As stated above, arms control - the process, objectives and outcomes - combines both political and technical elements. The first sections of this paper will discuss arms control in more "political" terms; the latter portions will present some of the technical means available for improving the understanding of arms control and its objectives. Before proceeding, however, we would note that two terms, arms race and crisis stability, appear repeatedly in arms control discussions.

- *Arms Race* relates to increasing military power in a system caused by an action-reaction mechanism based on psychological, economic, political or technological behavior of the opponents.
- *Crisis Stability*, at given military capabilities, is assumed to exist if in a given crisis neither side perceives advantage for either side to attack first. In other words, both sides perceive an advantage in striking second.

2.1 ARMS CONTROL OBJECTIVES

Arms control and military forces are two of many arms of our political body. Thus, the arms control process must be considered as one of many instruments of an holistic strategy for achieving and enforcing peace. Arms control in the literal sense of controlling arms can't serve as an end in itself. It is just one element to be used to achieve security goals.

The "classic" literature on arms control usually raises three basic concerns in which arms control was considered to be helpful. First, that arms control could help enhance stability in the strategic relationship between the U.S. and the Soviet Union. This notion was based on an assumption that the strategic situation could be improved (e.g., stability enhanced) through a series of qualitative limitations on the offenses of both sides, such that a situation would be created where neither side would perceive any advantage in attacking the other in a crisis. Second, that arms control could reduce damage if war should occur. This belief was based on the notion that it would always be better for both sides to be at lower rather than higher levels of offensive forces in the event that deterrence failed and war came about. Third, it was felt that arms control could and should reduce the costs of building and maintaining one's forces. In other words, by lowering the levels of forces on both sides, benefits would be achieved by shifting assets into other non-defense areas.

2.2 CONTRIBUTORS TO THE PAST SHORTCOMINGS OF ARMS CONTROL

A review of the past fiteen years of arms negotiations, especially nuclear negotiations, highlights the shortcomings in satisfying these concerns. Among these reasons are:

1) Problems caused by the fundamental adversarial US-Soviet relationship are probably beyond the reach of arms controls. Forces exist on both sides to support a particular military doctrine and strategy, and to satisfy the political need to demonstrate military power to the world. The Soviets in particular must rely on military might to demonstrate their superpower status because of their inherent weakness in ideological, political, and economic areas.

2) The two sides may have different concerns and objectives. Clearly, in addition to understanding our own needs and concerns, we need to understand the concerns of the Soviets. Thus the success of the negotiation

process depends on how much real understanding there is of positions held strongly by the opponent. Such positions need not be held just to extract concessions but may result from genuine concerns of the parties. Successful negotiations are more likely to result when each party makes its evaluation in a framework that is considered rational by both sides.

3) The realtionship between cost and the choice of force structures, particularly in the Soviet Union, is not clear. Nor is it clear how to assess the cost of weapons to the Soviets, or how U.S. spending for weapons motivates the Soviets to structure their forces. As Pastijn and Struys point out in their paper, Soviet decision making cannot be explained only as a reaction to NATO initiatives. Therefore, if the U.S. pursued arms control to reduce force costs, the Soviets would not necessarily reduce their expenditures. In fact, they conclude that it would be particularly dangerous for NATO to decrease its own defense effort if there are not fundamental changes in Warsaw Pact behavior.

4) The strategic arms control process has been primarily concerned with reducing numbers of weapons and secondarily with controlling the types. This roughly corresponds to primarily pursuing arms race stability and secondarily pursuing crisis stability, the reverse of the generally stated importance of the two goals.

2.3 LEGITIMATE CONCERNS OF ARMS CONTROL

As the SCOWCROFT Commission pointed out, we have in some sense moved to a less, not more, stable situation, particularly given the high level of MIRV forces on both sides. Further, the capability of forces to inflict damage has actually increased, not decreased, over the last 15 years. And finally, the costs of maintaining deterrence have, if anything, been raised rather than lowered.

But, the shortcomings of arms control need not mean giving up on the process. Rather, we need to consider what should be the legitimate concerns that arms control might be able to address, recognizing the very real limits on what arms control might achieve. Our working group identified some potentially fruitful subjects to explore:

1) Perhaps more than any single objective or outcome of negotiations, an arms control agreement should help both sides to *gain insights* into their opponents' motivations and future force directions, thus enabling the sides to better understand and be more able to predict the future threats

likely to be faced by each side.

2) Arms control negotiations can allow the two sides to better understand not just the dynamics of the process itself, but how that process can help create a better overall *diplomatic climate* between the two sides.

3) Arms control can help bring about a *more stable situation* between the two sides, not necessarily by focusing on qualitative improvements in the offenses but rather, as the Scowcroft Commission pointed out, by channeling the modernization of the forces of two sides into directions that create targets of reduced value to a potential attacker.

4) Arms control agreements should be *sufficiently robust* and flexible to be able to adjust to future environments and changes in the force postures of both sides.

5) At the same time, agreements must *allow* for *asymmetries* in the two sides' force posture requirements brought about by differences in geography, proximity to the threats, history, technology, etc.

6) Arms control negotiations and agreements must take into account the links between the security of the major powers and the *security of their alliance partners*.

7) Arms control negotiations must be designed to ensure *effective verification* of the two sides and also ensure that there are measures for dealing with questions of noncompliance. These features will be particularly necessary to guard against breakout from an agreement as the sides reduce their levels of forces. Also, *measures of compliance* in one area can provide a test of the broader relationship between the two partners.

8) Although *negotiability* should not become a driving US concern, negotiability is at least a factor that must be taken into account. In designing proposals, it is always important to recognize that both sides have legitimate concerns and interest in achieving possibly different outcomes.

9) The parties also need to consider the *effect* of high levels of Soviet and U.S. arms *on third countries* and their concerns regarding the effectivenes of their own weapons to deter either of the given parties. Stability at a high level of U.S. and USSR arms may be viewed as unstable to third nations and induce a larger weapon buildup by them. Such a reaction could affect the economic welfare of these nations and their overall strengths relative to each other.

2.4 SUMMARY OF ARMS CONTROL GUIDELINES

In sum, appropriate areas of application of arms control seem to be, for the near term, the achievement and enforcement of crisis stability and, in the longer term, the dampening and eventual curtailment of the arms race in such a way as to preclude the development of crisis-unstable postures. The mere pursuit of these goals will, at the least, maintain communication between parties.

Because military capability, arms control and international policy are all part of a tightly woven fabric, arms control proposals that consider limitet elements of total force structure must be evaluated in the context of the whole, i.e., all the other force elements, planned force acquisitions, other arms control initiatives and objectives, and other relevant elements of international policy. We also must carefully consider the interdependencies among all of these elements so that all avenues that could lead to a non-desirable objective are adequately circumscribed.

3. MEASURES OF NUCLEAR FORCE LEVELS

One outcome of the arms control process has been treaties. The documents generally embody some of the sentiments which led the signatories to desire to reach an agreement, as well as statements delineating what was agreed upon. These latter often include quantitative limits on the numbers of weapons to be deployed and on their design. The ABM Treaty, the Interim Agreement on Strategic Offensive Arms, and the second Strategic Arms Limitation Treaty are noteworthy examples.

In order to arrive at such numerics, the mainly political objectives of arms control are translated into numerical descriptors. For example, a rough measure of an arms race is a comparison of the total number of strategic weapons each side has deployed, as time passes. In addition, the ratio of these numbers, or their difference, or perhaps some other mathematical function, can be used as a quantitative measure of arms race. We will divide the measures of nuclear forces into three categories:

- The number and size of the systems in the force,
- the capability of the systems in the force, and
- the characteristics of the systems in the force.

3.1 NUMBER AND SIZE OF SYSTEMS

The number of systems in a force is measured by the number of nuclear delivery systems and the number of warheads or weapons that the force carries. The size of the force is usually measured by its throwweight and sometimes by the total megatonage in the force.

Nuclear Delivery Vehicles

For arms control counting purposes, nuclear delivery systems have been separated, based on range, into strategic systems and theater systems. While there is some disagreement as to exactly which systems belong in each category, in general it is understood that Strategic Nuclear Delivery Vehicles (SNDV) are comprised of ICBMs, SLBMs and Heavy Bombers with ranges greater than 5500km. The Theater Nuclear Delivery Vehicles (TNDV) are comprised of Intermediate Range and Medium Range Ballistic missiles, Bombers and Ground Launched Cruise Missile Launchers.
Often separate counts are taken of delivery vehicles with Multiple independently-Targetable Re-entry Vehicles (MIRVs) and those with single warheads. In this regard it should be noted that in SALT II heavy bombers carrying Air Launched Cruise Missiles are counted as MIVRs.

The issue of systems carried on naval vessels, such as long or short range Sea Launched Cruise Missiles, aircraft, or short range ballistic missiles has not yet been resolved.

Warheads

The number of warheads is the number of *independently* targetable weapons. This means that Multiple Re-entry Vehicles (MRVs) count only as one warhead, whereas MIRVs count as the number of re-entry vehicles on the system. The warheads on heavy bombers are the ALCMs, the air-to-surface missiles and the bombs.

Throwweight

The size of a nuclear force can be measured by the trowweight of its missile force and the payload of its bomber force. The throwweight of an ICBM was defined in SALT II as the sum of the weight of

1) its re-entry vehicle or re-entry vehicles;

2) any self-contained dispensing mechanism or other appropriate devices for

targeting one re-entry vehicle, or for releasing or for dispensing and targeting two or more re-entry vehicles; and

3) its penetration aids, including devices for their release.

A great deal of work has been done in trying to measure bomber payload in a way that will make it comparable to missile throwweight, but to date no acceptable procedures have been developed. Most of the suggested procedures calculate the required throwweight of a ballistic missile which could deliver the same size weapon as those on the bombers. The major problem with these estimates are that they do not take into account the fact that it takes the bomber much longer to deliver the weapon and that the bomber must penetrate through air defenses.

An example of how these latter two quantities, warhead numbers and throwweight, can be used, is presented in the paper by REVELLE and BARKER. In their paper, functions of numbers of warheads and throwweight are developed as measures for configuring U.S. and Soviet forces. They construct a linear program to generate force configurations whose measures approach most closely the overall limitations that they set.

3.2 CAPABILITY OF SYSTEMS IN FORCE

The greatest effort on static measures has gone into the development of indices which in some manner reflect the capabilities of nuclear forces. It is not possible to address all the force capability indices that have been proposed or investigated, but some of the more prominent ones are discussed below.

Equivalent Megatons (EMT)

This measure is probably the best know and most used capability index. For each weapon of yield Y, EMT is defined as

$$\text{EMT} \begin{cases} = Y^{2/3}, & \text{for Y less than 1 megaton} \\ = Y^{1/2}, & \text{for Y larger than 1 megaton} \end{cases}$$

where Y is the yield of the weapon.

The EMT of the force is the sum of the EMTs off all the weapons in the force. EMT is an index which is a good measure of the blast effect against urban-industrial targets.

While $y^{2/3}$ is the most common definition of EMT, other exponents have been studied to more accurately reflect the effects on specific target systems. It might be noted that when the exponent is 1, EMT equals the yield and when the exponent is 0, EMT equals the number of warheads.

As LIEBERMAN discusses in his paper, the Soviets use a measure in which the yield of various weapons is first summed, and then the sum is raised to the two-thirds power. This measure is quite different from EMT and can lead to quite different assessments of the desirability or utility of various force structures than would be calculated using EMT.

Lethal Area Potential

This index measures the area destroyed. It is defined as the area covered by blast overpressure for a nuclear weapon detonated at the optimum height of burst for blast overpressures in the 5 to 15 psi range.

Counter Military Potential (CMP)

CMP is an index of counterforce capability being defined as

$$CMP = EMT/CEP^2 ,$$

where EMT is the equivalent megatons and CEP the circular error probable in nautical miles (see section 3.3)

CMP is useful, of course, only when CEP>0. Furthermore, care must be taken with the CMP index when the CEP gets close to 0.

Hard Target Kill Capability (HTK)

This index measures the number of targets of a specified hardness (generally 2000 to 2500 psi) that a force can destroy. HTK is defined as

$$HTK = \sum_{i=1}^{W} R_i \, DE_i ,$$

where R_i is the reliability of the ith warhead, DE_i is the damage expectancy of the ith warhead, and W is the number of warheads in the force.

Often this measure is computed separately for ballistic missile (ICBM or SLBM) warheads and is then called "prompt hard target kill capability" (PHTK) since these warheads are much faster than those delivered by bombers.

The principal weakness of HTK is that it assumes that a hard target is available for each weapon.

Equivalent Weapons (EW)

EW is an index which measures the effectiveness of each weapon against a generalized target structure (see also PAYNE (1977)).
The EW for each weapon is defined as

$$EW = \frac{1}{\frac{a}{P_{ka}} + \frac{b}{P_{kb}} + \frac{c}{P_{kc}}}$$

where a represents the proportion of soft point targets in the total target set, b the portion of soft area targets and c of hard point targets. The P_k are the expected probabilities of kill against each of these targets.

Joint Throwweight and Warhead Measures

Two measures which combine the throwweight and the number of warheads in a force have been investigated. The first of these is the Index of Strategic Offensive Potential (ISOP) which is the cross product of the total throwweight and the number of warheads in the force, and the other is Destructive Potential (DP) which is the sum of the throwweight and the number of warheads (see LIEBERMAN (1981)). Appropriate normalization factors are used with these indices. They both represent weapons capability in an original manner and have interesting features from an arms control point of view (DSAI 1982).

Standard Weapon Stations (SWS)

The Standard Weapon Stations (SWS) index is a concept which attempts to calibrate the destructive potential of both ballistic missiles and bombers (see KENT (1984)). It is based on the following rules:

The number of standard weapon stations counted for each type of ballistic missile delivery vehicle would be the largest of the following four numbers:

1) The declared or agreed to number of weapons on the missile;
2) The maximum number of weapons tested on the missile;
3) The throwweight of a MIRVed missile in kilograms divided by 400 (500 for a singe RV missile;

4) The volume of a MIRVed missile in cubic feet divided by 400 for missiles with solid propellant and 500 for a single RV missile and for missiles with liquid propellant.

The number of standard weapon stations charged for each type of bomber would be either the

1) take-off gross weight in pounds divided by 25,000 if the bomber carries ALCMs or

2) take-off gross weight divided by 50,000 if the bomber does not carry ALCMs.

3.3 CHARACTERISTICS OF SYSTEMS IN FORCE

There are many other characteristics which need to be examined in the evaluation of a nuclear force. Some of these characteristics, either by themselves or in combination with others, provide measures of various aspects of the force.

Accuracy of a nuclear weapon system is measured in terms of its CEP. The CEP, circular error probable, is the radius of a circle centered on the target such that the probability is 0.5 that the point of impact of the weapon will lie within the circle.

Availability is a measure of the probability that the weapons system will be ready for use when required. The measure is very important in noting the difference between ICBMs which are almost always ready (probability of availability ≈ 1) and SLBM or bombers for which only a portion of the force is available at any given time.

Reliability is the probability that an available weapon will operate properly when fired. The reliability can be divided into factors such as probability of successful RV separation, probability of successful detonation, which are combined to form the total reliability.

Pre-launch Survivability is a measure of the vulnerability of a system to attack. The pre-launch survivability of a system is a function of many factors such as its hardness, mobility, concealment, defenses and warning time. Pre-launch survivability is also a function of the scenario of the nuclear weapon employment plan. This is a very significant feature in crisis stability since the more vulnerable a system is before it is launched, the more the incentive to launch it before it is lost.

Penetration Capability is the probability that a weapon system can penetrate defenses to reach its target. It is an important characteristic to consider since similar forces which face different defenses could have substantially different capabilities.

Timeliness is a measure of the time it takes a weapon to reach its target from the moment it is launched. This is a very significant feature in crisis stability since the shorter the flight time the less time there is for response.

Range is the distance which a weapon can reach from its point of launch. This measure is particularly important for theater systems since their ranges are short and, therefore, may have to be taken into account in measuring their capabilities.

4. TOOLS FOR ASSESSMENT

A number of promising tools have been developed through the years to explore military problems, including those tools structured to examine components of a weapon, or an entire weapon, or a weapon system, or an entire force. Of practical necessity, the larger the frame of reference, the less detail included. Therefore, if one is using a particular tool, it is critical to use it to help shed light on a issue for which the tool is appropriate. The tools can take the form of physical models or of mathematical models that may be computerized so that many different specific cases can be examined. These models may run through to the end on a computer or be interrupted by an individual who can change the status of various parameters, i.e., be non-interactive or interactive. The tool could be a game, played by many individuals divided into teams, with guidelines issued as the game progresses. While not exhaustive, this list provides an idea of the diversity available.

When choosing a method or tool to use to help understand an issue, among the criteria that should influence the choice are

- adequacy for the problem
- communicability
- transparency

- credibility
- effect on decision or decision processes.

Much of what is learned from analysis is not in the "answer" of the analysis. It is usually the hands-on analyst that learns the most. This individual is usually not the decision maker, thus much of the value of any analysis is lost if the analyst is unable to communicate the understanding of, and insights into, the problem that he gained through the doing of the analysis. A major area that needs to be addressed, particularly in the arms control area, is how to assure that a "politican" and a mathematician/modeler can communicate usefully.

While there are many tools available to address military capability, there are far fewer that focus specifically on arms control objectives. There is much work to be done to take the arms control objectives discussed earlier, define functions which mathematically represent these notions (for example as in the previous section), and combine these functions into an analytical tool to help shed light on some meaningful arms control issues.

4.1 CATEGORIZATION OF FORMS OF ANALYSIS

Most methodological approaches used to support military balance assessments are of one of two basic forms: static or dynamic analyses. The former simply compare numerical factors such as manpower or numbers of major weapon systems. The latter use the results of static analysis as inputs in order to produce "outcomes" of military conflicts between the two sides.

Today, the most prevalent form of force balance analysis is of the static type. However, one would expect dynamic analysis to be superior in the context of negotiations because of the possibility of consistently and rather quickly testing the relative impact of varying assumptions with regard to both quantitative and qualitative assessment factors. In contrast, in the absence of analysis where individual judgments are relied upon, the results are neither reproducible in a rigorous sense nor is it possible to arrive at more than ordinal (better, worse) judgments when confronted with questions related to the impact of varying assumptions.

With respect to force balance assessments, static and dynamic analyses are not alternative methodological approaches. Rather, they represent complementary tools in that static analyses provide the inputs for dynamic analyses. Static analyses develop the array of mutual forces and order of battle for each scenario to be analyzed. Then dynamic analyses are used to provide estimates of the outcomes of military conflicts or battles waged by the forces confronting each other in the various scenarios.

Depending upon the solution procedures and the representation of stochastic events, there are essentially four fundamental classes of dynamic analysis tools which are discussed in section 2.1.2 of the workshop directors' *Introduction:*

1) Deterministic Analytical Models (DAM)
2) Stochastic Analytical Models (SAM)
3) Deterministic Simulation Models (DSM)
4) Stochastic Simulation Models (SSM).

Models of the DSM and SSM varieties provide time histories of the simulated conflicts or battles in terms of average outcomes in the former, and of frequency distributions of possible outcomes in the latter case. Except for rather simple cases, DAM and SAM type models are usually restricted to providing just the outcomes - average or probability distributions thereof - but no time histories.

4.2 SOME EXAMPLES OF TOOLS OF ASSESSMENT

4.2.1 STRATEGIC NUCLEAR WARFARE

In the U.S., the most widely used model of strategic nuclear warfare ist the Arsenal Exchange Model (AEM). The model is comprised of approximately 50,000 FORTRAN statements, treating both ballistic missile and air breathing offensive forces as well as ballistic missile defenses and air defenses and is a two-strike model. It addresses the strategy optimization problem, which in a simplified form might be characterized as the first striker attacking with all of his weapons on the second striker's weapons and value targets, after which the second striker responds with his remaining weapons on the first striker's value targets. The first striker maximizes, and the second striker minimizes, an objective function such as damage to the second striker's value targets minus damage to the first striker's value targets.

A significant limitation of a two-strike model, even if the analyst withholds some of the weapons, is that the optimal execution of a many-stage war is not addressed. How many weapons to allocate at each stage of a many-stage war is an exceedingly difficult analytical question. One model which begins to address this problem is the MUSTEX model, but the general problem has not been fully addressed.

Another analytical issue underlying any assessment of a series of engagements, (e.g., layered defense against ballistic missiles) is the replacement of multi-stage stochastic processes by a series of deterministic equivalents. For instance, if missiles are launched and attacked by boost-phase defenders, then RVs and decoys are attacked by midcourse defenders and exoatmospheric area defenders, and finally RVs approaching individual targets are attacked by terminal defenders, can the outcome of each stage of this process be assessed as an expected value, and the expected value be used in the next stage, to finally result in a correct expected value of the process? In general, the answer is no, and the approximation can be particularly poor if the final damage is relatively small; the fewer RVs that impact after the multi-stage defense, the worse is the approximation. Monte Carlo methods offer some hope for correct assessment, but they take long to run and are difficult to incorporate in an optimization framework.

Unlike conventional warfare and tactical nuclear warfare, in a two-strike nuclear war involving all or substantially all of the forces there are not many qualitatively different war-fighting scenarios. An important case is a counterforce exchange, which can be analyzed by the use of a subset of the AEM or by separate models. An interesting conceptual problem which has not been widely addressed is defining the extent to which strategic nuclear employment would not be rigidly defined and stylized, and developing comprehensive, dynamic models flexible enough to address a broad range of scenarios, i.e. defining a strategic battlefield that approaches the tactical in complexity.

4.2.2 TACTICAL NUCLEAR WARFARE

Chemical weapons and tactical nuclear weapons are treated in several dynamic simulations. For example, the TACWAR model of the U.S.'s Institute for Defense Analysis (IDA) is a very detailed model, comprised of about 80,000 Fortran statements, with assessments every 12 hours (notionally, day and night). It represents ground units to the level of detail of the specific types of weapons comprising the units (e.g., tanks, armored anti-tank weapons, unarmored anti-tank weapons, and artillery), and represents aircraft by type and their assignment to a wide variety of missions. The conventional model in TACWAR is based on that of IDAGAM, which has evolved to the INBATIM model of the U.S.'s Joint Chiefs of Staff's Joint Analysis Division.

Analysis capabilities to address tactical nuclear war are important in arms control because the large number of tactical nuclear weapons on both sides make them natural candidates for arms control consideration. Delivery systems capable of projecting nuclear weapons deep into the opponent's territory, such as Medium Range Ballistic Missiles, Ground Launched Cruise Missiles and tactical fighter-bombers, are an integral part of tactical nuclear capabilities. The employment of these tactical nuclear systems may overlap substantially with strategic nuclear systems. Since the forces are composed of many diverse types of tactical nuclear weapons, assessment models should be able to address the effects of cuts in sufficient detail to distinguish among the various types of tactical nuclear weapons.

One important modeling issue which is basic to dynamic simulation of conventional/tactical nuclear warfare is the extent to which stochastic warfare processes are approximated by deterministic equivalents, and the possible error introduced by the approximations. For instance, a typical methodology for representing attrition within a dynamic conventional/tactical nuclear warfare model is the use of a deterministic heterogeneous Lanchester square model, period by period. To the extent that the process is deterministic there is no error introduced in the period by period evaluation. However, if the underlying model should more properly be stochastic heterogeneous Lanchester square, the replacement of the stochastic process by a deterministic equivalent might result in significant errors over a number of cycles. If the percent of attrition in each cycle is relatively small there might not be much effect over time, but if it is large there might be a significant effect.

Another tool for analysis of tactical nuclear warfare is a somewhat free-play war game, where the players have a menu of strategies available. The strategies might be conceptualized as the equivalent of playing cards in a deck. As the players play their cards, a control team assesses results and the game continues. Such games can be as detailed as the designer wishes. The principal weakness of such a war game is that it may not be replicable. A corresponding strength is that it is difficult if not impossible to build as much strategy flexibility into a dynamic model as can be built into such a war game.

For the past several years RAND has been addressing the construction of decision logics for nuclear employment. Such logics would be incorporated into a dynamic model and would replace to a large extent the human players of the war game. The logics would be built from many points of view, to attempt to span a broad range of possible employment styles. Tactical nuclear warfare is a natural focus of such approaches, being the "bridge" between conventional to strategic warfare escalation and is arguably the most difficult aspect of warfare to conceptually understand. The challenge to dynamic modeling is substantial, as is correspondingly the potential contribution of models to the policy makers.

4.3 OBSERVATIONS

In summary, the strategic exchanges are generally treated as snapshots, or sequences of snapshots. Flow or movement with time is not treated anywhere near continuously. However, mobile missiles and other moveable targets, as well as more diversity of weapon systems, are becoming more characteristic of strategic arsenals and target bases. Thus, the strategic battlefield is becoming more like the tactical, and will require tools that are more flexible and can account for the passage of time.

5. FURTHER RESEARCH

The preceding sections have just touched upon some of the issues that are of interest to both the politician and the analyst vis-à-vis arms control The following, non-exhaustive list, suggests areas that would be fruitful for further research:

- How to bridge the gap between analyst and policy maker;
- How to improve implementation of results of analysis;
- More structured ways of generating arms control options;
- Better mechanisms for predicting reception of arms control options;
- Better ways of integrating arms control with the totality of security objectices;
- Better understanding of opponent;
- Better ways of presenting information;
- Better understanding of the effect of different attitudes on acceptability of models and output;

- Impact of models and their outputs on changing or confirming attitudes;
- Development of models that incorporate both strategic offense and defense;
- Improvements to models to permit trade-offs between force structure and operational concepts;
- Development of fully linked strategic - theater nuclear - conventional - chemical models of warfare.

6. REFERENCES

Adelman, K.L. (1984): Arms Control with and without Agreement. Council on Foreign Relations, Inc.

Bennett, B.W. (1980): Assessing the Capabilities of Strategic Nuclear Forces: The Limits of Current Methods.Rand, June 1980

BDM (1979): "Gray-Area System Measures of Effectiveness", December 1979

Decision Science Applications, Inc. (1982): An Evaluation of the Index of Strategic Offensive Potential - A New Approach to Limiting Military Capability Through Arms Control.February 1982

Galiano, R. (1975): Counter Military Potential and Related Thoughts. U.S. Arms Control and Disarmament Agency, April 1975

Hughes, W. (Ed., 1984): Military Modeling. Military Operations Research Society

Kent, G. (1984): A New Approach to Arms Control. Rand, June 1984

Lieberman, A. (1981): Joint Throwweight and Warhead Limitations Concept. U.S. ACDA, August 1981

Payne, Fred, A. (1977): The Strategic Nuclear Balance: A New Measure. Survival, May/June 1977

Santa Fe Corporation (1983): A Review of Trends in U.S. and USSR Nuclear Force Levels and Related Measures. June 1983

Wolf, C. (1975): Perceptions of the Military Balance: Models and Anecdotes. Rand, March 1975

THE USE OF ARMS CONTROL NEGOTIATIONS SIMULATION AS A BRIDGE BETWEEN POLICY AND ANALYSIS

Frank W. Jenkins
The Center for National Security Negotiations
McLean, Virginia 22102, USA

1. INTRODUCTION

One key difficulty with any arms negotiations is determining the possible effect that an agreement might have on the military balance and hence the strategic relationship between the two sides. Part of the source of that difficulty is based on the inherent flexibility that an agreement provides for the sides to structure their forces. Another important ingredient stems from each side's estimate of how the other side might structure its forces. Hence, one positive outcome of an arms control agreement can be to provide a better understanding of what the other side intends to do. However, because there will always be significant flexibility within the bounds of most agreements likely to be negotiated, the sides will continue to desire the capability to assess a range of potential outcomes and capabilities.

This desire to know more about the potential impact of a negotiated agreement has brought about a dialogue between those who are responsible for formulating or carrying out arms control policy and those who possess the analytic skills and tools for assessing an agreement. This dialogue has, over time, fostered a language and understanding between many people in these otherwise disparate groups which has served the policy community quite well; at least until now.

Almost from the dawn of the nuclear age, the United States and the Soviet Union (followed rather quickly by the other nuclear powers) have relied on the threat of severe punishment to deter an attack. It is also the case that we must, of necessity, continue to rely on that form of deterrence well into the future, no matter what decision may ultimately be made regarding strategic ballistic missile defense deployment. What President Reagan has done, by elevating the level of debate to a matter of policy, is to question whether there is a better way to carry out deterrent strategy and, importantly, whether there is a way to ensure our security *even if de-*

NATO ASI Series, Vol. F 26
Modelling and Analysis in Arms Control
Edited by R. Avenhaus et al.

terrence should fail. Given this perspective on the President's initiative, it is instructive for the analyst to understand the alternative notions of deterrence that are involved.

1.1 Deterrence Based on Assured Destruction (MAD)

The combination of the SALT I Interim Agreement on Strategic Offensive Arms and the ABM Treaty had the effect of codifying deterrence based on the threat of punishment. By attempting to rule out any notion of a nation-wide defense, the ABM Treaty emphasized the requirement for increased capability in offenses, which is exactly what happened. The United States and the Soviet Union have continued to develop these offenses in terms of, for example, accuracy, RV-size for a given yield, and numbers of warheads.

Our current offense-based strategy depends on the perception by a potential adversary that the risk of nuclear conflict outweights any potential political gains to be achieved by using military force in the first place. As long as his calculus causes him to arrive at that conclusion, he remains deterred.

In other words, deterrence is based on two critical elements:

- One side desires to achieve some political objective through the use of his military forces.
- The capability of the other side's forces are such that they effectively "block" that action.

But, the existing strategy requires that stability during crisis depends on each side always arriving at the same conclusion: using my nuclear forces would be a net loss. Should the calculus change, or there be a miscalculation, it is conceivable that deterrence could fail.

Given this situation, the analytic focus since SALT I has been primarily on 1) the "strategic balance", and 2) stability during a crisis, e.g., whether either side has an advantage in attacking first. This emphasis has, in turn, led the analysts to focus on static measures before an exchange and dynamic measures based on war gaming various scenarios[1].

With the possibility that the President's Strategic Defense Initiative could lead to a greater reliance on defenses and, indeed, alter the very basis for

---

[1] See examples by Al Lieberman in the subsequent paper of this book.

deterrence it is not at all clear that these traditional methods of analysis will be appropriate for judging the possible outcome of future negotiations.

1.2 Deterrence Based on Assured Survival (MAS)

A strategy which incorporated major capability in strategic defense would introduce a shift along the following lines:

- Even modest strategic defenses could compound the potential attackers' problem by reducing his confidence in achieving his military objectives.
- Robust strategic defenses could eventually deny the potential attacker the ability to achieve his military objectives, and
- Very effective defenses would assure national survival even if deterrence were to fail.

The different stages of a transition to defense dominance have been described by members of the Administration as:

- A near-term phase - perhaps lasting a decade or more - during which the sides would reduce their offensive arsenals and stabilize the offense-defense relationship.
- A mid-term phase - perhaps several decades - during which strategic defenses would be deployed and the sides further reduce their offenses.
- An ultimate phase when ballistic missile as well as other nuclear weapons would be eliminated.

Figure 1 is the author's attempt to graphically portray the Administration's strategic concept for the transition as well as the key points in the transition as discussed above.

Given the President's desire to move the two superpowers away from assured destruction toward assured survival, and given at least the possibility that the USSR may choose to move in that direction as well, the real issue is: how might one structure a cooperative transition? Given that issue, it follows that we should search for ways in which innovative analytic tools and methodologies might help inform policy judgments. One useful way to bring out some of the needed insights is through interactive gaming or simulations.

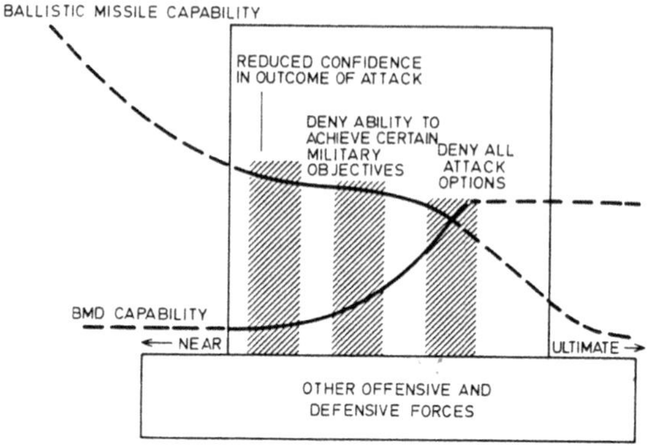

Fig. 1: Concept for the Transition from MAD to MAS

2. BACKGROUND

The President has said that he would be willing to share the fruits of the SDI research program with the Soviet Union and to work toward a cooperative rather than hostile or non-cooperative transition.

One perspective on this concept holds that the Soviet Union has no inclination or incentive for such cooperation. Rather, the Soviets may attempt to overcome or otherwise thwart our efforts. Those holding this perspective believe it will lead inevitably to a highly unstable, charged environment with the two sides racing to achive strategic superiority. The Soviets themselves have focused their debate on this potential outcome as a way to get the United States to drop the initiative altogether.

Given this perspective, it is difficult, if not impossible, to conceive of a negotiated, cooperative transition.

However, there is an alternative view that is also worth testing. First, the Soviet Union should actually find appealing the thought that the survival of their nation might somehow be restored to their control.

Second, a non-cooperative transition may not be very appealing to them. From their viewpoint, they may perceive:

- A US SDI research program that proves effective and feasible for rendering ballistic missiles "impotent and obsolete".
- A US which, despite the President insisting that a deployment decision must be reserved for a future administration, seems determined to move toward strategic defense if the concept *is* feasible.

- The possibility that their own technology will not keep pace.
- The undesirable prospect for having to fund increases in both offensive and defensive systems.
- The chance, at least, that they may lose the single measure of equality with the US as a superpower: military capability.

Given this perspective, the best choice may be for them to cooperate in some way that protects against a major shift in the strategic relationship.

3. A NEGOTIATIONS SIMULATION

This section describes a simulation of negotiations between the US and USSR on strategic forces that has been used by Science Applications International Corporation's Center for National Security Negotiations. The CNSN simulation has two purposes: 1) to develop insights about possible future negotiations; and 2) to identify the kinds of analysis that would be useful to decision makers and negotiating teams.

3.1 Scenario

The timeframe for the simulation is 1987. Progress toward an arms control agreement that might replace the SALT I and SALT II agreements has been slow, the negotiating situation can be characterized by a sense of stalemate in the talks. There is uncertainty about the very future of the arms negotiations process. It is the prevailing view within the US, the USSR and Western Europe that a new agreement must be achieved quickly if the arms control process is to avoid breaking down completely leaving an informal arms control regime at best.

Although the "umbrella" talks continue on START, INF and SPACE, no new agreements have been achieved. The sides are generally adhering to the SALT II Treaty limits and it is apparent that neither side wants to be the first to take actions which would be seen as "walking away" from the negotiations.

The Standing Consultative Commission is functioning, however the compliance issues raised by both sides in 1984-1985 remain unresolved. The focus of the talks on Space/Defense will soon turn to the next five year US-Soviet review of the ABM Treaty which was signed in 1972. The review is to take place only six months from the time the simulation begins.

3.2 Game Objectives

For the US: To undertake a transition to a new strategic regime in which deterrence is based on a mix of offensive and defensive forces. The US prefers that this transition be undertaken in the context of a cooperative agreement with the USSR.

Rationale for US Objective:

- President's vision of the future calls for a world free of nuclear weapons. As a first step, the SDI called for a comprehensive and intensive research program aimed at the eventual elimination of the threat caused by ballistic missiles.
- Since its inception, the SDI has made substantial progress (in the game) in research on technologies which can be applied to the interception of ballistic missiles and their warheads.
- As a result of this progress, the President will take an early decision to pursue the testing and deployment of SDI weapon system components. The US team is advised that in the very near term, the President intends to make a decision to proceed with testing of a space-based, non-nuclear defensive system. Testing will occur roughly one year from the start of the game and is judged to be contrary to the provisions of the ABM Treaty.

Other Key National Level Decisions:

- The US will seek in the negotiations to modify or replace the ABM Treaty.
- The US will continue to seek deep reductions in both sides' offensive forces - particularly ballistic missiles.
- Research, development, testing or deployment of anti-tactical ballistic missile systems should not be precluded by a future agreement.

For the Soviet Union: Different objectives are established for three USSR (Red) teams.

Red Team 1: To prevent any US deployment based on the SDI research and development program. To achieve this objective, the USSR would be willing to propose and/or accept major cuts in offensive forces.

Rationale: Through enormous investment in its strategic and theater forces, the USSR has achieved at least rough military parity with the US. This USSR team is concerned that SDI could undermine that parity and is not sure that additional offenses will be able to maintain or regain the balance.

Red Team 2: To prevent limits on Soviet nuclear offensive forces and programs involving nuclear or conventional defensive systems.

Rationale: This USSR team is convinced that the US has decided to pursue its SDI research efforts and eventually deploy ballistic missile defenses (as well as air defenses). Therefore, the team believes it is no longer possible to preserve the current strategic relationship based on offenses alone. Rather, the USSR must pursue its own defensive program while maintaining strong offensive forces.

Red Team 3: To establish a new strategic relationship based on a gradually increasing role for defenses. However, they will attempt to slow US momentum in SDI, especically in moving toward space based interceptors.

Rationale: As with Red 2, Red 3 is convinced that the US intends to pursue its SDI but questions whether the US can maintain such a policy decision over the long term. At the same time, the USSR believes its long term strategic interests are best served by deploying expanded ballistic missile defenses of its own.

3.3 Team Requirements

For Move One, each team:

- Formulates a desired outcome for the negotiations;
- Designs a range of alternative negotiating approaches;
- Adopts an in-going negotiating position.

For Move Two, each team:

- In negotiations with a counterpart team, attempts to achieve the major elements of an agreement which will satisfy the objectives outlined by the political authorities.

3.4 Game Play

The US side (Blue) is split into three separate teams, all with the same objectives as indicated above. In the first move all teams are required to formulate a desired outcome for the negotiations and design a range of alternative negotiating approaches. In the second move, each team in negotiating with a counterpart team, attempts to achieve the major elements of an agreement which will satisfy the objectives outlined by the political authorities. During the play, the control operating as a Green team (external to the game) can intervene, e.g., to represent NATO views or public opinion.

3.5 Observations from the Game

1) Most Blue teams are reluctant to reduce their offensive forces below the limits proposed in START. At the same time, they are reluctant to violate the ABM Treaty but typically want to negotiate the ability to conduct some space based testing. When forced (by the Control Team) to push for expanded ballistic missile defenses, Blue tends to be at a loss to create or even explain the desired offense-defense formulation. Blue is always looking for ways to assess the strategic situation with alternative levels of offense and defense for the two sides. They are somewhat reluctant to move from the "known" to the "unknown" in terms of concrete proposals.

2) Red Teams have far less difficulty formulating their positions:

   - Both Red 1 & Red 3 typically offer offensive reductions well below what Blue is prepared to adopt. The actual negotiations move will often involve tradeoffs being offered on both sides, but only between differing offensive capabilities; seldom between offenses and defenses.

   - Red 1 will frequently propose rapid cuts in offenses (as a sweetner) whereas Red 3 seeks a more measured pace in both the reductions and in the introduction of defenses. However, Red 3 tends to place the responsibility on Blue to propose an explicit formula for the offense-defense relationship. They insist that because the shift is a US initiative, it is incumbent upon the US to offer specific recommendations for doing so.

   - Red 2 & Blue 2 frequently end up with a "live-and-let-live" approach which codifies each side's offenses, while focusing on the pace of the defenses.

3) In post-game discussions with the Teams (principally Blue) the following kinds of analysis results have emerged as being potentially useful to the decision makers and negotiators (all figures are notional):

- The rate or actual number of warheads penetrating the defense, relative to the various target sets;
- The amounts of critical military targets surviving (CMT Surv) on both sides (see Fig. 2);
- Areas of stability (no first strike incentive) as a function of the shift from offensive to defensive capabilities for both sides (Fig. 3);
- Levels and difference of surviving assets (e.g., other military targets, recovery capability, resources, leadership (Fig. 4);
- Impact of defenses on the confidence of the attacker to achieve his objectives (Fig. 5).

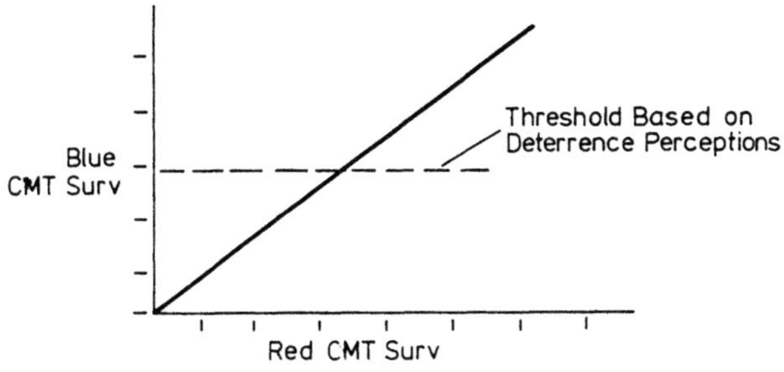

Fig. 2: Amounts of Critical Military Targets Surviving

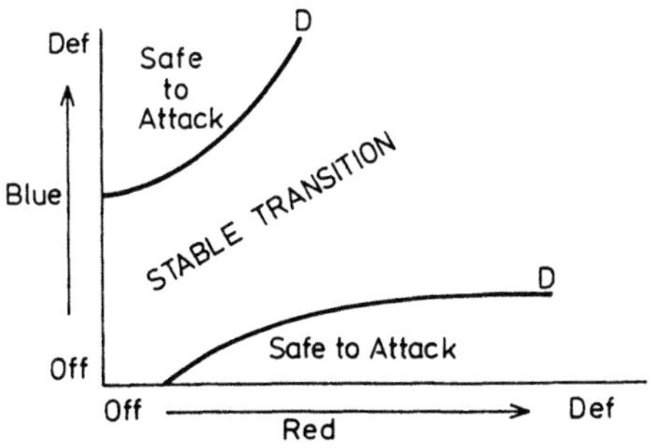

Fig. 3: Stability and the Shift from Strategic Offense to Defense

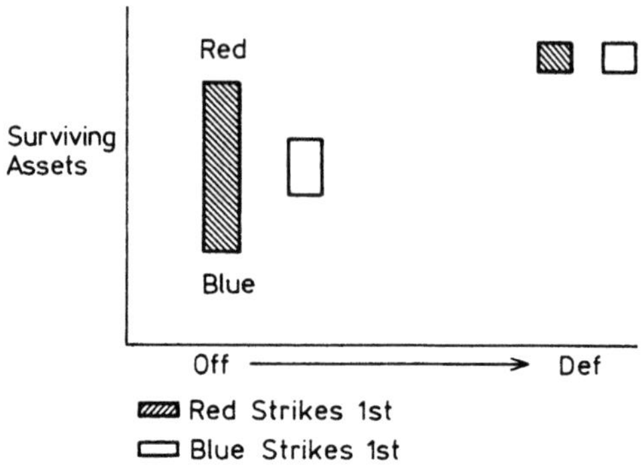

Fig. 4: Relative Surviving Assets (e.g., other military targets, recovery capability, resources, leadership)

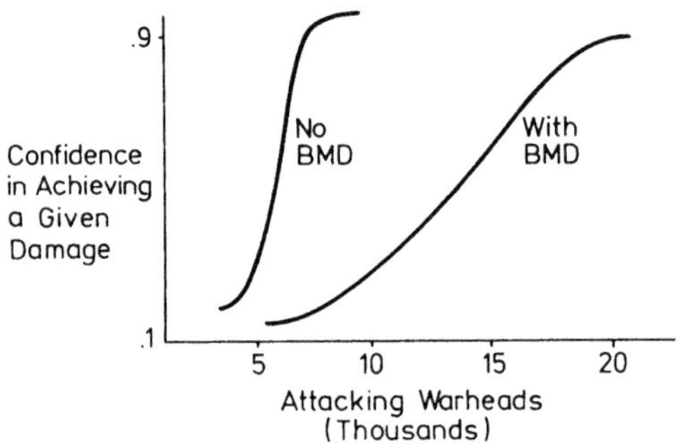

Fig. 5: Impact of Defenses on Attacker's Confidence

4. CONCLUSION

The traditional forms of quantitative analysis performed over the past several decades will continue to be useful to arms control policy makers and negotiators. However, the introduction of defenses into the strategic equation has provided both a challenge and an opportunity for those who wish to offer helpful analyses. This paper has highlighted the way that negotiations gaming techniques can help identify analytic tools and methodologies that might help illuminate the very complex strategic relationship, between the United States and the Soviet Union.

PRE-ARMS CONTROL ASSESSMENT OF THE STRATEGIC BALANCE: THE IMPACT OF OBJECTIVES AND APPROACHES

Alfred Lieberman

U.S. Arms Control and Disarmament Agency
Washington, D.C. 20451, USA

The role of models and analysis in the strategic arms control process will be examined by addressing two types of analyses:

1) The impact of strategic objectives on strategic exchange calculations and arms control;

2) The differences between the US and Soviet approaches to strategic analysis.

1. IMPACT OF STRATEGIC OBJECTIVES

The strategic objectives analysis will be illustrated by a simple example. Table 1 presents a weapon force structure. While it does not represent any real forces, it is a good example for showing the impact of strategic objectives on the arms control process. We have a force of 9000 warheads with 2000 on ICBMs, 4000 on SLBMs and 3000 on bombers, each with the assumed yields, accuracies, reliabilities and availabilities as indicated.

TABLE 1: EXEMPLARY WEAPON FORCE STRUCTURE

WEAPON TYPE	YIELD (KT)	CEP (NM)	RELIABILITY	AVAILABILITY	NO. OF WARHEADS
ICBM	300	0.10	0.8	1.00	2000
SLBM	100	0.15	0.8	0.75	4000
BOMBERS	200	0.05	0.8	0.80	3000
TOTAL					9000

NATO ASI Series, Vol. F 26
Modelling and Analysis in Arms Control
Edited by R. Avenhaus et al.

Table 2 shows the target data base developed for this example. Note that the 8100 targets are divided into 5 categories and each of these categories into subcategories. A value, number and a hardness for each type of target subcategory was assigned. The value represents the importance of each target, the number is the number of targets of that type and the hardness is the vulnerability of the target to overpressure given in pounds per square inch.

TABLE 2: EXEMPLARY TARGET DATA BASE

TARGETS	VALUE	NUMBER	HARDNESS (PSI)
COUNTERFORCE			
CF 1	10	1500	2000
CF 2	30	200	10
LEADERSHIP			
LDR 1	5	200	10
LDR 2	5	100	50
LDR 3	10	100	500
COMMAND & CONTROL			
CC 1	5	200	500
CC 2	2	800	10
OTHER MIL. TARGETS			
OMT 1	25	500	50
OMT 2	10	2500	10
INDUSTRY			
IND 1	25	1000	10
IND 2	5	1000	10
TOTAL		8100	

To attack this target system, it was decided that the counter-force targets should be attacked with ballistic missiles (ICBMs & SLBMs) since these were time-urgent targets that should be destroyed rapidly. Then three strategic objectives were selected. The first was to maximize the target value destroyed, the second was to destroy 90% of each of the top seven subcategories of targets and the third was to accomplish objective 2 and at the same time destroy the same percent of value as was obtained in objective 1.

Strategic exchange calculations were then run with the Arsenal Exchange Model (AEM) based on these input data and specifications.

The results of these calculations are given in Table 3. First, we can note that for objective 1 which maximizes the value destroyed, 75.7 of the target value was destroyed. In objective 2, we were able to reach the objectives of

90% destruction for 6 of the 7 target subsets. Only 76% of subset CF1 was destroyed. Note, however, that the total value destroyed was reduced to 25.7%. In other words, when we dictate part of the strategy - giving objective 2 - we reduce the value which is destroyed from what it was when the only goal was to maximize value destroyed.

TABLE 3: COMPARISON OF STRATEGIC OBJECTIVES

OBJECTIVE	VALUE DESTROYED (PERCENT)
1) BASE CASE: MAXIMIZE VALUE DESTROYED	75.7
2) DESTROY 90% OF 7 TARGETS (CF1&2, LDR1,2&3 AND CC1&2)	25.7 (OBJECTIVES MET, EXCEPT FOR CF1 ONLY TO 76%)

If now we want to establish the force that would be required to meet objective 2 and at the same time get us back to the 75% target value destruction that existed in the objective 1 case, we find that we need a force of 14,802 warheads (see Table 4). This calculation also assumes that we wish to keep the ratio of ICBM, SLBM and bomber warheads approximately equal to what it was in the base case. This strategic objective, therefore, requires a 70% increase in the number of warheads. This example illustrates the impact that strategic objectives have on the arms control process.

TABLE 4: FORCES REQUIRED TO MEET OBJECTIVE 2 AND GET BACK TO ORIGINAL VALUE DESTROYED

WEAPON SYSTEM / FORCES NEEDED	ICBM	SLBM	BOMBERS	TOTAL WARHEADS
BASE CASE	2000	4000	3000	9,000
OBJECTIVE 3	3427	6853	4522	14,802

The next part of this example examines the impact of strategic objectives on force reduction analyses and the difficulties in measuring which type of reduction might be more advantageous.

Table 5 shows an example of two reduction cases. We start with the same base case force of 9000 warheads. In case A, we reduce by 2000 ICBM warheads and in case B we reduce by 2000 bomber warheads. We now want to determine which of these two reduction cases is more advantageous.

TABLE 5: FORCE REDUCTION ANALYSIS

CASE \ WEAPON SYSTEM	ICBM	SLBM	BOMBERS	TOTAL WARHEADS
BASE CASE	2000	4000	3000	9000
CASE A	0	4000	3000	7000
CASE B	2000	4000	1000	7000

In Figure 1, we compare the base case and the two reduction cases in terms of a static measure, hard target kill capability. This measure represents the number of 2000 psi targets that the force could destroy. We find in this comparison that case A, the ICBM reduction, looks advantageous over case B, since it can destroy approximately 15% more hard targets.

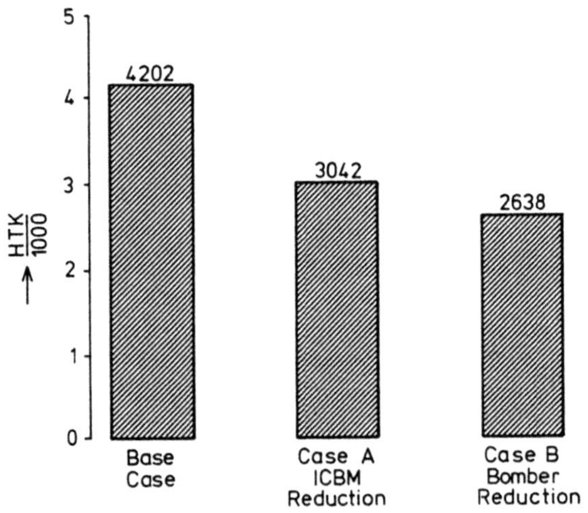

Fig. 1: Static Measure Hard Target Kill (HTK) Capability

These same forces submitted to strategic exchange calculation, however, present a different picture (see Table 6). We note that for value destroyed case B, the bomber reduction, give higher results, thereby being the preferred option.

TABLE 6: VALUE DESTROYED

CASE \ OBJECTIVE	1) MAX. VALUE DESTROYED	2) DESTROY 90% OF 7 TARGET SETS
BASE CASE	75.7	25.7
A: ICBM REDUCTION	64.3	18.1
B: BOMBER REDUCTION	68.7	21.1

When we examine the capabilities of the two reduction forces to accomplish objective 2, Table 7 shows that we get mixed results. Case B is substantially better against CF1, but not as good against CC1 and CC2.

TABLE 7: OBJECTIVE 2 RESULTS

TARGET \ CASE	BASE CASE	A ICBM REDUCTION	B BOMBER REDUCTION
CF1	.76	.29	.76
CF2	.90	.90	.90
LDR1	.90	.90	.90
LDR2	.90	.90	.90
LDR3	.90	.90	.90
CC1	.90	.90	.60
CC2	.90	.90	0.00

These examples illustrate the importance of strategic objectives to the arms control process and the complexity of measuring the benefits of alternative arms control options.

2. ARMS CONTROL IMPLICATIONS OF DIFFERENT US AND SOVIET APPROACHES TO STRATEGIC ANALYSIS

The second part of this paper deals with the different US and Soviet approaches to strategic analysis. This difference in approach can readily be seen by examining the actual counterforce capabilities of the strategic forces of the US and the Soviet Union.

In order to show the difference in US and Soviet strategic policy, it is worthwhile to examine the actual forces the two sides have developed. In order to compare these two force structures we have calculated the counterforce capabilities under the assumption - first, that both sides had forces which are similar to the US forces and second, that both sides had forces similar to the Soviet forces.

Figure 2 shows the results of a strategic counterforce exchange if both sides had the US strategic forces*). In the chart the equivalent megatonage (EMT) of the US forces are plotted along the vertical axis while the EMT of the Soviet forces are plotted along the horizontal axis. Therefore, whenever the graph is above the diagonal central line, the balance is to the US advantage and whenever it is below this central line, the balance is to the Soviet advantage. In this case the starting balance is, of course, even since both sides are using US forces.

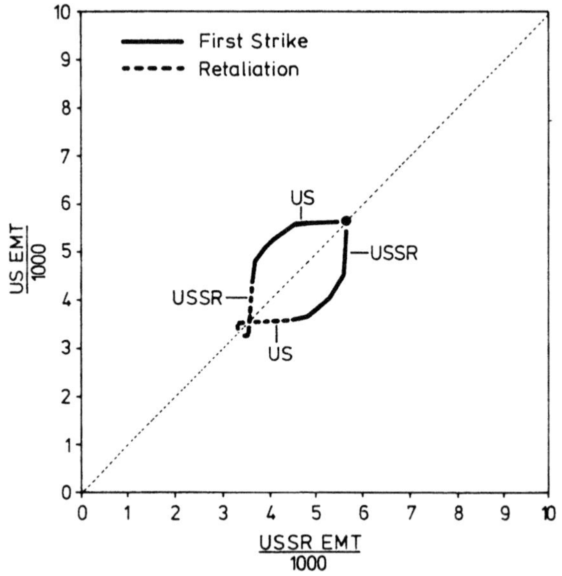

Fig. 2: Strategic Counterforce Exchange Both Sides have US Forces

*) Data obtained from "The Military Balance 1982-1983" IISS.

The nuclear exchange calculations start from the dot in the upper right hand corner of the figure. This is the balance of the forces before the attack. In the figure it represents approximately 5,500 EMTs. The chart then shows two possible situations, one is a Soviet first strike (solid line going downward) against US strategic forces (ICBM, SLBM and bombers) and a US retaliation (dashed line going across) against Soviet strategic forces. The other situation depicted in the chart is a US first strike (solid line going across) against Soviet strategic forces and a Soviet retaliation (dashed line going downward) against US strategic forces.

The separation between the end points of the dashed lines and their location with respect to the diagonal line give a measure of the advantage each side would gain by a first strike relative to what the other side would gain by a first strike. In this case the end points crossover and are close to the diagonal line, indicating that there is no advantage in a first strike. This is a situation which is considered very stable, since there is nothing to be gained by striking first.

In Figure 3 we have the results of a counterforce exchange if both sides had the Soviet forces. Clearly, this is a very unstable situation since the solid lines are very long indicating great losses of forces and the end points are far apart indicating that there is substantial advantage in striking first.

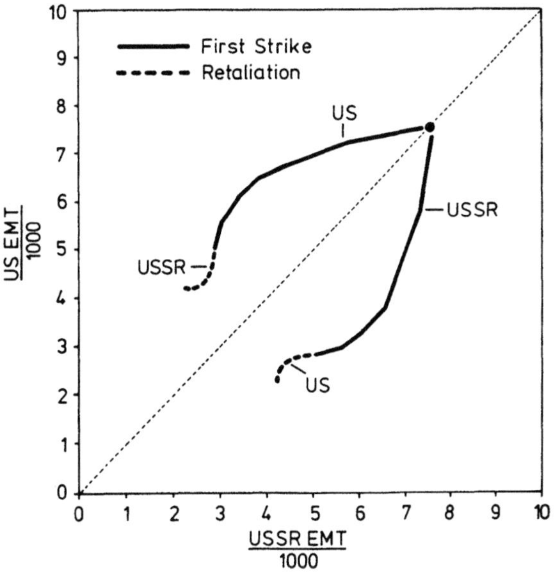

Fig. 3: Strategic Counterforce Exchange Both Sides have Soviet Forces

These two pictures clearly demonstrate the different route the US and the Soviet Union have taken in the development of their strategic forces.

The examination of the Soviet view will begin with an introduction to the Soviet correlation of forces methodology[2]. Next we will examine a documented example of a correlation of forces calculation which appears to be particularly relevant to the analysis of strategic nuclear forces. We will try to examine this Soviet example in some detail and compare its analytical structure, assumptions, and findings to similar US analytical structure. Finally, we will relate the analytical differences and similarities to possible problems and opportunities in arms control.

The Soviets are known to have many indices of the correlation of forces. These indices are used as part of a complex process of estimating the probability of accomplishing specific missions designed to achieve specific strategic goals. Figure 4 is adopted from a Soviet text by Tarakanov. It clearly illustrates the relationship that the Soviets have in mind between the probability of mission accomplishment and appropriate indices of the correlation of forces.

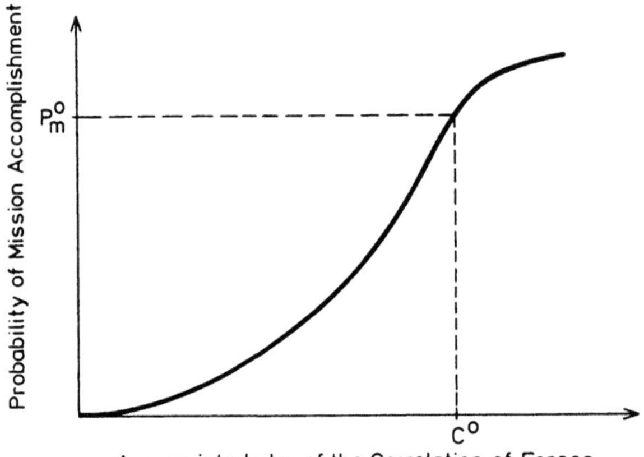

Fig. 4: Typical Soviet Pay-Off Function

---

[2] This section is based on work performed by Decision Science Application (DSA) and Science Application, Inc. (SAI).

At this point it should be stressed that we do not have the information suggested by this figure. We do not know the specific missions or goals to which the correlation of forces is related nor do we know the nature of such relationships between the index and probabilities of accomplishing possible missions.

Next we turn to an examination of a particular Soviet index which appears to be highly relevant to the analysis of strategic nuclear forces. This index is the "correlation of forces in terms of nuclear weapons". It was first introduced in 1967 by Major General I.I. Anureyev. Anureyev defined his index as "the relationship of the combat capabilities of the sides in terms of inflicting nuclear strikes with consideration of enemy countermeasures".

Fundamental quantities used in the formulation of the correlation of forces in terms of nuclear weapons are:

Y_{Fi} = Total weapon yield carried by all Delivery Vehicles of type i of side F

$Y_F = \sum_i Y_{Fi}$

$X_{Fi} = Y_{Fi}/Y_F$

P_{Fi} = Probability of nondestruction before launch for i-type delivery of side F

Q_{Fi} = Probability of overcoming enemy defense for i-type delivery vehicle of side F

Define Y_{Gj}, Y_G, X_{GJ}, P_{GJ}, O_{GJ}, as analogous quantities of J-type delivery vehicles of side G.

These quantities are defined for the two opposing sides which are designated by a subscripts F and G. Traditionally, side F would be the Soviets and side G would be the US. For both sides, the different types of delivery vehicles must also be designated. For each type of delivery vehicle the analyst must know the total yield carried, the probability of survivability to launch, and the probability of overcoming enemy defense. Note that the parameter Y_{Fi} is not the yield of individual weapons but the total yield carried by the totality of delivery vehicles of that type. The probabilities of survivability to launch and the probabilities of overcoming enemy defense will, of course, depend on the nature of the scenario being analyzed.

Using the quantities defined above, the formulae for the correlation of forces in terms of nuclear weapons are defined as follows:

$$C_0 = \frac{Y_F^{2/3}}{Y_G^{2/3}}$$

$$C = \frac{\sum_i X_{FI}^{2/3} P_{Fi} Q_{Fi}}{\sum_j X_{Gj}^{2/3} P_{Gj} Q_{Gj}} \cdot C_0$$

$$= \frac{\sum_i Y_{Fi}^{2/3} P_{Fi} Q_{Fi}}{\sum_j Y_{Gj}^{2/3} P_{Gj} Q_{Gj}}$$

The first formula defines C_0 the initial correlation of forces. The second formula defines the correlation of forces as C_0 times a modifying function which depends on the distribution of yield among the weapon types, the probabilities of survivability to launch and the probabilities of overcoming enemy defense. The final formula shows that, when C_0 is multiplied through, the measure becomes a ratio of lethal area associated with the weapon types modified by these same two probabilities.

These formulae all contain terms in which yield is raised to the two-thirds power. These terms are reminiscent of the equivalent megatonnage measure used in the West but they are really quite different. Western equivalent megatons is a measure of lethal area derived by taking the two-thirds power of the yield of each weapon and summing that quantity over the number of weapons being considered. This Soviet quantity is different because the yield of various weapons is first summed and the two-thirds power of the sum is then taken. The Soviet measure is a lethal area that the West might associate with placing all weapons in one place and detonating them simultaneously with an aggregate yield equal to the sum of the yields of the individual weapons. In the formula for C_0 we see such lethal areas associated with the total yield of each force. In the final formula we see such lethal areas associated with total yield deployed in each type of weapon. As you might expect, this measure of lethal area makes the correlation of forces in terms of nuclear weapons quite sensitive to the number of weapon types and the distribution of yield between the types. The Soviets try to express this sensitivity in terms of a quantity called the coefficient of distribution. These formulae suggest that the US and Soviets may have very different interpretations of the lethal area associated with nuclear weapons. This is a major potential source of analytical differences to which we now turn.

The difference between the US and Soviet measure of lethal area is that the US measure is a linear one while the Soviet measure is a nonlinear one. As shown by the graph in the upper right of Figure 5, as more weapons are deployed in a single type of delivery vehicle, the US measure would grow in proportion to the number of weapons. As shown by the graph in the upper left, for the same situation the Soviet measure would grow as the number of weapons raised to the two-third power.

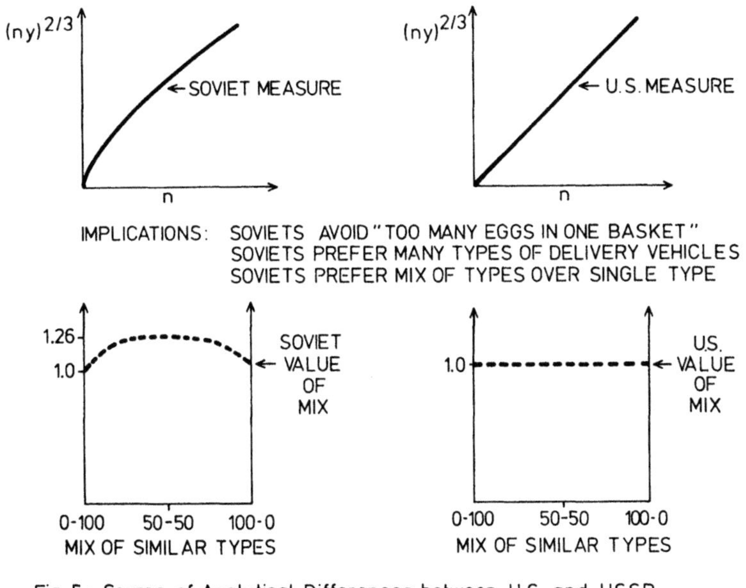

Fig. 5: Source of Analytical Differences between U.S. and USSR

This Soviet measure has significant implications for the preferred composition of nuclear forces. With a nonlinear function such as the one shown here, the marginal utility of each additional weapon of the same type steadily decreases and, no matter how effective that particular type of weapon is, it eventually becomes desirable to stop adding weapons of the same type to the force and begin adding weapons of a new type. Thus the general implications of the

Soviet nonlinear measure is that it may cause the Soviets to avoid placing "too many eggs in one basket". The Soviets would also tend to prefer many types of delivery vehicles and to prefer a mix of types over a single type.

The bottom graphs of Figure 5 illustrate the implied difference between US and Soviet preferences for weapons mixes. Suppose there were two types of delivery vehicles which carried the same number of weapons with the same yields. With the linear US measure of lethal area, all weapon mixes would have the same utility. However, with the nonlinear Soviet measure, a 50-50 mix of weapon types would be valued 26% more than a pure force of either type.

The Soviet preference for many weapon types may be analogous to the US desire for a TRIAD of strategic nuclear delivery vehicles. In both cases, the need for variety may be linked to the operational stability of the force.

The structure of the correlation of forces in terms of nuclear weapons suggests another difference between US and Soviet analytical approaches. According to the formulation of this index, launched weapons would be valued more than surviving weapons. This property arises because the probability of survivability to launch is the same for a launched weapon as for a surviving weapon and because launched weapons can reduce the probability of survivability to launch of opposing weapons. In fact, the correlation of forces in terms of nuclear weapons is optimized when one side launches all of its weapons in a counterforce attack against the other side.

To appreciate the meaning of this finding, consider two forces after a nuclear exchange. The value of each force can be broken down into three components, value which is launched during the exchange, value which survives but is not launched, and value which is destroyed. The Soviet and US indices for this case are as follows:

<u>Soviet Measure:</u>	<u>US Measure:</u>
$\frac{V_{FL} + V_{FS}}{V_{GL} + V_{GS}}$	$\frac{V_{FS}}{V_{GS}}$

The Soviet index appears to measure a ratio of value launched (L) plus value surviving (S).The US, however, is usually concerned with the ability of forces to guarantee stable deterrence by riding out an attack and having adequate force surviving to assure unaccepted retaliation. Accordingly, the US would tend to measure a ratio of only the value which survives an exchange.

The difference between these Soviet and US measures has a significant implication. In evaluating the same scenario both sides could perceive an advantage. The Soviets could have a force with lots of readily launchable assets like ICBMs and perceive an advantage according to the Soviet measure. Simultaneously, the US could have a force with lots of survivable assets like SLBMs and perceive an advantage according to the US measure.

The correlation of forces in terms of nuclear weapons can be calculated for many situations. As the formulae suggest, there are abbreviated forms of this index which can be calculated independent of possible strategic operations. These include the initial correlation of forces and the coefficient of distribution. Secondly, there are values which depend on the form of strategic operation which is to be modelled. Indeed, Anureyev's description of the index states that it should be used to select preferred forms of strategic operations. We have evaluated the index for several different kinds of operation including Soviet first strikes, meeting strikes in which both sides launch simultaneously, and US first strikes. We do not know how the Soviets conduct such an analysis but would like to discuss one possible way this might be done (Figure 6).

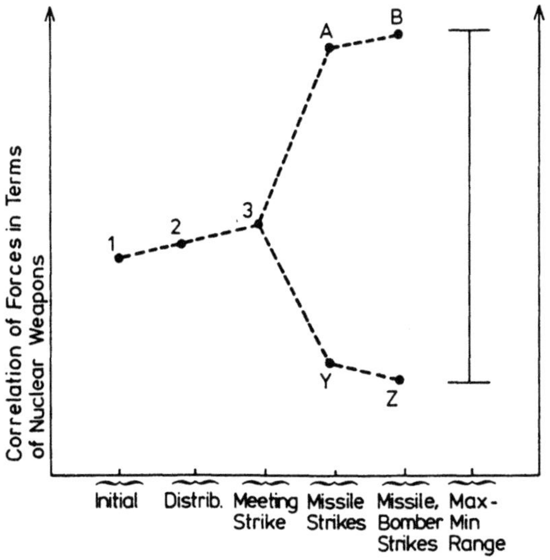

Fig. 6: Hypothetical Example of a Correlation of Forces Array

A correlation of forces array can be derived for any pair of opposing force structures. Interesting forms of the index calculation are listed along the abscissa and the actual values of the correlation of forces in terms of nuclear weapons are plotted accordingly along the ordinate. The array shows three important relationships. There is a "horizontal" relationship between points 1, 2, and 3. There is a vertical relationship between points B, A, 3, Y, and Z. Finally, there is a bounding relationship illustrated by the solid bar.

In the horizontal relationship between points 1, 2, and 3, the forces are evaluated on a par with each other. Point 1 is the initial correlation of forces. When the two sides have approximately equal total yield, this initial value can be quite close to one. It is not unreasonable to conjecture that, according to the principle of equality, the Soviets might accept unity as the value of the initial correlation of forces for situations that are subject to arms control. Point 2 is the coefficient of distribution which exhibits the effects of weapon distribution among various types. It is not unreasonable to expect point 2 to be higher than point 1 because the Soviets have more weapon types than the US. Point 3 is the value associated with a meeting strike in which both sides simultaneously launch their forces and neither side has weapons destroyed before launch. If, in a generated alert posture, the Soviets have more of their forces able to fire than the US does, point 3 would be higher still than point 2.

Points A and B are values associated with Soviet first strikes. In point A the US retaliates after Soviet ballistic missiles arrive. In point B the US retaliates only after both Soviet ballistic missiles and Soviet bomber weapons arrive. Points Y and Z are analogous values associated with situations in which the US strikes first.

The vertical relationship between points B, A, 3, Y, and Z is intended to illustrate the sensitivity of the correlation of forces to the Soviet concept of the balance of time. For point B to be achieved, the Soviet strike would have to be ten hours ahead of the US strike. For point A to be achieved the Soviets would have to be about one hour ahead. For point 3 to be achieved the two forces would have to be launched approximately simultaneously. For points Y and Z the US would have to be ahead of the Soviets by about one hour and ten hours, respectively. The sensitivity of the correlation of forces in terms of nuclear weapons to the balance of time helps us understand why the Soviets are so concerned about US systems like Pershing II. The Soviets are probably afraid that systems which can strike in only a few minutes can prevent or delay launch operations. The presence of only a few such systems could thus change the Soviet perception that the probable correlation of forces in terms of nuclear weapons would not be point A but, instead, point 3 or possibly point Y.

This topic brings us to consider different US and Soviet concepts of crisis stability. According to Soviet concepts of stability, they are apparently concerned with maximizing the probability that their forces can accomplish their assigned missions in the face of operational uncertainties and enemy counteractions. In the present context this probably means that the Soviets would try to guarantee the successful launch of their ballistic missiles so that the most probable value of the correlation of forces in terms of nuclear weapons is point A. The US concept of crisis stability is concerned with reducing the incentive to strike first. The correlation of forces array is useful in assessing this US concept because the vertical distance between point A and point Y is a measure of the incentive to strike first.

As a final topic associated with the correlation of forces array, we would like to consider some problems and opportunities which might be associated with agreeing on a common US and Soviet approach to the concept of crisis stability (see Figure 7). What would happen if both sides pursued a unilateral concept of stability, like the apparent Soviet concept? In that case,

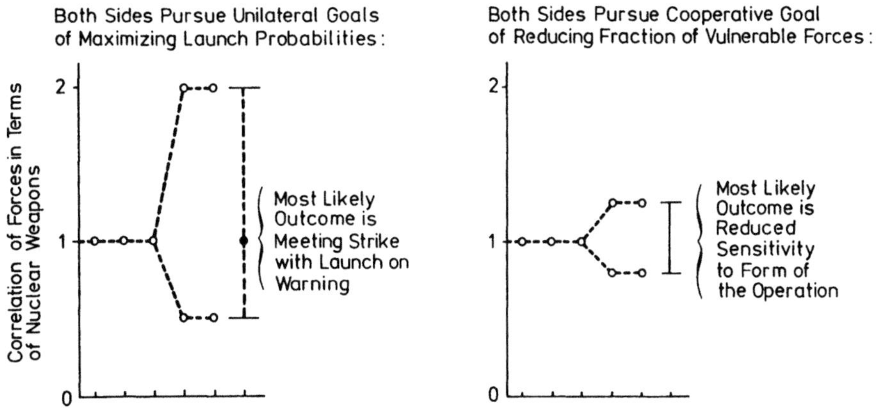

Fig. 7: Arms Control Problems / Opportunities Associated with a Common Approach to Crisis Stability

both sides might well try to maximize the launch probabilities of their own forces. The result, shown on the left in Figure 7, is that the most likely outcome of a conflict would be a meeting strike in which both sides launch their forces nearly simultaneously as in a launch on warning posture. However, if both sides pursued a US concept of crisis stability they would try to reduce the incentive to strike first by reducing the fraction of vulnerable forces. The results, shown on the right would be a restructuring of the correlation of forces array. The result of this restructuring would be much reduced sensitivity to the different forms of strategic operation. Obviously, the results shown on the two sides of this slide are very different from each other. It would be very useful to discuss such results with our Soviet counterparts in order to get their perceptions of them.

This discussion indicates that there are significant differences in the ways the US and the USSR evaluate the strategic nuclear relationship. This situation suggests two disparate courses of action regarding the future of arms control. One course of action would be to exploit analytical differences by constructing arms control proposals which both sides view as beneficial by virtue of their different methods and approaches to strategic analysis. Another course of action would be for both sides to reach agreed definitions of such concepts as equality and stability as well as agreed procedures for evaluating these concepts. Arms control proposals could then be formulated to promote the agreed concepts.

3. THE ROLE OF MODELS AND ANALYSIS

In summary, the analyses discussed in this paper lead to the following issues:

The strategic objectives analysis shows how these objectives drive the weapon requirement. The arms control process, therefore, needs to start at the time that strategic objectives are established. While the arms control process should not drive the strategic objectives, it must, nevertheless, be taken into account. This analysis also shows how in an arms control reduction case, static measures can lead to contradictory results from those obtained with dynamic calculation.

The differing US and Soviet approaches to strategic analysis show that there are significant differences in the ways the US and USSR evaluate the strategic nuclear relationship. This situation suggests two disparate courses of action regarding the future of arms control. One course of action would be to exploit analytical differences by constructing arms control proposals which both sides view as beneficial by virtue of their different methods and approaches to strategic analysis. Another course of action would be for both sides to reach agreed definitions of such concepts as equality and stability as well as agreed procedures for evaluating these concepts. Arms control proposals could then be formulated to promote the agreed concepts.

REFERENCES

Anureyev, I.: Determining the Correlation of Forces in Terms of Nuclear Weapons. Voyenna Musl (Military Thought), No. 6, 1967, Translated in Foreign Press Digest, 11 August, 1968.

Bozovich, J.F.: The Arsenal Exchange Model (AEM) User's Manual. The Stonehouse Group, Inc., November 1985.

Hughes, W. (Ed.): Military Modeling. Military Operations Research Society, 1984.

GENERATION OF ALTERNATIVE FORCE CONFIGURATIONS FOR ARMS CONTROL NEGOTIATIONS USING LINEAR PROGRAMMING

Charles ReVelle
Joanne Barker

The Johns Hopkins University
Baltimore, Maryland 21218, USA

1. INTRODUCTION

Harold Brown and Lynn E. Davis (1984) propose a strategy for arms control that they refer to as "Overall Equivalence". This strategy requires the United States and Soviet Union to agree to overall limits on nuclear weapons systems for each side instead of individual limits for each type of weapon, as in the past. Brown and Davis suggest three such Overall Equivalence limits:

(1) Total Equivalent Missile and Bomber Warheads not to exceed 6500;

(2) Total Equivalent Throw-Weight not to exceed 8,000,000 lbs.;

(3) Total Missile Warheads (excluding Bomber Warheads) not to exceed 6000.

Further, Brown and Davis propose hypothetical configurations of weapons for the United States and the Soviet Union which satisfy these three Overall Equivalence limits. One such configuration is proposed for the United States, and two configurations are laid out for the Soviet Union, all three configurations meeting the three limits enumerated above. It is the problem of generating such hypothetical weapons configurations that is addressed in this paper.

2. METHODOLOGY

Linear Programming, a well-developed and widely-used optimization procedure, was utilized to find weapons configurations which push as closely as possible toward the Overall Equivalence limits. In this initial work, the optimization procedure is used for the United States and again for the Soviet Union. With one minor exception, the counting rules for weapon warheads and throw weights were those developed by Brown and Davis.

These rules are used to detail the number of warheads per weapon for each

NATO ASI Series, Vol. F 26
Modelling and Analysis in Arms Control
Edited by R. Avenhaus et al.

weapon type and the throw-weight per weapon for each weapon type. The three constraints of "Overall Equivalence" are built up using the counting rules in the following way:

(1) The total equivalent missile and bomber warheads is the sum over all weapon systems of the warheads per weapon multiplied by the number of weapons of each type. Weapon types include each land-based system, each sea-based system and each bomber type. The sum of all warheads is to be less than 6500.

(2) The total equivalent throw-weight is the sum over all weapon systems of the throw weight per weapon multiplied by the number of weapons of each type. The sum is formed over all land-based, all sea-based and all bomber-based weapons systems, and is not to exceed 8,000,000 lbs.

(3) The total missile warheads is the the sum of the warheads per weapon of each type multiplied by number of weapons of each type. The sum of warheads, formed only over the land-based and sea-based missiles, is not to exceed 6000.

As upper bounds for the various weapons systems, Brown and Davis' projection of weapons counts in 1990 were used for both the US and USSR (see Tables 1 and 2). Their projection assumes that no new arms control agreement has been concluded. It should be pointed out that Brown and Davis had not assigned an equivalent throw-weight to the Bear and Bison bomber of the USSR. However, a comparison of the equivalent throw-weights and the gross take-off weights (GTW) of the US bombers and the Soviet Blackjack indicates that they used an average of about 4% of the GTW. Thus, the same figure was applied to the Bear and Bison, the GTW of which were obtained from Aviation Week (1983).

The objective of meeting the Overall Equivalence limits as closely as possible was modeled using simply a minimization of slack variables with one slack variable being assigned to each of the three Overall Equivalence limits. The respective linear program with upper bound and non-negativity constraints is expressed as

$$\text{Minimize} \quad S_1 + S_1 + S_3 \qquad (1)$$

Subject to

Table 1: NUCLEAR WEAPONS SYSTEMS OF THE UNITED STATES

LAND-BASED MISSILES Weapon Name	Projected 1990 Level of Weapons	Warheads per Weapon	Total Warheads	Throw-weight per Weapon (1000 lbs)	Total Throw weight (1000 lbs)
Minuteman II	450	1.0	450	1.6	720
Minuteman III	550	3.0	1650	2.4	1320
MX Missile	100	10.0	1000	7.9	790
Subtotal, Land-Based Missiles:			3100		2830
SEA-BASED MISSILES					
Poseidon C-3	304	14.0	4256	3.3	1003
Trident C-4	384	8.0	3072	2.9	1114
Trident D-5	48	9.0	432	6.0	288
Subtotal, Sea-Based Missiles:			7760		2405
BOMBERS					
B-52 (ALCM)	120	10.0	1200	20.0	2400
B-52 G/H	121	5.0	605	20.0	2420
B-1	100	5.0	500	20.0	2000
Subtotal, Bombers:			2305		6820
		TOTAL WARHEADS:	13,165	TOTAL THROW-WEIGHT:	12,055

Table 2: NUCLEAR WEAPON SYSTEMS OF THE SOVIET UNION

LAND-BASED MISSILES Weapon Name	Projected 1990 Level of Weapons	Warheads per Weapon	Total Warheads	Throw-weight per Weapon (1000 lbs)	Total Throw weight (1000 lbs)
SS-11	340	1.0	340	2.0	680
SS-13	60	1.0	60	1.0	60
SS-17	150	4.0	600	6.0	900
SS-18	308	10.0	3080	16.7	5144
SS-19	540	6.0	3240	8.0	4320
SS-X-24	150	10.0	1500	8.0	1200
SS-X-25	100	1.0	100	1.5	150
Subtotal, Land-Based Missiles:			8920		12,454
SEA-BASED MISSILES					
SS-N-6	384	1.0	384	1.5	576
SS-N-8	298	1.0	298	1.5	447
SS-N-17	12	1.0	12	2.5	30
SS-N-20	200	9.0	1800	6.5	1300
SS-N-18	256	7.0	1792	5.0	1280
Subtotal, Sea-Based Missiles:			4286		3633
BOMBERS					
Blackjack	50	10.0	500	20.0	1000
Bear	100	2.0	200	14.0	1400
Bison	43	2.0	86	10.0	430
Subtotal, Bombers:			786		2830
		TOTAL WARHEADS:	13,992	TOTAL THROW-WEIGHT:	18,917

$$\sum_{j \in J} W_j X_j + S_1 \leq 6500$$

$$\sum_{j \in J} T_j X_j + S_2 \leq 8000 \qquad (2)$$

$$\sum_{j \in LUS} W_j X_j + S_3 \leq 6000$$

$$X_j \leq U_j \quad \forall_j$$

$$X_j \geq 0 \quad \forall_j$$

with

S_i = slack variable of Overall Equivalence limit i (i=1:total equivalent warheads; i=2:total throw-weight; i=3:total missile warheads)

X_j = number of weapons of type j employed $j \in J$;

W_j = number of warheads per weapon j;

T_j = number of 1000 lbs of throw-weight per weapon j;

U_j = upper bound of variable j, the 1990 level of weapon j;

J = set of all weapons systems;

L = set of land-based weapons;

S = set of sea-based weapons;

B = set of bombers.

It should be noted that the slack variable S_2 representing the second Overall Equivalence limit is measured in units of 1000's of pounds. Because all three slack variables are minimized simultaneously, all three limits are implicitly given equal importance. The implication is that one warhead from limit S_1 or from limit S_3 is as important as 1000 lbs. of throw-weight. There is no *a priori* reason that this is the correct relative importance, and a multi-objective approach in which each limit is considered individually may be appropriate. Alternatively, any particular specification of weights could be used.

3. GENERATING WEAPONS CONFIGURATIONS

3.1 United States Configurations

Three possible postures of the United States were explored, all with the

Overall Equivalence limits as the base constraints on weapons configurations. The first United States Model, USA1, includes only the three Overall Equivalence constraints plus upper bounds. Total slack was minimized to approach the three limits as closely as possible.

Weapons assignments for USA1 and Brown and Davis' option are shown in Table 3. It indicates that total slack in the United States' weapon system can be driven down to a minimum of 557. In comparison, total slack of Brown and Davis' proposed United States weapons configuration amounts to 1725. We do not claim that the configuration with the smallest sum of slack is necessarily the best solution since other values and factors may have influenced the Brown and Davis configuration. Among these values and factors may be cost and degree of modernization. Nonetheless, the solution of USA1 comes close to dominating (in a mathematical sense) the Brown and Davis proposal in that the slacks in two categories of the USA1 solution are much less than the corresponding slacks of the Brown and Davis proposal and the slacks in the third category are comparable.

Table 3: WEAPON ASSIGNMENT STRATEGIES - UNITED STATES

	1990 Projection from Brown and Davis	Brown and Davis Proposal	USA1 3 Constraints	USA2 = USA1 + 10% Triad Con.	USA3 = USA2 + MX = 100
Minuteman II	450	0	450	450	450
Minuteman III	550	0	550	418	82
MX	100	100	100	0	100
Poseidon C-3	304	0	0	3	4
Trident C-4	384	384	240	384	384
Trident D-5	48	48	48	48	48
B-52 Bomber with ALCM	120	120	0	14	13
B-52 G/H	121	59	109	121	121
B-1B	100	100	100	100	100
Total Warheads	13,165	6449	6497	6495	6491
S_1 = Slack	N.A.	1	3	5	9
Total Throw-weight	12,055	7772	7994	7834.7	7801.6
S_2 = Slack	N.A.	228	6	165.3	199.4
Sub-ceiling Warheads	10,860	4504	5452	5250	5256
S_3 = Slack	N.A.	1496	548	750	744
Total Slack	N.A.	1725	557	920.3	952.4

The second model, USA2, attempts to address the goal of achieving a balanced weapons system, balanced in the sense that the weapons are distributed across the basing modes (land, sea, bombers) in a desirable way. This is accomplished by including triad ratio constraints. In order to determine limits for the triad ratio constraints, we examine the 1990 weapons systems mix hypothesized by Brown and Davis. This mix, which was assumed to have a desirable balance of force among land-based missiles, sea-based missiles, and bombers, implies the following ratios:

Total Warheads (TWH)

- land-based missiles (L) $R_{LTWH} = 0.235$
- sea-based missiles (S) $R_{STWH} = 0.590$
- bombers (B) $R_{BTWH} = 0.175$

Total Throw-Weight (TTW)

- land-based missiles (L) $R_{LTTW} = 0.235$
- sea-based missiles (S) $R_{STTW} = 0.200$
- bombers (B) $R_{BTTW} = 0.565$

Constraints were developed to insure that the weapons system would be distributed within ±10% of these triad ratios. That is, weapons patterns were forced into a distribution that matched, within 10%, the distribution of weapons between and among the basing modes in the 1990 scenario. Thus, using the total warheads of land-based missiles as an example, we may write

$$0.9\, R_{LTWH} \le \frac{\sum\limits_{j\varepsilon L} W_j X_j}{\sum\limits_{j\varepsilon J} W_j X_j} \le 1.1\, R_{LTWH}\ .$$

In standard form these two constraints are:

$$\left(1 - 0.9R_{LTWH}\right) \left[\sum_{j\varepsilon L} W_j X_j\right] - 0.9R_{LTWH} \left[\sum_{j\varepsilon SUB} W_j X_j\right] \le 0$$

$$\left(1 - 1.1R_{LTWH}\right) \left[\sum_{j\varepsilon L} W_j X_j\right] - 1.1R_{LTWH} \left[\sum_{j\varepsilon SUB} W_j X_j\right] \le 0\ .$$

Each of the six ratios requires two such constraints, resulting in twelve triad ratio constraints that were included in the linear program of Eqs. (1) and (2).

Thus, USA2 incorporates the Overall Equivalence constraints of USA1 plus the 12 triad ratio constraints. Since USA2 is more highly constrained than USA1, the solution will not be expected to come as close to the Overall Equivalence limits as the USA1 model, resulting in a higher value of total slack. This is indeed the case; total slack of USA2 is 920.3, still much less in value than the Brown and Davis option, but much higher than USA1.

In the third model, USA3, the effect of the MX missile on the United States weapon system was explored. Model USA3 incorporates the triad constraints of USA2 plus a requirement on MX missile deployment. Because the United States will want to modernize its forces, the MX is likely to be added to the United States weapons system. Although the MX did not appear in USA2, Brown and Davis chose the MX as the *only* United States land-based missile in 1990. For this reason, we forced the MX to appear in the solution at its upper bound of 100 in USA3 to examine its effect on the solution. Total slack rose only slightly to 952.4. A graphical summary of all three United States models is shown in Figure 1.

Figure 1: USA WEAPON ASSIGNMENT STRATEGIES

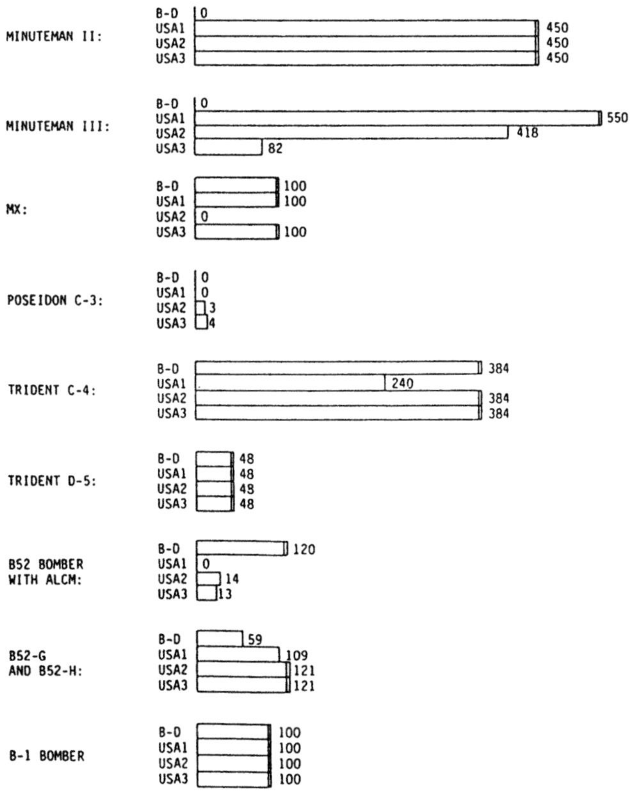

3.2 The Soviet Configurations

The results for the Soviet weapon mixes are shown in Table 4 and Figure 2.

As in the USA1, the model USSR1 includes only the three Overall Equivalence constraints along with upper bounds from the 1990 USSR scenario. Minimizing slack in the Soviet weapons system yields a total slack of 27, dramatically lower than any United States slack, and much lower than the slack in either of the Brown and Davis options for the Soviet Union (929 and 224).

Table 4: WEAPON ASSIGNMENT STRATEGIES - SOVIET UNION

	No Arms Control 1990	Brown and Davis Option A	Brown and Davis Option B	USSR1 3 Con-straints Only	USSR2 3 + 10% Triad Ratios
SS-11	340	0	0	0	0
SS-13	60	0	0	0	0
SS-17	150	0	0	0	150
SS-18	308	210	285	270	211[a]
SS-19	540	275	0	0	0
SS-X-24	150	0	75	150	138[a]
SS-X-25	100	0	0	0	0
SS-N-6	384	0	0	0	0
SS-N-8	298	0	0	0	0
SS-N-17	12	0	0	0	12
SS-N-20	200	0	80	0	11[a]
SS-N-18	156	256	224	256	256
Blackjack/CM	50	50	50	50	34[a]
Bear	100	0	0	0	28[a]
Bison	43	0	0	0	0
TWH	14,992	6042	6388	6492	6389
Slack = S_1	--	458	112	8	111[a]
TTW	16,087	7987	8000	7989	7981.2
Slack = S_2	--	13	0	11	18.8[a]
SWH	13,206	5542	5888	5992	5993
Slack = S_3	--	458	112	8	7[a]
Total Slack	--	929	224	27	136.8[a]

[a] These numbers have been rounded from original fractional values.

Figure 2: USSR WEAPON ASSIGNMENT STRATEGIES

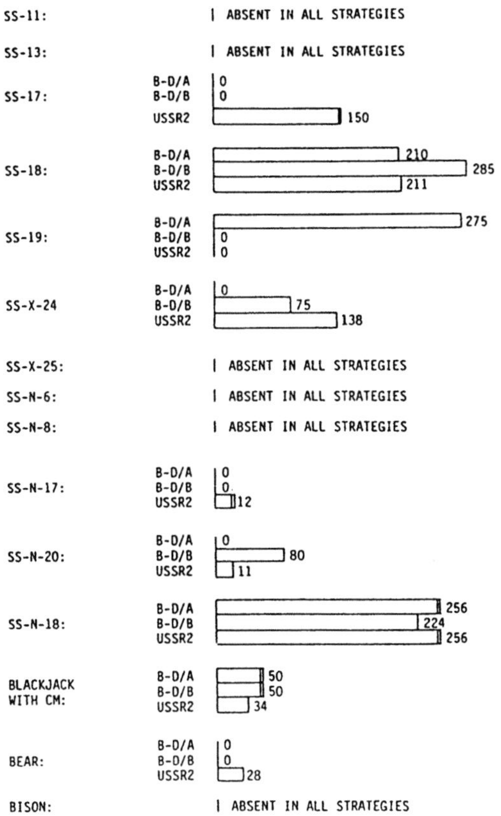

In the same manner as USA2, USSR2 incorporates triad ratio constraints, based on the 1990 proportions of warheads and throw-weight in each of the three weapons categories:

$$R_{LTWH} = 0.638$$

$$R_{STWH} = 0.306$$

$$R_{BTWH} = 0.056$$

$$R_{LTTW} = 0.658$$

$$R_{STTW} = 0.192$$

$$R_{BTTW} = 0.150$$

Total slack in USSR2 rose to 136.8, still lower than any United States slack.

3.3 Interpretations

Efficient weapons configurations for both the United States and Soviet Union were generated under varying constraints. The most striking conclusion is the flexibility of the Soviet Union system which allowed all three limits to be very closely met simultaneously.

One experience is that the wide range of Soviet weaponry with differing characteristics (fifteen Soviet weapons systems compared to nine U.S. weapons systems) made possible a closer approach to the limits. However, the model USSR1 utilized only four different weapons systems while the model USA1 used seven different weapons systems. Another possible explanation is that some Soviet weapons, like the SS-X-18, the SS-X-24, and the SS-N-18, have a favorable combination of warheads and throw-weight that happen to match the combination of warheads and throw-weight in the Overall Equivalence limits.

In fact, three "ideal" weapons could be designed to meet all three limits exactly. For instance, let L be a land-based missile, S be a sea-based missile, and B be a bomber. Suppose L has 10 warheads/missile and 15,000 lbs throw-weight/missile; S has 5 warheads per missile and 2000 lbs throw-weight per missile; B has 10 warheads/bomber and 2100 lbs throw-weight/bomber; then a system of 500 L's, 200 S's and 50 B's will yield a slack of zero under the Overall Equivalence constraints.

A second conclusion is that, in the United States system, emphasizing land-based missiles, as USA1, USA2, and USA3 do, is preferred to emphasizing bombers, as Brown and Davis do, to achieve less slack in the system. Of course, there may be strategic reasons for the Brown and Davis configuration.

Thirdly, the MX missile has only a small effect on the slack of the United States system. It can be easily substituted for Minuteman III missiles without significantly increasing total slack. Fourthly, the models reveal "strategically inefficient" weapons, or those weapons that appear at a level of zero in the models' solutions. These weapons might be favorable choices for future arms reductions.

4. SUMMARY AND CONCLUSION

We have extended the Overall Equivalence concept of Brown and Davis' proposal by utilizing linear programming to generate alternative weapons configurations that fall under the limits for total warheads, total throw-weight, and missile warheads. Weapons configurations were produced for both the United States and the Soviet Union under the objective of approaching as closely as possible the Overall Equivalence limits. Additional models included constraints to insure a desirable distribution of warheads and throw-weight in the three basing categories.

The work presented here is basic in concept and forms the foundation for more complex analyses. Other factors reflecting desirability of weapons, such as accuracy, vulnerability, and cost, as well as different objectives, may be included.

A particularly appealing approach would be one which considers interactive goals and constraints between the two countries. For example, the US might wish to retain the same relative bomber advantage over the Soviets while the Soviets might want to maintain the same relative land-based missile advantage over the US. These twin constraints could be considered simultaneously. A possible joint objective might be to minimize imbalances in all categories between the United States and Soviet Union weapons systems as a means to increase overall stability. Modifications of this sort, which consider both the US and USSR forces at once, could provide realistic and useful alternative weapons configurations that could be considered in arms control negotiations.

REFERENCES

Aviation Week and Space Technology, March 14, 1983, p. 124

Brown, H. and Davis, L.E. (1984): Nuclear Arms Control Choices. SAIS Papers in International Affairs, Number 5, Westview Press/ Foreign Policy Institute, School of Advanced International Studies, The Johns Hopkins University, 1984

STABILITY, SDI, AIR DEFENSE AND DEEP CUTS

Jerome Bracken
Institute for Defense Analyses
Alexandria, Virginia 22311, USA

1. INTRODUCTION

This paper treats two-sided issues of the transition from current strategic force structures to alternative strategic force structures.

The baseline situation involves the first striker attacking, with all of his ballistic missiles, the vulnerable ballistic missiles, vulnerable air breathers and value targets of the second striker, and, with all of his air breathers the value targets of the second striker. The second striker responds with all of his remaining vulnerable ballistic missiles, his invulnerable ballistic missiles, his remaining vulnerable air breathers and his invulnerable air breathers in an attack on the value targets of the first striker. The ballistic missiles of both strikers are opposed by a ballistic missile defense and the air breathers of both strikers are opposed by an air defense.

Three stability measures are defined. The first two measures involve net gains to the two sides from optimally allocated first strikes followed by second strikes on value targets by the opponent. The third measure involves incentives to strike first in order to secure a better return than obtained if the opponent strikes first.

2. APPROACH

The approach is to define a two-strike exchange process with a minimal number of force structure and effectiveness parameters, to optimize the first strikes by both sides, and to integrate the results as represented by stability measures for the set of policy variables being studied.

2.1 Stability

Stability is employed as the underlying criterion for evaluation of changes from current strategic force structures on both sides to force structures which include from very small to very large ballistic missile defenses and air defenses. Also, substantially reduced strategic offensive forces are considered. Thus the analysis treats current offensive forces, substantially

NATO ASI Series, Vol. F 26
Modelling and Analysis in Arms Control
Edited by R. Avenhaus et al.

reduced offensive forces, a wide range of ballistic missile defense forces (in more refined detail than the other aspects of the analysis) and several levels of air defense forces.

The measures of stability capture two very different considerations of nuclear weapons: (1) the net gain from striking first, and (2) the incentive for both sides to strike first to either capture a net gain or deny a net gain to the opponent. The first consideration addresses the issue that if upon calculation it can be determined that there is a net gain to one side from striking first, but not to the other side from striking first, then the former side can coerce or threaten the latter side. Also, the latter side may be motivated to change the state of affairs by building up his forces (engaging in an arms race). Thus, the measure evaluates both the static situation and the motivation for changing that situation. The second consideration addresses the issue that if, for both sides, striking first results in an end state which is preferred to the end state if the opponent strikes first, in a crisis both sides might be motivated to preempt.

The second aspect of stability is the principle focus of this analysis, for if both sides are either retaining current offensive forces or transitioning to smaller offensive forces, while substantially building up defensive forces, the force structure situations in which one side dominates the other are fairly clear. It is the two-sided force structure situations leading to payoffs from striking first in a crisis which are of most interest.

2.2 Scope of Analysis

The offensive forces of the model are composed of vulnerable and invulnerable ballistic missiles (for instance, ICBMs and SLBMs) and vulnerable and invulnerable air breathers (for instance, bombers on bases and cruise missiles on land, ships or submarines). The ballistic missiles are characterized by number of RVs per missile and the air breathers are characterized by number of weapons per air breather.

The defensive forces of the model are represented by overall threshold parameters and by marginal effectiveness parameters per incoming offensive weapons after the threshold has been surmounted. The physical situation should be conceptualized as the first striker utilizing all of his ballistic missiles and all of his air breathers in the first strike. The number of ballistic missile RVs exceeding the ballistic missile defense threshold is allocated to vulnerable ballistic missiles, vulnerable air breathers, and value targets. The number of air breathing weapons exceeding the air defense threshold is allocated to value targets.

The marginal damage parameters govern the destruction of the targets. The RVs destined to attack vulnerable weapons achieve a specified yield per attacker, which decreases as the number of attackers increases. The RVs and air breathers destined to attack value targets are combined; they also achieve a specified yield per attacker, which decreases as the number of attackers increases. Since the vulnerable weapon targets are many in number, dispersed, and in some cases hardened, the marginal damage parameter is small. For value targets, the marginal damage parameter is relatively large.

This simplified attrition process can be best conceptualized as the attacker paying a certain price, the defense threshold, and then achieving damage which approaches an upper bound of the total number of vulnerable weapons or the total amount of value. The attrition process does not include leakage by RVs. In the counterforce role this is not important, but in the countervalue role a relatively small amount of leakage, if the attacker concentrates his weapons on a high-value subset of the value targets, can yield significant damage. The analysis, therefore, is most appropriately thought of as a combined counterforce/countervalue analysis, and does not directly address a predominantly countervalue exchange (to the extent the latter might be possible by leakage through the substantial defenses considered herein).

A significant strength of the model is that it incorporates investigation of the best tactics of the first striker. While not formally optimizing, in each force structure situation it chooses the best option from a menu of options which can be constructed to span the space of alternatives considered feasible. The potential analytical problem of algorithmic convergence to a local optimum allocation, perhaps far from the global optimum allocation, is avoided by this approach.

2.3 Character of Inputs

The investigation is carried out with offensive and defensive forces which very roughly correspond to the strategic forces of both sides in order to shed light on qualitative considerations of the strategic planning issues.

The main dimensions of the offensive forces (for instance, number of ICBMs and number of RVs per ICBM) are represented in order to capture the aggregate counterforce/countervalue interactions. The highly-aggregated defense thresholds are the principle variables of the analysis. The marginal damage parameters, and the aggregated forms of the attrition process, are characteristics which influence the detailed outputs of the model but to which overall conclusions may not be greatly sensitive.

3. THE MODEL

3.1 Definitions

There are two sides, which are called Blue and Red. Definitions are as follows:

X,Y = Number of Blue, Red vulnerable missiles with k,l RVs each

X',Y' = Number of Blue, Red invulnerable missiles with k',l' RVs each

R,S = Number of Blue, Red vulnerable air breathers with m,n weapons each

$R'S'$ = Number of Blue, Red invulnerable air breathers with m',n' weapons each

P,Q = Threshold capability of Blue, Red SDI

P',Q' = Threshold capability of Blue, Red air defense

p_1,p_2,q_1,q_2 = Parameters for marginal capability of Blue, Red SDI to protect vulnerable ballistic missiles and air breathers from first strike (equivalently, marginal factional damage to Blue, Red ballistic missiles and air breathers per counterforce RV beyond SDI threshold)

p_3,q_3 = Parameter for marginal combined capability of Blue, Red SDI and air defense to protect value targets from second strike (equivalently, marginal factional damage to Blue, Red value targets per countervalue RV and/or air breathing weapon beyond SDI and air defense thresholds)

$u = u_1,u_2,u_3$, $v = v_1,v_2,v_3$ = Fractional allocation of Blue, Red first strike RVs to vulnerable ballistic missiles, vulnerable air breathers and value targets, where

$u_1 + u_2 + u_3 = 1$ and $v_1 + v_2 + v_3 = 1$

U,V = Set of permissible Blue, Red allocations

A,B = Amount of Blue, Red value (in this analysis $A = B = 1$).

3.2 Payoff for Blue First Strike, Red Second Strike

For a particular allocation u of Blue ballistic missile RVs the number of Red vulnerable ballistic missiles killed, the number of Red vulnerable air breathers killed and the amount of Red value killed are as follows (where

$(x)^+$is x when x is positive and 0 when x is 0 or negative):

$$Y_k = Y(1-\exp(-q_1u_1(Xk + X'k' - Q)^+))$$

$$S_k = S(1-\exp(-q_2u_2(Xk + X'k' - Q)^+))$$

$$B_{k1} = B(1-\exp(-q_3[u_3(Xk + X'k' - Q)^+ + (Rm + R'm' - Q')^+])).$$

The amount of Blue value killed on the second strike is

$$A_{k2} = A(1-\exp(-p_3[((Y - Y_k) + Y'l'-P)^+ - ((S-S_k)n + S'n'-P')^+])).$$

The payoff from a Blue first strike and Red second strike is

$$P_{XY} = \max_{u \varepsilon U}(B_{k1}-A_{k2}).$$

3.3 Payoff for Red First Strike, Blue Second Strike

For a particular allocation v of Red ballistic missile RVs the number of Blue vulnerable ballistic missiles killed, the number of Blue vulnerable air breathers killed and the amount of Blue value killed are as follows:

$$X_k = X(1-\exp(-p_1v_1(Yl + Y'l' - P)^+))$$

$$R_k = R(1-\exp(-p_2v_2(Yl + Y'l' - P)^+))$$

$$A_{k1} = A(1-\exp(-p_3[v_3(Yl + Y'l'-P)^+])) + (Sn+S'n'-P')^+])).$$

The amount of Red killed on the second strike is

$$B_{k2} = B(1-\exp(-q_3[((X-X_k)k+X'k' - Q)^+])) + ((R-R_k)m+R'm' - Q')^+])).$$

The payoff from a Red first strike and Blue second strike is

$$P_{YX} = \max_{v \varepsilon V}(A_{k1}-B_{k2}).$$

3.4 Stability Measures

Three measures of stability are presented throughout, as follows:

(1) P_{XY}, the payoff from an optimized Blue first strike followed by a Red second strike $(-1 \leq P_{XY} \leq +1)$

(2) P_{YX}, the payoff from an optimized Red first strike followed by a Blue second strike $(-1 \leq P_{YK} \leq +1)$

(3) $S = P_{XY} + P_{YX}$, the incentive to strike first in a crisis to avoid relative gains by the other side $(-2 \leq S \leq +2)$.

The result $P_{XY} = 1$ is obtained when $B_{k1} = 1$ and $A_{k2} = 0$. The result $P_{XY} = -1$ is obtained when $B_{k1} = 0$ and $A_{k2} = 1$. The result $P_{XY} = 0$ can be obtained for $B_{k1} = 1$ and $A_{k2} = 1$, for $B_{k1} = 0$ and $A_{k2} = 0$, or for any other case where $B_{k1} = A_{k2}$. The measure P_{XY} is a relative one, measuring how much better off Blue is than Red is after Blue strikes first.

The value P_{XY} can also be interpreted as the threatening ability of Blue, or the ability of Blue to coerce. It might be argued that any positive value of A_{k2} would negate Blue threats (i.e., that finite deterrence is sufficient to invalidate nuclear threats). It will be assumed here, however, that Blue forces which result in positive values of P_{XY} possess nuclear first-strike strength.

Similar interpretations can be offered for P_{YX}. Red forces which have positive values of P_{YX} possess nuclear first-strike strength.

The measure $S = P_{XY} + P_{YX}$ is quite different. If for a particular two-sided force posture $P_{XY} = 1$, $P_{YX} = -1$, and thus $S = 0$, there is no incentive for either side to strike first in a crisis to prevent the other from striking first. Blue can threaten because he is a sure winner in a first strike, and Red cannot threaten because he is a sure loser in a first strike, but neither side gains from striking first to prevent the other from striking first. Alternatively, if for a particular force structure $P_{XY} = 1$, $P_{YX} = 0$, and thus $S = 1$, both sides have an incentive to strike first to prevent an outcome favorable for the other side. (Similar interpretations can be made for all S between -2 and +2).

4. INPUTS

Current Offensive Forces

					Warheads
Blue	X = 1000	k = 3	X' = 600	k' = 10	9000
	R = 400	m = 20	R' = 1000	m' = 1	9000
Red	Y = 1300	l = 5	Y' = 300	l' = 10	9500
	S = 200	n = 20	S' = 100	n' = 1	4100

Deep Cut Offensive Forces

					Warheads
Blue	X = 500	k = 3	X' = 300	k' = 10	4500
	R = 200	m = 20	R' = 500	m' = 1	4500
Red	Y = 700	l = 5	Y' = 150	l' = 10	5000
	S = 100	n = 20	S' = 100	n' = 1	2100

Defensive Forces

Blue and Red SDI thresholds to be explored parametrically:

$$P = 0, 1000, 2000, \ldots, 10{,}000$$
$$Q = 0, 1000, 2000, \ldots, 10{,}000.$$

Marginal damage parameters against weapons:

$$p_1, p_2 = .001$$
$$q_1, q_2 = .001.$$

Marginal damage parameters against value targets:

$$p_3 = .01$$
$$q_3 = .01.$$

Current Air Defenses

$$P' = 200, \ Q' = 1000$$

Larger Air Defenses

$$P' = 3000, \ Q' = 3000.$$

Permissible First Strike RV Allocations

Let the allocations of first strike RVs to targets be chosen from within the following set of seven options (U and V):

To Ballistic Missiles	To Air Breathers	To Value Targets
.10	.30	.60
.10	.60	.30
.30	.10	.60
.30	.60	.10
.60	.10	.30
.60	.30	.10
.33	.33	.33

This set of permissible allocations limits the optimality of the Blue and Red choices. It can be expanded to analyze the problem in more detail.

5. RESULTS

Four broad cases comprise the first part of the analysis, as follows:

Case I,I	Current Forces, Current Air Defenses
Case I,II	Current Forces, Larger Air Defenses
Case II,I	Deep Cuts, Current Air Defenses
Case II,II	Deep Cuts, Larger Air Defenses.

For each case, the Blue and Red SDI threshold is varied from 0 to 10,000, resulting in an 11 x 11 matrix of outcomes of values of P_{XY}, P_{YX} and S.

In addition, excursions are made for much larger air defenses for both, current forces and deep cuts.

Case I.I Results

Figure 1 presents P_{XY}, P_{YX} and S in the most aggregated form for Case I,I. Results are given only in terms of + or 0 (there are no negative values in Case I,I). Interpreting the figure, considering P_{XY}, if Red SDI is 0 while Blue SDI is 3000 or more, then P_{XY} is positive. But when Red SDI is 6000 or more (regardless of Blue SDI) P_{XY} is always 0. If Blue has a large SDI while Red has none or a small one, then P_{XY} is positive and Blue can threaten or coerce Red.

For P_{YX}, results are similar to those for P_{XY}. When Red has a large SDI and Blue has none or a small one, then P_{YX} is positive and Red can threaten or coerce Blue.

The most dangerous results in Case I,I are associated with S. When these values are positive there is an incentive for both sides to strike first. In the lower left corner, Blue wishes to strike first to achieve $P_{XY} = +$ while Red wishes to strike first to achieve $P_{YX} = 0$. In the upper right corner, Blue wishes to strike first to achieve $P_{XY} = 0$ while Red wishes to strike first to achieve $P_{YX} = +$.

Figure 2 adds more information to Figure 1 for Case I,I. Areas are described in more detail by 0, + < 1 and + 1. Areas with payoffs equal + < 1 are not as dangerous as those with payoffs equal + 1.

Numerical Results for All Cases

Tables 1 through 4 in the Appendix document the numerical results underlying the first part of the analysis. In Table 1, for instance, the lower left

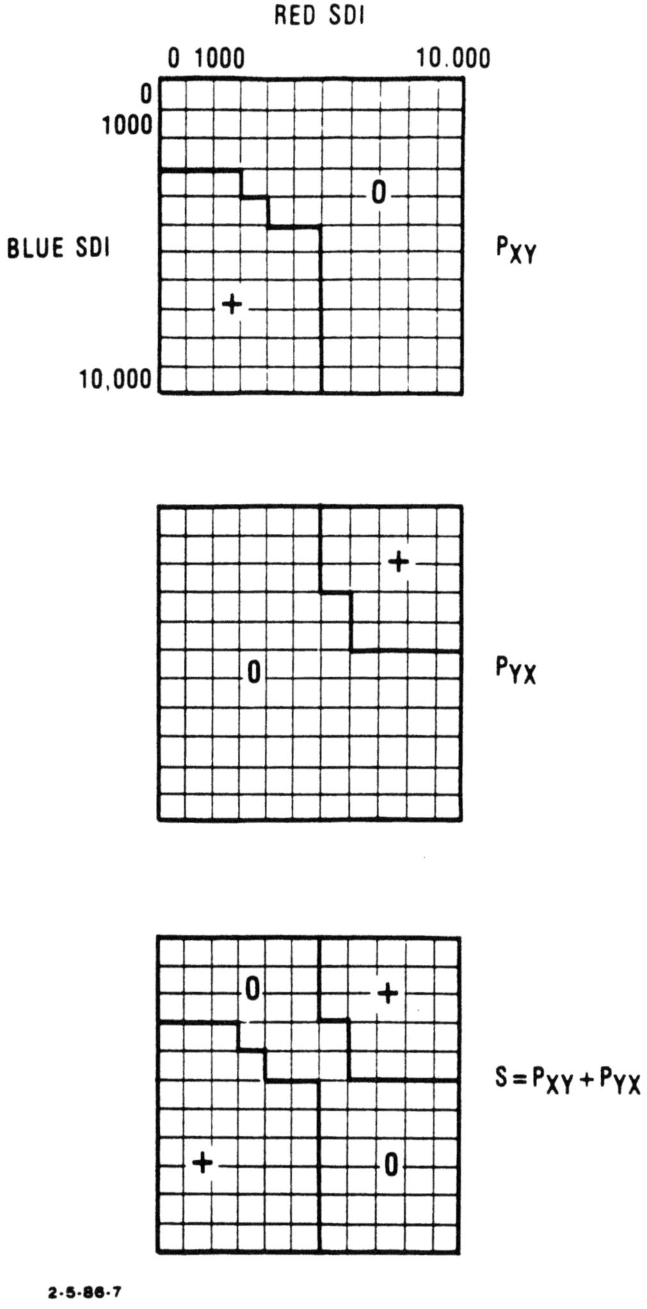

Figure 1: RESULTS FOR CASE I,I

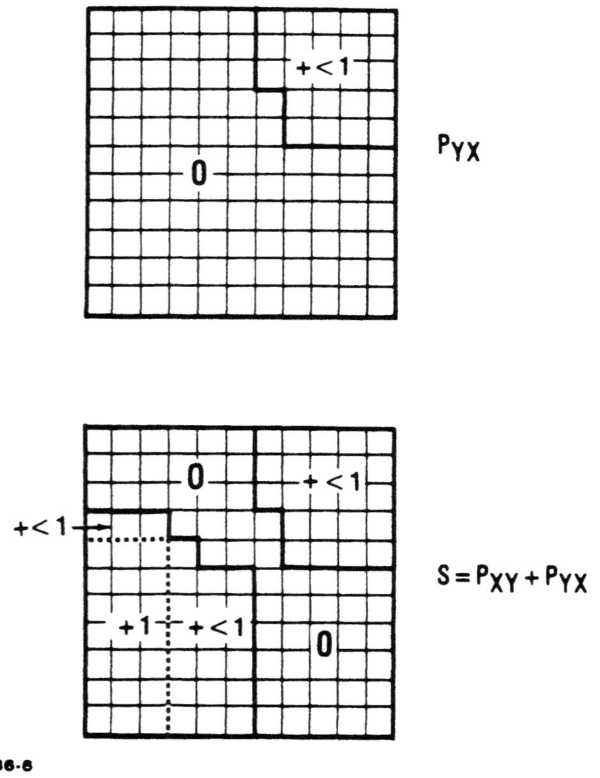

Figure 2. RESULTS FOR CASE I,I--MORE DETAIL

corner of P_{XY} is comprised of entries equal 1.00(the borders of the area containing 1.00 values are positive but less than 1.00). The upper right corner of P_{YX} is comprised of entries which are positive but less than 1.00. The values of S are the sum of P_{XY} and P_{YX}.

Synthesis

First consider Figure 3. Proceeding from Case I,I to Case II,I several results hold. For P_{XY} the positive region is smaller, while for P_{YX} the positive region changes shape but has exactly the same area. In both cases, since there are fewer offensive forces on both sides, the side with a somewhat smaller SDI striking the side with no SDI can obtain positive payoff. But most notable is the total area in which S equals 0, which is much larger in Case II,I than in Case I,I. The top left corner of S in Case II,I contains a smaller stable region when there are deep cuts than for current forces, which indicates that the transition during which SDI is being deployed must be more carefully coordinated. Considering the situations where the distance between areas with positive values of S is smallest, note that in Case I,I they occur when SDI thresholds are about 6000 while in Case II, I, they occur when SDI thresholds are about 3000.

Now proceed from Case I,I to Case I,II. There are much larger areas of positive P_{XY} and P_{YX}. But most dramatic is that when both sides have small SDI thresholds or very large SDI thresholds S equals 0 while for all of the other levels of Blue and Red SDI the value of S is positive. In many cases there is an incentive to strike first, for taking punishment from a first strike and then carrying out a second strike against a substantial SDI threshold and larger air defense is too hard.

Now consider Case II,II which can be reached from Case II,I or Case I,II (or perhaps diagonally from Case I,I). P_{XY} is positive in a very large area, for Red has insufficient surviving ballistic missiles to surmount the Blue SDI threshold an insufficient surviving air breathers to surmount the Blue air defense. P_{YX}, however, is negative in a large area because Red cannot attack over the Blue SDI threshold and kill enough ballistic missiles and air breathers to stave off the retaliation. With respect to S, Case II,II has some of the same properties as Case II,I. Namely, in a large midrange area the values of S are positive.

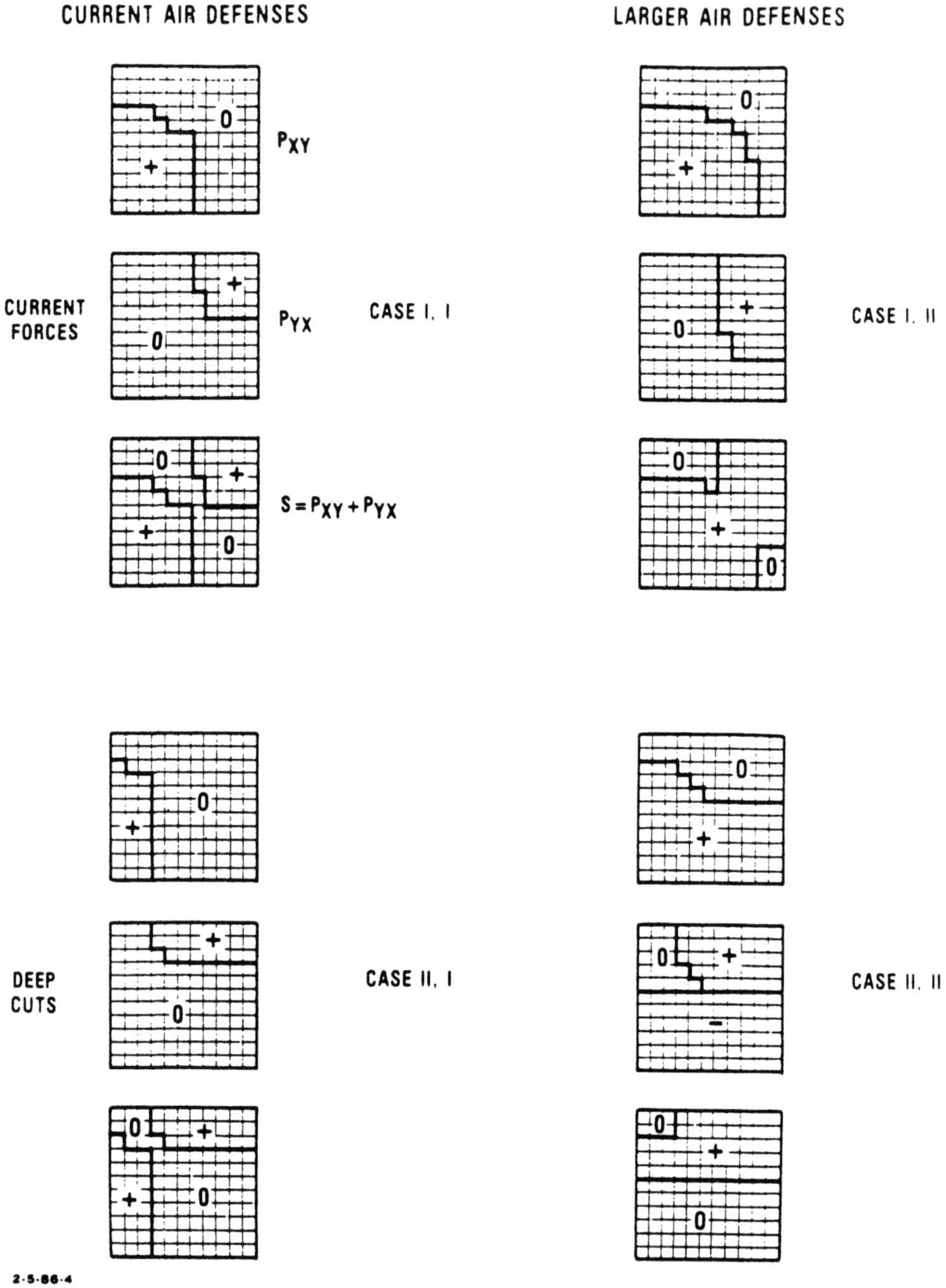

Figure 3: SYNTHESIS OF RESULTS

Figure 4 presents more detail than Figure 3. Two conditions are especially noteworthy:

a) In Case I,I P_{XY} has many +1 values while in Case II,I P_{YX} has many +1 values. Blue is stronger in Case I,I while Red is stronger in Case II,I.

b) Case I,II contains a +2 in S. There is the strongest possible desire to preempt, Blue to achieve P_{XY} = +1 and Red to achieve P_{YX} = +1, when Blue SDI is 5000 and Red SDI is 7000.

The overall interpretation of these results is that Case II,I is quite stable if both sides have very small SDI thresholds or both sides have medium-to-large SDI thresholds. Case I,I is stable for more of the small SDI thresholds. To proceed most safely with respect to measure S, Blue and Red should keep current forces, deploy medium SDI, then make deep cuts. They should do this with very careful coordination to avoid positive values of S. They should not deploy larger air defenses.

Results for Much Larger Air Defenses

There are two cases, as follows:

Case I,III Current Forces, Much Larger Air Defenses
Case II,III Deep Cuts, Much Larger Air Defenses.

Much larger air defenses are P' = 6000, Q' = 6000, twice as many interceptors on both sides. Figures 5 and 6 synthesize the results for these new cases. Tables 5 and 6 contain the numerical results.

Essentially, the interpretation of Case I,III is that the areas in which P_{XY} and P_{YX} are positive in increased somewhat. Also, P_{XY} becomes negative for very large Blue SDI due to Red's inability to surmount the Blue air defense in a second strike. The shape of S does not change substantially from Case I,II to Case I,III; crisis stability is only marginally improved.

Results for Case II,III are very interesting. The top right corner of P_{XY} and the bottom left corner of P_{YX} become negative. Considering the top right corner of P_{XY}, if Blue strikes first there is little or no damage to Red, but Blue is relatively unprotected against the second strike. The change in shape of S from Case II,II to Case II,III is also interesting. There is a much smaller area of crisis instability. With deep cuts, therefore, much larger air defenses increase stability.

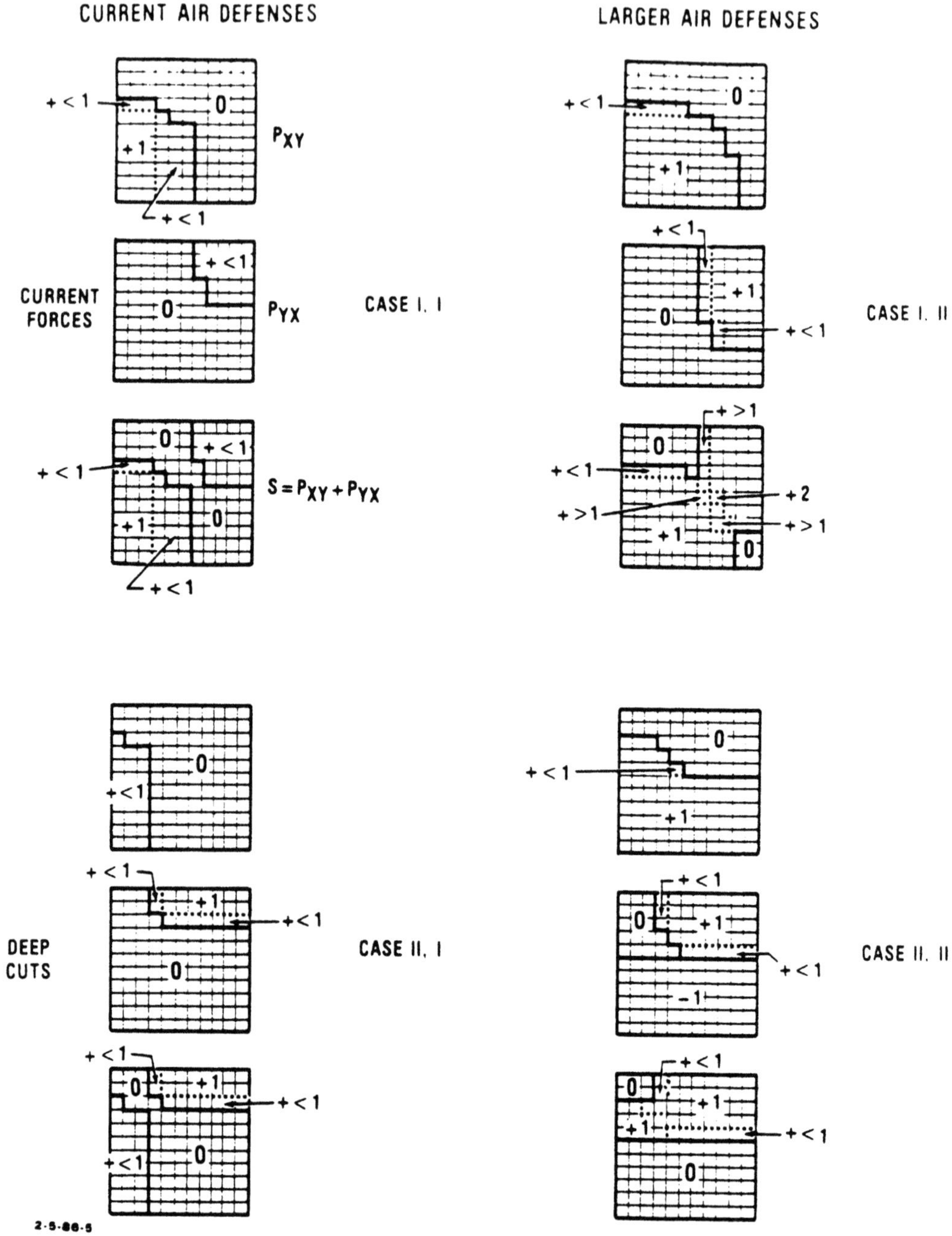

Figure 4: SYNTHESIS OF RESULTS--MORE DETAIL

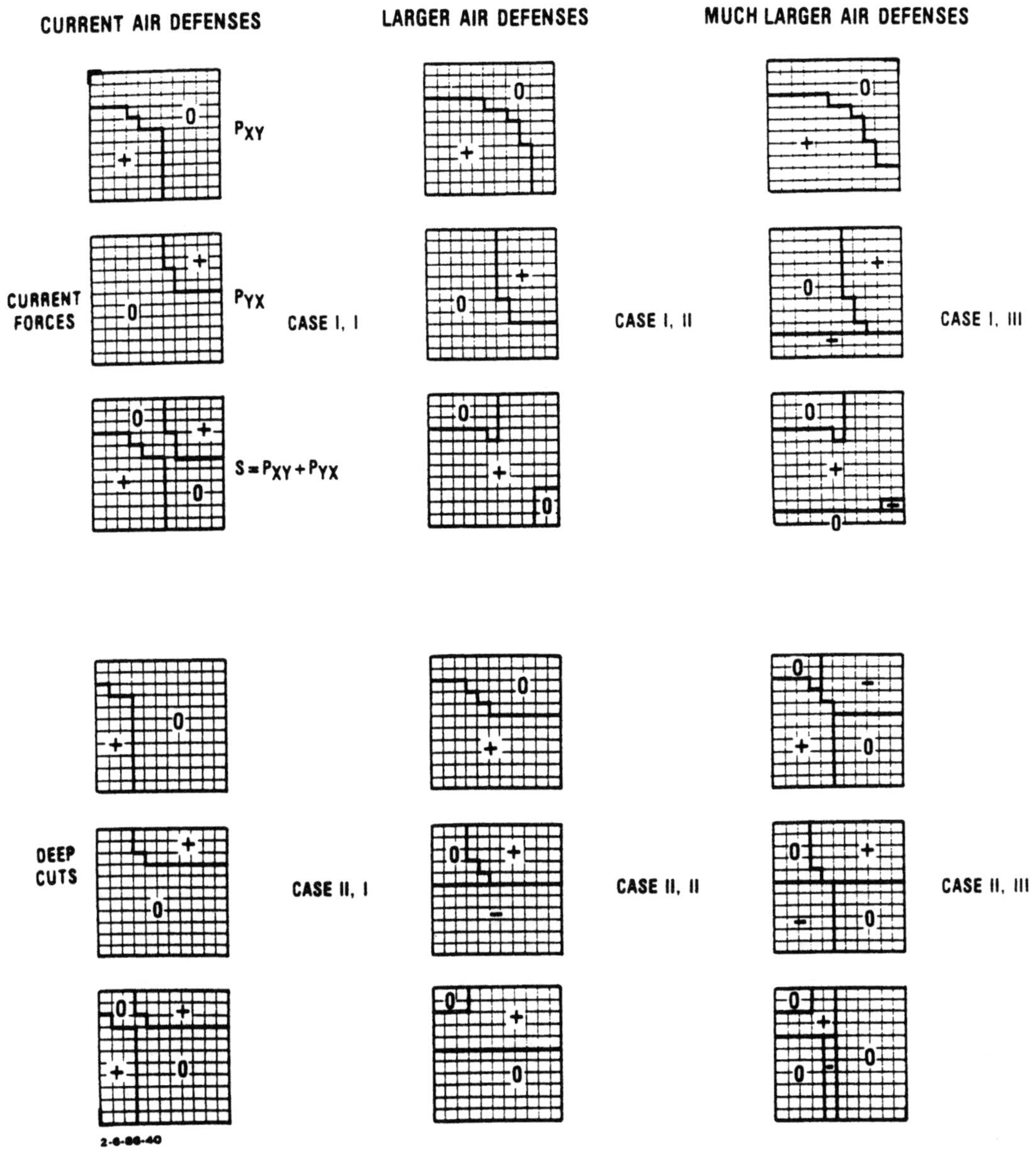

Figure 5: SYNTHESIS OF RESULTS WITH MUCH LARGER AIR DEFENSES

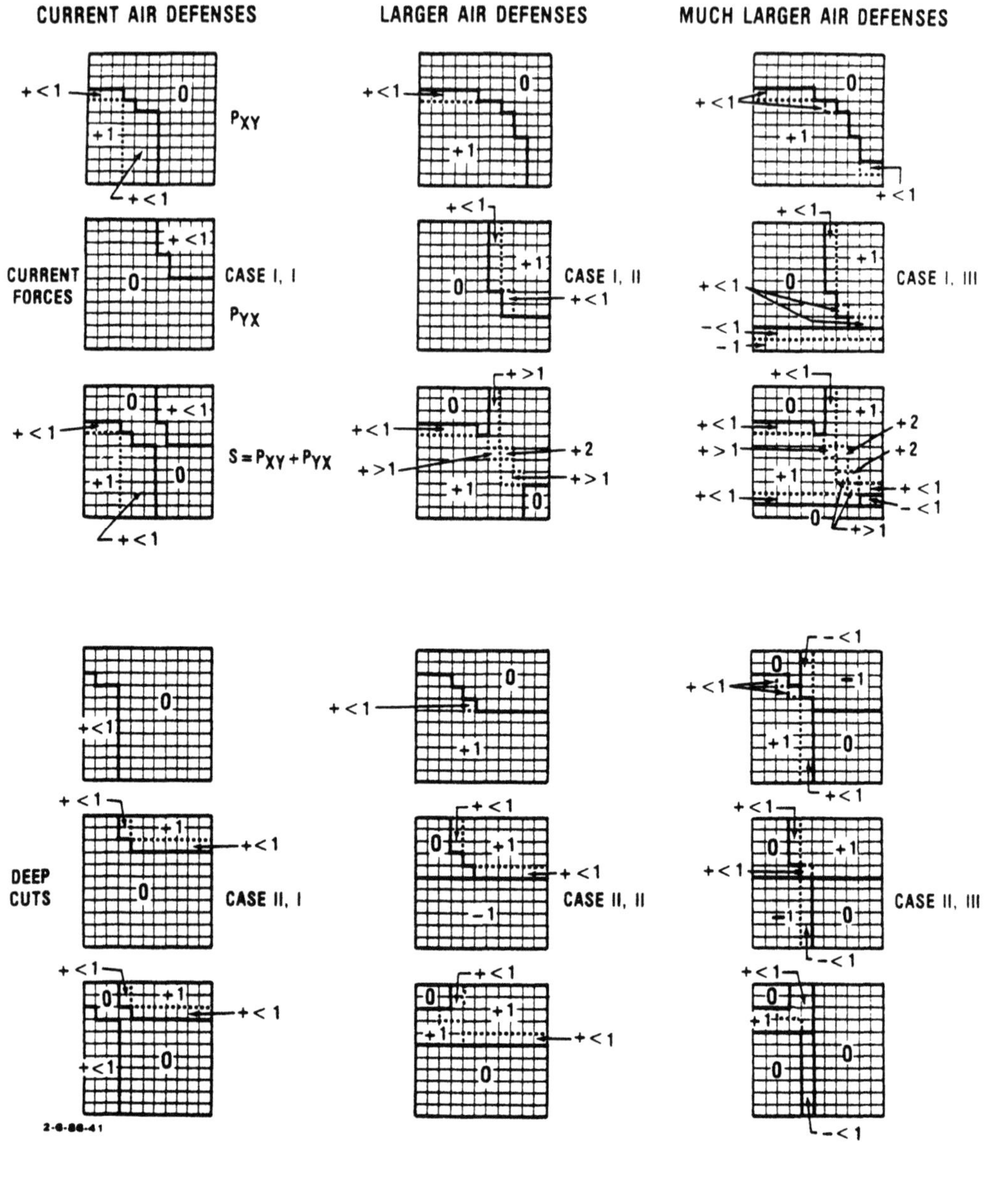

Figure 6: SYNTHESIS OF RESULTS WITH MUCH LARGER AIR DEFENSES--
MORE DETAIL

Finally, it is important to note that in Case II,III the bottom right corner of S involves no damage to either side. In the other five cases stability is induced by the total destruction of both sides in the optimized exchange, while in this case there are sufficient ballistic missile defenses to avert this occurrence. Rather than stability being provided by a state of "Mutual Assured Destruction" it is provided by a state of "Mutual Assured Survival". Achieving the latter is expensive in resources and difficult with respect to making a stable transition.

6. SENSITIVITIES AND LIMITATIONS

Sensitivity of results to variations in the inputs is of interest. Though a great deal of experimentation has not been performed, it is believed that qualitative results will not differ substantially for moderate changes in almost all of the inputs. In particular, sensitivities to changes in offensive force structures should not be too great.

The marginal damage parameters against value targets, p_3 and q_3, directly affect the amount of blue killed on the first and second strikes. Performing a limited experiment for Case I,I, when the marginal damage is twice as large ($p_3 = q_3 = .02$) the values in P_{XY} and P_{YX} are smaller due to the second striker being able to retaliate more readily, and the stable regions in S are larger. Correspondingly, when the marginal damage is twice as small ($p_3 = q_3 = .005$) the values in P_{XY} and P_{YX} are larger due to the second striker being able to retaliate less readily, and the stable regions in S are smaller. In this latter situation there is no transition path from the top left corner to the bottom right corner of S for Case I,I. Similar results hold for Case II,I, but a narrow stable transition path is still present.

It would be desirable to explore larger sets of permissible attack allocations. Limited explorations adding to the previous set of options the "corner point" allocations 1,0,0, etc. and the "mid-edge" allocations .5,.5,0, etc., which completely span the space of options (though not filling it in), yield small increases in the areas of P_{XY} and P_{YX}. Increasing the number of alternatives will always result in at least as much payoff to the first striker and further analysis should be performed with more options. However, the qualitative conclusions are not expected to be changed significantly.

The payoff functions P_{XY} and P_{YX}, from which S is determined, are composed of damage to the second striker minus damage to the first striker. The first striker, however, might value damage to himself differently than damage to the second striker. For instance, he might weight damage to the second striker less than damage to himself in the payoff function. If new functions were introduced which incorporated this consideration, P_{XY} and P_{YX} would be smaller, and in most cases S would be larger. In general, alternative payoff functions should be explored.

Similarly, perceptions might influence the views of both sides of possible future occurrences. For instance, Blue might perceive Red's defense to be better than it is and his own to be worse than it is. In this case P_{XY} would be smaller and P_{YX} would be larger. Correspondingly, Red might perceive P_{XY} to be larger and P_{YX} to be smaller. Each would thus perceive a different shape of S. The joint perception would produce an S which is the intersection of the two shapes, and the stable region would be smaller. There would be more combinations of ballistic missile defenses which induce the weaker side to strike first in order to avoid a relatively worse outcome.

An important limitation is associated with the threshold aspect of the damage function. The attacker and defender strategies have not been explored in detail with respect to the two-sided aspects of denying or imposing a damage function of this type. The overall qualitative insights might be sensitive to this limitation, as well as to the inclusion of leakage in a more general damage function. This area of improvement should be emphasized in further work.

Acknowledgement

The author is grateful for suggestions by Frank Albini, Lowell Bruce Anderson, Sydell Gold, Jeffrey Grotte, William Lynn, Albert Perrella, Richard Soland and Amy Woolf.

APPENDIX
NUMERICAL RESULTS

Table 1: NUMERICAL RESULTS FOR CASE I,I

	Red SDI Threshold											
Blue SDI Threshold	0	1000	2000	3000	4000	5000	6000	7000	8000	9000	10000	
0	0.00	0.00	0.00	0.00	0.00	0.00	0.00	0.00	0.00	0.00	0.00	
1000	0.00	0.00	0.00	0.00	0.00	0.00	0.00	0.00	0.00	0.00	0.00	
2000	0.00	0.00	0.00	0.00	0.00	0.00	0.00	0.00	0.00	0.00	0.00	
3000	0.14	0.04	0.01	0.00	0.00	0.00	0.00	0.00	0.00	0.00	0.00	
4000	1.00	1.00	1.00	0.43	0.00	0.00	0.00	0.00	0.00	0.00	0.00	P_{XY}
5000	1.00	1.00	1.00	0.91	0.37	0.07	0.00	0.00	0.00	0.00	0.00	
6000	1.00	1.00	1.00	0.91	0.37	0.07	0.00	0.00	0.00	0.00	0.00	
7000	1.00	1.00	1.00	0.91	0.37	0.07	0.00	0.00	0.00	0.00	0.00	
8000	1.00	1.00	1.00	0.91	0.37	0.07	0.00	0.00	0.00	0.00	0.00	
9000	1.00	1.00	1.00	0.91	0.37	0.07	0.00	0.00	0.00	0.00	0.00	
10000	1.00	1.00	1.00	0.91	0.37	0.07	0.00	0.00	0.00	0.00	0.00	
0	0.00	0.00	0.00	0.00	0.00	0.00	0.13	0.77	0.77	0.77	0.77	
1000	0.00	0.00	0.00	0.00	0.00	0.00	0.06	0.61	0.61	0.61	0.61	
2000	0.00	0.00	0.00	0.00	0.00	0.00	0.02	0.41	0.41	0.41	0.41	
3000	0.00	0.00	0.00	0.00	0.00	0.00	0.00	0.20	0.20	0.20	0.20	
4000	0.00	0.00	0.00	0.00	0.00	0.00	0.00	0.05	0.05	0.05	0.05	P_{YX}
5000	0.00	0.00	0.00	0.00	0.00	0.00	0.00	0.00	0.00	0.00	0.00	
6000	0.00	0.00	0.00	0.00	0.00	0.00	0.00	0.00	0.00	0.00	0.00	
7000	0.00	0.00	0.00	0.00	0.00	0.00	0.00	0.00	0.00	0.00	0.00	
8000	0.00	0.00	0.00	0.00	0.00	0.00	0.00	0.00	0.00	0.00	0.00	
9000	0.00	0.00	0.00	0.00	0.00	0.00	0.00	0.00	0.00	0.00	0.00	
10000	0.00	0.00	0.00	0.00	0.00	0.00	0.00	0.00	0.00	0.00	0.00	
0	0.00	0.00	0.00	0.00	0.00	0.00	0.13	0.77	0.77	0.77	0.77	
1000	0.00	0.00	0.00	0.00	0.00	0.00	0.06	0.61	0.61	0.61	0.61	
2000	0.00	0.00	0.00	0.00	0.00	0.00	0.02	0.41	0.41	0.41	0.41	
3000	0.14	0.04	0.01	0.00	0.00	0.00	0.00	0.20	0.20	0.20	0.20	
4000	1.00	1.00	1.00	0.43	0.00	0.00	0.00	0.05	0.05	0.05	0.05	$S=P_{XY}+P_{YX}$
5000	1.00	1.00	1.00	0.91	0.37	0.07	0.00	0.00	0.00	0.00	0.00	
6000	1.00	1.00	1.00	0.91	0.37	0.07	0.00	0.00	0.00	0.00	0.00	
7000	1.00	1.00	1.00	0.91	0.37	0.07	0.00	0.00	0.00	0.00	0.00	
8000	1.00	1.00	1.00	0.91	0.37	0.07	0.00	0.00	0.00	0.00	0.00	
9000	1.00	1.00	1.00	0.91	0.37	0.07	0.00	0.00	0.00	0.00	0.00	
10000	1.00	1.00	1.00	0.91	0.37	0.07	0.00	0.00	0.00	0.00	0.00	

Table 2: NUMERICAL RESULTS FOR CASE I,II

Blue SDI Threshold	Red SDI Threshold 0	1000	2000	3000	4000	5000	6000	7000	8000	9000	10000	
0	0.00	0.00	0.00	0.00	0.00	0.00	0.00	0.00	0.00	0.00	0.00	
1000	0.00	0.00	0.00	0.00	0.00	0.00	0.00	0.00	0.00	0.00	0.00	
2000	0.00	0.00	0.00	0.00	0.00	0.00	0.00	0.00	0.00	0.00	0.00	
3000	0.75	0.59	0.38	0.17	0.04	0.00	0.00	0.00	0.00	0.00	0.00	
4000	1.00	1.00	1.00	1.00	1.00	1.00	0.48	0.00	0.00	0.00	0.00	
5000	1.00	1.00	1.00	1.00	1.00	1.00	1.00	1.00	0.00	0.00	0.00	P_{XY}
6000	1.00	1.00	1.00	1.00	1.00	1.00	1.00	1.00	0.53	0.00	0.00	
7000	1.00	1.00	1.00	1.00	1.00	1.00	1.00	1.00	1.00	0.00	0.00	
8000	1.00	1.00	1.00	1.00	1.00	1.00	1.00	1.00	1.00	0.00	0.00	
9000	1.00	1.00	1.00	1.00	1.00	1.00	1.00	1.00	1.00	0.00	0.00	
10000	1.00	1.00	1.00	1.00	1.00	1.00	1.00	1.00	1.00	0.00	0.00	
0	0.00	0.00	0.00	0.00	0.00	0.00	0.90	1.00	1.00	1.00	1.00	
1000	0.00	0.00	0.00	0.00	0.00	0.00	0.83	1.00	1.00	1.00	1.00	
2000	0.00	0.00	0.00	0.00	0.00	0.00	0.72	1.00	1.00	1.00	1.00	
3000	0.00	0.00	0.00	0.00	0.00	0.00	0.54	1.00	1.00	1.00	1.00	
4000	0.00	0.00	0.00	0.00	0.00	0.00	0.33	1.00	1.00	1.00	1.00	P_{YX}
5000	0.00	0.00	0.00	0.00	0.00	0.00	0.06	1.00	1.00	1.00	1.00	
6000	0.00	0.00	0.00	0.00	0.00	0.00	0.00	0.61	1.00	1.00	1.00	
7000	0.00	0.00	0.00	0.00	0.00	0.00	0.00	0.02	1.00	1.00	1.00	
8000	0.00	0.00	0.00	0.00	0.00	0.00	0.00	0.00	0.00	0.00	0.00	
9000	0.00	0.00	0.00	0.00	0.00	0.00	0.00	0.00	0.00	0.00	0.00	
10000	0.00	0.00	0.00	0.00	0.00	0.00	0.00	0.00	0.00	0.00	0.00	
0	0.00	0.00	0.00	0.00	0.00	0.00	0.90	1.00	1.00	1.00	1.00	
1000	0.00	0.00	0.00	0.00	0.00	0.00	0.83	1.00	1.00	1.00	1.00	
2000	0.00	0.00	0.00	0.00	0.00	0.00	0.72	1.00	1.00	1.00	1.00	
3000	0.75	0.59	0.38	0.17	0.04	0.00	0.54	1.00	1.00	1.00	1.00	$S=P_{XY}+P_{YX}$
4000	1.00	1.00	1.00	1.00	1.00	1.00	0.81	1.00	1.00	1.00	1.00	
5000	1.00	1.00	1.00	1.00	1.00	1.00	1.06	2.00	1.00	1.00	1.00	
6000	1.00	1.00	1.00	1.00	1.00	1.00	1.00	1.61	1.00	1.00	1.00	
7000	1.00	1.00	1.00	1.00	1.00	1.00	1.00	1.02	1.53	1.00	1.00	
8000	1.00	1.00	1.00	1.00	1.00	1.00	1.00	1.00	1.00	0.00	0.00	
9000	1.00	1.00	1.00	1.00	1.00	1.00	1.00	1.00	1.00	0.00	0.00	
10000	1.00	1.00	1.00	1.00	1.00	1.00	1.00	1.00	1.00	0.00	0.00	

Table 3: NUMERICAL RESULTS FOR CASE II,I

Blue SDI Threshold	Red SDI Threshold: 0	1000	2000	3000	4000	5000	6000	7000	8000	9000	10000	
0	0.00	0.00	0.00	0.00	0.00	0.00	0.00	0.00	0.00	0.00	0.00	
1000	0.00	0.00	0.00	0.00	0.00	0.00	0.00	0.00	0.00	0.00	0.00	
2000	0.02	0.00	0.00	0.00	0.00	0.00	0.00	0.00	0.00	0.00	0.00	
3000	0.71	0.23	0.01	0.00	0.00	0.00	0.00	0.00	0.00	0.00	0.00	P_{XY}
4000	0.71	0.23	0.03	0.00	0.00	0.00	0.00	0.00	0.00	0.00	0.00	
5000	0.71	0.23	0.03	0.00	0.00	0.00	0.00	0.00	0.00	0.00	0.00	
6000	0.71	0.23	0.03	0.00	0.00	0.00	0.00	0.00	0.00	0.00	0.00	
7000	0.71	0.23	0.03	0.00	0.00	0.00	0.00	0.00	0.00	0.00	0.00	
8000	0.71	0.23	0.03	0.00	0.00	0.00	0.00	0.00	0.00	0.00	0.00	
9000	0.71	0.23	0.03	0.00	0.00	0.00	0.00	0.00	0.00	0.00	0.00	
10000	0.71	0.23	0.03	0.00	0.00	0.00	0.00	0.00	0.00	0.00	0.00	
0	0.00	0.00	0.00	0.04	1.00	1.00	1.00	1.00	1.00	1.00	1.00	
1000	0.00	0.00	0.00	0.01	1.00	1.00	1.00	1.00	1.00	1.00	1.00	
2000	0.00	0.00	0.00	0.00	0.20	0.20	0.20	0.20	0.20	0.20	0.20	
3000	0.00	0.00	0.00	0.00	0.00	0.00	0.00	0.00	0.00	0.00	0.00	
4000	0.00	0.00	0.00	0.00	0.00	0.00	0.00	0.00	0.00	0.00	0.00	P_{YX}
5000	0.00	0.00	0.00	0.00	0.00	0.00	0.00	0.00	0.00	0.00	0.00	
6000	0.00	0.00	0.00	0.00	0.00	0.00	0.00	0.00	0.00	0.00	0.00	
7000	0.00	0.00	0.00	0.00	0.00	0.00	0.00	0.00	0.00	0.00	0.00	
8000	0.00	0.00	0.00	0.00	0.00	0.00	0.00	0.00	0.00	0.00	0.00	
9000	0.00	0.00	0.00	0.00	0.00	0.00	0.00	0.00	0.00	0.00	0.00	
10000	0.00	0.00	0.00	0.00	0.00	0.00	0.00	0.00	0.00	0.00	0.00	
0	0.00	0.00	0.00	0.04	1.00	1.00	1.00	1.00	1.00	1.00	1.00	
1000	0.00	0.00	0.00	0.01	1.00	1.00	1.00	1.00	1.00	1.00	1.00	
2000	0.02	0.00	0.00	0.00	0.20	0.20	0.20	0.20	0.20	0.20	0.20	
3000	0.71	0.23	0.01	0.00	0.00	0.00	0.00	0.00	0.00	0.00	0.00	
4000	0.71	0.23	0.03	0.00	0.00	0.00	0.00	0.00	0.00	0.00	0.00	$S=P_{XY}+P_{YX}$
5000	0.71	0.23	0.03	0.00	0.00	0.00	0.00	0.00	0.00	0.00	0.00	
6000	0.71	0.23	0.03	0.00	0.00	0.00	0.00	0.00	0.00	0.00	0.00	
7000	0.71	0.23	0.03	0.00	0.00	0.00	0.00	0.00	0.00	0.00	0.00	
8000	0.71	0.23	0.03	0.00	0.00	0.00	0.00	0.00	0.00	0.00	0.00	
9000	0.71	0.23	0.03	0.00	0.00	0.00	0.00	0.00	0.00	0.00	0.00	
10000	0.71	0.23	0.03	0.00	0.00	0.00	0.00	0.00	0.00	0.00	0.00	

Table 4: NUMERICAL RESULTS FOR CASE II,II

Red SDI Threshold

Blue SDI Threshold	0	1000	2000	3000	4000	5000	6000	7000	8000	9000	10000	
0	0.00	0.00	0.00	0.00	0.00	0.00	0.00	0.00	0.00	0.00	0.00	
1000	0.00	0.00	0.00	0.00	0.00	0.00	0.00	0.00	0.00	0.00	0.00	
2000	1.00	1.00	0.06	0.00	0.00	0.00	0.00	0.00	0.00	0.00	0.00	
3000	1.00	1.00	1.00	1.00	0.00	0.00	0.00	0.00	0.00	0.00	0.00	
4000	1.00	1.00	1.00	1.00	0.40	0.00	0.00	0.00	0.00	0.00	0.00	
5000	1.00	1.00	1.00	1.00	1.00	1.00	1.00	1.00	1.00	1.00	1.00	P_{XY}
6000	1.00	1.00	1.00	1.00	1.00	1.00	1.00	1.00	1.00	1.00	1.00	
7000	1.00	1.00	1.00	1.00	1.00	1.00	1.00	1.00	1.00	1.00	1.00	
8000	1.00	1.00	1.00	1.00	1.00	1.00	1.00	1.00	1.00	1.00	1.00	
9000	1.00	1.00	1.00	1.00	1.00	1.00	1.00	1.00	1.00	1.00	1.00	
10000	1.00	1.00	1.00	1.00	1.00	1.00	1.00	1.00	1.00	1.00	1.00	
0	0.00	0.00	0.00	0.47	1.00	1.00	1.00	1.00	1.00	1.00	1.00	
1000	0.00	0.00	0.00	0.24	1.00	1.00	1.00	1.00	1.00	1.00	1.00	
2000	0.00	0.00	0.00	0.03	1.00	1.00	1.00	1.00	1.00	1.00	1.00	
3000	0.00	0.00	0.00	0.00	1.00	1.00	1.00	1.00	1.00	1.00	1.00	
4000	0.00	0.00	0.00	0.00	0.00	0.95	0.95	0.95	0.95	0.95	0.95	
5000	-1.00	-1.00	-1.00	-1.00	-1.00	-1.00	-1.00	-1.00	-1.00	-1.00	-1.00	P_{YX}
6000	-1.00	-1.00	-1.00	-1.00	-1.00	-1.00	-1.00	-1.00	-1.00	-1.00	-1.00	
7000	-1.00	-1.00	-1.00	-1.00	-1.00	-1.00	-1.00	-1.00	-1.00	-1.00	-1.00	
9000	-1.00	-1.00	-1.00	-1.00	-1.00	-1.00	-1.00	-1.00	-1.00	-1.00	-1.00	
10000	-1.00	-1.00	-1.00	-1.00	-1.00	-1.00	-1.00	-1.00	-1.00	-1.00	-1.00	
0	0.00	0.00	0.00	0.47	1.00	1.00	1.00	1.00	1.00	1.00	1.00	
1000	0.00	0.00	0.00	0.24	1.00	1.00	1.00	1.00	1.00	1.00	1.00	
2000	1.00	1.00	0.06	0.03	1.00	1.00	1.00	1.00	1.00	1.00	1.00	
3000	1.00	1.00	1.00	1.00	1.00	1.00	1.00	1.00	1.00	1.00	1.00	
4000	1.00	1.00	1.00	1.00	0.39	0.95	0.95	0.95	0.95	0.95	0.95	
5000	0.00	0.00	0.00	0.00	0.00	0.00	0.00	0.00	0.00	0.00	0.00	$S=P_{XY}+P_{YX}$
6000	0.00	0.00	0.00	0.00	0.00	0.00	0.00	0.00	0.00	0.00	0.00	
7000	0.00	0.00	0.00	0.00	0.00	0.00	0.00	0.00	0.00	0.00	0.00	
8000	0.00	0.00	0.00	0.00	0.00	0.00	0.00	0.00	0.00	0.00	0.00	
9000	0.00	0.00	0.00	0.00	0.00	0.00	0.00	0.00	0.00	0.00	0.00	
10000	0.00	0.00	0.00	0.00	0.00	0.00	0.00	0.00	0.00	0.00	0.00	

Table 5: NUMERICAL RESULTS FOR CASE I,III

Red SDI Threshold

Blue SDI Threshold	0	1000	2000	3000	4000	5000	6000	7000	8000	9000	10000	
0	0.00	0.00	0.00	0.00	0.00	0.00	0.00	0.00	0.00	0.00	0.00	
1000	0.00	0.00	0.00	0.00	0.00	0.00	0.00	0.00	0.00	0.00	0.00	
2000	0.00	0.00	0.00	0.00	0.00	0.00	0.00	0.00	0.00	0.00	0.00	
3000	0.75	0.59	0.38	0.17	0.04	0.00	0.00	0.00	0.00	0.00	0.00	P_{XY}
4000	1.00	1.00	1.00	1.00	1.00	1.00	0.48	0.00	0.00	0.00	0.00	
5000	1.00	1.00	1.00	1.00	1.00	1.00	1.00	1.00	0.00	0.00	0.00	
6000	1.00	1.00	1.00	1.00	1.00	1.00	1.00	1.00	0.00	0.00	0.00	
7000	1.00	1.00	1.00	1.00	1.00	1.00	1.00	1.00	1.00	0.00	0.00	
8000	1.00	1.00	1.00	1.00	1.00	1.00	1.00	1.00	1.00	0.00	0.00	
9000	1.00	1.00	1.00	1.00	1.00	1.00	1.00	1.00	1.00	0.01	0.01	
10000	1.00	1.00	1.00	1.00	1.00	1.00	1.00	1.00	1.00	1.00	1.00	
0	0.00	0.00	0.00	0.00	0.00	0.00	0.90	1.00	1.00	1.00	1.00	
1000	0.00	0.00	0.00	0.00	0.00	0.00	0.83	1.00	1.00	1.00	1.00	
2000	0.00	0.00	0.00	0.00	0.00	0.00	0.72	1.00	1.00	1.00	1.00	
3000	0.00	0.00	0.00	0.00	0.00	0.00	0.54	1.00	1.00	1.00	1.00	
4000	0.00	0.00	0.00	0.00	0.00	0.00	0.33	1.00	1.00	1.00	1.00	P_{YX}
5000	0.00	0.00	0.00	0.00	0.00	0.00	0.12	1.00	1.00	1.00	1.00	
6000	0.00	0.00	0.00	0.00	0.00	0.00	0.00	1.00	1.00	1.00	1.00	
7000	0.00	0.00	0.00	0.00	0.00	0.00	0.00	0.92	1.00	1.00	1.00	
8000	0.00	0.00	0.00	0.00	0.00	0.00	0.00	0.00	0.99	0.99	0.99	
9000	-0.05	-0.05	-0.05	-0.05	-0.05	-0.05	-0.05	-0.05	-0.05	-0.05	-0.05	
10000	-1.00	-1.00	-1.00	-1.00	-1.00	-1.00	-1.00	-1.00	-1.00	-1.00	-1.00	
0	0.00	0.00	0.00	0.00	0.00	0.00	0.90	1.00	1.00	1.00	1.00	
1000	0.00	0.00	0.00	0.00	0.00	0.00	0.83	1.00	1.00	1.00	1.00	
2000	0.00	0.00	0.00	0.00	0.00	0.00	0.72	1.00	1.00	1.00	1.00	
3000	0.75	0.59	0.38	0.17	0.04	0.00	0.54	1.00	1.00	1.00	1.00	
4000	1.00	1.00	1.00	1.00	1.00	1.00	0.81	1.00	1.00	1.00	1.00	$S=P_{XY}+P_{YX}$
5000	1.00	1.00	1.00	1.00	1.00	1.00	1.12	2.00	1.00	1.00	1.00	
6000	1.00	1.00	1.00	1.00	0.00	1.00	1.00	2.00	1.00	1.00	1.00	
7000	1.00	1.00	1.00	1.00	0.00	1.00	1.00	1.92	2.01	1.00	1.00	
8000	1.00	1.00	1.00	1.00	1.00	1.00	1.00	1.00	1.99	0.99	0.99	
9000	0.95	0.95	0.95	0.95	0.95	0.95	0.95	0.95	0.95	-0.04	-0.04	
10000	0.00	0.00	0.00	0.00	0.00	0.00	0.00	0.00	0.00	0.00	0.00	

Table 6: NUMERICAL RESULTS FOR CASE II,III

Red SDI Threshold

Blue SDI Threshold	0	1000	2000	3000	4000	5000	6000	7000	8000	9000	10000	
0	0.00	0.00	0.00	0.00	-0.05	-1.00	-1.00	-1.00	-1.00	-1.00	-1.00	
1000	0.00	0.00	0.00	0.00	-0.05	-1.00	-1.00	-1.00	-1.00	-1.00	-1.00	
2000	1.00	1.00	0.06	0.00	-0.05	-1.00	-1.00	-1.00	-1.00	-1.00	-1.00	
3000	1.00	1.00	1.00	0.99	-0.05	-1.00	-1.00	-1.00	-1.00	-1.00	-1.00	
4000	1.00	1.00	1.00	1.00	0.17	-1.00	-1.00	-1.00	-1.00	-1.00	-1.00	P_{XY}
5000	1.00	1.00	1.00	1.00	0.95	0.00	0.00	0.00	0.00	0.00	0.00	
6000	1.00	1.00	1.00	1.00	0.95	0.00	0.00	0.00	0.00	0.00	0.00	
7000	1.00	1.00	1.00	1.00	0.95	0.00	0.00	0.00	0.00	0.00	0.00	
8000	1.00	1.00	1.00	1.00	0.95	0.00	0.00	0.00	0.00	0.00	0.00	
9000	1.00	1.00	1.00	1.00	0.95	0.00	0.00	0.00	0.00	0.00	0.00	
10000	1.00	1.00	1.00	1.00	0.95	0.00	0.00	0.00	0.00	0.00	0.00	
0	0.00	0.00	0.00	0.47	1.00	1.00	1.00	1.00	1.00	1.00	1.00	
1000	0.00	0.00	0.00	0.26	1.00	1.00	1.00	1.00	1.00	1.00	1.00	
2000	0.00	0.00	0.00	0.08	1.00	1.00	1.00	1.00	1.00	1.00	1.00	
3000	0.00	0.00	0.00	0.01	1.00	1.00	1.00	1.00	1.00	1.00	1.00	
4000	0.00	0.00	0.00	0.00	0.95	1.00	1.00	1.00	1.00	1.00	1.00	P_{YX}
5000	-1.00	-1.00	-1.00	-1.00	-0.99	0.00	0.00	0.00	0.00	0.00	0.00	
6000	-1.00	-1.00	-1.00	-1.00	-0.99	0.00	0.00	0.00	0.00	0.00	0.00	
7000	-1.00	-1.00	-1.00	-1.00	-0.99	0.00	0.00	0.00	0.00	0.00	0.00	
8000	-1.00	-1.00	-1.00	-1.00	-0.99	0.00	0.00	0.00	0.00	0.00	0.00	
9000	-1.00	-1.00	-1.00	-1.00	-0.99	0.00	0.00	0.00	0.00	0.00	0.00	
10000	-1.00	-1.00	-1.00	-1.00	-0.99	0.00	0.00	0.00	0.00	0.00	0.00	
0	0.00	0.00	0.00	0.47	0.95	0.00	0.00	0.00	0.00	0.00	0.00	
1000	0.00	0.00	0.00	0.26	0.95	0.00	0.00	0.00	0.00	0.00	0.00	
2000	1.00	1.00	0.06	0.08	0.95	0.00	0.00	0.00	0.00	0.00	0.00	
3000	1.00	1.00	1.00	1.00	0.95	0.00	0.00	0.00	0.00	0.00	0.00	$S=P_{XY}+P_{YX}$
4000	1.00	1.00	1.00	1.00	1.12	0.00	0.00	0.00	0.00	0.00	0.00	
5000	0.00	0.00	0.00	0.00	-0.04	0.00	0.00	0.00	0.00	0.00	0.00	
6000	0.00	0.00	0.00	0.00	-0.04	0.00	0.00	0.00	0.00	0.00	0.00	
7000	0.00	0.00	0.00	0.00	-0.00	0.00	0.00	0.00	0.00	0.00	0.00	
8000	0.00	0.00	0.00	0.00	-0.04	0.00	0.00	0.00	0.00	0.00	0.00	
9000	0.00	0.00	0.00	0.00	-0.04	0.00	0.00	0.00	0.00	0.00	0.00	
10000	0.00	0.00	0.00	0.00	-0.04	0.00	0.00	0.00	0.00	0.00	0.00	

PRE-ARMS CONTROL ASSESSMENT OF THE CONVENTIONAL BALANCE IN EUROPE

John W. Gibson
Sevenoaks, Kent, United Kingdom

1. TRENDS IN THE MILITARY BALANCE

There is general consensus in the West that there has been an adverse trend in the NATO/WP military balance over the past 15 years, but less agreement on the sizing of NATO's deficiencies. The strategy of flexible response (MC 14/3) developed in 1967, argued that each leg of the triad (strategic nuclear, theatre nuclear - TNF, conventional forces) should offer both independent and mutually supporting deterrent and defence roles. It has always recognized quantitative inferiority in readily deployable conventional forces, offset at the outset by a measure of strategic and theatre nuclear superiority and qualitative advantages stemming from NATO's lead in technology.

It was argued some years ago[1] that the NATO offsets have been eroded, due to Soviet modernisation and expansion of nuclear assets, advantages in chemical weapons, and that the qualitative gap in conventional weapons has been eliminated in some areas and narrowed in many others. However, the West probably remains well ahead in fields of high technology and their application to system development. MC 14/3 continues to call for

- effective conventional defence that would additionally force the burden of escalation onto the other side;
- the capability for deliberate escalation;
- general nuclear response, being the ultimate guarantor of deterrence.

It is assumed that NATO objectives with conventional forces are related to possessing a credible capability to

- prevent loss of NATO territory for "as long as necessary", in a posture of forward defence, implying the ability to retain viable command and control, reinforcement/re-supply assets;

---

1) Record,J.: Force Reduction in Europe: Starting Over. Insitute for Foreign Policy Analysis Inc., 1980

NATO ASI Series, Vol. F 26
Modelling and Analysis in Arms Control
Edited by R. Avenhaus et al.

- preserve TNF assets and posture.

The WP objectives are seemingly aimed at retaining the lead in deployed and mobilisable conventional forces, and achieving superiority in nuclear and chemical weapons.

2. THE OPPOSING FORCES: OBJECTIVES AND ASYMMETRIES

This section and the following two draw and expand on some of the arguements put forward in a presentation to the German Strategy Forum workshop on "Long Term Development of NATO's Forward Defence"in December 1984[2). They develop criteria of relevance to a major aggression aimed at territorial acquisition, the "design contingency" that has largely dictated NATO's force posture and the bulk of its defence expenditure. However, it is important to consider a diversity of scenarios, variants of those related to a major aggression, as well as other "off-design" contingencies involving more limited objectives, pre-cursor actions and out-of-area activities. Force assessments, other than those based on relative numbers of men and equipment, are necessarily founded on political factors and on questionable assumptions about why and how a conflict might start - assumptions that could never be a basis for negotiation.

Current views on the future threat reflect a consensus among the assessment community that in order to succeed in a major aggression against the Alliance, it would be necessary for the WP to neutralise NATO assets quickly in order to avoid a situation in which the US military industrial potential could be brought to bear, and to avoid escalation into a general nuclear exchange. This would call for speed, surprise and deception in Soviet operational strategy. The objectives of WP forces on the Central Front would aim to exploit NATO's weakness and to choose the most advantageous time to attack.

Studies are made on the basis of various warning scenarios : surprise attack by WP in-place forces; attack after partial mobilisation; or after full build-up. The first appears to be well suited to Soviet force design and deployment, but it could be a high risk option if based on a misjudgement

2) Gibson,J.W. (1984): Criteria for the Evaluation of Conventional Forces and Quantification. In: Modeling and Analysis of Conventional Defense in Europe (Huber,R.K., Ed.), Plenum Press, New York and London, 1986, pp. 15-24

of NATO's ability to respond and if it failed to achieve operational surprise. It is this question of surprise that poses the most difficult problem for the analyst attempting to develop effectiveness criteria. Soviet preparations for war would provide indications to NATO unless, as they undoubtedly would be, they were ambiguous, involving various forms of deception. With advances in overhead sensor technology, this will pose increasing problems for a would-be aggressor. NATO's ability to counter surprise is related to its alert system and to political decision-making. And if this process could be improved as a consequence of arms control negotations, it should be given high priority.

Other factors can influence perceptions of the military balance, some relating to the structures of the respective alliances and the asymmetries between them. In NATO, national contributions and their employment have to be coordinated through a democratic process of collective discussion and agreement that can lead to protracted decision-making. In respect of the conduct of military operations, NATO forces are less controlled by standardised doctrines and concepts, which might be perceived as exploitable weakness but which could present problems to the WP facing a variety of countermeasures. A further asymmetry stems from relationships within each alliance and the reliability of the constituent allies. There are differences between the two military postures relating to the lack of depth in NATO's defences, the commitment to forward defence and to maldeployment in peacetime - weaknesses that the structure and deployment of WP forces are fully tailored to exploit. NATO is seeking to redress these weaknesses by measures designed to increase readiness of in-place forces, the early arrival of reinforcements, and to provide for a more cohesive defence across NORTHAG and CENTAG.

Perhaps the most significant difference between the opposing forces, in respect of force design, concerns the structure of the NATO and WP divisions, the widely different manpower to equipment ratios in the teeth arms (with the WP deploying on the order of less than half the men per major weapon system than NATO), and the seemingly much larger investment by NATO in support and logistics, resulting in a much smaller "teeth to tail" ratio. These factors are clearly important in any arms control negotiations concerned with force reductions and their constituent parts.

3. EVALUATION CRITERIA FOR CONVENTIONAL FORCES

Calculations on the military balance or "correlation of forces" may be based on

- static measures and force ratio comparisons;
- deterrence criteria that extend on force ratio comparisons to include consideration of the drawdown of forces over time;
- analysis that is scenario-dependent but which takes account of operational factors, military objectives and doctrine.

Many people outside the defence community are familiar with static indicators of relative force capability. Various institutes produce statistics of numbers of men, ground equipments, aeroplanes, missiles, ships, that provide some numerical estimates of relative strength or force ratio. For ground equipments, attempts have been made to allow for quantitative and qualitative differences between NATO and WP divisions, based on computing combat potential expressed typically in armoured division equivalents. These are based on historical data and judgment relating to firepower, mobility and vulnerability estimates. In the context of discussions on "balanced" force reductions, it should be noted that numbers of men, other than those required to man equipments, do not have a driving effect on the calculations. These static measures take no account of unquantifiable factors such as the quality of men, training, morale, readiness; they are unrelated to scenarios, to the projectability of forces and to the dynamics of combat. But they convey an impression of the likelihood of a force being able to *deter* aggression. and rules of thumb have been developed which relate perceptions of the chance of success to specified force ratio levels.

Gibson argues (1984) that opinions vary on whether an effective conventional posture for deterrence differs in any significant respect from an effective war fighting/winning capability. It appears that the Soviets have never accepted such a difference, believing the former to be a by-product of the latter. The idea of deterrence has evolved around nuclear weapons, long range delivery means of mass destruction, the effects of which are amenable to comparable calculation by both sides. It could be argued that a viable deterrent posture with conventional weapons should be based more on an assessment of demonstrable capabilities that would be involved in the development of a confrontation than on the less predictable dynamics of action after war start. Obvious factors included in perceptions of deterrence are the forces and their composition (in-theatre, mobilisable, reinforcement) and crisis management, the political and military responses affecting action and the build-up of forces. The NATO objective can be related to an ability to sustain conventional operations to the extent that Soviet planning could not confidently perceive a conflict development leading to successful termination. This can be interpreted into evaluation criteria that relate to NATO's capability to

- hold forward for a specified period in the main defence positions;
- achieve after that time an improving ground force ratio development.

4. METHODOLOGIES

These criteria could be examined on the basis of a range of dynamic analysis methodologies, from the use of differential equations, Lanchester laws, to more complex simulations or war games. The simpler differential equation techniques have the attraction of being amenable to a wide range of threat assumptions, parametric variation, and force improvement options, including political issues (e.g. reductions in warning and reaction times) and various forms of force enhancement. They are certainly amenable to the study of force reduction options and provide for a simple and transparent means of comparing disparate force enhancements or measures aimed at improving the *deterrent* posture of conventional forces. They may be regarded as relating to necessary conditions for an effective *defence*, but they are not sufficient conditions. They do not take account of

- operational and tactical concepts; the use of manoevre to breakthrough, fracture and envelop defensive deployments; surprise attack;
- linkages with TNF.

Analytical studies that include such factors entail complex simulations of combat (that may be difficult to validate) or wargaming techniques that may be driven by the judgment of the players. Various studies have demonstrated that an adequate deterrent posture, as defined by the above attrition criteria, could fail in various scenarios to provide for an effective defence, and vice versa (see Gibson (1984)).

This suggests that evaluation criteria, descriptive of the balance or correlation of forces, and their translation into "quasi-dynamic" measures of effectiveness, as rehearsed above, are meaningful in relation to sizing force deficiency and assessing alternative prescriptive options. They imply that in order to deter aggression with conventional forces, NATO must be seen to possess sufficient force in respect of defensive and offensive firepower. However, the choice between various improvement options that would redress an imbalance should be influenced by other factors, operational and political, including

- evolving WP operational concepts, e.g. the need to counter surprise;
- demographic trends;
- future technology : opportunities and WP responses;
- effects on stability : possible negotiations.

In respect of the last of these Huber and Hofmann[3] argue that in order to improve NATO's conventional posture with least risk of de-stabilising the balance, emphasis should be given to the adoption of defensive as distinct from offensive solutions. Their arguements are exemplified using criteria and methodology comparable with that discussed above.

5. ASSESSMENT OF CONVENTIONAL ARMS CONTROL OPTIONS

The discussions on Mutual and Balanced Force Reductions (MBFR) over more than a decade, aimed at increasing the stability of the military balance, though largely motivated by national objectives, have considered

- definition of the Guidelines Area (GA);
- reduction or withdrawal of ground force units within the GA;
- reduction or withdrawal of manpower and equipment within the GA;
- some trade-off between conventional and TNF forces;
- inspection procedures that would reduce the possibility of a surprise attack.

---

[3] Huber, R.K. and Hofmann, H.W.: Gradual Defensivity - An Approach to a Stable Conventional Force Equilibrium in Europe? Operational Research '84 (Brans, Ed.), Elsevier 1984, pp. 197-211

In respect of force reductions, it would seem that pre-occupation with counting the numbers of men in the GA is counterproductive. The numbers of equipments are less relevant than the relative numbers of effective units, in-place or readily reinforcable, that could be built up to a situation in which an attack would be likely to succeed. The key to conventional arms control arrangements should relate to relative force projectability, i.e. build-up capability. History has shown that discussions about the balance or correlation of forces based on comparisons of numbers have failed to achieve agreements. Attempts to extend beyond numerical assessment would involve scenarios that would be quite impossible to agree. And there is conflict from the NATO viewpoint in seeking to develop a deterrent posture that would persuade the WP that the likelihood of their succeeding in an aggressive action would be insufficiently high - and at the same time, postulating force reductions based on admission of failure to achieve the former. But the peacetime locations of the respective forces and the restrictions on build-up imposed by geography should be more amenable to reasonable discussion, and NATO should focus attention on measures designed to reduce the possibility for covert build-up and surprise attack.

Of the measures considered to date on MBFR those relating to information, inspection and other factors concerning the knowledge by each side of changes in the status of forces, are the most important and may offer the best opportunities for agreement. Record (1980) argued convincingly that the "... fundamental issue is not the presence of opposing forces but the presence of growing military incentives to use force .... . Military incentives to initiate hostilities in time of crisis increasingly have become more of a function of specific capabilities that endow a military force of whatever size with a real or perceived ability to destroy quickly and at a single blow an opponent's capacity to offer decisive resistance." Variants of this view of the WP threat are now widespread. The NATO response should continue to be aimed at providing a sufficiency of military capability in respect of firepower, but through force design and/or, if possible, through negotiation, should seek to embody a counter surprise capability.

6. SUMMARY

This paper on conventional arms control problems represents an excursus from the main body of discussions at the workshop which was primarily concerned with strategic nuclear issues, but it is interesting to observe the similarities and differences between the two problem areas. The strategic systems are deployed in peacetime and the arms race balance is related to an action-reaction mechanism aimed at parity. The Workshop defined arms race stability as a state in which, over a finite sequence of moves, reaction does not exceed action. Crisis stability is assumed to exist if, in a given crisis, neither side perceives advantage for either side to attack first. In the case of conventional weapons, relative total force capability is less relevant than the ability to project force to an area where destruction is aimed at territorial acquisition. In respect of the NATO/WP balance in Allied Command Europe, it is argued that the principal aims in arms control discussion should relate to crisis stability.

ON STRATEGIC STABILITY IN EUROPE WITHOUT NUCLEAR WEAPONS

Reiner K. Huber
Institut für Angewandte Systemforschung und Operations Research
Fakultät für Informatik
Universität der Bundeswehr München, 8014 Neubiberg, FRG

1. INTRODUCTION

In order to deter a Soviet attack of Western Europe, NATO strategy relies on a sequence of essentially three responses: *conventional defense, nuclear defense, nuclear retaliation*. The credibility of this strategy of 'Flexible Response' depends on a firm and timely linkage of those responses.

There are several developments and trends which have been contributing to an erosion of 'Flexible Response' as a viable defense strategy for the Atlantic Alliance. For one thing, the steady modernization of conventional and strategic nuclear forces and the rather dramatic build-up of theater nuclear forces provide the Soviets with the capability to dominate whatever response NATO chooses. For the other, Soviet efforts to obtain the capability for short warning attacks tend to reduce the credibility of nuclear responses. This is because such a capability would make situations more likely in which, in order to make sense militarily, nuclear release decisions would have to be made fairly early in a conflict. However, for political as well as technical and organizational reasons, the credibility of a nuclear response must be considered to be the lower, the less time has elapsed since the opening of hostilities.

In addition, the credibility gap brought about by Soviet military efforts is widened because of a waning public support in Western societies of a strategy that relies on using nuclear weapons first thereby possibly initiating a process that might result in the end of mankind. This is obvious, for example, from the wide approval with which the Gorbachev proposal of January 1986 (to abolish all weapons of mass destruction until the end of this century) was met by the Western publics which, by and large, are unaware of the real magnitude of the conventional imbalance between NATO and the Warsaw Pact.

In this situation, there seem to be basically two options for NATO which, judging from the arguments of their proponents, are usually regarded as

NATO ASI Series, Vol. F 26
Modelling and Analysis in Arms Control
Edited by R. Avenhaus et al.

disjunct alternatives. One is to restore the credibility of NATO's present strategy of 'Flexible Response' (see, e.g., the American Academy of Arts and Sciences (1983 and 1985) European Security Study). The other is to develop and adopt a new strategy (see, e.g., BUNDY et al. (1982), several European 'alternatives' such as AFHELDT (1983) who propose a 'defensive defense', and HUNTINGTON (1984) who recommends an 'offensive defense'[1]).

Reaching consensus on a change of strategy is a difficult and cumbersome process in an alliance of sovereign nations. It carries with it the risk of jeopardizing the cohesion of the alliance. Therefore, the administrations of most NATO nations not only prefer therapeutic measures to preserve the implemented and agreed upon strategy, they frequently even consider thinking about new strategies as counter-productive. However, at the same time many of them support the Strategic Defense Initiative (SDI) which does indeed imply a change of the strategic paradigm. One can not ignore the fact that, in the long term, there is the possibility that the implementation of more or less effective strategic defenses by the superpowers in exchange for deep cuts in their strategic arsenals might render 'Flexible Response' obsolete and make the conventional balance, or rather imbalance, in Europe assume strategic significance. For this reason, NATO's two basic options of response to the Soviet military efforts must not be considered as alternatives but rather as elements of one *long-term package of a strategic evolution*.

Trying to restore the credibility of 'Flexible Response' is really an immediate issue the resolution of which cannot wait until a new strategy has been developed and agreed upon. However, the measures taken to accomplish that goal in the near- and intermeditate-term must not jeopardize the long-term evolution of a new strategy. Thus, all near-term programs and proposals need to be assessed conditional to their compatibility with potential long-term strategy alternatives which one may envision as a result of the variance of the strategic situation. Another, and perhaps more important, reason for such a conditional assessment is that near- and intermediate-term programs may provide some leverage for making the Soviets reciprocate in a manner that is

---

[1] HUNTINGTON actually classifies his proposal as 'Reconstituted Flexible Response' suggesting that it does not involve a change in strategy. However, as the schematic characterization of his proposal (p.41) shows, he does not aim at reconstituting the credibility of the links between conventional and nuclear forces, but rather at creating a new link between conventional 'defense' and 'retaliatory' forces which is to provide conventional deterrence through the threat of invasion.

conducive to the emergence of a mutually acceptable strategic situation. In fact, properly conceived military programs can be powerful elements of an implicit arms control negotiations process[2].

In light of the above indicated trends one possible alternative of the long-term strategic situation may be characterized by the absence of an effective nuclear retaliatory capability on both sides. Whether this is a desirable situation or not depends on whether and under what conditions strategic (crisis and arms race) stability can be obtained in a post-nuclear world, or whether man would in fact run the risk of reverting to the situation of the pre-nuclear days when Europe was characterized by periodic occurrences of increasingly devastating wars.

Some insights as to the principal conditions of strategic stability in Europe without nuclear weapons may be obtained from the results two research projects which this author has undertaken jointly with AVENHAUS and HOFMANN. One was devoted to the issue of conventional force equilibria in Central Europe and their stability. Its results suggested that arms race and crisis stability may eventually be obtained by gradually restructuring the opposed military forces toward a 'reactive defense', i.e. forces specialized in defense at the expense of offensive capabilities (gradual defensivity[3]). There would be an economically as well as militarily compelling reason to do so if

---

[2] A remarkable part of the arms control negotiations progress has not been in the form of explicit treaties or agreements but rather a sequence of unilateral moves or non-moves. A current (June 1986) example seems to be the Reagan administration's announcement to proceed with the strategic ALCM-program beyond the limits imposed by SALT II and the subsequent Gorbachev offer of a 30% cut of strategic offensive systems (see also KETTELLE in this volume).

[3] The term 'defensivity' is meant to characterize a state in which the respective (defensive) party's military forces are incapable of large scale invasion and occupation of the opponent's territory. A conventional deep attack capability (e.g. FOFA) for the destruction of high value military targets at some distance would not be incompatible with defensivity. On the contrary, it might be a necessary prerequisite for a successful defense by reactive (land) forces since it would provide a non-nuclear means to keep the attacker/defender force ratio within manageable bounds. Only in conjunction with all 'active' land forces capable of mounting large scale invasions must deep attack systems be considered as offensive.

the so-called *'Defense Efficiency (DE) Hypothesis'*[4] were validated (see AVENHAUS et al. (1983), HUBER and HOFMANN (1984)).

Thus, in the second project a testbed for that hypothesis was developed in form of a rather detailed combat simulation model. So far, several hundred combat experiments have been simulated which involved battalion-size reactive and active defense modules being attacked by a sequence of Soviet motor rifle and/or tank regiments under varying environmental conditions (see HOFMANN et al.(1986)). As a number of the reactive defense modules closely resemble some of the structural variants forwarded by various proponents of so-called "defensive defense" concepts, the simulation results provide some insights as to their relative effectiveness in the initial phase of a non-nuclear conflict. However, at this time any conclusions must be considered as preliminary at best. This is because most experiments to date were restricted to the employment of fielded weapons technology. Only now are we beginning to include hypothetical systems employing emerging technologies.

2. A CONCEPTUAL MODEL OF CONVENTIONAL STABILITY

It is not unreasonable to assume that, in a military conflict in Europe, both NATO and the Warsaw Pact would have to fight the war with whatever military means are available to them at the outbreak of hostilities. This is to say that losses of major weapon systems and units cannot be replaced in time to become effective in the same war. Thus, the useful military capabilities of both sides must be expected to deteriorate as a result of attrition as the war goes on, a process which may be characterized by a certain trajectory in the phase space of the mutual military capabilities as illustrated in Fig. 1. There, each trajectory corresponds to a different initial capability state x and y of the sides X (NATO) and Y (Warsaw Pact). Its functional form depends, among others, on the relative operational skill of the opponents in the employment of their capabilities. The trajectory S which ends in annihilation of both sides (x=0,y=0) symbolizes equilibrium states. It separates (S=separatrix) the initial conditions (x,y) which lead to a victory for Y (above S) from those which lead to a victory for X (below S).

---

4) The DE-hypothesis implies that "reactive" military forces specialized in defensive operations can exploit the inherent defense advantage more efficiently than "active" (multi-purpose) forces designed for employment in all combat modes.

Of course, Fig. 1 is but a highly idealized representation of the course of a military conflict or battle as it may be generated from conflict and battle simulations by means of deterministic models. However, in reality military conflict is hardly a deterministic process but subject to a great many chance events including intelligence on the instantaneous conditions (x,y) of both sides. Therefore, the separatrix may be better interpreted as containing the initial states for which there is an equal victory probability $P_X=P_Y=50\%$ for both sides. For higher victory probabilities, the initial conditions become more demanding for the victor. This is illustrated in Fig. 2 which shows that increasing the victory probability from 50% to a higher value, say 90%, requires a corresponding increase of the initial capabilities by either side. Thus, if we assume that neither side would go to war unless its victory probability were at least 90%, then all capability states (x,y) within the cross-hatched area of Fig. 2 can be considered to represent mutually acceptable (equilibrium) states.

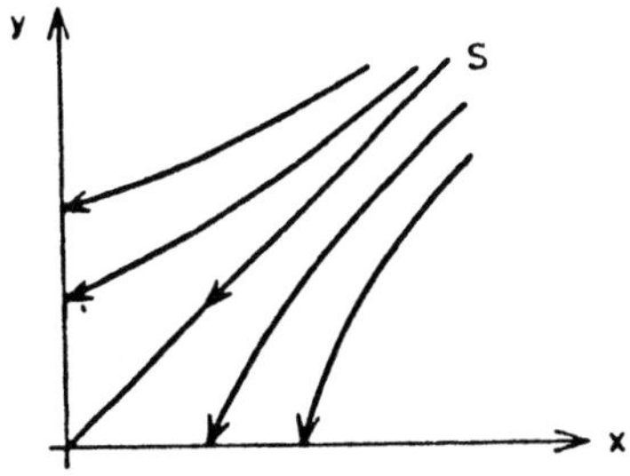

Fig. 1: Military conflict trajectories in terms of the opposed capabilities x and y

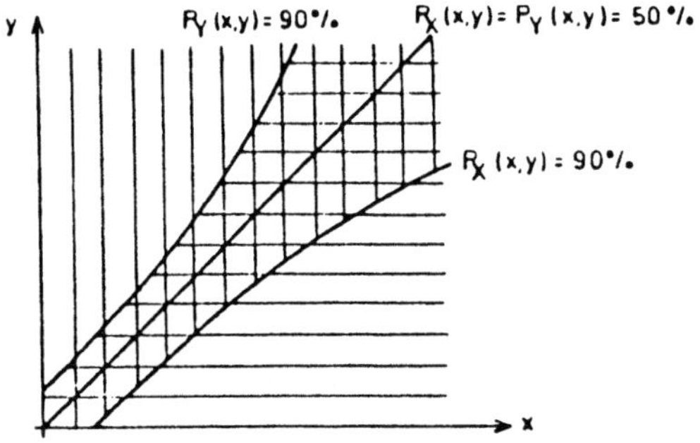

Fig. 2: Equilibrium states for victory-oriented attitudes (cross-hatched area)

It is obvious that such a *victory-oriented* assessment of equilibrium states by one side depends strongly on its risk evaluation of the other. For this reason, it might seem more rational to adopt a *security-oriented* attitude which prefers a high probability W_X and W_Y for being able to successfully defend oneself irrespective of the opponent's risk attitude. However, this leads to the situation depicted in Fig. 3 in which there are no equilibrium states. It suggests that arms races might be the result of the mutual desire to have sufficiently large armament states for a successful defense.

However, at least theoretically there is an escape from this security dilemma, if one assumes that a prepared defense has an inherent advantage over the attacker. Therefore, depending on which side attacks and which defends, we must actually distinguish two separatrices. This is illustrated in Fig. 4 where S_1 holds for Y attacking and X defending and S_2 for X attacking and Y defending. S_1 and S_2 divide the phase space into three different areas. The states above S_1 permit Y a successful attack of X. For states below S_2 the opposite holds true. States between S_1 and S_2 denote situations in which the defending side is successful.

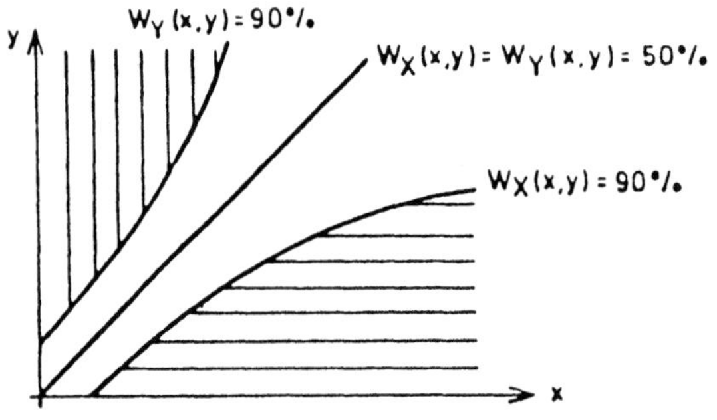

Fig. 3: Situation for security-oriented attitudes (no equilibrium states)

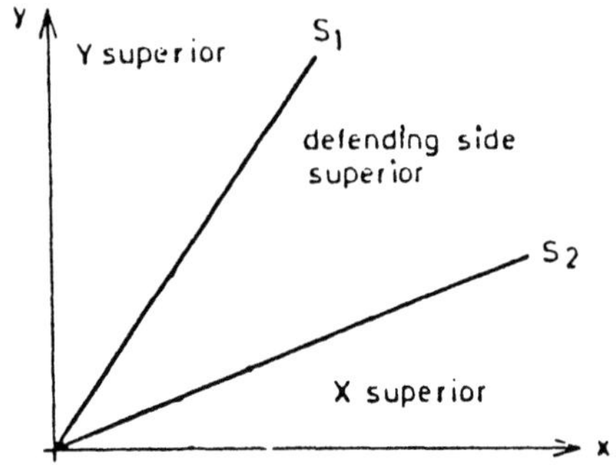

Fig. 4: Battle superiority when defending side is at an advantage

If we enter, as done in Fig. 3, the curves for sufficiently high probabilities of a successful defense W_X and W_Y for sides X and Y we arrive at the results illustrated in Fig. 5 for two situations i and k. In situation k the defending side's forces are more efficient in exploiting the inherent defense advantage than in situation i. This leads to a considerable increase in the stable area of mutually acceptable capability states as well as to a reduction in the minimum stable force levels for both sides.

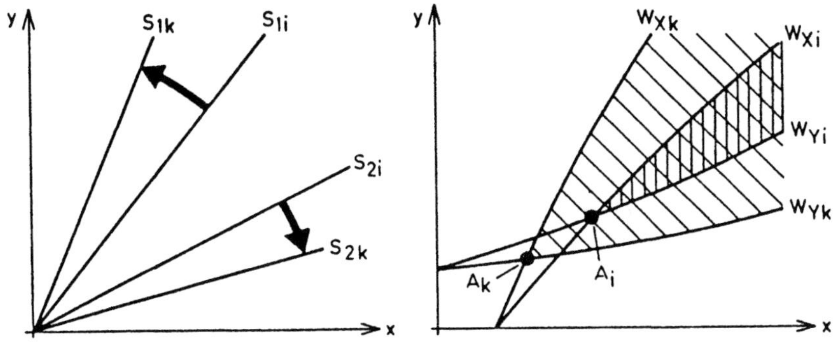

Fig. 5: Effect of an increasing defense advantage as force structure moves from situation i to k

Thus, if the DE-hypothesis were true that reactive defenses are more efficient in exploiting the inherent defense advantage than active ones, the gradual conversion of active land force elements into reactive ones on both sides would lead to an ever increasing size of the 'stable' area of equilibrium states with the minimum levels of mutually acceptable armaments approaching zero. Ultimately, the armaments levels of the opponents would be immaterial to their security.

3. EXPERIMENTAL TESTS OF THE DE-HYPOTHESIS

The basic idea for testing the defense efficiency (DE) hypothesis implies a comparative evaluation of the courses and outcomes of simulated defense battles fought by active and reactive units under a series of identical circumstances each.

The simulator is a stochastic Monte Carlo-type battle model (BASIS) which permits the (closed) simulation of battalion-size ground forces defending against a sequence of regimental-size attacker forces accounting, on both sides, for organic as well as higher-echelon fire support. The smallest element explicitly modelled is a so-called *combat group* which might be a mounted or dismounted infantry group or an individual combat vehicle such as an APC, tank, helicopter, or an artillery piece. Each element is described by a set of attributes which characterize its performance under a set of environmental conditions, its vulnerability and sustainability etc.

The elements are usually controlled at platoon level by means of so-called *Tactics Programs* which resemble formalized versions of the operations plans of both sides. Presently, the simulator provides for four different pieces of West German real estate (about 60 km^2 each) in form of digital maps containing elevation and terrain vegetation and trafficability data for grid sizes of 25, 50 and 100 m at an altitude resolution of 10 cm.

The battalion-size defender modules tested so far include four active ones (3 types of reinforced armoured infantry battalions and a reinforced tank battalion, all of the German Army) and ten reactive ones belonging to one of four basic categories of *Static Area Defense (SAD)*, *Dynamic Area Defense (DAD)*, *Continuous (C)* and *Selective (S) Fire Barriers (FB)*, the basic characteristics of which are summarized in Fig. 6 and Table 1. In all cases the defenders were assumed to be fully deployed and prepared.

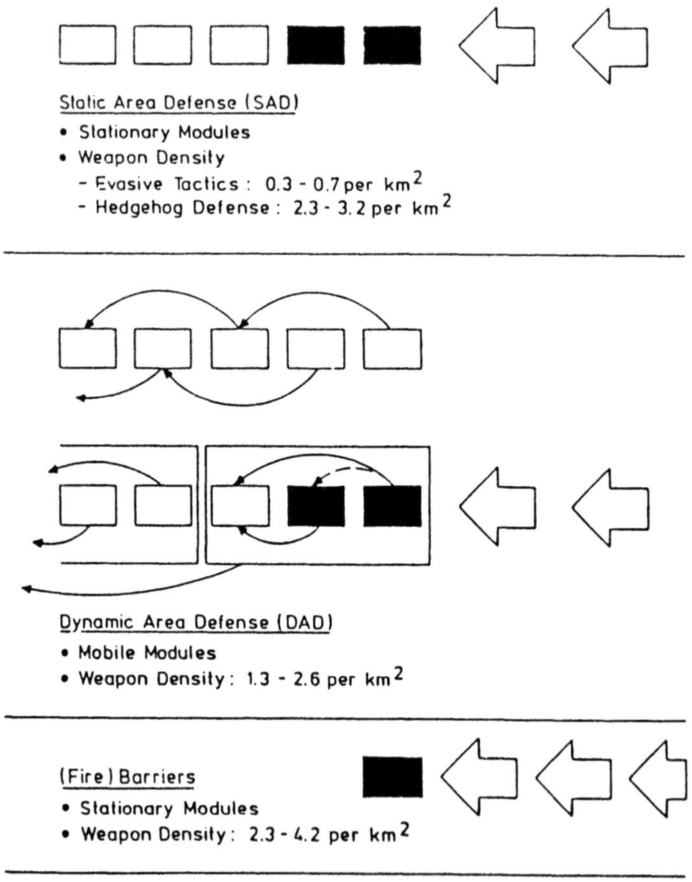

Fig. 6: Reactive Defense Concepts

Category	Type	Depth [km]	Direct Fire Wps No DFW	Direct Fire Wps Dens [l/km²]	Fire Support No IFW	Fire Support No Hel	Inv. Cost Factor
Active	A (RAI Btl)	5	82	3.3	32	7	16.5
	B (RAI Btl)	5	77	3.1	32	7	25.4
	C (RTK Btl)	5	61	2.4	26	7	30.2
	D (RAI Btl 90)	5	70	2.8	32	7	36.0
Reactive SAD	E (Afheldt)	10	14	0.3	7	-	1.0
	F (Swiss TD)	5	80	3.2	30	-	3.0
	G (SAS Inf)	8	27	0.7	7	4	4.2
	H (Austrian AD)	5	57	2.3	24	-	6.2
Reactive DAD	I (Löser)	7	50	1.4	6	6	12.0
	K (SAS Cav)	5	64	2.6	17	7	12.4
	L (Füreder)	8	50	1.6	29	7	21.6
Reactive CFB	M (Gerber)	8	134	3.4	30	6	18.6
	N (Hannig)	8	90	2.3	36	8	24.6
Reactive SFB	P (IASFOR)	5	106	4.3	32	-	10.4

Table 1: Equipment Summary for Defense Modules

3.1 Reactive Defense Modules

The SAD-class modules pursue a defense which is characterized by small combat teams fighting from a network of prepared positions and field fortifications taking advantage of reinforced terrain obstacles and mine barriers. Within this category, two fairly distinct subcategories must be distinguished: In one, the combat teams have, within their stationary area of operations, about two alternate positions to which they evade whenever they are threatened to be overrun or their losses approach 35-40%. The options E ('Technokommandos') of AFHELDT's (1983) *Area Defense Concept* and G (the infantry forces) of the SAS[5] proposal belong to this category[6]. In the other, the combat teams re-

[5] Studiengruppe für Alternative Sicherheitspolitik (1984).

[6] When they run out of alternative positions, AFHELDT's combat teams move into prestocked hideouts from which they attempt to harass the enemy forces in their rear. According to the SAS proposal, they are supposed to withdraw from their area of operations to reinforce identical forces further back. However, the proposal's transportation capability of two half-ton commercial vehicles per platoon of 28 men hardly seems sufficient for such an operational movement.

main stationary in their positions and continue fighting until they are virtually wiped out (hedgehog defense). This is the case in options F (the infantry forces of the *Swiss Territorial Defense System* (see MARTI (1979) and SENN (1979)), and H (the infantry forces of the *Austrian Area Defense* (see MAROLZ (1978) and HOCHAUER (1979)).

The options of the DAD-class are distinguished by their tactical mobility and the utilization of space in order to maintain a favourable loss exchange ratio. Fighting a mobile attrition-oriented delaying battle by falling back, through a series of prepared and partially reinforced positions, the options I (the so-called shield forces in LÖSER's (1980 and 1982) *Area Defense Concept*, K (the battalion-size cavalry regiment of the SAS proposal) and L (the anti-tank teams of FÜREDER's (1983) *Cellular Defense Concept* adhere to a tactical philosophy that may be described as *dynamic density defense*[7]).

The CFB-category includes concepts that foresee a continuous fire belt along the demarcation line acting as a barrier that the attacker has to penetrate. In option M (GERBER's (1984) *ATK-Sam Belt*), the forward edge of the belt (16 km) is reinforced by minefields and obstacles and defended by highly mobile anti-tank battalions equipped with light fighting vehicles capable of quickly digging themselves in and having elevated ATGW-platforms. A substantial number of LARS and heavy mortars are available to these battalions for fire support. Option N (HANNIG's (1981 and 1984) *Fire Barriers*) is characterized by 4 km deep belt in which attacking formations

---

[7]) This concept was theoretically substantiated in a joint working paper by Vector Research and BDM (May 1976). Accordingly, it takes advantage of the observation that the instantaneous offense/defense-exchange ratio as defined by the quotient of the fractional loss rates of defender versus attacker increases as a function of elapsed battle time since the concealment advantage accrued the defender wears off. For the same reason, the instantaneous exchange ratio is less dependent on the force ratio early in the battle. In fact, due to additional advantages to the defender (e.g., first shot and delayed reaction of the attacker), it must be assumed as being initially almost independent of the force ratio and very low. Therefore, an outnumbered defense should be deployed over some depth and fight a series of short battles as its units evade, thus continually increasing its density and improving the force ratio for a decisive battle.

are showered by artillery-delivered anti-tank mines and, when thus halted or slowed down, hit by long-range anti-tank weapons delivered by anti-tank defense battalions deployed behind the fire belt. These battalions also target and control a very substantial higher echelon fire support by LARS and heavy mortars. When incapacitated or having spent their ammunition, the battalions withdraw and the fire barrier is taken over and maintained by the battalions of a second wave in standby behind those of the first. Upon having been resupplied, the former first wave battalions will eventually replace, as a third wave, the second wave battalions, etc. (ladder tactics).

In contrast to the latter two options designed as continuous fire barriers, option P represents a light infantry battalion which, as part of a *'barrier brigade'* counting four of those battalions and one engineer battalion, would be employed to provide a selective fire barrier (SFB). It was developed at this author's institute by Prof. Hans W. HOFMANN based, among others, on the insights gained from the experiments. The barrier brigades are to be considered as additional forces assigned to the (possibly somewhat reduced) divisions of the active defenses. They would be deployed by the division commander or the commander of the superordinate corps consistent with the tactical situation. In suitable terrain, these brigades would be assigned to fight the initial forward defense battle largely from field fortifications assembled prior to combat from prefabricated (commercially available) structures stored in the vicinity of their usage. Thus, the armoured battalions of the active defense could assume the role of tactical and operational reserves for reinforcing the barrier brigades and for counterattacks.

3.2 Active Defense Modules

In order to provide a reference basis for a comparative assessment of the reactive defense options, three active defense alternatives were defined that resemble structural variants implemented within today's German Army Structure 4 (see GREINER et al. (1978) and BAHR (1981)). Of these, case A corresponds to the (normal) reinforced armoured infantry battalion (verst. PzGrenBtl) and case B to the mixed reinforced armoured infantry battalion (verst. gem. PzGrenBtl) of the armoured infantry brigade (PzGrenBrig). They differ primarily in that the latter battalion contains a mix of armoured personnel carriers (APC) and main battle tanks (MBT), while the former has no MBTs and a somewhat higher share of anti-tank guided weapons (ATGW) and recoilless rifles (RCL). Case C is identical to the mixed reinforced tank battalion (verst. gem. PzBtl) of the tank brigade (PzBrig). In all cases weapons are either mounted on armoured fighting vehicles or transported, together with their crews, in armoured personnel carriers. Their high mobility reflects the German Army's preference for a mobile defense requiring that all of its combat units must be employable in each of the three basic phases of a defense battle: 1) the initial *delaying phase;* 2) the *defense phase;* 3) the *counterattack phase.*

In addition to these current structural variants, a further hypothetical active defense option has been defined based upon the proposals by KOCH (1983 and 1984). This option D, the so-called reinforced armoured infantry battalion 90 (verst. PzGrenBtl 90), may be considered as a modernized version of option B. The latter's APCs and self-propelled mortars are replaced by new combat vehicles equipped with 25 mm automatic cannons, 120 mm anti-tank guns and improved 120 mm mortars. In addition, there are twelve 120 mm self-propelled anti-tank guns. The ATGWs available from higher-echelon fire support are launched from elevated platforms. Its operational employment and tactics are essentially identical to those practiced by today's German Army.

Of the three phases in a defense battle, our experiments on the active defense options simulate the second, and in a tactical context, sometimes the third phase. It is assumed that the terrain has been prepared (strong points, alternate firing positions for MBTs and ATGWs, mine barriers, etc.) and forces are fully deployed when the attack commences. Their primary objective is to stall the attack within the battalion defense sector of 5 km depth. Consistent with the tactical situation, the battalion commander may redeploy his forces to meet the enemy's main effort or for tactical counterattacks.

3.3 The Threat Forces

The threat forces considered in the combat simulation experiments consist either of motor rifle regiments (BMP) of the Soviet motor rifle division or tank regiments of a Soviet tank division. Their organization, equipment and tactics was specified from WIENER (1977), HARTUNG (1978), KREKER (1983), BAGINSKI (1983), and KARBER (1983).

In the simulation experiments, the typical regimental attack has two reinforced battalions attacking abreast as first-echelon forces over a sector of 5 km width. The third battalion follows as a second echelon force attacking in either one of the sectors of the two forward battalions. The attack is supported by organic and higher-echelon artillery forces and by attack helicopters.

The attack of the reinforced motor rifle battalion is spearheaded by the tank company followed closely by two motor rifle companies as first echelon elements, and by the third motor rifle company as a second echelon element.

The reinforced tank battalion's attack is spearheaded by two tank companies operating abreast, one being closely followed by the reinforcing motor rifle company. The third tank company follows as second echelon force.

3.4 The Scenarios

In addition to the threat forces and their operations as outlined in the previous section, the main parameters describing a BASIS scenario are related to

- terrain
- visibility conditions
- artillery environment
- the tactical organization of operations.

Presently, digital maps of four 6x10 km pieces of real estate in West Germany are available for simulation experiments. They resemble the following terrain types:
- mountaineous/wooded (Furth i. Wald)
- rolling hills/partly covered (Bubach)
- flat/partly covered (Donnersdorf)
- flat/open (Grettstadt.

Except for a few excursions involving attacks by tank regiments in the Grettstadt terrain, to date most experiments were performed in the Bubach area under three visibility conditions in each case, namely

- good visibility (≥ 5.000 m)
- dirty battlefield (initial visibility of 1.000 m deteriorates down to 350 m at a rate of 10% per minute)
- poor visibility (350 m).

In the standard experiment, the maneuver units of both sides are supported by artillery fire controlled by forward observers. In order to test their artillery sensitivity, the respective defense options were subjected to additional experiments involving artillery barrages preceding the attack. Tactical variations mainly involved local counterattacks by the defenders and different defense organizations.

4. SELECTED SIMULATION RESULTS

With a view to testing the DE-hypothesis, we were primarily interested in two questions:

(1) Do reactive defenses improve the direction in which the initial forward defense battle is moving?

(2) What operational depth is required for the various area defenses in order to attrite an identical number of enemy forces?

With regard to the first question we analysed the terminal states of the opponents and determined the *relative force value ratio (RFVR)* and the *relative loss exchange ratio (RLER)* at the end of the battles:

RFVR = Relative Value of Blue : Relative Value of Red

RLER = Relative Losses of Red : Relative Losses of Blue .

The relative values and losses are measured in terms of the respective module's relative investment cost saved respectively lost (including ammunition spent and destroyed by the enemy). This relative (to the initial value) measurement provides a direct indication of the situation development (>1 in favour of Blue; <1 in favour of Red).

As an example, Fig. 7a shows the RFVR-values for each of the 10 reactive defense modules from a test in a partly covered rolling hill terrain under good visibility conditions involving one Soviet motor rifle regiment (standard scenario). The test results are plotted over the respective module's direct fire weapon density. They support the old military truism that the effectiveness of a defense increases monotonically as the number of weapons available to the defender increases. For weapon densities ≥ 1 the relationship between effectiveness (RFVR) and weapon density is linear, an indication that none of the options are 'over-equipped' in the sense of diminishing (effectiveness) returns on weapon density. H (Austrian AD) falls outside the general pattern because its equipment does not include any ATGW.

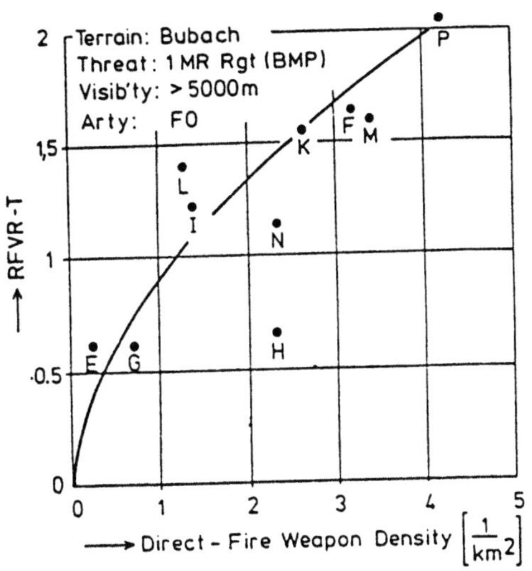

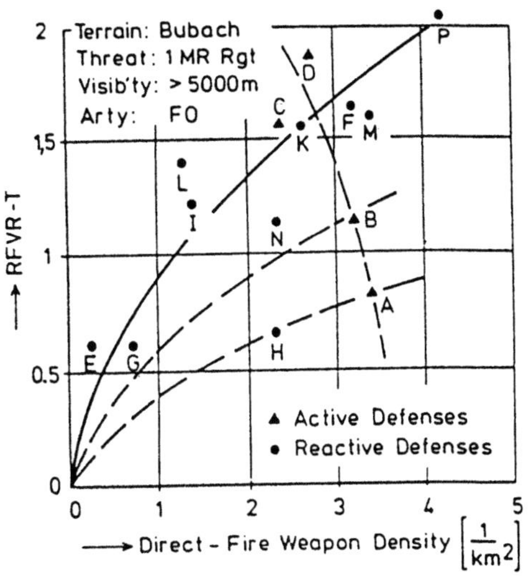

Relative Force Value Ratio (RFVR)
as a Function of the Direct Fire Weapon Density

Fig. 7a: Reactive Defense Options

Fig. 7b: Reactive and Active Defense Options

Fig. 7b shows the same results for both the reactive and active defenses. It is interesting to note that, with regard to the return-on-investment characteristics, the active options A and B obviously do not belong to the set of options of 'contemporary' technology and/or efficient tactics to which most reactive options belong. Option A could be of the same set as option H which, being deprived of modern ATGWs, had turned out to be among the least (cost-) effective of the reactive defense options under standard scenario conditions. Option B might be attributable to an intermediate set that also includes the continuous fire barrier option N, the latter not for reasons of inferior technology but because of its very one-sided structure and inflexible tactics. Therefore, the proposed evolution of the active defense forces toward option D can be interpreted as what it is meant to be: the attempt to incorporate modern contemporary weapons technology into the existing force structure. It is for this reason that the evaluation of the comparative effectiveness of reactive defense options should be based on the active defense options C and D. In some cases, both are capable to attrite up to three consecutively attacking MR regiments within an operational depth of less than 5 km before reaching their breakpoints. Of the reactive modules only P has a similar capability. All others require considerably more operational depth (see Fig. 8).

For the same (standard) scenario as in Fig. 7, Fig. 9 shows the relative offense/defense loss exchange ratio RLER for all active and reactive modules over their relative (to option E) investment cost. Since it dominates all other active defense options in terms of the RLER to be obtained for the (monetary) investment, option D may be considered to represent a point on their so-called *'efficient frontier'*. Being the set of options that are not dominated, the efficient frontier is also known as the 'Pareto optimal set'. There exists no active defense option which would, for a given amount of capital investment, yield a higher RLER than the (hypothetical) options on the efficient frontier. However, we notice that this efficient frontier is dominated by all but two of the reactive defense options. Due to their rather one-sided equipment structure, these two options are extremely sensitive toward visibility degradations and of little tactical flexibility.

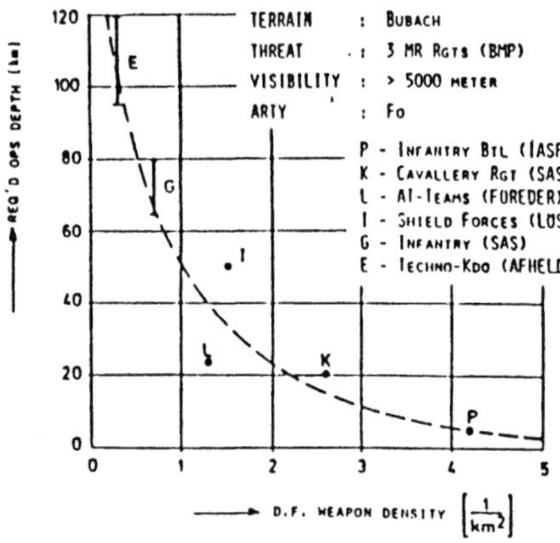

Fig. 8: Operational depth required for the attrition of three consecutively attacking Soviet MR regiments

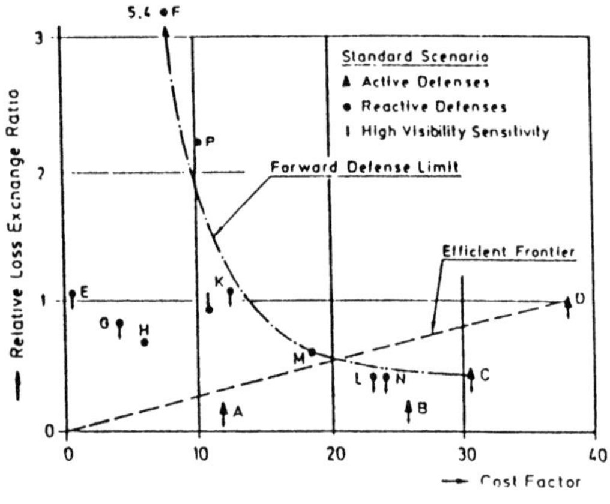

Fig. 9: Offense/Defense Loss Exchange Ratio versus the Relative Investment Cost of Btl-size defense modules

Based on the simulations so far and subject to the results of further experiments designed to test the threat and terrain sensitivity of the options, one may consider the defense efficiency hypothesis as not having been falsified, if not validated, at least in the economic terms of capital investment. However, based upon some preliminary estimates of the personnel losses to be expected for the various options, it seems very likely that the active defenses would dominate several reactive options, in particular those of the SAD category. For this reason, it is strongly recommended that empirical models be developed for the estimation of permanent and temporary personnel losses.

Strictly on the basis of economic considerations, the results also support the old military wisdom that a defense may be practised the more efficiently, the more operational depth a defender has available. This is evident when one compares, for the reactive options E, G, I, and K, the ratio of the RLER to the investment cost obtained from Fig. 9 and the required operational depth depicted in Fig. 8. We note that for both of these parameters the value sequence results as E > G > I ≥ K[8], and as a corollary, that there is a limit to the pursuit of efficiency, depending upon the available operational depth.

For example, let us assume that a fair chance for a successful forward defense were given if we had the capability to repulse, at some probability, the initial assault of two consecutively attacking Soviet motor rifle regiments at essentially no loss of terrain (i.e., less than 5 km). In that case the options F, P, M, and C would be members of the set defining the *forward defense limit* (see Fig. 9). If the forward defense criteria would be relaxed (e.g., by reducing the probability and/or the number of regimental attackers to be repulsed), this limit would shift to the left. In any case, only reactive defense options located in the sector 'north' of the efficient frontier and 'east' of the forward defense limit (including these bounds) could be considered as militarily and economically viable candidates for the design of a reactive defense component that is to supplement and, in the long term, even partially replace the traditional active defenses.

5. ON THE IMPLEMENTATION OF REACTIVE DEFENSES

The transition process from today's all active defenses to an ever more reactive defense can be characterized by a 'degree of defensivity' that is indicative of the relative size of the force restructuring effort toward a

---

[8] However, if in addition to the military capital investments the defender losses would also include the damage to the civilian infrastructure, the value sequence of RLER would presumably be reversed. Since approximately 25-30% of West Germany's economic infrastructure is located within a belt of 100 km west of the demarcation line, option E's extended RLER might indeed not be far from zero.

more reactive posture. Fig. 10 shows an illustration of the effects that the degrees ρ_X and ρ_Y of conversion of active land force units into reactive ones should have on the overall defense capability of side X (NATO)[9]. This overall defense capability E_X can be thought of as the capability of maintaining and restoring NATO's territorial *status quo ante*.

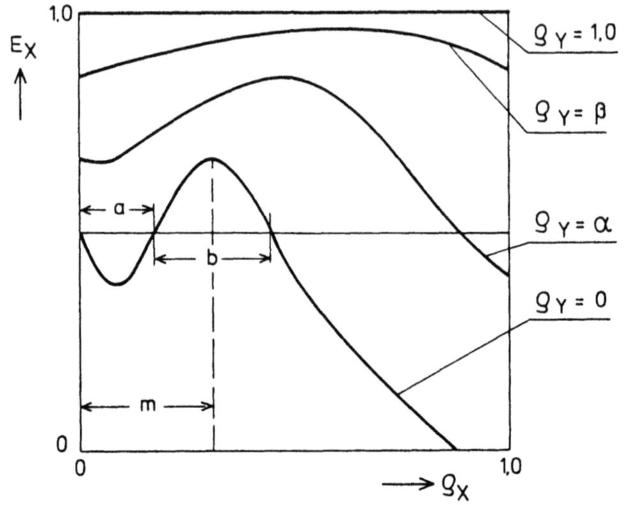

Fig. 10: Relative Defense Capability E_X of side X as a function of its degree of defensivity ρ_X for given degrees of defensivity ρ_Y of the opposing side Y $(0 \leq \rho_X, \rho_Y \leq 1; 0 < \alpha < \beta < 1)$.

Thus, as long as the Soviets maintain their present force structure and doctrine, their degree of defensivity is zero. Therefore, NATO must not extend its restructuring effort beyond a degree that makes it impossible to re-establish its territorial integrity. But it also must not be implemented to a degree too low for an effective operational exploitation of the superior defense advantage provided by properly designed reactive defense modules. This case is symbolized by the curve $\rho_Y=0$. The state $\rho_X=0$, $\rho_Y=0$ corresponds to today's situation in which the land forces of

[9] In order to validate these presumed effects, simulation experiments need to be performed on a higher level which permit to also test the operational implications of reactive defenses such as, for example, interfacing their operations with those of the active defense acting as operational reserves. Thus, the tactical-level BASIS experiments discussed above must be considered as the first step taken to determine whether the higher-level experiments (e.g., corps) would make sense at all.

both sides have the technical and tactical capability for defensive and offensive operations[10]. As side X becomes more defensive ($\rho_X > 0$), its overall defense capability E_X decreases to a certain minimum value to rise again and eventually exceeding the initial value at $\rho_X = a$. It reaches a maximum value at $\rho_X = m$ and falls below the initial value for $\rho_X > a+b$ when the active forces retained become too few to be able to regain lost territory through counter-attacks.

For $\rho_Y > 0$, the width a of the sector of initial defense capability deterioration diminishes gradually as the force structure of the opponent Y becomes more defensive ($\rho_Y \rightarrow 1$). Similarly, the width b of the sector with a positive defensivity pay-off grows. For $\rho_Y = 1.0$, the values of ρ_X would be immaterial to the defense capability E_X of X because Y is technically and operationally incapable of an attack of X.

Were Fig. 10 a fair description of reality, beginning an implementation of more defense-oriented force structures unilaterally would involve marginal security risks only, especially if the sector b is not too small and appropriate steps are taken to maintain the original defense capability during the process of restructuring the military forces. For example, side X might start the process at $\rho_X = 0$, $\rho_Y = 0$ by restructuring its force so that $a < \rho_X < a+b$, preferably $\rho_X = m$. Only if the opposing side Y would respond by also assuming a more defense-oriented posture would side X proceed in-

---

10) This is not to say that this author believes that NATO now has any capability whatsoever to sustain an operational offensive into Eastern European territory (invasion). However, it is doubtful whether the Soviets can be convinced that NATO's increasing land force mobility is only meant to off-set its numerical inferiority in a defensive battle, especially if they should come to the conclusion that this would be an inefficient way for NATO to prepare for such a battle. A rather unstable situation might exist if they should, irrespective of the limited logistic capabilities, perceive NATO's technical and tactical land-force parameters as being characteristic for an offensive force. HUBER (1983) forwards the thesis that imbalanced military forces which are perceived as being offensive in nature by the opposing sides represent a highly unstable situation. This is because the stronger party must assume that the inferior party, in order to preserve her chances for victory, will attack preemptively. That, in turn, makes the stronger party attempt to forego the assumed preemption by a preemptive attack of her own. It is for this reason that HUNTINGTON's proposal of 1984 is considered to be extremely detrimental to crisis stability.

crementally to a higher degree of defensivity $\rho_X > m$. After a series of moves and reciprocal moves, such a process could converge toward the state $\rho_X = 1$, $\rho_Y = 1$ when neither side has any capability left for invasions into the other side's territory.

In order to avoid the increased security risk for $0 < \rho_X < a$, X could pursue a restructuring strategy as illustrated schematically in Fig. 11. For example,

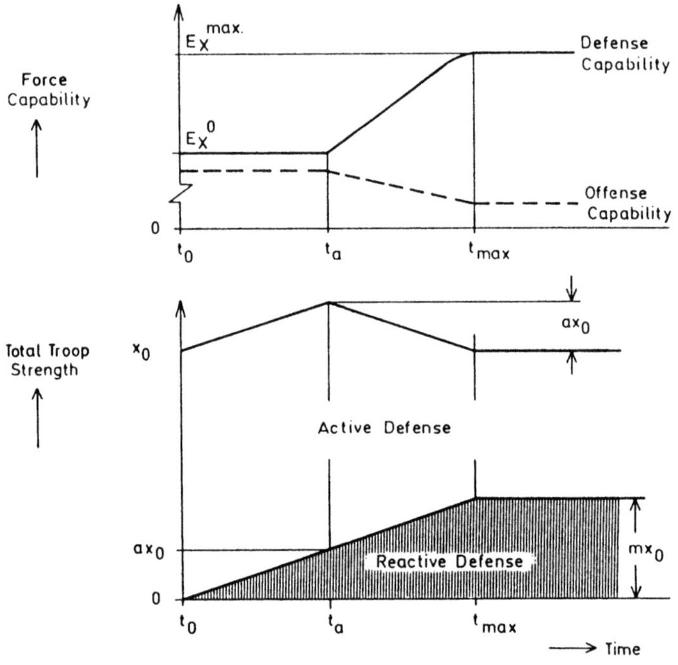

Fig. 11: Introduction of Reactive Defense Modules into an Active Defense Force: In order to maintain the original defense capability E_X^O, reactive defense elements are added until they reach a strength ax_O at ρ_X=a when the overall defense capability begins to rise at time t_a. Only then will active defense elements be converted into reactive ones and phased out until the force reaches its maximum capability E_X^{max} for ρ_X=m.

the structural changes might consist in a limited conversion of *active defense* forces into *reactive* ones. However, the existing active defenses are maintained at their initial level x_0 while reactive defenses are added until they reach the strength ax_0 at ρ_X=a when the overall defense capability E_X begins to increase at time t_a. Only then would active defense units be partly converted and partly phased out so that, at time t_{max}, the force mix corresponds to the maximum defense capability value E_X^{max} for $\rho_X = m$. In our example, ρ_X might indicate the relative size of the reactive defense forces. At no time would the original force level x_0 be exceeded by more than ax_0 of strictly defensive units incapable of operational offense. The offensive capability of X would initially remain at its original level and begin to decrease at time t_a, i.e., at no point in time is Y's security affected by the restructuring efforts of X. Thus, if accompanied by appropriate measures[11], the temporary increase of X's force levels should be acceptable to Y.

6. PRELIMINARY CONCLUSIONS

Based on the results of the analyses discussed above and subject to further simulation experiments, in particular also on higher operational levels, the following preliminary conclusions may be reached:

1) With due regard to the initial conditions underlying our experiments to date, properly designed reactive defenses can be expected to exploit the inherent defense advantage more efficiently than active ones.

2) Thus, if sufficient preparation time is available to the defender, the land forces of the opposing sides may be gradually restructured, on a reciprocal basis, toward ever more reactive postures without any impairment of mutual security[12]. On the contrary, since both sides would gradually give up whatever offensive capabilities they have, crisis and arms race stability would be enhanced.

3) Under certain conditions, a limited incorporation of properly designed reactive defenses into NATO's existing force structure might contribute to a significant improvement of NATO's forward defense at acceptable cost and even without having to rely on 'emerging technologies', the operational performance of which tends to be overestimated, especially

---

[11] For example, the introduction of the additional reactive forces could be accompanied by a (gradual) redeployment of the active defense units to areas behind designated lines further back.

[12] Whatever active defenses are retained in a force at any stage during the transition period, their relation to the reactive defenses would become one of operational reserves deployed further back. Therefore, the operational capability for mounting surprise or short warning attacks would necessarily diminish the more the less active forces are available to the attacker.

with regard to enemy adaptability and the demands of a battlefield environment (see HUBER and HOFMANN (1984), pp. 206-207).

4) For this reason, NATO may well initiate restructuring of its land forces as a first step in a longer-term process that the West might propose as a condition to accepting the Gorbachev proposal (of January 1986) on the abolition of weapons of mass destruction before the end of this century. Such a counter-proposal extending Gorbachev's vision to include the conventional arena should help the West to regain the political initiative. In case the Soviets accept, the Western goal of improving crisis and arms race stability would be achieved. If they reject it, they have to accept the burden of adverse public opinion that the West is now carrying.

REFERENCES

Afheldt, H. (1983): Defensive Verteidigung in Europa. Hamburg

Avenhaus, R., Fichtner, J., Huber, R.K. (1983): Conventional Force Equilibria - Some Arms Control Implications of Analytical Combat Models. Workshop on Supplemental Ways for Improving International Stability. IFAC-IIASA. Laxenburg, Sept. 1983, pp. 205-211

Baginski, E. (1983): Die Panzerabwehr der Kampftruppen. Wehrtechnik 8/83, pp. 18-25

Bahr, J. (1981): Gedanken zur Verteidigung der gepanzerten Kampftruppen. Kampftruppen/Kampftruppenunterstützungstruppen 3/31, pp. 105-110

Bundy, M., Kennan, F.G., McNamara, R., Smith, G. (1982): Nuclear Weapons and the Atlantic Alliance. Foreign Affairs 7 (1982), pp. 753-768

Füreder, G. (1983): Non-Nuclear Defense of Europe: Example Germany, Part I and II. Working Paper

Gerber, J. (1984): Fordert die Wirtschaftlichkeit eine neue Struktur des Heeres? Heere International, Band 3, Herford, pp. 39-52

Gerber, J. (1984): Bundeswehr im Atlantischen Bündnis, Abschnitt 10: Analytischer Rückblick und prognostischer Ausblick. Regensburg

Greiner, D. et al. (1978): Die gepanzerten Kampftruppen und Kampftruppenunterstützungstruppen im Heeresmodell 4. Kampftruppen/Kampftruppenunterstützungstruppen 1/78, pp. 8-27

Hannig, N. (1981): Die Verteidigung Westeuropas mit konventionellen Feuersperren. Internationale Wehrrevue 11 (1981), pp. 1439-1443

Hannig, N. (1984): Abschreckung durch konventionelle Waffen: Das David-Goliath Prinzip. Berlin

Hartung, H.-J. (1978): Sowjetische Grundsätze für die Gefechtsgliederung von Panzern im Angriff. Kampftruppen/Kampftruppenunterstützungstruppen 4/1978, pp. 174-177 and 5/1978, pp. 217-220

Hochauer, G. (1979): Raumverteidigung und Landwehrkonzept. Österreichische Militärische Zeitschrift, Heft 1/1979, pp. 11-19

Hofmann, H.W., Huber, R.K., Steiger, K. (1986): On Reactive Defense Options - A Comparative Systems Analysis of Alternatives for the Initial Defense against the First Strategic Echelon of the Warsaw Pact in Central Europe. Modeling and Analysis of Conventional Defense in Europe (R.K. Huber, Ed.), New York and London, pp. 97-100

Hofmann, H.W. et al. (1984): BASIS - Ein Gefechtssimulationsmodell auf Btl/Rgt-Ebene, Band 1: Beschreibung des Gefechtsmodells. Bericht 8401, Institut für Angewandte Systemforschung und Operations Research, Fachbereich Informatik, Hochschule der Bundeswehr München

Huber, R.K. (1983): Some Hypotheses regarding the Effect of the Structures of Antagonistic Military Forces on the Stability in a Bipolar World. Working Paper, Washington, D.C., May 1983

Huber, R.K., Hofmann, H.W. (1984): Gradual Defensivity - An Approach to a Stable Conventional Force Equilibrium in Europe? Operational Research '84 (J.P. Bran, Ed.). Amsterdam - New York - Oxford, pp. 197-211

Huntington, S.P. (1984): Conventional Deterrence and Conventional Retaliation in Europe. International Security, Vol. 8, No. 3, pp. 33-56

Karber, P.A. (1983): To Lose an Arms Race: The Competition in Conventional Forces Deployed in Central Europe 1965-1980. In: The Soviet Asset - Military Power in the Competition over Europe (U. Nerlich, Ed.). Cambridge, MA, pp. 31-87

Kreker, H.-J. (1983): Hinter den Panzern steht die Artillerie. Kampftruppen/Kampftruppenunterstützungstruppen 1/83, pp. 29-31

Koch, G. (1983): Panzergrenadiere 90. Truppenpraxis 12/83, pp. 880-885

Koch, G. (1984): Konzeptionelle Vorstellungen für die gepanzerten Kampftruppen der 90er Jahre. Europäische Wehrkunde/WWR 2/84, pp. 90-94

Löser, J. (1980): Vorneverteidigung der Bundesrepublik Deutschland. Österreichische Militärische Zeitschrift, Heft 2/1980, pp. 116-123

Löser, J. (1982): Weder Rot noch Tot - Eine sicherheitspolitische Alternative, München 1982

Marolz, J. (1978): Raumverteidigung und Mechanisierung. Österreichische Militärische Zeitschrift, Heft 5/1978; pp. 374-379

Marti, P. (1979): Schweizer Armee 80. Frauenfeld

Studiengruppe Alternative Sicherheitspolitik (1984): Strukturwandel der Verteidigung - Entwürfe für eine konsequente Defensive. Opladen, pp. 156-173

Senn, H. (1979): Kann die Armee ihren Auftrag erfüllen? In: Beilage zur Allgemeinen Schweizerischen Militärzeitschrift Nr. 3/1979, pp. 1-14

The American Academy of Arts and Sciences (1983 and 1985): Strengthening Conventional Defense in Europe. New York

Wiener, F. (1977): Das sowjetische MotSchützenregiment BMP. Truppendienst 5/1977, pp. 339-341

DEFENSE EXPENDITURE DYNAMICS BETWEEN TWO POTENTIAL OPPONENTS

H. Pastijn and W. Struys
Royal Military Academy, Brussels, Belgium

An arms race model should, in the first place, provide an insight into the mutual behaviour of two potential opponents - in our case NATO and the Warsaw Treaty Organization - which we try to describe and explain. Our model meets the keep-it-simple principle, knowing that "with 4 parameters you can fit an elephant and with 8 you can make him wiggle his tail" ; but despite its simplicity, our aim is to improve the understanding of the observed real life phenomenon. This requires that every term in the various equations have a meaningful social, economic and political definition. More particular emphasis should be on the question whether unilateral measures in certain sets of circumstances would make it possible to attain certain equilibrium points. In this respect, we try to give some elements of answer to the questions asked by AVENHAUS and FICHTNER [1].

1. The basic assumptions of the model.

The pioneer in mathematical theory of arms races is L.F. RICHARDSON [14]. He proposed to formalize the complex issues of competitive military expenditure into a simple mathematical model by reducing this topic into the following assumptions :

a. In an armament race between two powers, each of them is attempting to increase its armament proportionally to the size of the armament of the other.

b. There is an economical constraint on armament that tends to reduce the growth rate of armament by an amount proportional to the size of the existing forces.

NATO ASI Series, Vol. F 26
Modelling and Analysis in Arms Control
Edited by R. Avenhaus et al.

c. A nation is building up an armed force, by ambition, grievances and hostilities, even without threat from any potential opponent.

However formally described by the same type of equations, the interactions of the armament levels in RICHARDSON's model can be substituted by the expenditure dynamics [12].

In mathematical terms, a two-bloc model can thus be written as follows :

$$\begin{cases} \dfrac{dx}{dt} = ky - ax + g & (1) \\[2em] \dfrac{dy}{dt} = mx - by + h & (2) \end{cases}$$

all parameters are supposed to be positive when the three assumptions are verified.

In the context of the NATO - Warsaw Pact dynamics, equation (1) denotes the increase of the defense expenditure level over time for NATO, while equation (2) is denoting the same for WTO. The variables x and y represent the absolute levels of defense expenditure while their derivatives are the corresponding rates of increase. According to assumption (a), the defense coefficients k and m are the degree to which a nation is forced by the opponent's defense effort to increase its own military expenditure. The parameters a and b are fatigue or expense coefficients and show the extent to which the level of a nation's military expenditures inhibits any further increase in spending ; g and h are the grievance terms, measuring the natural tendency of a nation to build up or decrease its military expenditure level when the opponent achieves total disarmament.

2. The overall data collecting problems.

2.1. Problems of data reliability.

Quantitative studies in this area founder on the basic inadequacy of the available data, since they are unreliable in many countries [2]. Another obstacle is the limited number of data available. It should be stated that since defense expenditures are published annually, the number of available observations is too small to test a model of a certain complexity and to capture with sufficient rigor the dynamics of an arms race. As a consequence, our analytical approach will hardly be in the position to provide accurate quantitative predictions of military expenditure. Let us, however, keep in mind that our first aim is to describe, to understand and to explain.

The most valuable information in defense matters is provided by aggregates such as the national defense budgets or expenditures. However, the methods used in measuring and comparing military expenditure have a significant influence on the behaviour of our model. It is appropriate, therefore, to investigate the utility and the representativity of the available data in order to interpret them with due caution.

Different indicators can be used in order to have an idea of the defense capability of a nation or an alliance. They generally belong to two main categories :

- qualitative indicators, which "qualify" the operational value of the armed forces ; they are impossible to quantify and to integrate in a mathematical model ;

- quantitative indicators, such as means devoted to the military, stated in terms of manpower, weapon systems, or available resources, expressed in financial terms.

For obvious reasons, only the latter are operational for our purpose. The aggregate figures for NATO member countries, being based on a common definition of defense expenditure to assess each nation's defense contribution, do not set particular conceptual problems, since we do not have to take into account any disparity of national defense budgets. Unfortunately, the same remark cannot be applied to the Warsaw Pact, where military spending is derived from national definitions. This problem is especially hard to solve in the case of the Soviet Union.

It should also be stated that, as well for NATO as for WTO, the mere defense expenditure figures cannot be regarded as a perfect estimate of the arms race or of the defense burden in economic terms, since they do not give an accurate idea of the so-called opportunity costs. This concept in economics stems from the fundamental postulate that resources are scarce ; as a consequence, the use of resources in one activity has a "cost" in terms of output they might have produced in some other activity. Stated military expenditure cannot be an adequate mesure of opportunity costs, since national economies do not offer, neither on a quantitative nor on a qualitative basis, exactly the same alternatives for resources allocation.

2.2. Time series problems.

This RICHARDSON-type model is deterministic and does not permit forecasting in a probabilistic way. The equations state that a precise, inevitable relationship exists between increases in military spending and their assumed causes. However, value aggregates are composed of price and quantity variables. Changes over time thus could be the result of either of them. The best way to isolate a quantitative evolution is to express values in constant prices, with the help of price indices. Unfortunately, appropriate indices do not exist for military goods and services ; most authors use national accounts price indices, or any composite index instead. This method is not satisfactory, since military prices are far from following the other price trends. As a matter of fact, only personnel costs can be deflated in a satisfactory way by the known price indices. The high degree of specialization of operating methods, as well as the extremely sophisticated technology involved in defense capital goods cannot but make the classic deflators obsolete. Furthermore, the fact that the military produces no tangible output and uses equipment that frequently has no civilian counterpart, results in an even more arbitrary deflation procedure, which provides "real" expenditure series without any clear conceptual meaning [7][15]. Moreover, even if we had a military price index at our disposal, we could not be sure that the prices of the military goods would fully reflect their real value in military capacity terms. This restriction is even more valid for the opportunity costs : since no attempt has resulted in a way to assess them on both sides, the use of military indices could lead us to even more inaccurate comparisons [15].

Changes over time however are not limited to changes in the quantities and prices of the product. Many goods and services are subject to quality changes which modify their physical characteristics. Typical military goods such as major weapon systems are more subject to this phenomenon than civil products. It is very difficult, not to say impossible, to evaluate the size of any numerical adjustment needed when there is a modification in the quality of the military effort.

2.3. International comparison problems.

Comparison problems become worse when several countries are involved. Little successful work has been done to establish a framework for intercountry comparisons of defense expenditures, except in the case of nations with similar economic structures and macro-economic aggregates. Key comparative data as defense expenditures per capita or expressed as a percentage of gross domestic or of national products, or military budgets as a percentage of government expenditure, could assumably lead to satisfactory evaluations between most of the NATO member countries. They represent nevertheless an often unsatisfactory measure for a great amount of underlying social, demographic, economic and political factors as well as for differences in the scope of the public sector, that make even similar economies so different.

The main problem, however, belongs to the monetary. International comparisons are easily made with monetary aggregates converted to a common currency ; defense expenditures comparisons, like most others, are based on U.S. dollar exchange rates. However, many factors do affect the validity of an exchange rate whose imprecision results from the official value of one currency in terms of another, based on the international exchange of goods, services and capital. For most countries, export and import only represent a small fraction of the total output or expenditure. Exchange rates thus are only a very imperfect guess of what they would be if all goods were taken into account. Moreover, price relations between goods and services, which do not participate in international trade, are very different from the official exchange rates : these are not an accurate reflection of the internal purchasing power of the respective currencies, since they do not give an accurate idea of the actual volumes of goods and services produced and consumed in different countries. Consequently, it is indispensable to eliminate the differences in price levels : this can be achieved by using <u>purchasing power parities</u>. Unfortunately, they do not exist for the Warsaw Pact countries. Anyway, price differencies at any point in time are not the same for all commodities, so there exists potentially for any year a whole family of specific purchasing power parities [7], which brings us back to a similar problem as that of a specific military price index.

The breakdown of macro-economic aggregates into a classification where specific military goods and services would be related to their prices and purchasing power parities, is not possible with the existing methods and the available data.

2.4. Specific WTO and Soviet Union problems.

Even if not perfect, comparisons between NATO countries are relatively satisfactory. More and new problems arise when one has to deal with data from the Warsaw Pact countries. The case of the Soviet Union is especially explicit in this respect [3][6]. The difficulty of correctly estimating Soviet defense expenditure stems from two factors :

(a) The considerable uncertainty over what is covered by the official military budget, which only covers the operating and military construction costs of the armed forces and excludes of other defense expenditures, such as military R&D, which is included in other budgets.

(b) The completely different Soviet pricing practices. Macro-economic data cannot be correctly derived without international price comparisons tailored to each purpose. Soviet pricing practices are quite different from those in the West. Objectives are set in real terms with no requirement for money prices to coincide with the real costs of goods and services. As a result of this, the rouble cost of the defense effort does not reflect the real cost of any alternative production ; even a rouble value of defense expressed as a percentage of Gross Domestic Product does not reflect the true burden. If roubles are then converted into dollars, the difficulties are compounded, because the official exchange rates are inadequate.

2.5. The final choice of the data.

Since our aim is to compare two coalitions whose political, economical and military structures are fundamentally different, we had to use data which avoid as much as possible errors or misinterpretations, but which still allow mutual comparisons. With respect to this double constraint and taking into consideration that although it is better to take into account real rather than nominal expenditure for an accurate evaluation of the arms race between two military alliances, the unavailability of "realistic real" figures has led us to base our figures on homogeneous data belonging to a period during which the same collecting methods have been used [17].

3. The validation of the model.

The mathematical implications of the equations must correspond to reality. The model must be examined for its validation. A measure of this is how well the response of the model fits the real world observations.

For the estimation of the parameters of the model, we used the method of MARQUARDT-LEVENBERG which is appropriate for non linear parameter estimations ([9][11]). This iterative algorithm needs a first guess of the parameter values.

An attempt to obtain good first guesses of these parameters with multiple regression between successive Δx (resp. Δy) versus the mean levels of x and y at the same instant, on the basis of crude data [12] is disappointing, since values of the FISHER ratio (mean squares attributable to regression on mean squared deviations from regression) for degrees of freedom (2,7), are in the range of [1.2,1.6] and the 90 % level of F(2,7) is 3.26.

We therefore smoothen the crude data by a stepwise polynomial regression of the levels of expenditure as a function of time, yielding 5th degree curves. These polynomials, as well as their first derivatives are plotted (See Figure 1). With these smoothened data given by the ordinates of the 5th degree polynomials and with the first derivative as a local measure of the increase rate of the expenditures, we investigated multiple regressions between increase rate and level of variables. This time we find rather significant regressions. The F-scores are respectively for equations (1) and (2) : 3.28 and 3.6 (notice $F_{.90}$ (2,8) = 3.11) for the period 1965-1975.

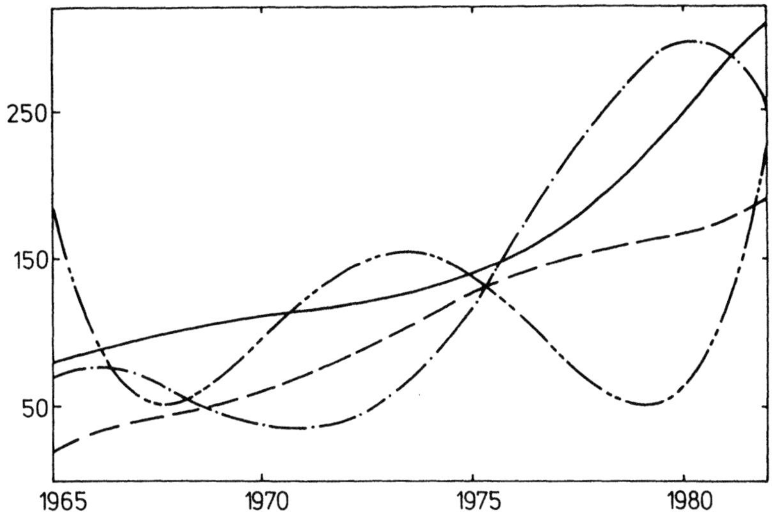

Fig. 1: Smoothened real defense expenditure data in current US $ billion for NATO (——) and Warsaw Pact (---). The first derivatives of the defense expenditures are also given for both NATO (-····-) and Warsaw Pact (-······-).

We stress the fact that these regression procedures can only give a first guess of the parameter values, because no interaction between the two equations is taken into account by these regressions. For an alternative approach of the causality analysis in arms race modelling, we refer to [13], where difference equations are taken into account, introducing time lags. We feel that the poor quality and the low amount of data do not justify this method for our problem.

We observe also that a Box-and-Jenkins approach is not considered because of the limited amount of data.

With this initial guess the iterative MARQUARDT method converges to the following model fit for the period 1965-1975

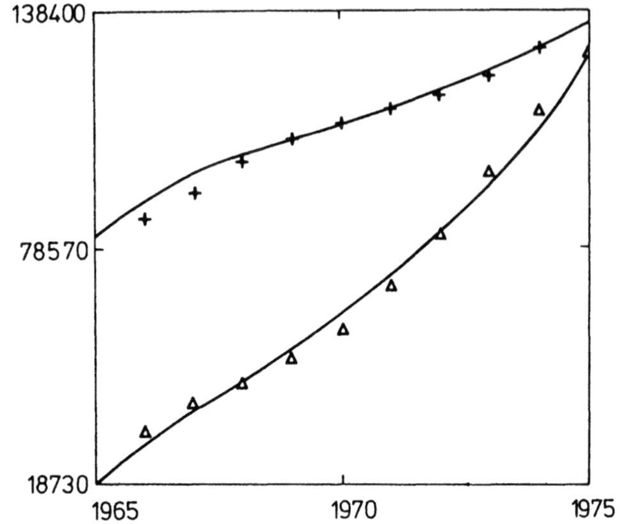

Fig. 2: Defense expenditures (in current US $ billion) of NATO (++++) and Warsaw Pact (ΔΔΔΔ) as resulting from an integration of equations (5) and (6).

$$\frac{dx}{dt} = (0.21)\ y + (-\ 0.36)\ x + 31334 \qquad (5)$$

$$\frac{dy}{dt} = (-\ 0.65)\ x + (0.38)\ y + 57067 \qquad (6)$$

For the period from 1965 to 1981, the model (1),(2) is fitting very poorly on the set of observed values, undoubtedly due to a lack of homogeneity between the sets of data before and after 1976, since most of the evaluating methods of the WTO defense expenditures have been changed, inducing a lack of permanency of the model [3][8].

4. Simulation results and interpretation.

Simulation by integration of the system of differential equations (5) and (6) is yielding the plotted results (See

Figure 2). The smoothened observed values are plotted on the same picture for comparison with the solid lines of the integration results.

When compared with RICHARDSON's initial assumptions about the sign of the coefficients in the model, we observe that NATO is behaving "normally" as to the signs of both its coefficients ("defense" and "fatigue"). Moreover, the Warsaw Pact is seeming to behave "abnormally" as to both :

- the sign of the fatigue coefficient seems to indicate that the Warsaw Pact, during the period 1965-1975, was eager to increase its military effort (negative expense coefficient b = - 0.38) because its existing expenditure level was stimulating its own expenditure growth rate ;

- the sign of the defense coefficient is indicating that the Warsaw Pact defense expenditure is backing down when it has the impression to be threatened by a high level of defense expenditure achieved by its potential opponent (negative defense coefficient m = - 0.65).

One could be attempted to explain the higher value of the so-called "grievance" term h in (6) according to g in (5) by the fact that the WTO military bureaucracy, together with a basic suspicious behaviour about traditional sea-powers like most of its potential opponents, imposes to provide a high level of minimal defense effort. One should however keep in mind our discussion about the reliability of the data, and consequently relativate this last interpretation.

Since our aim is neither to prove any apriorism nor to uphold preconceived favourable or unfavourable opinions, we should be conspicuous to the following caveat : even if our method is scientific and thus presents the highest possible rate of objectivity, the simulation results still are subject to misinterpretations. As the data we used are influenced as well by military as by political, economical and social realities, it should be useful to compare our interpretations with those of specialists in the other aspects of the arms race. In this respect, we can refer to D. HOLLOWAY's original publication [4] and its Dutch translation [5], in which an epilogue was added about the late developments of Soviet politics.

It is interesting to ascertain that our interpretations confirm some of HOLLOWAY's, which -incidentally- are not based upon quantitative methods.

Our conclusion about the Warsaw Pact not behaving accordingly to the RICHARDSON original model is confirmed by HOLLOWAY [4, p. 101].

The Soviet leaders thus do not let their political decision-making be determined by the behaviour of NATO. This explains also why - at least to a certain extent - the economic crisis does not affect the Warsaw Pact defense expenditure as it should [4, p. 102]. Since the military take a prominent part in the Soviet foreign policy, the financial aspect of their defense effort cannot but express this important constraint ; even détente is deemed to be the logical consequence of the growing Soviet overall - thus military - power. NATO, on the other hand, obviously does not grant the same role and importance to the military. As a result of this, international political and diplomatic efforts, together with the economic constraints, are the cause of the "normal" behaviour, from the viewpoint of RICHARDSON's model, of the NATO-equation.

The foregoing evidence however only gives proof to the fact that the Warsaw Pact does not react to the NATO-behaviour, and takes its own decisions in an autonomous way. But in this case, the coefficients b and m should be equivalent to zero ! How can we then explain our negative coefficients b and m ? HOLLOWAY provides a political explanation : pointing out that " There are elements of the action-reaction phenomenon (...) in the history of Soviet-American nuclear weapons competition, with the Soviet Union less innovative, and therefore more reactive, than the United States.", he finds it " (...) more difficult to trace the interaction for the later decisions than for the earlier ones, but the evidence is strong that interaction exists."[4, p. 178].

Our study tends to prove that these interactions find their expression in the overall Soviet defense expenditure, which represent about 90 percent of the WTO expenditure, for the period 1965-1975, but in the opposite way than what RICHARDSON suggested. We can thus conclude, together with HOLLOWAY, that " it is not helpful, therefore, to view Soviet policy as autistic, unresponsive to external stimuli." [4, p. 178].

5. Stability analysis.

What about the tendency of this system towards an equilibrium ? The theoretical equilibrium point of the model (5),(6) is located on the intersection of the loci $\frac{dx}{dt} = 0$ and $\frac{dy}{dt} = 0$ in the phase space (x,y). These are the two straight lines representing the equations

$$y = 1.714\, x - 149\,209.52 \qquad (7)$$

$$y = 1.711\, x - 150\,176.32 \qquad (8)$$

Since these straight lines are quasi parallel, and even coinciding, we should not expect to reach an equilibrium of this system in a finite time period. When we represent the trajectory of the point (x,y) from 1965 up to 1975, we remark that we never leave the quadrant where the increase rate of defense expenditure for both opponents is positive. It is also easy to show that this phenomenon is entirely in relation with the eigenvalue analysis of the matrix of coefficients of x and y in the system (5),(6). We can conclude that this system is obviously not tending towards a stable equilibrium, but is on a theoretically never ending linear drift parallel to the straight lines (7) and (8). If no drastic changes in basic attitudes of one or both partners are to be expected, no tendency towards a stable "statu quo" can ever be expected.

If we perform some more detailed sensitivity analysis on the hypothesis of an unilateral NATO behavioural change, our model (5),(6) reduces approximately to

$$\begin{cases} \dot{x} = - a.x + k.y + r.u_1 & (9) \\ \dot{y} = -pa.x + pk.y + pr.u_2 & (10) \end{cases}$$

where u_2 is slightly larger than u_1 and both constant,

with r, p, a and $k > 0$ and with $pk - a = 0.02$.

Assuming, for the purpose of simplicity, that $pk - a = 0$, we observe that the general solution of (9),(10) can be found easily :

$$\begin{cases} x = \frac{a.r}{2}.(u_2 - u_1).t^2 + (r.u_1 + k.y_0 - a.x_0).t + x_0 & (11) \\ y = \frac{a^2 r}{2k}.(u_2 - u_1).t^2 + \frac{a}{k}.(ru_2 + k.y_0 - a.x_0).t + y_0 & (12) \end{cases}$$

where x_0 and y_0 are the initial values.

From (11) and (12) we obtain the evolution of the difference between the two expenditure levels which could be considered as a measure of the "danger" :

$$\Delta = y - x = \frac{a.r}{2}.(\frac{a}{k} - 1).(u_2 - u_1).t^2$$

$$- [(u_1 - \frac{au_2}{k}).r + (1-\frac{a}{k}).(ky_0 - ax_0)].t$$

$$+ (y_0 - x_0) \qquad (13)$$

and consequently,

$$\dot{\Delta} = ar.(\frac{a}{k} - 1).(u_2 - u_1).t$$

$$- [(u_1 - \frac{au_2}{k}).r + (1-\frac{a}{k}).(ky_0 - ax_0)] \qquad (14)\ .$$

From (14), we conclude that

since r and $a > 0$, $\frac{a}{k} = \frac{.36}{.21} > 1$ and $u_2 > u_1$, there is

an instant t_1 for which Δ is an ever increasing function of time for all $t > t_1$.

From (13) we conclude that the coefficient of t^2 can increase drastically (and consequently increase international tension) when NATO reduces unilaterally its defense effort by increasing $|a|$ ("fatigue") or decreasing k ("defense") or decreasing u_1 ("grievance"), or any combination of some or all of these components of NATO policy.

From (9) and (10) we obtain the relation

$$\dot{y} \approx (1.81)\ \dot{x} + 353$$

This means that, even if $\dot{x} = 0$, the increase rate of the opponent is still positive because of his higher grievance.

When we assume $u_2 \approx u_1$ then

$$\Delta = (\frac{a}{k} - 1).(ru_1 + ky_0 - ax_0).t + (y_0 - x_0)$$

and since $\frac{a}{k} - 1 > 0$

Δ is decreasing if $ru_1 + ky_0 - ax_0 < 0$

otherwise

Δ is increasing if $ru_1 + ky_0 - ax_0 > 0$,

conditions which are strongly depending on the "initial" status (x_0, y_0) of the system. In our case of model (5),(6) we notice that Δ is increasing if $u_1 \approx u_2$.

6. Conclusion.

As RAPOPORT [13] stressed, the RICHARDSON model of two blocs is isolating an arbitrary couple of opponents out of the population of possible (and existing) coalitions. We are aware of this critique but we have the strong feeling, induced by our simulation results, that our actual choice constitutes a very relevant approximation of the studied cross-section of the global dynamics of arms race on world level.

Since our first aim was to describe, understand and explain, we feel that our approach provides objective evidence for some real-life events.

Nevertheless, the Soviet decision-making may not be explained only as a reaction to NATO initiatives. Even if their deep motivations are not always easy to identify, it should be emphasized that their political decisions always find their military expression in their defense expenditure, which we may consider as nothing less than the financial expression of a defense policy. In this respect, we consider that the military expenditure indeed plays the role of an explanatory variable of the Soviet action-reaction behaviour.

The stability analysis performed above shows that if no fundamental changes in the behaviour of the Warsaw Pact is to be expected for the decade 1975 - 1985 and later on, it would be particularly dangerous for NATO to decrease its own defense effort, consequently speeding up the growth rate of the Warsaw Pact defense expenditure.

ACKNOWLEDGMENT.

The authors wish to express their indebtedness to Professor J. CHARLES of the Royal Military Academy in Brussels for his most valuable comments which allowed them to improve the clarification of the results interpretation.

LITERATURE REFERENCES

[1] AVENHAUS, R. and FICHTNER, J., A Review of Richardson Models", in "Quantitative Assessment in Arms Control" (Mathematical Modeling and Simulation in the Analysis of Arms Control Problems), Ed. R. Avenhaus and R. K. HUBER, Plenum Press, New York - London, 1984.

[2] BUSCH, P.A., Mathematical Models of Arms Races, in RUSSETT, B., What Price Vigilance ? (Appendix), Yale University Press, London, 1970.

[3] DOENGES, B., Soviet Resource Allocation - Military versus Civilian, in The Soviet Economy after Brezhnev, NATO Colloquium, Economic Directorate, Brussels, April 11-13, 1984.

[4] HOLLOWAY, D., The Soviet Union and the arms race, Yale University Press, London, 1983.

[5] HOLLOWAY, D., De Sovjetunie en de bewapeningswedloop, Uitgeverij Jan Mets, Amsterdam, 1984.

[6] HOLZMAN, F.D., Soviet Military Spending : Assessing the Numbers Game, in International Security, Spring 1982.

[7] KRAVIS, I.B., Comparative Studies of National Incomes and Prices, in Journal of Economic Literature, Vol. XXII 4, N° 1, March 1984.

[8] LEE, W.T., The Estimation of Soviet Defense Expenditures 1955-1975 : An Unconventional Approach, New York, Praeger, 1977.

[9] LEVENBERG, K.A, Method for the solution of certain non-linear problems in least squares, Quart. Appl. Math. 2, pp. 164-168, 1944.

[10] MAJESKI, S.J., Arms Race Modeling, Causality analysis and model specification, The Journal of Conflict Resolution, Vol. 25 Nr 2, June 1981.

[11] MARQUARDT, D.W., An Algorithm for Least-Squares Estimation of Non- Linear Parameters, J. SIAM, Vol. 11, Nr 2, pp. 431-441, 1963.

[12] PASTIJN, H. and STRUYS, W., Modelling the Defense Expenditure Dynamics between two Potential Opponents, in Quantitative Defense Economics, Brussels, 1984.

[13] RAPOPORT, A., Fights, games and debates, University of Michigan Press, 1960.

[14] RICHARDSON, L.F., Arms and Insecurity - A Mathematical Study of the Causes and Origins of War, Atlantic Books, Stevens and Sons Ltd, London, 1960.

[15] STRUYS, W., Aspects économiques de la production de systèmes d'arme dans l'Europe des Neuf, Dissertation présentée en vue de l'obtention du grade de Docteur en Sciences Economiques, Université Libre de Bruxelles, 1977.

[16] STRUYS, W., Les dépenses de défense dans les pays du Marché Commun : analyse globale des déterminants et évaluation de la charge économique, in Cahiers Economiques de Bruxelles, N° 78, 1978.

[17] The Military Balance, Annual publications of The International Institute for Strategic Studies, London.

DETERRENCE AND INCOMPLETE INFORMATION
THE GAME THEORY APPROACH

Werner Güth
Staatswissenschaftliches Seminar
der Universität Köln

1. Introduction

Game theoretical studies of international military conflicts usually assume simple game structures, such as 2 x 2 - bimatrix games (cf. Brams, Davis and Straffin 1979, Brams and Davis 1984, Brams and Kilgour 1985a-d, and Brams 1985 for an excellent overview and introduction to the game theoretic approach). Such simple models inevitably neglect institutional aspects of real-life international armed conflicts. They still deserve attention, since they help to explain why no significant disarmament has occurred thus far.

There are however important questions which cannot be answered by models comprising only two countries with two strategies each. Why for instance in a world comprising many sovereign states are there only two antagonistic super-powers? Furthermore, this type of model ignores problems of setting up and maintaining international military alliances. Restricting analysis to only two strategies appears less harmful than assuming the existence of only two countries, since most analyses can easily be extended to cover more than two strategies, and even in day-to-day politics discussion is often limited to two alternatives.

Completeness of information is another assumption requiring more further consideration. States are assumed to have precise knowledge of their opponents' objectives, strategic options and information resources. In other words, given complete information, the players know everything about their opponents. In the present situation there are two opposing super-powers, the USA and the USSR. Completeness of information means that both countries have certain knowledge of whether the other merely

NATO ASI Series, Vol. F 26
Modelling and Analysis in Arms Control
Edited by R. Avenhaus et al.

wants to defend its own territory or is endeavouring to expand the area under its control. Neither of them can have any doubt regarding the other's type. In many countries, however, policy is determined by various competing groups whose relative strength and intentions are difficult to assess. Here, assuming complete information would mean neglecting significant uncertainties which exist in the real world and might strongly influence day-to-day political decision-making.

Models which include incomplete information, i.e. uncertainties about the types of other players are not necessarily complex. We shall illustrate this with 2 x 2 - bimatrix games with incomplete information whose complete information analogues have already been analysed in the literature on international armed conflicts.

We then discuss an extensive game with incomplete information which attempts to model the recent debate on nuclear deterrence and the deployment of additional nuclear missiles in Western Europe. In this extensive game the decision process is sequential and not static, as in normal form games. (Dynamic analyses of situations based on 2 x 2 - bimatrix games can be found in Brams and Hessel 1984, as well as Brams and Kilgour 1985b.)

In all the examples incomplete information may be inconsistent, i.e. players need not revise their subjective probabilities until they can be shown as conditional probabilities of the same chance move. The inconsistent case of incomplete information gives much more freedom in modelling international armed conflicts (cf. Güth 1985, for a more detailed and formal description of consistent and inconsistent incomplete information.)

2. 2 x 2 - Bimatrix Games With Incomplete Information

Incomplete information can be described as uncertainty regarding the rules of the game, i.e. a player might not know for sure which strategies are available to his opponents, on what knowledge their decisions are based and how they evaluate possible outcomes of the game. These uncertainties can all be remodelled as uncertainties regarding the opponents' payoff functions (Harsanyi 1968). Assume for instance that one country is uncertain as to whether another country has the equipment to produce nuclear weapons. To capture the inability to produce nuclear weapons one will allow all types to produce them, except that one type will produce them only at prohibitively high cost, thus ensuring that this type will never choose this option. Thus different types of player can be represented by different payoff functions.

Although games with incomplete information are often mentioned, games which are actually solved are always those with complete information. This is done by transforming the incomplete information game into a strategically equivalent game with complete information by introducing a fictitious intial chance move which determines the types of players (Harsanyi 1968). By informing players of their own types and less fully of the types of the others which correspond to their subjective beliefs, uncertainties concerning the types of others are adequately shown. In other words, incomplete information has been transformed into stochastic uncertainty by including a fictitious chance move.

If at least two types of one opponent behave differently, one may expect that this opponent is using a mixed strategy. Incomplete information together with type-differentiating equilibria can therefore substitute for mixed strategy equilibria, which appear rather unlikely in international armed conflicts. Studies based on the use of mixed strategies (e.g. Brams 1984, and Brams and Kilgour 1985a) could therefore be remodelled as games with incomplete information, the solution of which does not require mixed strategies.

2.1 Is Disarmament Impossible Where There Is Uncertainty About The Opponent's Type ?

Countries 1 and 2 can both choose between d (disarmament) and $\bar{d}$ (no disarmament). The payoffs for the possible strategy vectors are shown in the following bimatrix:

	d	$\bar{d}$
d	c_1 c_2	d_1 1
$\bar{d}$	1 d_2	0 * 0

Figure 1: 2 x 2 - 'prisoner's dilemma' games with $1 > c_i > 0 > d_i$ for $i = 1$ and 2

The payoff of player 1 (2) choosing rows (columns) is given in the upper left (lower right) corner for all strategy vectors. Games of this type are often considered typical paradigms of international armed conflicts (cf. for instance, Brams, Davis and Straffin 1979, Brams 1985, Brams and Kilgour 1985c). Since utilities are only determined up to affine transformations, there is no loss of generality in assuming that both players evaluate a military advantage by 1 and the status quo $(\bar{d},\bar{d})$ by 0. The game has a unique equilibrium point $(\bar{d},\bar{d})$ in dominant strategies which is payoff dominated by (d,d). In Figure 1 equilibrium behavior is indicated by '*'.

Since $1 > c_i$, both players are assumed to prefer a military advantage to mutual disarmament (d,d), i.e. both countries are of an aggressive type. Politicians however, at least in their public statements, usually declare that their army's only purpose is to protect the country from foreign aggression. If this is taken seriously, there is no reason why anyone should strive for military superiority. A country i which is merely trying to protect itself should therefore evaluate a military advantage by $1-\varepsilon_i$ instead of by 1 where $c_i + \varepsilon_i > 1$, i.e. mutual disarmament is better than a military advantage.

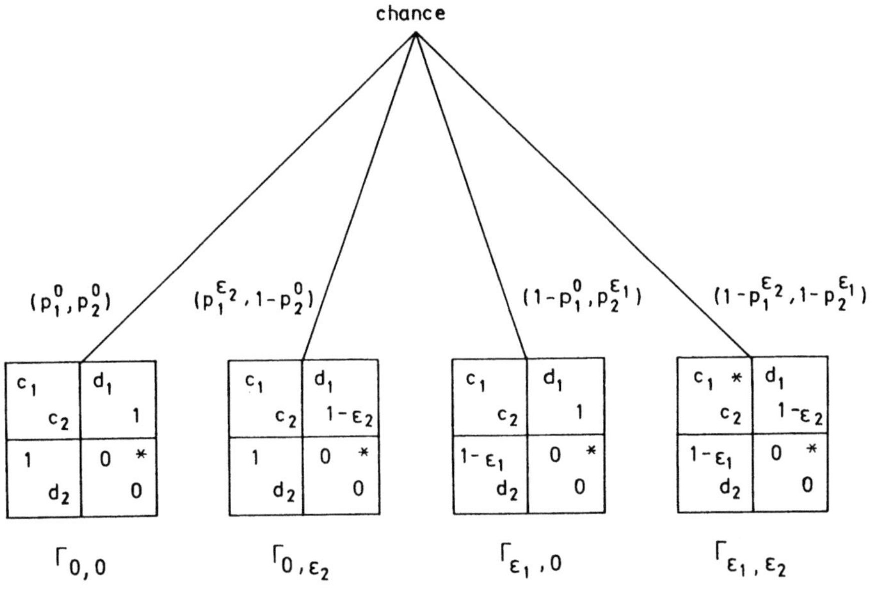

Figure 2: 2 x 2 - bimatrix game with incomplete information with two types of both players differing in their evaluation of a military advantage ($1 > p_i^{t_j} > 0$ for $t_j = 0$ and $t_j = \varepsilon_j$ and $c_i + \varepsilon_i > 1 > c_i > 0 > d_i$ for $i = 1,2$)

Incomplete information is introduced by assuming that a country j does not know whether its opponent i evaluates a military advantage by 1 or by $1-\varepsilon_i$ with $c_i + \varepsilon_i > 1$. Type t_j of country j expects the type which enjoys a military advantage with probability $p_i^{t_j}$ and the other type with probability $1-p_i^{t_j}$ where $0 < p_i^{t_j} < 1$. This situation is illustrated by Figure 2. First, a chance move determines the type vector (t_1,t_2) where the types $t_i = 0$ or $t_i = \varepsilon_i$ are identified by the discount from the evaluation of a military advantage. Given the type vector (t_1,t_2) the resulting game is the 2 x 2 - bimatrix game $\Gamma(t_1,t_2)$. The probability vectors at each chance move give the conditional probabilities for the other's type, given its own type. The probability with which type $t_i = 0$ is expected by $t_{j(\neq i)}$ is denoted by $p_i^{t_j}$. For type $t_i = \varepsilon_i$, this probability is $1-p_i^{t_j}$. The information conditions are such that a player is only aware of his own type. Thus he knows that two of the four games $\Gamma_{(t_1,t_2)}$ are impossible, but not which of the two remaining games he is actually playing. He only has probabilistic information concerning the other player's type and thereby about the true game. This clearly illustrates that uncertainty about the other's type is adequately shown.

We have again indicated the equilibrium points of the various games $\Gamma_{(t_1,t_2)}$ by '*. But this only tells us of the game structure which the two players would face if they knew the other's type. If information is incomplete, a player does not know the actual game $\Gamma_{(t_1,t_2)}$ for sure. His decision will therefore be optimal with respect to the set of possible games $\Gamma_{(t_1,t_2)}$ and not to a single game $\Gamma_{(t_1,t_2)}$ alone.

Of course, for a type $t_i = 0$ the strategy $\bar{d}$ is still dominant. Thus in equilibrium the aggressor types $t_i = 0$ will always choose $\bar{d}$. For the types $t_i = \varepsilon_i$ the situation is different. Although the general choice of $\bar{d}$ is always in equilibrium, there also exists a non-degenerate range of parameters where both types $t_i = \varepsilon_i$ choose disarmament d. The strategy vector $((\bar{d},d), (\bar{d},d))$ according to which types $t_i = 0$ choose $\bar{d}$ and types $t_i = \varepsilon_i$ choose disarmament d is a strict equilibrium for all parameter constellations satisfying the following condition.:

$$c_i+\varepsilon_i-1 > -d_i p_j^{\varepsilon_i}) \text{ for } i,j = 1,2 \text{ and } i \neq j \qquad (1)$$

Thus mutual disarmament is no longer impossible. Given condition (1) and that players select the equilibrium point $((\bar{d},d), (\bar{d},d))$, the result may be any possible military constellation: mutual disarmament (d,d), preserving the status quo of high general armament $(\bar{d},\bar{d})$ as well as a military advantage for one of the two countries ($(\bar{d},d)$ or $(d,\bar{d})$). The specific result will depend on the type vector (t_1,t_2) which is actually present. But in equilibrium it is impossible that one type $t_i = \varepsilon_i$ chooses disarmament whereas the other type $t_j = \varepsilon_j$ with $j \neq i$ does not.

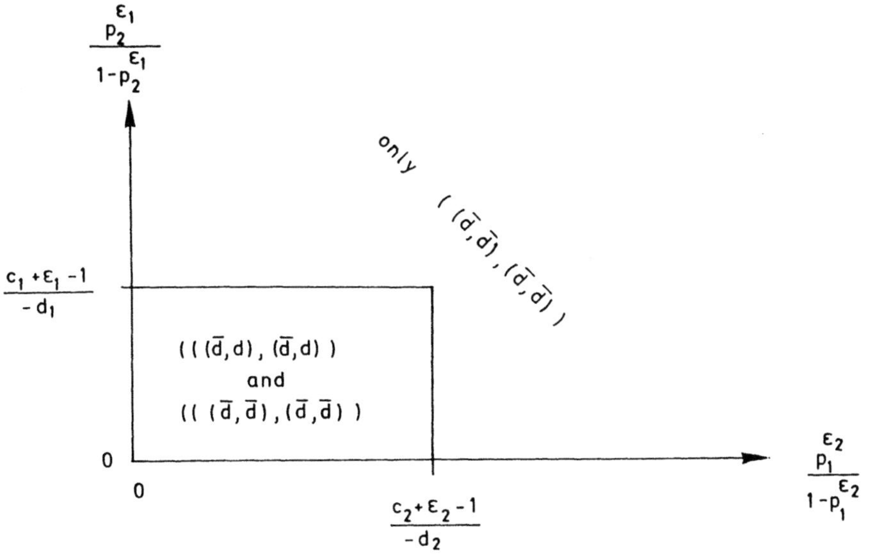

Figure 3: The set of strict equilibria in the game shown in Figure 2 as depending on the model parameters

Figure 3 illustrates the dependence of the set of strict equilibria on the model parameters. In the region where condition (1) is satisfied the strategy vector $((\bar{d},d), (\bar{d},d))$ is a strict equilibrium in addition to $((\bar{d},\bar{d}),(\bar{d},\bar{d}))$. Whenever one of the two conditions in (1) is not true, $((\bar{d},\bar{d}),(\bar{d},\bar{d}))$ is the only equilibrium point.

Since in range (1) there are two strict equilibria one might apply equilibrium selection to solve the game uniquely (cf. Güth and Stephan 1984, and Güth and Seifert 1984, for easy applications of equilibrium selection theory).

Substituting Figure 2 for Figure 1 derives from the assumption that the other country might not be a "greedy" conqueror. The objection to assuming that the other country is peaceful would be that the consequences of a military disadvantage are so dire that the gamble should not be taken.

In other words, even if Figure 2 is a better description of the actual situation, political decisions should be based on the game in Figure 1, which assigns maximum probability to the worst assumptions about the other country's type. The gist of this argument is that in military conflicts one should expect the worst and not weigh one risk against another.

This viewpoint seems however inconsistent with logic, since modern forms of defence themselves imply serious risks. A nuclear bomb can explode by accident, or be misused by military leaders who are dissatisfied with the political situation. Thus opting for nuclear defence itself implies a willingness to balance risks. If the risk of a military disadvantage is considered so serious, this should be represented by the pay-off function of the game. If, for instance the pay-off parameter d_i is small enough, i.e. d_i is rather large, condition (1) is no longer true, i.e. even the peaceful types will not dare to choose nuclear disarmament.

2.2 Attacking First Without Knowing The Other's Type

Assume now that in the case of a military conflict the attacking country wins by destroying most of the other country's military potential with its first blow, as in the following 2 x 2 - bimatrix game:

	$\bar{a}$	a
$\bar{a}$	d_1 ; d_2	c_1 ; 1 *
a	1 ; c_2 *	0 ; 0

Figure 4: The 'battle of the sexes' - game with $1 > d_i > c_i > 0$, $i = 1,2$

Here 'a' stands for attacking first and '$\bar{a}$' for refraining from such a move. Of course, if both countries attack, (a,a), the consequences are disastrous; 0 is the worst pay-off for both players. This game has two strict equilibria, namely ($\bar{a}$,a) and (a,$\bar{a}$). A peaceful world (a,a) is unstable, since both countries would prefer to attack first, i.e. deviate to their strategy a.

Let us introduce incomplete information once again by assuming that it is not sure whether the other country really prefers being the only aggressor threatening world peace ($\bar{a}$,$\bar{a}$). Such a situation is described by the following game with incomplete information with two possible types t_i = 0 and $t_i = \varepsilon_i$ of both countries:

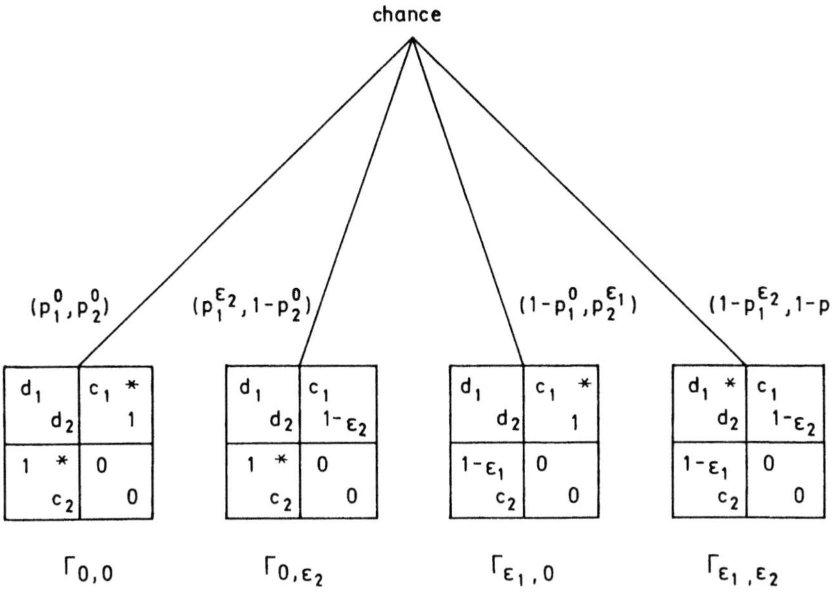

<u>Figure 5</u>: 2 x 2 - bimatrix game with incomplete information and two types of both players differing in the payoff of a successful aggression; $d_i + \varepsilon_i > 1 > d_i > c_i > 0$ and $0 < p_i^{t_j} < 1$ for $t_j = 0$ and $t_j = \varepsilon_j$ and i = 1,2

It is an interesting fact that although the games of Figures 1 and 4 are quite different, their incomplete information analogues have much in common: in both games (cf. Figures 2 and 5) there are type games $\Gamma_{(t_1,t_2)}$ with dominant strategies for both players and type games $\Gamma_{(t_1,t_2)}$ with two strict equilibria. This shows that in a world of incomplete information one often will not face one simple game structure. Depending on the types actually present the conflict situation can change fundamentally. Since players do not know their opponents for sure they therefore must consider different conflict situations when deciding whether a given policy is good or not.

Observe that in Figure 5 the strategy $\bar{a}$ is dominant for both peaceful types $t_i = \varepsilon_i$. Nevertheless in equilibrium not all types can be peaceful, since then an aggressor of type $t_i = 0$ would like to deviate. The possible equilibria of the game in Figure 5 are graphically illustrated in Figure 6.

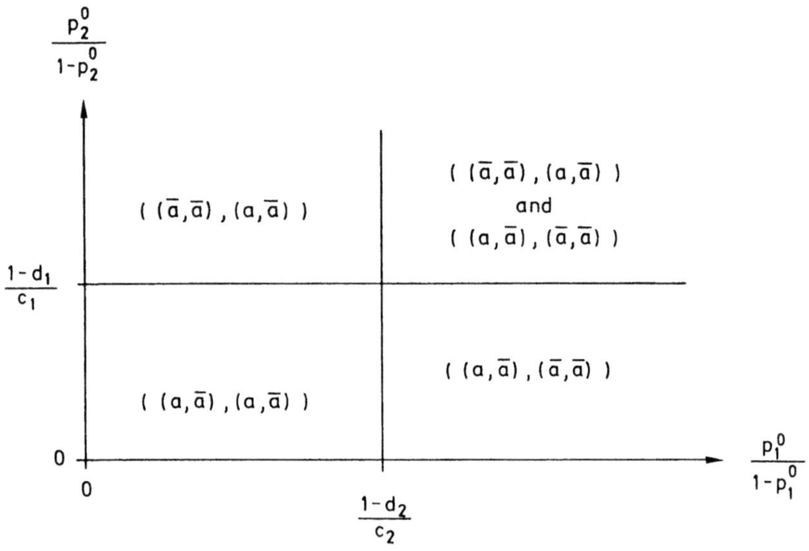

Figure 6: Four different parameter regions with different sets of strict equilibria in the Figure 5 game.

In the parameter region $((a,\bar{a}), (a,\bar{a}))$ where

$$(1-p_j^0)(1-d_i) > p_j^0 c_i \quad \text{for } i,j = 1,2 \text{ and } i \neq j, \qquad (2)$$

the strategy vector $((a,\bar{a}), (a,\bar{a}))$ is the only equilibrium point. In the other two regions with only one strict equilibrium, only one of the two conditions in (2) is satisfied. Here one aggressor type is also peaceful, whereas the other attacks first. In the remaining region where both inequalities in (2) do not hold, the game has two strict equilibria. Thus only here does the Figure 5 game have a similar structure as its complete information analogue of Figure 4.

3. The Nuclear Deterrence Debate As An Extensive Game

We shall now briefly describe an extensive game approach to modelling the nuclear deterrence debate on new nuclear missiles in Western Europe (cf. Güth 1985, for a more detailed analysis). Whereas the previous examples concentrate on the more abstract aspects of international armed conflicts, we shall here attempt to capture all significant features of a real-life situation.

There are three players:

USA - the United States of America

SU - the Soviet Union

E - Western Europe

The model treats Western Europe as one player to simplify the game's graphical presentation. Information is incomplete since neither USA nor SU are sure of player E's type. Type $\hat{E}$ of player E is expected with probability p and q by players SU and USA, respectively. The probabilities for the other possible type $\tilde{E}$ of player E are 1-p and 1-q with $0 < p < 1$ and $0 < q < 1$. The decision process is graphically illustrated in Figure 7 in the usual way of completed game trees.

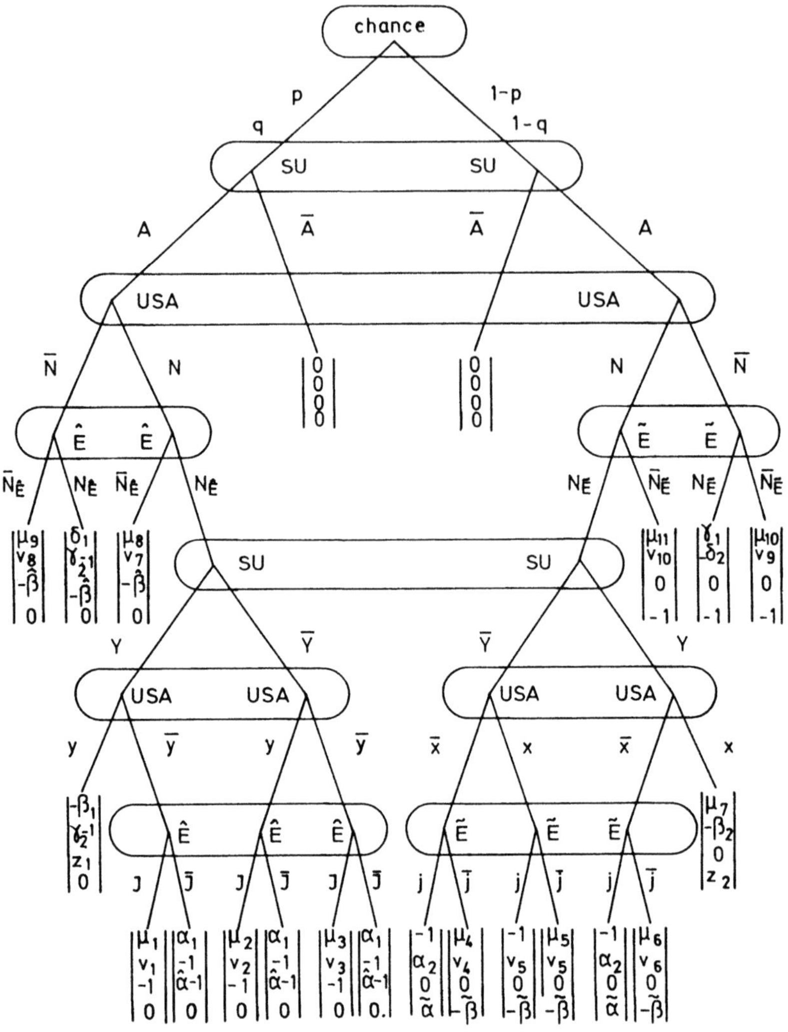

<u>Figure 7</u>: The completed game tree of the nuclear deterrence game. A play is a chain of moves from the origin (the top) to an endpoint (a corner where the tree ends); the pay-offs which a play implies are attached to the end-point; pay-offs are given in the order SU, USA, $\hat{E}$, $\tilde{E}$; 0 is the pay-off of the status quo, -1 the worst result; probabilities of chance moves are attached to the branches in the order SU, USA; information sets are illustrated by encircling corners, a player only knows that he is in the set but not at which corner; the moves are explained in Table 1.

p,q	probabilities by which SU, USA expect type $\hat{E}$
$A(\bar{A})$	SU increases (does not increase) nuclear armament
$N(\bar{N})$	USA threatens (does not threaten) to balance nuclear potentials
$N_{\hat{E}}(\bar{N}_{\hat{E}})$ or $N_{\tilde{E}}(\bar{N}_{\tilde{E}})$	$\hat{E}$ or $\tilde{E}$ threatens (does not threaten) to balance nuclear potentials
$Y(\bar{Y})$	SU proposes (does not propose) an agreement which balances nuclear potentials at the previously lower level
$y(\bar{y})$	USA, knowing that E is of type $\hat{E}$, proposes (does not propose) an agreement which balances nuclear potentials on the previously lower level
$x(\bar{x})$	USA, knowing that E is of type $\tilde{E}$, proposes (does not propose) an agreement which balances nuclear potentials on the previously lower level
$J(\bar{J})$ or $j(\bar{j})$	$\hat{E}$ or $\tilde{E}$ accepts (does not accept) new nuclear missiles in Western Europe

Table 1: The moves in the nuclear deterrence game illustrated by Figure 7

All plays start with the initial fictitious chance move and proceed without backward movements to an end point (a corner without downward-reaching branches). The pay-off function attaches a pay-off vector to every play. Since plays can be identified by end points, the pay-off function can be determined by assigning a pay-off vector to every end point. In Figure 7 the pay-offs are given in the order SU, USA, $\hat{E}$, $\tilde{E}$ from top to bottom. Information sets are graphically illustrated by encircling decision corners (corners where the name of a player appears). When a player has to move, he only knows that he is at one of the corners in the set but not exactly at which one. Pay-offs have been normalised such that 0 is the status quo pay-off (pay-off after move $\bar{A}$ of SU) and -1 is the worst pay-off of all players. It is a pure convention that the non-existent type of E always receives 0.

The possible moves in the course of a play are explained in Table 1: after the initial chance move determining player E's type SU must decide whether to increase nuclear armament in Europe (A) or not ($\bar{A}$). It is essential that SU does not know the type of E when choosing between A and $\bar{A}$. After move A of SU the NATO team (USA and E) does not react immediately. They first can only threaten to react with new nuclear missiles in Europe. For this threat to be effective, both NATO partners must agree to it, i.e. one must have N and $N_{\hat{E}}$ in the case of $\hat{E}$ and N and $N_{\tilde{E}}$ in the case of $\tilde{E}$.

Only in the case of an effective threat from NATO can both, SU and USA, bargain (in Geneva) on whether to balance nuclear potentials in Europe on the previously lower level or not. To achieve agreement on the previously low level, both the bargaining parties have to propose this agreement (decisions Y and y or x of SU and USA respectively). When bargaining in Geneva, USA knows the true type of its ally E, whereas SU is still unaware of E's true type.

If there is no agreement in Geneva, NATO is asked to carry out its threat. Although E did agree to this threat it will not necessarily accept the new nuclear missiles in Western Europe. In democratic countries the government deciding between J or $\bar{J}$ (j or $\bar{j}$) is not necessarily the same one which threatened to increase nuclear armament. E might just have tried to regain the status quo situation, although it considers new nuclear missiles on its territory to be unacceptable. If $\hat{E}$ or $\tilde{E}$ do not accept new nuclear missiles in Western Europe SU stabilizes its military advantage. Otherwise nuclear potentials are balanced on the high level as determined by SU's initial move A.

The model parameters are restricted by

$$\begin{gathered}\hat{\alpha} > 0,\ \hat{\alpha}+\hat{\beta} > 1,\ \tilde{\alpha} > -1,\ \tilde{\alpha}+\tilde{\beta} > 0,\ \alpha_1+\beta_1 > 0, \\ \gamma_1 > 0,\ \delta_1 > 0,\ \alpha_2+\beta_2 > 0,\ \alpha_2+\delta_2 > 0,\ \gamma_2 > 0, \\ q \neq \frac{\alpha_2+\delta_2}{\alpha_2+\delta_2+\gamma_2},\quad p \neq \frac{1}{1+\alpha_1}\end{gathered} \tag{3}$$

Since pay-off parameters are not numerically specified, the complete game tree of Figure 7 together with the parameter restrictions in (3) define a class of games and not just one game. Due to the special assumptions and restrictions on parameters this is, of course, a rather narrow class of games. But a model which tries to capture institutional richness has to be specific.

The solution of the nuclear deterrence game can be easily derived by first determining the decisions in the final information sets, then the choices in the second last informations sets by anticipating the final decisions, etc. Proceeding in this way one derives:

- $\hat{E}$ does not accept new nuclear missiles in Western Europe, $\tilde{E}$ does;
- USA does not aim at an agreement in Geneva when $\tilde{E}$ is present, but it does when knowing that Western Europe is of type $\hat{E}$;
- SU prefers conflict in Geneva, i.e. bargaining in Geneva has to fail;
- both types, $\hat{E}$ and $\tilde{E}$, want USA and SU to bargain in Geneva about regaining the status quo situation of low nuclear armament.

Anticipating these results, the game situation is reduced to a conflict between USA and SU only (cf. Figure 8). In the reduced game of Figure 8 only USA and SU are strategically interacting. The equilibrium behavior of this game is graphically illustrated by Figure 9: in parameter region (A,N) the Soviet Union SU increases its nuclear potential in Europe and USA reacts with the threat of new nuclear missiles in Western Europe. In region $(\bar{A},N)$ there would have been no nuclear deterrence debate because of SU's first move $\bar{A}$. Whereas $(\bar{A},N)$ results from SU's low trust in type $\hat{E}$, the solution $(A,\bar{N})$ is characterized by USA's low level of confidence in E's actually carrying out its threat, i.e. that type $\tilde{E}$ is present.

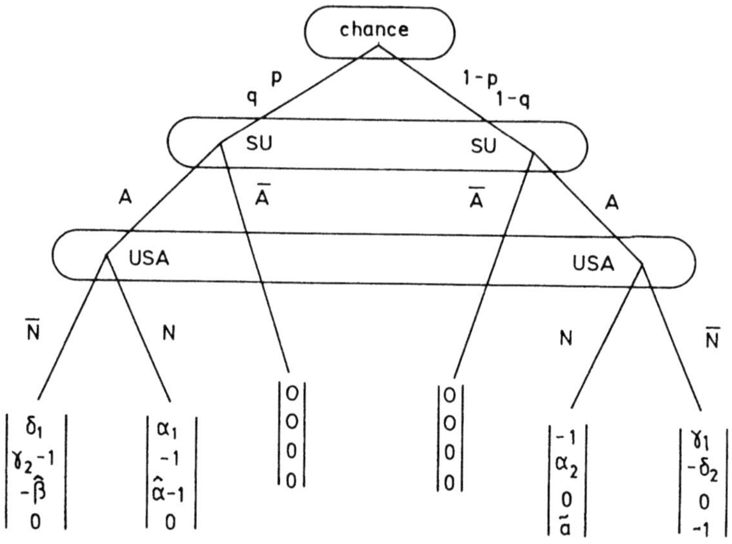

Figure 8: The completed game tree of the reduced nuclear deterrence game resulting from Figure 7 by repeated elimination of dominated strategies

Assume that the model correctly reflects the decisive aspects of the nuclear deterrence debate in the years 1982 and 1983. From the political results of this debate (SU has chosen A, USA and E have threatened to adjust their nuclear potential in Europe) one can conclude that the actual situation was in region (A,N) of Figure 9. So the a priori beliefs of USA and SU have to satisfy certain conditions: SU was expecting the unwilling type $\hat{E}$ of E and USA the willing type $\tilde{E}$ of E with significantly positive probability. The final political result in region (A,N) of Figure 9 is, of course, different when $\hat{E}$ or $\tilde{E}$ is present. For more countries of Western Europe at least, actual results reveal that E is of type $\tilde{E}$.

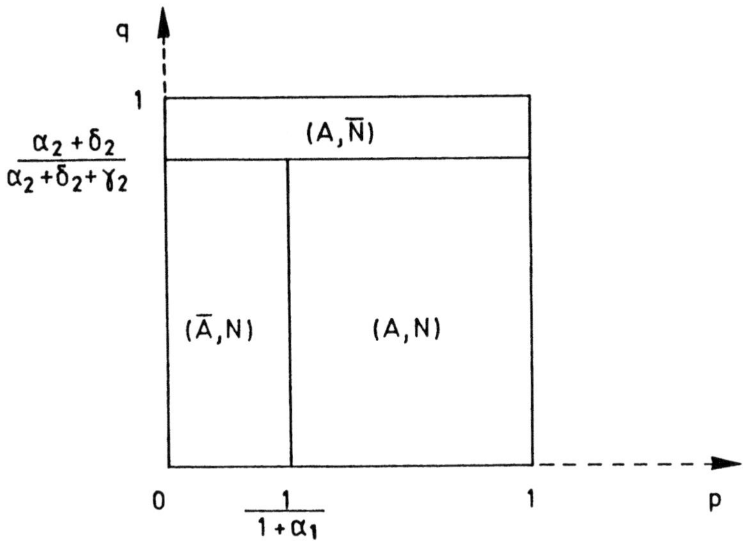

Figure 9: The equilibrium point of the reduced nuclear deterrence game, illustrated by the p-q - diagram in Figure 8 (regions are distinguished by the equilibrium point of the reduced nuclear deterrence game)

Political opinions in the Federal Republic of Germany are well reflected in the equilibrium strategies of the two types $\hat{E}$ and $\tilde{E}$ of player E. The policy of the government (Christian Democrats, Liberals) is closely related to the solution strategy $(N_{\tilde{E}},j)$ of type $\tilde{E}$, whereas the policy of the Social Democratic Party is represented by the solution strategy $(N_{\hat{E}},\bar{J})$ of the type $\hat{E}$. Thus political disagreement can be traced to different evaluations of political actions and military constellations. The main difference is that $\hat{E}$ does not want new nuclear missiles in Western Europe even though the Soviet Union has increased its nuclear threat potential in Europe. On the other hand type $\tilde{E}$ fears a military advantage of SU and accepts therefore the risk of additional nuclear missiles in Western Europe. Political analysis of the solution indicates that incomplete information about policy in Western Europe seems to be crucially important. One can represent ambiguous views about military opponents and analyse how these influence political decisions. Splitting up political agents into several types offers moreover a unique way of explaining different political opinions.

References:

S.J. Brams: Superpower games - Applying game theory to superpower conflicts, Yale University Press 1985.

S.J. Brams: Deterrence and uncertainty: A game-theoretic analysis. Discussion paper (1984).

S.J. Brams - M.D. Davis: The verification problem in arms control: A game-theoretic analysis. Discussion paper (1983).

S.J. Brams - M.D. Davis - P.D. Straffin: The geometry of the arms race, International Studies Quarterly, Vol. 23 (1979), 567-588.

S.J. Brams - M.P. Hessel: Threat power in sequential games, International Studies Quarterly 28 (1984), 23-44.

S.J. Brams - D.M. Kilgour: Optimal deterrence, Social Philosophy and Policy 3 (1985a), 118-135.

- , The path to stable deterrence, in: Dynamic Models of International Conflicts (ed. U. Luterbacher and M.D. Ward), Boulder 1985b.

- , Rational de-escalation, IPDM Report No. 27 (1985c), University of Haifa, Israel.

- , Winding down if pre-emption or escalation occurs: A game-theoretic analysis, Research Report No. 30 (1985d), Department of Economics, New York University, N.Y. 10003, USA.

W. Güth: An extensive game approach to model the nuclear deterrence debate, to appear in Zeitschrift für die gesamte Staatswissenschaft/Journal of Institutional and Theoretical Economics.

W. Güth - H.G. Seifert: Equilibrium selection for bargaining games with unbiased threats, Methods of Operations Research, 51 (1984), 315-346.

W. Güth - J. Stephan: Equilibrium selection in the "one seller and many buyers" game, Zeitschrift für Nationalökonomie/Journal of Economics 44 (1984), 267-281.

J.C. Harsany: Games with incomplete information played by "Bayesian" players, Parts I, II, III, Management Science (1968), 159-182, 320-334, 486-502.

PART III

NEGOTIATIONS

WORKING GROUP MEMBERS:

KETTELLE, John D. (Chairman)

ALBERS, Wulf
BROWN, Scott
COLLINGRIDGE, David
DOMPKE, Uwe
FRASER, Niall
GORI, Umberto
GÜNDOGDU, Hasim
JEANCLOS, Yves
PRINS, Gwyn
REVELLE, Charles
RUDNIANSKI, Michel
SCHMIDT, Christian

REPORT OF THE CHAIRMAN: NEGOTIATION ISSUES

J.D. Kettelle
Ketron, Inc., Arlington, Virginia 22209, USA

1. BACKGROUND

The Negotiation Section of the workshop was charged with looking for negotiation concepts that can be relevant and helpful in the arms control process. We tried to concentrate on logically-structured concepts and procedures, simply because the workshop as a group had attempted to represent the particular contributions of the analytic community, rather than for example the diplomatic community.

We all brought working papers to the workshop, and some of us did additional writing after the workshop. This section presents a selection of some of these papers, and this report will comment briefly on how they relate.

In addition to the included papers a number of ideas were developed within the workshop itself. Although some of them were triggered by the papers themselves (and therefore are addressed to some extent in the collection herewith presented), the primary goal of this report is to present some of the thoughts that actually grew out of the workshop meetings.

A presentation of the substantive workshop material would be incomplete without some description of its participants and the dynamics of the discussions. There were two relevant dimensions - national and professional. About half of the participants (including the chairman) had backgrounds in mathematics or operations analysis. (This group was once referred to by the chairman as "warm human beings.") The rest of the group had backgrounds in other disciplines in which negotiation is somehow pertinent--political science, law, and philosophy. (The chairman never found a satisfactory collective adjective for this group). In one sense the first group provided procedural expertise, and the second provided experiential, or database expertise. One form and the other substance. Somehow the workshop generated some very positive chemistry, wherein each group stimulated the other. The diversity of nationalities was an equally positive feature. Although we consciously concentrated on process rather than current specific issues, the quite different views of historical and current arms control negoti-

NATO ASI Series, Vol. F 26
Modelling and Analysis in Arms Control
Edited by R. Avenhaus et al.

ations as seen for example by the British, French, and German participants very definitely provided additional varieties of "substance" that led to very useful expanded insights into "process". This was particularly true regarding our newly-found concerns about climate, linkage, and multi-national negotiations.

2. THOUGHTS DEVELOPED AT THE WORKSHOP

This section presents various concepts which grew out of the workshop itself. In some cases we have pursued them subsequent to the workshop, but in all cases they were either initiated or significantly advanced during the course of the discussions.

The negotiation subgroup of the workshop identified at least seven aspects of arms control negotiations to which the analytic community might be able to make helpful contributions:

Linkage
Sequential Unilateral Actions
Climate
Information Management
Multi-lateral Negotiations
Secondary Pay off Functions
Negotiations in Peace and War.

2.1 LINKAGE

Any treatise on negotiation theory quickly establishes the advantage of widening the issues that are to be put on the negotiating table. In fact, that is the grist for the "yes-yes" results that third-party negotiators relish - modifications that benefit both sides. A simple case: a buyer and seller argue over the price of a house. The negotiator finds the seller wants to brag that he got a high price. He then introduces a new issue-asking the seller in effect to provide the mortgage. By structuring the mortgage at a low interest rate, the theoretical price can be high even though the actual payments are low. Both sides win. More generally, the possible results of any multi-issue negotiations can be plotted as follows:

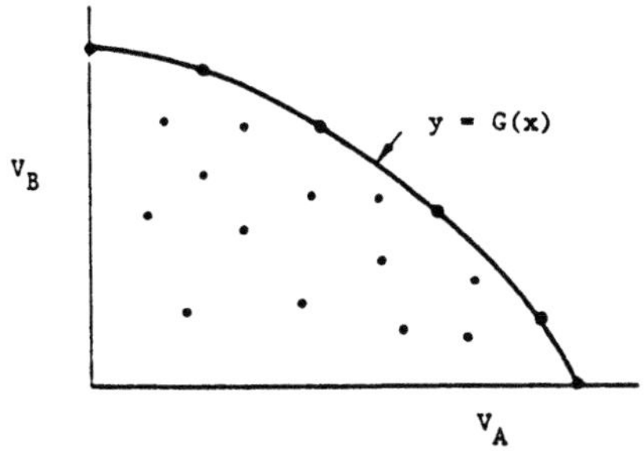

where V_A is the value of a deal to side A,
V_B is the value of a deal to side B, and
$y = G(x)$ is the convex hull of all possible deals.

G is called the Pareto frontier. For any deal on the frontier, side B is getting the highest possible value consistent with the value realized by side A. Putting it another way, for any deal not on the frontier, there will be a deal on the frontier (or weighted average of two such deals) that is better for both sides.

The cooperative forces associated with this search for efficient deals are always theoretically enhanced by increasing the scope of the negotiation. All issues thereby put on the same table are ipso facto "linked". There are of course contrary forces that counter-indicate linkage. The simplest is that linkage complicates the negotiations. If the theoretical advantage (always present) is in fact sufficiently compelling, the "complication" will be justified. A more compelling deterrent is that one side (or both) may have some reason not to let an issue on the table, in spite of its logical relevance. Often the problem is associated with the publicity that unfortunately accompanies such negotiations. This problem may be addressed by some of our ideas presented below in the section on "information management".

Even at best, we must concede that there are prices for adding issues to the table. So how to economize on issues? A natural analytical approach is to partition the negotiations into goal-oriented groups. This means putting onto one table all issues that are centrally relevant to one goal. Present partitions are typically by weapon types, or by geography. Although these tend to separate by goals, the exceptions are too obvious to belabor.

Possible examples of goal-oriented groups:

(a) Maximize times of flight for weapons directed at critical targets within the U.S. or the USSR. Consequently put on the same table restrictions on nuclear missiles in European countries that can reach Moscow, and restrictions on Soviet submarines off the coast of the U.S.

(b) Minimize threat of "blitzkrieg" incursions into Western Europe, or into Eastern Europe. Consequently explore ways to deploy existing mechanized and artillery forces as far back from the present "boundary" as possible - in the Soviet case well east of Moscow.

(c) Maximize warning times of both sides with respect to first strikes. Consequently include on the same table agreements about locations of deployed weapons and locations of warning devices. Perhaps even cooperate by furnishing platform locations to facilitate each other's warning abilities.

2.2 SEQUENTIAL UNILATERAL MOVES

A remarkable part of the arms control negotiations process has not been in the form of explicit treaties or even agreements, but rather a sequence of unilateral moves, or non-moves. A current (March 1986) example, is the Soviet announcement of its cessation of underground testing, and the U.S. decision to nevertheless proceed with its planned test. Which was the move and which the non-move is a nice question. Even within the context of explicit agreements, there has been a long history of such unilateral moves. Some of these are near what might be called the boundaries of the agreements, and have the effect of refining or revising the agreements. An obvious example would be the Soviet encoding of missile telemetry data. Others involve actions not subject to agreements, but which are clearly relevant to arms control. Here continuing examples are annual defense expenditures of NATO on the one hand and the Warsaw Pact countries on the other.

What can be said about this form of de facto negotiations? Recent work in game theory has addressed what seems to be a similar problem, namely repeated plays of the Prisoner's Dilemma game. The result seems to be a consensus that the best strategy (or at least a robust and effective one) is "tit-for-tat": if the other player (we avoid calling him an adversary) double crosses you on one play, you double cross him on the next; conversly, if he makes a cooperative move you make one on the next play. Although this seems to be <u>suggestive</u>

for the case of sequential unilateral moves, it is irrelevant when viewed by strict logic. With tit-for-tat, a positive move on one side would lead to a reciprocal positive move on the other, which would lead to another positive move by the first and so on indefinitely; conversely for a single negative move. Although the analytic community does not seem to have any ready-made theoretical contribution to the process of unilatered moves, we do seem at least to have some problems to work on. A partial list:

(a) What have been the historic sequences of such moves, and their responses? To what extent have these moves been communicative, such as invitations to cooperate, or such as reprimands for precedent moves which were viewed as hostile? To what extent, on the other hand, were they dictated by internal (in a sense exogenous) considerations?

(b) How effective have various sequences of unilateral moves been, as a form of communication, or as an influence on the other side's behavior?

(c) What can be learned about the tactics of such moves. Are many small moves effective than a single large one (equal to the sum of the small ones?) Is a large positive move enhanced if it is preceded by a small hostile move?

(d) What time constants, or delays, are to be expected for responses to positive moves? To negative moves?

(e) What are effective combinations of actions and words? When should words precede, accompany, or follow actions?

(f) Can you make a case that the essential nature of relations between super powers is in fact only unilateral actions? If not, to what extent are treaties useful (as opposed to action patterns, accompanied by appropriate "words"). To the extent treaties are useful, how can unilateral actions expedite the formation of treaties?

Work on those problems must either be led by a remarkably eclectic individual, or be the combined effort of experts in political science, diplomacy, negotiation theory, and operations research.

2.3 CLIMATE

The political scientists in our workshop emphasised the importance of climate in the conduct of international negotiations. This leads us to search for a quantitative way to characterize climate. Our first reaction has been to characterize it in terms of the values each side assigns to the various possible outcomes of the negotiation. Typically an outcome will be assigned different values α and β by sides A and B. In more detail, the value α assigned by side A will itself have two components:

$$\alpha = f\,(a,b),$$

where a may be thought of as the internal value of the outcome to side A and b the internal value of outcome to side B, as perceived by A. The extent to which α depends on b can characterize the climate: If a positive b decreases α, one can say the climate is hostile, or competitive. If α increases with b, the climate may be considered cooperative. This concept cries for an example. Suppose that there are two alternative arms control agreements that will have precisely the same result with respect to stability--that they differ only with respect to the financial costs each side would incur.

	Agreement 1	Agreement 2
Cost to A	$100B	$120B
Cost to B	$ 80B	$150B

If the "total" value α_i to A of each deal is only a_i, then he clearly will prefer Agreement 1. On the other hand, if the climate is hostile, α_2 may well exceed α_1, because A perceives that costing B an extra $70B is somehow worth more than the extra $20B it costs A. Paradoxically, if B is sufficiently rich and hostile, even B may prefer Agreement 2.

There would seem to be little argument that the post World War II East-West climate has been primarily hostile. Nevertheless, significant arms agreements have been effectuated. All this logic provides a structure for both sides to examine how to control whatever (exogenous to arms control) hostility is unavoidable, and to balance it more rationally against the otherwise obvious payoffs of significant arms reductions.

To be somewhat more specific, one might characterize actual or potential conflicts between two super powers as being threedimensional: military, economic, and political. Arms control agreements are necessarily structured in military terms. An amelioration of the arms race can provide differing economic consequences to the two sides, differing internal political consequences, or differing implications for relations with other countries. Those who are interested specifically in strong arms control agreements must recognize that economic and political concerns are significant as determinants of the arms control payoff matrices.

As an aside, this consideration of "climate" led our group to consider a rather perverse motivation for more progress in arms control - it may help if arms control measures can require expenditures commensurate with those demanded in the arms race itself. If the Space Defense Initiative can be regarded as an arms control program (which paradoxically it can), it certainly qualifies as a high expenditure component. Such components, if they force similar expenditures by the other side, at least permit some decoupling of arms control from economic "warfare".

2.4 INFORMATION MANAGEMENT

A particular difficulty with arms control negotiations (as opposed, for example, to trade negotiations) is the background of sensitive military secrets that presumably underlie the logic each side must apply to the assessment of potential agreements. Just as centrally, any negotiation typically suffers if your adversary knows your bargaining position - the values you put on the various components of a possible deal, and the limits to which you are prepared to go. The search for efficient treaties - ones on the Pareto frontier-is thus complicated by the nonavailability of information about the desires of both sides. In other contexts this dilemma is often addressed by using a "trustworthy" third party - trustworthy in the sense that each side can tell him its value functions, and depend on his not relaying them directly to the opponent.

The possibility of the superpowers entrusting their secrets to such a third party is too remote even to consider. Even if there were someone (or some agency) they both considered sufficiently neutral, the possibility of inadvertant compromise of the necessary sensitive information would be unacceptable.

One solution to this problem was presented to the group - that of designing a system that could serve as a computerized third party (CTP). The CTP would have to be demonstrably (to both sides) inacessable except by mutual agreement. Each side would need confidence that its inputs could not be ascertained by the other. Only questions mutually agreed to could be asked of the CTP. At any stage, a central such question would be: Given the limits both sides have stated, is there room for an agreement? There is a rich variety of issues regarding a CTP:

(a) Is it technically feasible, given its confidentiality requirements?

(b) How could dimensions of arms control agreements be structured to lend themselves to efficient valuations to be put on the results?

(c) What negotiating strategies, other than straightforward input of sincere values and limits, should be used with a CTP?

(d) To what extent is it necessary or useful for each side to present the CTP with its own highly classified models of strategic warfare, that reflect its calculation of the impact of arms limitations.

Enough thought has been directed to these questions to make the concept of CTP very intriguing; much more could usefully be applied.

2.5 MULTILATERAL NEGOTIATIONS

One result of the multi-national constituency of the workshop itself was the concern with the treatment of multilateral aspects of arms control negotiations. Simply put, an efficient treaty for NATO as a whole may have very inefficient implications, or very uncomfortable disparaties, for individual countries within NATO. (Although we regard the countries within the Warsaw Pact as less autonomous, it would be simplistic to assume that some version of this problem does not bedevil the Soviets.) As with the previous issue of "climate", this one must recognize economic and political concerns as well as military. A sampling of issues of concern to NATO members:

(a) With the principal exception of the Greek-Turkish dispute regarding Crete, (and perhaps the fishing dispute between the United Kingdom and Iceland), the Western Alliance has had a remarkable record of lack of internal military discord. On the other hand, each member country has an understandable interest in a reasonably balanced force of its own. These balanced forces may add up to totals that are interfered with by an over-all East-West arms control treaty.

(b) The "military-industrial complex" of the United States has its counterparts in the other members of the Western alliance. The economic benefits (and sometimes hardships) of arms control agreements can parse themselves out in ways that make various members very nervous.

(c) The Pershing deployments have been a recent example of the impact of arms control agreements (or sequences of unilateral actions) on internal politics of member countries. Even if regimes, or administrations currently in power, ratify NATO decisions regarding arms control, one must anticipate the political consequences within each member nation - consequences that may not accrue until subsequent elections.

Multi-lateral negotiations can of course be conducted either simultaneously or sequentially--in this arena there are at least a few techniques that operations analysts and negotiation theorists have thought about. For arms control one natural procedure would be first to get agreements among component members of one side, and then negotiate with the opposing side. An essential complication of this natural procedure ist secrecy - not just "military" secrets, but negotiating policy secrets such as reserve prices and tradeoff values. An elegant solution to this problem might be a variant of the computerized third party (CTP) discussed above. A less elegant (but perhaps likely) approach is exemplified by the workshop itself. Although the workshop was partially sponsored by NATO, it had no official status with respect to the component members. Conceivably similar "workshops" could sharpen the issues of concern to member countries - with clearly no official implications, but with the benefit of well-informed and well-structured analysis. Subsequently the group that must be small in order to be secret can exploit the thinking of this broader community.

2.5 SECONDARY PAYOFF FUNCTIONS

It is self-evident that any negotiator wants to have the clearest possible picture of what he is trying to achieve. In the context of negotiation theory this means knowing one's payoff functions--knowing the various results that can arise from a possible agreement and knowing how to compute the value of these results. The computation needs to be estimated for the opponent's side as well as calculated for one's own. Theoretically, the payoff has to be structured as a single combined variable - otherwise there may be no way to decide whether one treaty is better than another. In practice several variables are needed, and the negotiator delays the necessary overall evaluation until a particular comparison becomes really difficult.

The calculation of payoffs has been the primary concern of the assessment subgroup of the workshop. However, these assessments have addressed primarily the military outcomes of the possible conflicts that the armament postures would permit. In a realistic set of negotiations it is essential that a more complete array of payoffs be recognized. There seems to be a tendency to divorce the non-military payoffs from arms control discussions.

This is probably because there are two primary and obvious payoffs to arms control: (1) avoidance of war, and (2) avoidance of an arms race. For either side to admit to other concerns payoffs might make it vulnerable to the criticism of letting secondary issues interfere with the avoidance of nuclear war. What are some of these secondary payoffs?

(1) Establishment or preservation of regional hegemonies

(2) Ability to deal militarily with third countries

(3) Development of technology with non-military payoffs

(4) Support of one's military-industrial complex for reasons that are not strictly military, such as national economics.

The last one may in fact be the most important and troublesome. Although it may appear to be illegitimate a case can be made for its being extremely legitimate. Legitimate or not, any arms control treaty will have tough sledding getting "ratified" by its respective superpowers if it threatens the economic viability of their respective military industries. As things presently stand this problem is implicity recognized by the two sides, but is completely ignored in any negotiation agenda. More specifically, in the typically hostile "climate" characterizing arms control negotiations, both sides may well rejoice in whatever economic difficulties they may perceive the other side is likely to encounter as a result of possible treaties. In fact, one payoff to each side associated with the current relatively large military expenditures may be the damage it perceives that is being done to the other side's economy.

At a minimum, an arms control negotiator should be provided with some estimates of the economic consequences of various treaties--to his country as well as his opponents. If these consequences are to be realistically assessed, and if the treaty is one that "threatens" to generate a really large reduction in defense expenditures, one must hypothesize either a laissez-faire attitude or deliberate programs to utilize the idled capabilities of the military-industrial community. Programs of this nature in the United States (although not necessarily constructed for this reason) have been the "War on Proverty" initiated in the 1960's, the space program, certain elements of the health budget, and various programs of the by-now-defunct Department of Energy (such as the Synfuel Corporation). Fortunately or otherwise, none of these programs would have been large enough to replace adequately the expenditure reductions likely to be associated with a really successful arms control treaty. Postulation of large programs of this nature, that are alternatives to defense-oriented projects, is beyond the scope of this working group, but it is our legitimate reccommendation that someone search for such programs.

There are alternatives closer to home - that is, projects that are related to military security but which in fact are not strictly projects nor projects that would demonstrably increase the consequences of a nuclear war. These projects include surveillance systems, systems for conducting negotiations, and systems for verification. Interestingly enough all of these above projects could conceivably involve joint efforts - there could be jointly structured surveillance systems, jointly structured verification systems, and of course negotiation systems would necessarily be cooperatively put together. By the same token it is conceptually clear that the non-military economic alternatives could also include joint projects. Including these elements as an inherent part of the negotiation process may well be an example of the kind of healthy linkage that is discussed elsewhere in this report.

3. COMMENTS ON THE PAPERS PRESENTED IN THIS SECTION

The disparate disciplines and nationalities generated correspondingly disparate papers. Not surprisingly, almost none of them were received in the technical and linguistic style that would be comfortable to any single participant, or for that matter to any one reader of this report. A first reaction was simply to reject the uncomfortable papers for publication. That would have been a tragic loss. Our linguistic editing has been severe, and not entirely separable from our technical editing. In the latter we have exercised almost unprofessional restraint, so as not to filter out nuances just because our own background was insufficient to assess them. We made a conscious effort to avoid letting game theory dominate the negotiation analysis. Nevertheless, the game structure clearly deserves major effort, and continues to be a helpful way to organize negotiation concepts. Fraser's paper provides the arms negotiation analyst with an invaluable reference background of the complete set of essentially different two-by-two games, specifically addressing arms control. If we characterize "climate" as the assignment of payoff functions in two-by-two games, Fraser's paper thereby gives us a quantitative way to evaluate and react to changes in climate. Of course, Gori's paper addresses climate head-on, from the background of a political scientist.

Rudnianski and Schmidt submitted a paper entiled "A Logic of Arms Negotiations between USA and USSR". It is indeed very much of logician's paper, and as such exceeded even our above-explained high tolerance levels for disparate disciplines. Unfortunately, its length and typographic complexity preclude its inclusion in this report. They use the normal two-person game-theory structure to characterize the arms-control process. They then define similar games for the arms-using (or arms-abstaining) process. For these latter games they characterize the outcome of pairs of moves as 0 or 1 for each respective player. This defines a partial ordering of the arms-using process- an ordering, by the way, that depends on the degree of hostility (or cooperation) between the players. This partial ordering is therefore imposed on the outcomes of the moves of the arms-control game. They propose using this logic to systematize an examination of all possible structures of the arms control games. There is no question that a partial ordering of arms-using results is a helpful concept. Although it would appear that Fraser's paper addresses this very issue, the work by Rudnianski and Schmidt may provide a stimulus for game theorists to study games in which the value of the outcomes to the two sides is only partially ordered.

The payoff functions of game theory were also central to the group's deliberation on linkage. Not only can linkage improve possible outcomes for both players, it can also make possible discrete shifts from one category of a two-person game to a more cooperative category. Albers' paper deals with the pressures implicit in the negotiation process itself, and ways in which these pressures can lead systematically to a compromise which reflects the respective strengths of the two sides, and at the same time follows them to share efficiently the "non-zero" sum. This of course is precisely the kind of thing that game theory tries to address. A principal message in Collingridge's paper is the balance between preventing conflict and minimizing damage if conflict occurs. Clearly, deterrence has been pre-occupied with prevention, to the extent of accepting unholy damage if prevention fails. Since deterrence is a primary element of arms control logic, Collingridge may be suggesting that we find a more explicit logic for damage minimization when we develop the payoff functions for arms control.

Brown and Fisher bring expertise derived from a variety of actual negotiations. Much of their language is that of "human behavior", as opposed to payoff functions and strategy. It would seem to be the job of our analytic community to effect a two-way translation between their language and that of the game theorists. An example is Brown and Fisher's advice one should not link procedural issues with substantive issues. In game-theory terms this may be like saying changing the rules of a game should not be considered as a legitimate move of the game itself. The very thought is intriguing. They shouldn't have told us not to do it. Kettelle's paper addresses the conduct of negotiations from the concern of information management--how to get an efficient treaty without "giving away the store" with respect to one's own information.

"Thousands at His bidding speed o'er land and ocean without at rest; they also serve who only stand and wait". The workshop participants whose papers are not included here indeed serve the cause fully as well. In addition to written work, each delegate gave a thoughtful presentation to the group and acted as a foil for the others. Their contributions are less explicit in this report than the published papers, but were in our judgment were often even more helpful. We herewith acknowledge them with gratitude to the participants, and commend to the readers of this book any opportunity they may have to discuss arms control negotiations with any of the participants of the group. Finally, but not least, the contribution of Gwyn Prins demands special acknowledgement. As vice-chairman of the working group he was doubly valuable --first as the discussion spokesman for the non-mathematicians, and second for the formulation of some of the best ideas that were finally hammered out.

4. NEGOTIATIONS IN PEACE AND WAR

Some fresh insight on arms control negotiations can come from hypothesizing the negotiations that might take place pursuant to the termination of an actual war. Following this approach one starts with various possible outcomes of a conflict, and works one's way backward all the way to appropriate negotiations regarding the means for conducting a conflict. Arms control is typically motivated by avoiding conflicts. This particular logical process pursues the conflicts themselves to their "logical" conclusion. The negotiations ending the conflict are of course described as armistice or peace-treaty negotiations. Any logical conflict needs to be waged in a way that negotiations can be concluded whenever a cessation of hostilities is preferable to both sides. Clearly, a "preconflict" phase (suchas the present) is one in which a continuation of no-conflict is preferable to both sides. It clearly makes sense to integrate a study of the conflict-avoidance negotiations, including arms control, with a study of the conflict-termination negotiations that automatically are appropriate once the discontinuity of conflict initiation has occured.

When the rest of a war is completely predictable there is logically a settlement that both sides will prefer to continuation of the conflict. This principle can define efficient "battles" as those which improve the predictability of a war's outcome for a relatively small damage incurred during the battle by one or both sides. Concepts of deterrence, such as the capability for mutually assured destruction, are almost the epitome of inefficient battles. Paradoxically, this very characteristic appears to be essential to their deterrent power.

An "efficient" strategic war would appear to be one whose first battle would be a sample combat, involving only a few weapons and perhaps conducted in a relatively harmless area. Theoretically, each side could derive from this "joint maneuver" an accurate projection of the results of successive battles. If the separate calculations of the two sides were sufficiently similar, a peace treaty could be logically negotiated without having to fight the war itself.

Clearly, this is all very theoretical. For one thing the "sample battle" would have to be conducted in cold blood - an unlikely choice even for two hostile countries. Beyond that, there are all kinds of reasonings as to whether one should deploy one's best weapons, in order to convince the opponent that he should accede to a favorable peace treaty, or whether one should withold them in order to provide an element of surprise in case the peace treaty fails.

No matter how strong the theoretical difficulties the above logic does provide a coherent framework for evaluating opposing force structures--the very evaluations that are central to arms control negotiations. Furthermore, this logic can address the combined chase of warfare avoidance and reduction of damage if warfare occurs. There is a three-step set of negotiations that are inextricably related:

(1) Arms control negotiations on the mutual development, production and deployment of weapons, forces, and related systems.

(2) "Pre-conflict" negotiations, in which adversaries accede to their respective opposing interests in a way that avoids the outbreak of military hostilities.

(3) Conflict termination negotiations, in which the two sides search for agreements which will permit military operations to cease in a way acceptable to both parties.

The first-phase negotiations (arms control) cannot be properly designed without anticipating the goals and strategies of the other two kinds of negotiations. None of these negotiations can be properly strategized without some logical conjectures regarding the strategic uses of the armaments in actual conflict (which is already well-understood), and corresponding conjectures regarding acceptable ways that a conflict can be terminated (which may not be well understood).

TWO-PERSON BARGAINING BETWEEN THREAT AND FAIR SOLUTION

Wulf Albers
Universität Bielefeld

Summary: The paper gives a model of bargaining involving threats. Two types of solution concepts are introduced, one models bargaining in conflict situations, the other models fair solutions.
Experimental results indicate that the conflict-concept seems to be adequate, if the problems discussed include all issues which have to be ruled between the opponents. It does not make sense to apply the conflict-concept to single issues, since then logrolling is neglected.

The fairness concept only has its place as a helpful tool which can be applied to single issues to obtain overall results corresponding to the conflict-concept. It does, however, not generally lead to these solutions, so that additional arrangements are necessary.

1 Introduction:

Bargaining in two-person or two-party bargaining can be modeled from different points of view. The bargaining strength is the main criterion in the theory of HICKS (1932), who considers the possible costs of a strike as a determinant of the wage level. This approach has been extended by CHAMBERLAIN (1951) and in the bargaining model of CARTTER and MARSHALL (1972). In these concepts the solution of the wage problem is that amount where each player has the same threats, measured as possible lengths of a strike a player would involve.

Other theories, as those of ZEUTHEN (1930), PEN (1952) and SHACKLE (1964) refer more to the risk that a player takes when he starts a strike in order to reach his aims. Here the solution is that point, where both players have the same probability to escalate the conflict. Game theoretic-axiomatic approaches are given by ZEUTHEN (1930), NASH (1953), SHAPLEY (1953), RAIFFA (1953), HARSANYI (1956), HOMANS (1963), CROTT-KALAI-SMORODINSKI (1975) and

NATO ASI Series, Vol. F 26
Modelling and Analysis in Arms Control
Edited by R. Avenhaus et al.

(1976), SCHMITZ (1977) and PERLES/MASCHLER (1979). All these theories only refer to the set of possible outcomes. In addition, ADAMS (1965) refers to the stake of the players. In this context the two-step bargaining procedure of NASH (1980) is worthy of note, where in a first round of bargaining the players determine a threat point and then select a cooperative solution which gives equal improvements with respect to the threat point to both players. HARSANYI and SELTEN (1972) generalized this approach to games with incomplete information. The concession-behavior has been modeled by STEVENS (1963) and in the aspiration adjustment theory of SAUERMANN and SELTEN (1962), and its extension by TIETZ (1975) and by OSGOOD (1959). The possible length of a strike is also the main criterion of BISHOP (1964) and FOLDES (1964), they however, model the bargaining process by stepwise concessions of the player with the -in the sense of the theory- weaker position. Dynamic theories of bargaining within time using differential equations have been given by CROSS (1965) and CODDINGTON (1966).

In this approach we model the solution as that point where both players get equal losses if the conflict escalates (fair solution) and as the point that the players reach, if both of them concede such that they just avoid a tremendous escalation of the conflict (threat-solution). Similar to the two step-NASH-procedure we predict that in view of the threat-solution (which gives both players the same utility as if they accept the ideal position of the other in the beginning of the escalation) the players find a cooperative solution, which gives both players equal surplus compared to the threat point.

2. Two-Person Bargaining

Let a bargaining-situation be given by

- X space of alternatives
- $D = \mathbb{R}_+$ degrees of escalation (which can be used without extending the conflict essentially)
- $U_i : X \to \mathbb{R}$, $V_i : D \to$ utility functions of players $i = 1,2$ on X and D respectively.

The utility functions U_1, U_2 are supposed to be strictly quasi concave and to have unique maxima on X. The corresponding points, in which the maxima are attained are denoted as x^1 (for U_1) and x^2 (for U_2). We assume that x_1 and x_2 are the initial demands of the players in the bargaining procedure.

Possible threats are supposed to be orderable in a linear way according to the degree of escalation. At a certain degree of escalation all threats corresponding to that of a lower degree are imposed. $V_i(d)$ gives the utility of all threats belonging to d for player i. V_i is assumed to be monotonically decreasing and continuous.

Example:

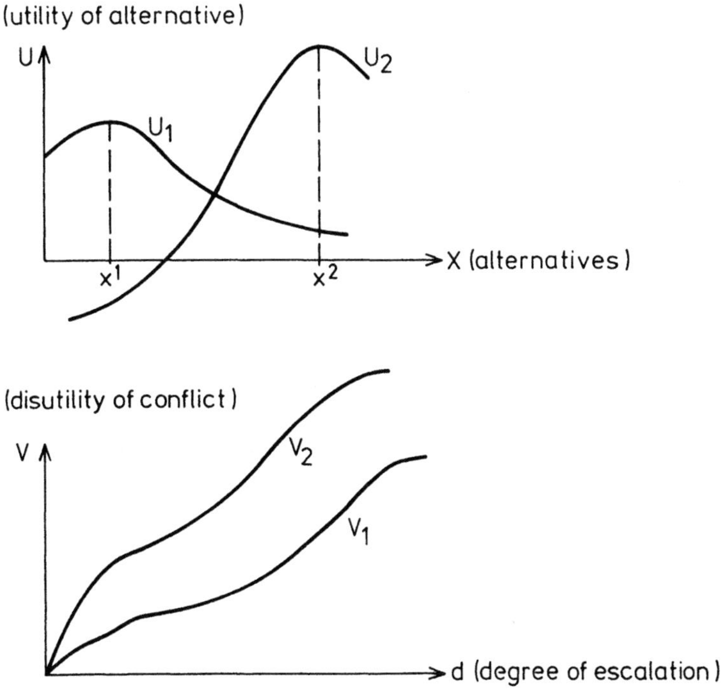

Fig. 1: a) utilities of two players 1, 2 on the space of alternatives
b) disutilities of a conflict as a function of the degree of escalation

3 The Fair Solution (for $X = \mathbb{R}$)

We assume now that $X = \mathbb{R}$ and introduce a "fair solution" by the following two assumptions:

(F1) In view of an extension of the conflict to a degree $d \in D$ the players agree to avoid the conflict by reducing their initial demands x^1 (in favor of the respective other player) to a new demand $x^i(d)$ in such a way that

$$U_i(x^i(t)) = U_i(x^i) - V_i(d)$$

I. e. each player reduces his demand in such a way that his positional loss equals the loss he would suffer, if the threat corresponding to the degree d of escalation would be verified.

(F2) The solution is given by that degree d^F of escalation, for which

$$x_i(d^F) = x_i(d^F) =: x^F.$$

4 The Threat-Solution (for $X = \mathbb{R}$)

Let still $X = \mathbb{R}$. The second solution-concept models a more conflicting situation. This approach models a bargaining process combined with an escalation of conflict. The assumption is that a player escalates the conflict to an essentially higher degree than modeled in D (which imposes essentially higher costs than the degrees of D), if the net-effect of the offers of the other (utility reduced by the disutility of the imposed threats) gets worse than the utility of the initial offer of the opponent. We assume that the disadvantage of this further escalation is so high that during an escalation following the steps of D both players reduce their demands in such a way that the other (just) does not initiate the further escalation.

Thus, we get the following conditions:

(T1) A player i escalates the conflict to a high degree (which is not modeled in D), if during the escalation of the conflict the other player j does not react on an escalation $d \in D$ by an offer $\tilde{x}^j(d)$ with

$$U_i(\tilde{x}^j(d)) - V_i(d) \geq U_i(\tilde{x}^j)$$

(T2) Each player j tries to give in as slowly as possible, i. e. he selects $\tilde{x}^j(d)$ in such a way that

$$U_i(\tilde{x}^j(d)) - V_i(d) = U_i(\tilde{x}^j)$$

for all $d \in D$.

(T3) The threat-solution is given by that degree $\tilde{d} \in D$ of the extension of the conflict, for which

$$\tilde{x}^i(\tilde{d}) = \tilde{x}^j(\tilde{d}).$$

So $\tilde{d}$ is the highest degree of conflict for which it is possible to avoid the further extension of the conflict to alternatives outside D. In $\tilde{d}$ the corresponding offers $\tilde{x}^i(\tilde{d})$ and $\tilde{x}^j(\tilde{d})$ of the players coincide, but for each player the utility of the solution is the same as if he had accepted the opening offer of his opponent before the escalation of the conflict.

An example of such an escalated conflict is a strike, where the set D is given by the possible lengths of strike. The essentially higher escalation can be for instance to close or destroy the firm. In this example the conflict is automatically escalated (to a higher length of strike) if the players do not reach an agreement.

Example:

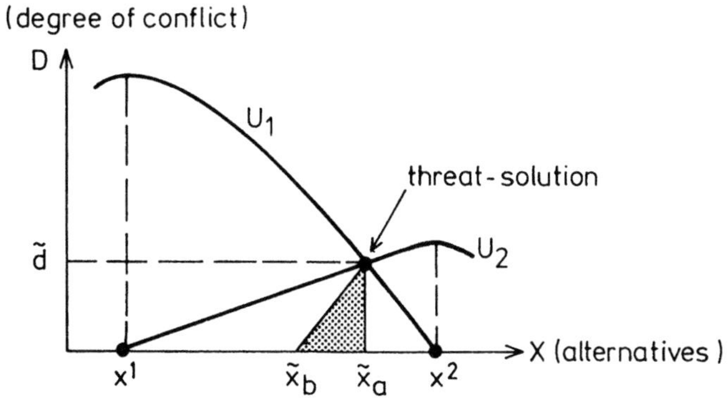

Fig. 2: Iso-utility lines of the players in the space of alternatives x degree of conflict.
(For each player his level of utility is given his value of the ideal position of the other if the conflict is not escalated (d = 0).)

It should be remarked that finding the cooperative solution "below" the threat point with equal improvements of utility for both players involves a comparison of the utility scales. In the situation given here, two extreme alternatives for such a comparison can be suggested:

(a) Utility comparison via degree of threat: Here we assume that the players evaluate their improvements as equal if both of them can avoid the same degree of escalation. The corresponding solution is $\tilde{x}_a$;

(b) Utility comparison via a natural scale of the space of alternatives: If the space of alternatives has a natural scale (as the amount of wages) then the concessions can be measured by the distances on the x - scale. This way of utility comparison gives the mid-point of the ideal positions of the players as a solution, since (for fixed d = 0) the distances to the iso-utility lines U^1 and U^2 through the threat point are equal. The corresponding solution is $\tilde{x}_b$.

Experimental results indicate that condition (T2) is usually met by real behavior. Players try to avoid the maximal possible conflict and then usually find a cooperative solution below the threat point (which improves the utilities of both of them). The problem of this cooperation is, however, how to compare the advantages of the players with respect to the threat point.

5 Differences of the Two Concepts

We illustrate the differences of the two concepts by an example: (see figure 3).

It can easily be seen that the fair solution and the threat-solution favor different players. The fair solution corresponds to the bargaining theory of HICKS (1963). Experimental results, SCHWIND (1977), support the threat-solution. In this experiment the space of alternatives had a natural measure and the solutions where between $\tilde{x}_a$ and $\tilde{x}_b$.

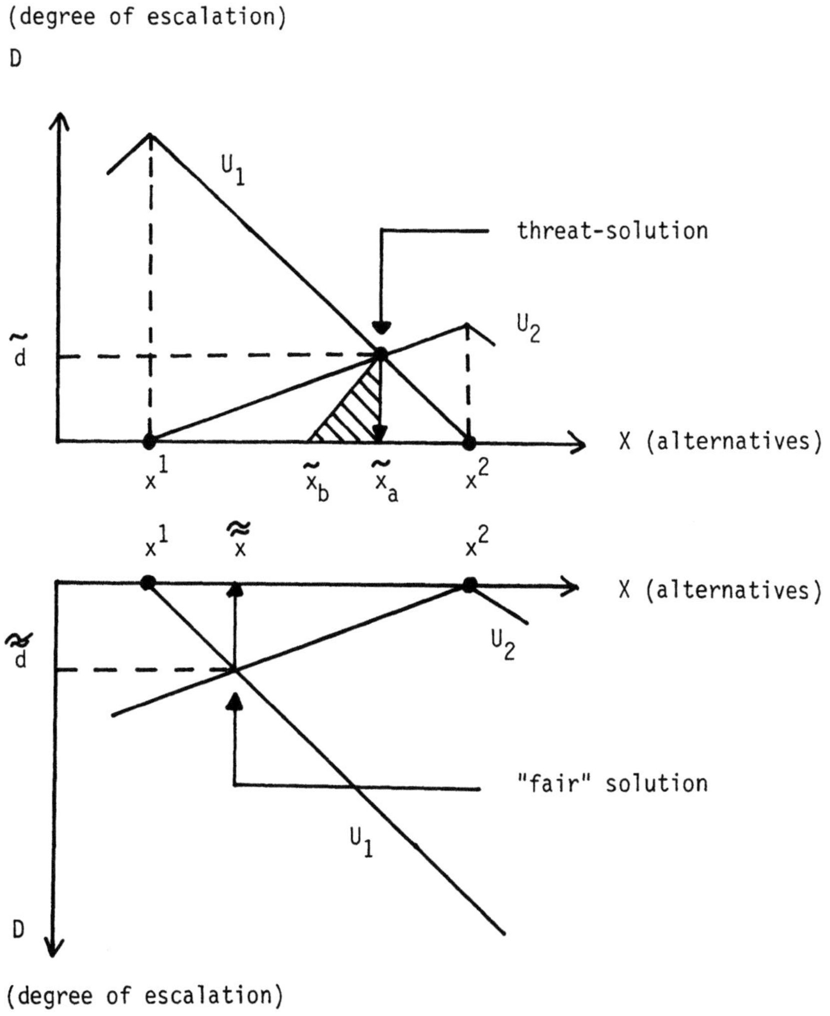

Fig. 3: Threat-solution and conflict solution and the corresponding isoutility lines of the players in the 1-dimensional case.

6 Threat-Solutions for $X = \mathbb{R}$

We now consider the threat-solution for $X = \mathbb{R}^n$. In this case (if for example no threats are imposed) the situation looks as in the following example:

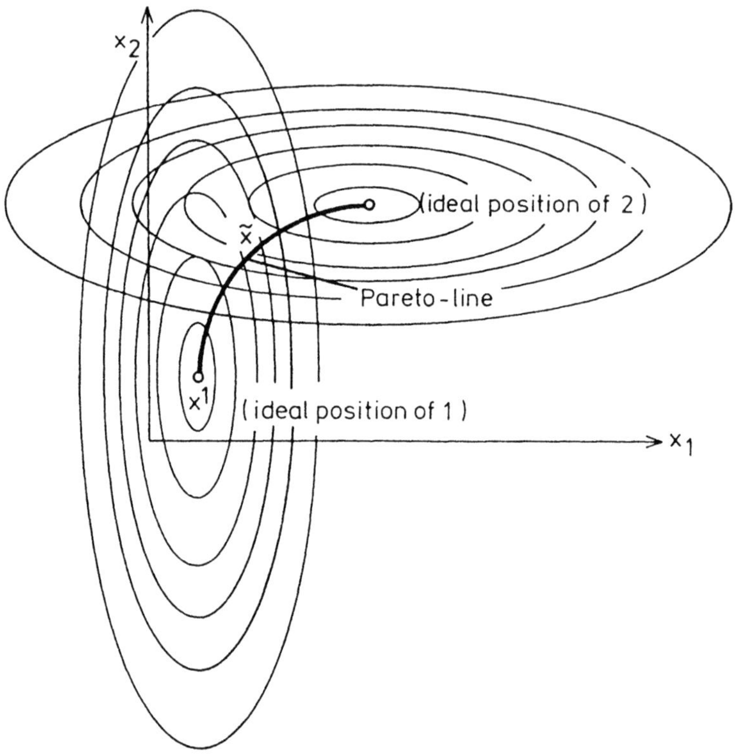

Fig. 4: Iso-utility lines of two players in a two dimensional space if no threats are involved.

To apply the threat-theory we assume that rational players will bargain on a solution point on the Pareto line x^1 x^2. We stretch this line and model the solution point as in the 1-dimensional case. [1] Thus, we get the threat-solution above $\tilde{x}$ on the Pareto-line: [2]

---

1) This reduction to the 1-dimensional case is generally possible, if the utility functions are strictly quasi concave, since the Pareto-frontier is 1-dimensional in also n-dimensional case.
2) Since there is no natural measure on the Pareto-line, we only predict the cooperative solution $\tilde{x}_a$.

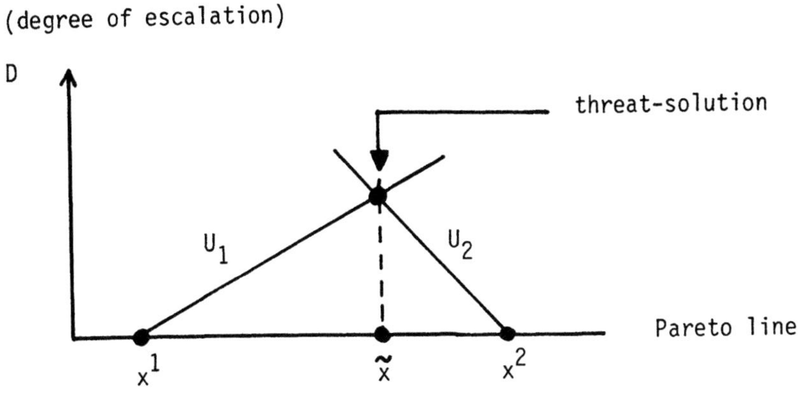

Fig. 5: Threat-solution on the Pareto-line of the multi-dimensional conflict.

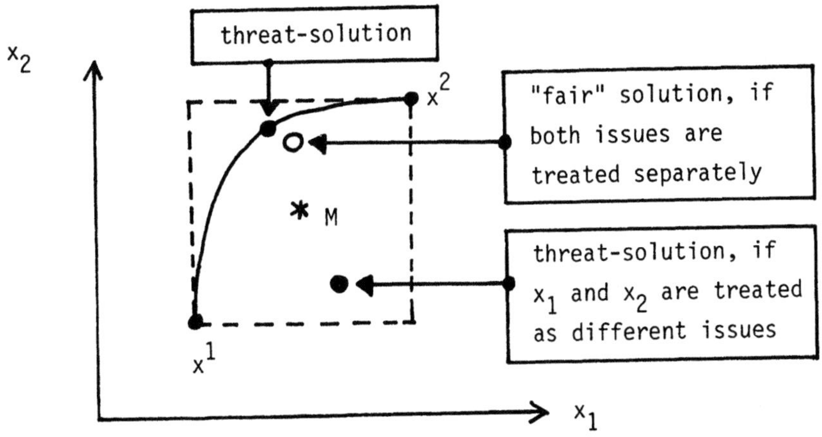

Fig. 6: Solution points corresponding to different solution concepts in case of a two-dimensional space of alternatives.

We remark that the threat-solution selects a point which gives to players 1 and 2 higher utility than the mid-point M of x^1 and x^2. (If the dimensions of the space X would have been bargained separately the solution point would have been worse than M for both players.)

The fair solution, which is obtained, if both issues are treated separately leads to a result, which is "quite near" to the threat-solution of the global

(2-dimensional) problem.

Our opinion is, that generally the threat-solution models possible bargaining results adequately.
However, if problems become too difficult, so that they must be splitted up into different issues (and this is generally the case for the permanent bargaining situation between states) each issue may be treated by the fairness-concept.

This is, however, only a convention and not directly justified by strategic power. To establish a balance of concessions the overall concessions must be counted and eventually corrected by additional arrangements - as for instance the introduction of interest spheres.

Essential new problems will not necessarily be solved on the conventional and unreflected basis of a "fair" solution, but will follow considerations as outlined in the threat-solution concept.

REFERENCES

Adams, S.J. (1965): Inequity in Social Exchange. In: *Advances in Experimental Social Psychology*, Vol. 2, (Leonrad Berkowitz, Ed.), pp. 267-299, New York

Albers, W. (1977): Eine Anti-Hicks-Theorie für bilaterale Verhandlungen mit Zeitkosten. *Arbeitspapiere für mathematische Wirtschaftsforschung*, 26. Augsburg

Bishop, R.L. (1964): A Zeuthen-Hicks Theory of Bargaining. *Econometrica* 32, pp. 410-417

Boulding, K.E. (1963): Towards a Pure Theory of Threat Systems, *American Economic Review, Papers and Proceedings*, pp. 424 ff.

Buchanan, J.M., G. Tullock (1962): *The calculus of consent*. Ann Arbor

Coddington, A. (1966): The Theory of the Bargaining Process: Comment *American Economic Review* 56, pp. 522-536

Contini, B. (1968): The Value of Time in Bargaining Negotiations: Some experimental Evidence. *American Economic Review* 58, pp. 374-393

Cross, J.G.(1965): The Theory of the Bargaining Process. *American Economic Review* 55, pp. 67-94

Crott, H.W. (1972): Der Einfluß struktureller und situativer Merkmale auf das Verhalten in Verhandlungssituationen. *Zeitschrift für Sozialpsychologie*, pp. 134-158 und pp. 227-244

Foldes, L. (1964): A Determinate Model of Bilateral Monopoly. *Economica* 31, pp. 117-131

Harsanyi, J.C. (1956): Approaches to the Bargaining Problem Before and After the Theory of Games: A Critical Discussion of Zeuthen's, Hicks', and Nash's Theories. *Econometrica* 24, pp.144-157

Harsanyi, J.C., Selten, R. (1972): A Generalized Nash Solution for Two-Person-Bargaining Games with Incomplete Information. *Management Science* 18, No. 5, Jan. Part 2, pp. 80-106

Hicks, J.R. (1963): *The Theory of Wages*. Second Edition, London

Homans, G.C. (1963): Social Behavior as Exchange. *American Journal of Sociology*, pp. 597-606

Kalai, E., Smorodinski, M. (1975): Other Solutions to Nash's Bargaining Problem. *Econometrica* 43, pp. 513-519

Nash, J.S. (1953): Two Person Cooperative Games. *Econometrica* 21, pp. 128-140

Nash, J.S. (1960): The Bargaining Problem. *Econometrica* 28, pp. 155-162

Perles, M., Maschler, M. (1979): *A Superadditive Solution to Nash Bargaining Games*. Manuscript

Osgood, C.E. (1959): Suggestions for Winning the Real War with Communism. *Journal of the Conflict Resolution* 3, pp. 295-325

Pen, J. (1952): A General Theory of Bargaining. *American Economic Review* 42, pp. 24-42

Raiffa, H. (1953): Arbitration Schemes for Generalized Two Person Games. In: *Contributions to the Theory of Games* (Kuhn, H.W., Tucker, A.W., Eds.), pp. 361-387

Roth, A.E. (1979): *Axiomatic Models of Bargaining*. Berlin,Heidelberg, New York

Sauermann, H., Selten, R. (1962): Anspruchsanpassungstheorie in der Unternehmung. *Zeitschrift für die Gesamte Staatswissenschaft*, pp. 557-597

Schmitz, N. (1977): *Bemerkungen zum Zweipersonen-Verhandlungsproblem: I. Verhandlungen ohne Drohungen*. Arbeitspapier S15, Münster

Schwind, C. (1977): *Zur Gültigkeit verschiedener Modelle für bilaterale Verhandlungen mit Verhandlungskosten*. Diplomarbeit, Augsburg

Shackle, G.L.S. (1964): *On the Nature of the Bargaining Process*.

Shapley, J.S. (1953): A Value for n-Person Games. *Annals of Math. Studies* 28, pp. 307-318

Stevens, C.M. (1963): *Strategy and Collective Bargaining Negotiations*. New York,Toronto,London

Tietz, R. (1975): An Experimental Analysis of Wage Bargaining Behavior. *Zeitschrift für die Gesamte Staatswissenschaft* 131, pp. 44-91

Tietz, R., Weber, H.J. (1978): Decision Behavior in Multi-Variable Negotiation. In: *Bargaining Behavior* (Sauermann, H., Ed.), Tübingen, pp. 60-87

Walton, R.E., McKersie, R.B. (1965): *A Behavioral Theory of Labor Negotiations. An Analysis of a Social Interaction System*. New York

Young, O.R. (1975): *Bargaining - Formal Theories of Negotiation*. Urbana, Chicago, London

Zeuthen, F. (1930): *Problems of Monopoly and Economic Warfare*. London

GENERAL ORDINAL 2x2 GAMES IN ARMS CONTROL APPLICATIONS

Niall M. Fraser
Department of Management Sciences
University of Waterloo
Waterloo, Ontario
N2l 1G3 Canada

1. INTRODUCTION

The most common model of human behavior employed in game theory is the normal form, introduced by von NEUMANN and MORGENSTERN (1953). An example of a two player, two strategy game ("2x2 game") in normal form is illustrated in Table 1. This particular game is called "Prisoners' Dilemma". The possible outcomes are the four cells of the matrix. Player 1 must choose between row R1 and row R2, while player 2 must choose between column C1 and column C2. If Player 1 chooses R1 while 2 chooses C1, the resulting outcome is the upper left cell of the matrix, which, in Prisoners' Dilemma, is marked 3,3. The numbers in each cell (called "payoffs") denote the relative preference of each player for the outcome; the first number is for Player 1 and the second for Player 2. The higher the number, the more preferred the outcome. Thus, the most preferred outcome for Player 1 is represented by the (R2, C1) cell, which is marked 4,1. This is Player 2's least preferred outcome.

		Player 2	
		C1	C2
Player 1	R1	3, 3	1, 4
	R2	4, 1	2, 2

Table 1: An Example 2x2 Game (Prisoner's Dilemma)

Although the 2x2 game model may seem highly restrictive, it has been found to present many strategic situations in a usefully clear manner. (See, for example, BRAMS and DAVIS (1983), SNYDER (1971), ZAGARE (1981, 1985), as well as the enormous literature on Prisoners' Dilemma and Chicken, referred to below). SNYDER and DIESING (1977) generally favor the 2x2 game over any

NATO ASI Series, Vol. F 26
Modelling and Analysis in Arms Control
Edited by R. Avenhaus et al.

other model for the study of international conflict. Consequently, much research has been done on 2x2 games. Some particular games, such as Prisoners' Dilemma and Chicken, have been subjected to extensive study by many authors (e.g., RAPOPORT and CHAMMAH (1965, 1966), AXELROD (1984) and BRAMS (1985)), particularly in arms control applications.

The purpose of this paper is to expose the reader to some important new developments in the study of conflicts using general ordinal 2x2 games, and to suggests avenues of application of these to arms control problems.

2. THE MODELLING PERSPECTIVE

In the traditional point of view of the normal form game, the strategic options available to a player are only thought of as alternatives for one-shot choices ("strategies"), to be selected once and for all, in ignorance of the opponent's reaction. Under this viewpoint, the only decision available to a player is the determination of a strategy, or a random mixture of strategies. The methods of determining these strategies are very limited, and include ideas of rationality and dominance.

Many interesting lines of inquiry have been developed from this paradigm of behavior over the last three decades. However, commencing with HOWARD's (1971) work on Metagame Theory, and reinforced by SNYDER and DIESING (1977), BRAMS (1977), BRAMS and WITTMAN (1981), FRASER and HIPEL (1979, 1984), KILGOUR (1984) and ZAGARE (1981, 1984), an alternative approach was implicitly developed.

One major change in this new use of the normal form model concerns a subtle reworking of the meaning of both strategies and outcomes. In this alternative approach the options in a game are thought of as "policies", perhaps to be selected initially but in any case permitting the players the opportunity to change policies (once or more than once) at a later time. Such a change implies, of course, a change of outcome (Fraser et al, 1985). The interpretation creates a substantive alteration in the way in which the normal form representation is used. Under the traditional interpretation each element of the matrix is a final outcome of the entire process, and not subject to change within the context of that game. Under the second interpretation, the matrix is a structure for retaining various possible states of affairs, and the situation may pass through some or all of these states before possibly settling on one.

Also, in this new interpretation of the normal form, a different kind of assessment must be made. Instead of determining which is the most reasonable strategy for a player to employ, the question now centers on special characteristics of each outcome. For instance, since the result of a game can move from one outcome to another, one particular important characteristic is stability. An outcome is stable if it can be expected to persist, should it arise. That is, it is stable if the players, individually or collectively , would rationally prefer to hold the game at that position rather than to cause it to move elsewhere.

As a consequence of this new viewpoint, methods for the analysis of game models have proliferated in recent years. Originally, there was only one procedure relating a game model to a real-world outcome - the "Nash" equilibrium (NASH, 1951). A Nash equilibrium is any outcome at which each player can be said to maximize his payoff, under the assumption that his opponent's strategy is fixed. For example, (R2, C2) in Table 1 is the only Nash equilibrium of Prisoners' Dilemma. However, in recent years many other "stability" concepts have been defined. These help to identify other outcomes that have some kind of inherent stability - their individual applicability may depend on how the 2x2 game model is to be interpreted. For example, most stability concepts identify outcome (R1, C1) in Table 1 as also having some stability properties. Different stability properties are significant under different circumstances. KILGOUR et al. (1984) have rigourously compared several such solution concepts.

The consequences of all of these changes taken together is the creation of a somewhat distinct area of applied game theory, which is often called "conflict analysis" (FRASER et al., 1985). Included in this eclectic new field are the work of engineers (FRASER and HIPEL, 1979, 1984), political scientists (BRAMS, 1977; BENJAMIN, 1981; KNIGHT and POWELL, 1974), operations researchers (BENNETT and DANDO, 1977; 1979; BENNETT et al., 1980), business consultants (RADFORD and FINGERHUT, 1980), and mathematicians (HOWARD, 1971; KILGOUR, 1984). Their common focus is the use of game theory for dealing with real world conflict, and their intellectual environment features a relaxation of many of the traditional assumptions constraining game theoretic modeling.

3. THE EXHAUSTIVE ANALYSIS OF THE 2x2 GAME

A 2x2 game is traditionally constructed using ordinal preference information. Thus, only the fact that a player prefers one outcome to another is known, and there is never any meaningful measure how much a player prefers one outcome over another. In Table 1, the outcome preferences are numbered from 1 to 4 for each player. This implies that each player has a definite preference between any two outcomes. Such a preference ordering is referred to as "strict ordinal". It is clear that there are only finitely many different 2x2 game matrices involving strict ordinal preferences. The numbers 1, 2, 3 and 4 can be placed in the four cells in 4! = 24 different ways for Player 1 and again for Player 2, resulting in 24 x 24 = 576 different matrices. However, many of these are essentially the same. For example, the decision problem faced by the players (as a group) is no different if Player 1 is called Player 2 and Player 2, Player 1. Similarly, strategy R1 could have been interchanged with R2 and/or C1 with C2. By such considerations, the number of "strategically non-equivalent" strict ordinal 2x2 games is only 78. RAPOPORT and GUYER (1966) gave the original enumeration of the 78 strategically distinct strict ordinal 2x2 games, which was expanded upon by RAPOPORT et al. (1976). Another enumeration of the 78 games was given by BRAMS (1977)).

In recent years, interest has extended beyond the set of strict ordinal 2x2 games. A player may be indifferent between two or more of the four outcomes in the game. Thus, each player may have any one of the following eight preference orderings:

1,1,1,1 all outcomes equally preferred
1,1,1,2 indifferent among the three least preferred
1,1,2,2 indifferent between two least and two most
1,1,2,3 indifferent between two least preferred
1,2,2,2 indifferent among three most preferred
1,2,2,3 indifferent between two middle
1,2,3,3 indifferent between two most preferred
1,2,3,4 distinct level of preference for each outcome.

GUYER and HAMBURGER (1968) calculated that the number of strategically non-equivalent games when both players may have nonstrict ordinal preferences is 726, out of 5625 apparent possibilities. Table 2 illustrates exactly how many non-equivalent games there are for every possible combination of preference orderings for the two players - a grand total of 726.

Payoff set	1111	1112	1122	1123	1222	1223	1233	1234
1111	1	1	3	3	1	3	3	6
1112		3	6	12	4	12	12	24
1122			8	18	6	18	18	36
1123				21	12	36	36	72
1222		Number of games			3	12	12	24
1223						21	36	72
1233							21	72
1234								78

Table 2: Number of Different Games for Each Pair of Payoff Sets

FRASER and KILGOUR (1985) wrote several computer programs to generate and analyze all of these general ordinal games. First, the set of 726 strategically non-equivalent games had to be identified and enumerated. The main program performing this function was POS (Pay Off Sets). Secondly, the calculations applying the various forms of analysis to strategies, outcomes and games were carried out. The main computer program for this purpose was PROP (PROPerties).

The PROP program determines a remarkable number of properties for players, outcomes and games. For references detailing the sources of each of these stability concepts, the reader is referred to the original paper by FRASER and KILGOUR (1985). These include:

For each game:

- symmetric
- mutually ordinal
- strict ordinal
- no conflict
- complete opposition

For each game and player:

- minimax value
- minimax strategy
- maximin value
- dominant strategy
- best outcome
- worst outcome

For each outcome and player:

- rational (R)
- general metarational (GMR)
- symmetric metarational (SMR)
- Fraser-Hipel sequential stability (FHQ)
- Stackelberg (ST)
- Non-myopic stability (NM)
- Extended non-myopically stable (XNM)
- Limited-horizon stability, foresight 1-6 (L1-L6)
- Disaster stability (D)

For each outcome:

- group rational (R)
- group general metarational (GMR)
- group symmetric metarational (SMR)
- group Fraser-Hipel sequential stability (FHQ)
- group Fraser-Hipel simultaneous stability (FHM)
- group Stackelberg stability (ST)
- group Non-myopic stability (NM)
- group Extended non-myopic stability (XNM)
- group Limited-horizon stability (L1-L6)
- group Disaster stability (D)

The results of all these calculations are presented in a simple chart form as illustrated in Table 3. This shows only one of the 726 games; the complete output consumes 243 pages. (A legend for interpreting Table 3 is given in Table 4). After listing each game, classification information is given for indexing purposes. (More information about the taxonomy scheme can be found in KILGOUR and FRASER (1985)). For each game, general characteristics are listed first, followed by the maximin and minimax values, and dominant strategies. Then six lines of characters display individual and group stability and other information for each outcome. The four large columns on the left contain the individual properties of each outcome, and the two large columns on the right show group properties.

For individual properties, the chart's first two columns (from the left) and top three rows correspond to the upper left outcome (R1, C1) in the 2x2 game. Of these, the first three lines of the extreme left column show the individual results for Player 1, while the same lines in second column contain the results for Player 2. In the same manner, the original matrix is visually mapped onto the four columns and six lines so that there is space for

```
215) 2,2 1,3
     3,1 1,1
    DD-4442-Sy
    maxmin values = (1, 1); strategies = (R1&R2, C1&C2)
    minmax values = (1, 1)
    dominant for 1: R2;     dominant for 2: C2
   ( GS    ) ( GS    )    (RGSQ T)  (RGSQ T)          ( GSM   ) (RGSQ T)
   (      3) (      3)    (NXD W2)  (NXD BO)          (       P) (NXD  P)
   (       ), (       )   (123456), (123456)          (        ) (123456)
   (RGSQ T)  (RGSQ T)     (RGSQ T)  (RGSQ T)          (RGSQ T) (RGSQ T)
   (NXD BO)  (NXD W2)     (NXD W1)  (NXD W1)          (NXD  P) (NXD W )
   (123456), (123456)     (123456), (123456)          (123456) (123456)
```

Table 3: PROP Program Output for 2x2 Game Properties

```
                 Legend

          AA, BB, ... , HH = Class

          2222, 3222, ... , 5555 = Key Number

Game:     Sy = Symmetric
          Mo = Mutually Ordinal
          So = Strict Ordinal
          Co = Complete Opposition
          Nc = No Conflict

Individual:                              Group:

1) R            7) Nm                    1) R            7) Nm
2) Gmr          8) Xnm                   2) Gmr          8) Xnm
3) Smr          9) D                     3) Smr          9) D
4) fhQ         10) not used              4) fhQ|fhM     10) not used
5) not used 11) B|W|E                    5) not used 11) B|W|E
6) sT          12) type (0|1|2|3|C)      6) 1|2|sT      12) Pareto superior
13) to 18) L1 to L6                      13) to 18) L1 to L6
        maxmin values = (maxmin(1), maxmin(2))
        minmax values = (minmax(1), minmax(2))
```

Table 4: PROP Program Legend

18 characters to indicate the various individual properties for each outcome in the game, with respect to each player. Similarly, the two columns and six lines to the right provide 18 characters for each outcome to indicate group properties.

The Legend in Table 4 indicates the meanings of each of the symbols used in the output. B/W/E stands for Best/Worst/Equal. The Type is used in the NM and XNM calculations. FHQ and FHM are displayed in the same location in the group stability section since they are often applied together and cannot be simultaneously exhibited by one outcome. Group ST is indicated by a 1 or a 2, corresponding to an equilibrium with Player 1 as leader or Player 2 as leader, respectively, or by a T, meaning a dual ST equilibrium. Positions 5 and 9 in the individual stability matrices and positions 5, 9 and 10 in the group stability matrices are reserved for future solution concepts.

There are several benefits to having the data set of all 726 games available (FRASER and KILGOUR, 1985):

1) Previously, a real world situation such as an arms control problem had to fit a strict ordinal model if the available literature was to be of use in assessing its strategic implications. Now any appropriate 2x2 model can be used.

2) Results are easily available for games which are similar to a game under consideration. This makes it easy to perform sensitivity analyses to ensure the robustness of a particular result, or to see how it depends on the particular model chosen.

3) It is often of great value to be able to assess how different behaviour assumptions, as reflected in the different stability concepts, would affect action in conflicts. An enumeration of the stability results for every 2x2 game permits convenient comparisons in a particular situation without extensive calculations.

4) Certain games are of particular interest because of some strategic principle that they demonstrate. The games of Prisoners' Dilemma and

Chicken are most famous in this regard, but Battle of the Sexes, Hero, the Cookie Conflict and many others might be included in the list. Very few non-strict ordinal games have been identified as being of special interest, and part of the explanation may simply be that no comprehensive listing was available. A complete enumeration permits the freer examination of all 2x2 games. As an illustration, a game "midway between" Prisoners' Dilemma and Chicken is identified by Fraser and Kilgour (1985), and is presented below in an arms control application.

5) New solution concepts can more easily be developed and compared to existing ideas.

6) Proofs by exhaustion have been convenient for strict ordinal 2x2 games (eg, (BRAMS and WITTMAN, 1981)), but until now have been virtually impossible for the general case. Fraser and Kilgour (1985) present many interesting such results.

7) New concepts in science are often the result of observing raw data and noting patterns or inconsistencies. This data is now available, and can be manipulated in a variety of ways.

8) A complete enumeration may help to systematize current knowledge of 2x2 games, and current techniques for their application.

4. EXAMPLE - SUPERPOWER CONFLICT

As an example of the use of this data base in arms control problems, consider the 2x2 game shown in Table 5. This game is game number 215 from Table 3, formatted as a superpower conflict.

The strict ordinal 2x2 games known as "Prisoners' Dilemma" and "Chicken" have frequently been used to model the strategic problems that arise in arms control problems. Game number 215 is a general ordinal game that is strategically similar to both Prisoners' Dilemma and Chicken. Like the game of Chicken, if both players improve from the 2,2 payoff position, the worst outcome for both will result. However, similar to Prisoners' Dilemma, if only one of the players deviates, the other player is left at his least preferred outcome. The game thus might be called "Chicken's Dilemma".

		USSR: no preemptive strike	USSR: preemptive strike
USA	no preemptive strike	2, 2	1, 3
USA	preemptive strike	3, 1	1, 1

Table 5: Chicken's Dilemma

In the model in Table 5, the situation represents the strategic consideration on the part of the two superpowers of whether to make a preemptive nuclear strike on the other. In this case, it is assumed that the players have identical interests, including the Machiavellian one of most preferring to nuke the other to cinders. However, any other model the reader prefers could have also been employed.

In this model each player is indifferent to the two outcomes mathematically available when the other player preemptively strikes. The idea here is that the firepower of either side is so great that the other will be totally destroyed anyhow. It is immaterial to the destroyed side whether they strike back or not.

Reference to the stability information in Table 3 indicates the forces at play in determining the stability of this strategic relationship. All outcomes except the one with a payoff of 2,2 are very stable under all of the stability concepts. The desired outcome (with a payoff of 2,2), is stable only under general metarationality, symmetric metarationality and Fraser-Hipel simultaneous stability. The knowledge of this can guide policy makers to reinforce these forms of stability. For example, it is clear that comprehensive intelligence and fast deployment reinforce stability in this case.

5. CONCLUSIONS

The exhaustive analysis of the 2x2 game provides a large database of information for use in the study of arms control problems and other conflicts. One can determine the consequence of some strategic relationship between two participants from a wide range of points of view. Additionally, one can find a basic strategic relationship that can result in some desired end.

A particular application of a general ordinal 2x2 game to a superpower conflict demonstrated the potential of the approach.

6. REFERENCES

Axelrod, R. (1984): The Evolution of Cooperation. New York: Basic Books

Benjamin, C.M. (1981): Developing a Game/Decision Theoretic Approach to Comparative Foreign Policy Analysis: Some Cases in Recent American Foreign Policy. Ph.D. Dissertation, University of Southern California

Bennett, P.G. and Dando, M.R. (1977): Fall Gelb and other games: A hypergame perspective of the fall of France, 1940. Journal of the Conflict Research Society, Vol. 1, No. 2, pp. 1-32

Bennett, P.G. and Dando, M.R. (1979): Complex strategic analysis: a hypergame perspective of the fall of France. Journal of the Operational Research Society, Vol. 30, No. 1, pp. 23-32

Bennett, P.G., Dando, M.R. and Sharp, R.G. (1980): Using hypergames to model difficult social issues: an approach to the case of soccer hooliganism. Journal of the Operational Research Society, Vol. 31, pp. 621-635

Brams, S.J. (1977): Deception in 2x2 games. Journal of Peace Science, Vol. 2, pp. 171-203

Brams, S.J. (1985): Superpower Games: Applying Game Theory to Superpower Conflicts. New Haven CT: Yale University Press, 1985

Brams, S.J. and Davis, M.D. (1983): The verification problem in arms control: a game theoretic analysis, presentation to the Joint National Meeting of the Operations Research Society of America and the Institute of Management Sciences, Orlando, Florida, Nov. 7-9, 1983

Brams, S.J. and Wittman, D. (1981): Nonmyopic equilibria in 2x2 games, Conflict Management and Peace Science, 1981, Vol. 6, pp. 39-62

Fraser, N.M., Benjamin, C.M. and Powell, C.A. (1985): Optimizing the decision process: structure and stability in complex conflict. IS Notes, in press (accepted October, 1985)

Fraser, N.M., Benjamin, C.M. and Powell, C.A. (1985): Optimizing the decision process: structure and stability in complex conflict. Proceedings, Society for General Systems Research International Conference. Los Angeles, May 27-31, 1985, pp. 1061-1070

Fraser, N.M. and Hipel, K.W. (1979): Solving complex conflicts. IEEE Transactions on Systems, Man and Cybernetics, 1979, Vol. SMC-9, pp. 181-185

Fraser, N.M. and Hipel, K.W. (1984): Conflict Analysis: Models and Resolutions. New York: North-Holland, 1984

Fraser, N.M. and Kilgour, D.M. (1985): Nonstrict ordinal 2x2 games: a comprehensive computer assisted analysis of the 726 possibilities. Theory and Decision, in press (accepted October, 1985)

Guyer, M. and Hamburger, H. (1968): A note on a 'Taxonomy of 2x2 Games', General Systems, 1968, Vol. 13, 205-208

Howard, N. (1971): Paradoxes of Rationality. Cambridge, Mass.: The MIT Press, 1971

Kilgour, D.M. (1984): Equilibria for far-sighted players, Theory and Decision. 1984, Vol. 16, pp.135-157

Kilgour, D.M. and Fraser, N.M. (1985): A taxonomy of all ordinal 2x2 games, Department of Management Sciences, University of Waterloo, Waterloo, Ontario, Canada, 1985

Kilgour, D.M., Hipel, K.W. and Fraser, N.M. (1984): Solution concepts in 2x2 games, Large Scale Systems, 1984, Vol. 6, No. 1, pp. 49-72

Knight, K. and Powell, C.A. (1974): Metagame theory and the metagame/options analysis technique: A basic introduction and an application: Bandladesh, World Studies, 1974, Vol. 1, No. 1

Nash, J.F. (1951): Non-cooperative games, Annals of Mathematics, 1951, Vol. 54, pp. 286-295

Radford, K.J. and Fingerhut, B. (1980): Analysis of a complex decision situation - the Simpsons/Simpsons-Sears merger proposal. OMEGA, 1980, Vol. 8, No. 4, pp. 221-231

Rapoport, A. and Chammah, A.M. (1965): Prisoner's Dilemma. Ann Arbor: University of Michigan Press, 1965

Rapoport, A. and Chammah, A.M. (1966): The game of Chicken. American Behavioral Scientist, 1966, Vol. 10, pp. 23-28

Rapoport, A., Guyer, M.J. and Gordon, D.G. (1976): The 2x2 Game. Ann Arbor: The University of Michigan Press, 1976.

Rapoport, A. and Guyer, M.J. (1966): A taxonomy of 2x2 games. General Systems, 1966, Vol. 11, pp. 203-214

Snyder, G.H. (1971): Prisoner's Dilemma and Chicken models in international politics. International Studies Quarterly, 1971, Vol. 15, No. 1, pp. 97

Snyder, G.H. and Diesing, P. (1977): Conflict Among Nations. Princeton, N.J.: Princeton University Press, 1977

Von Neumann, J. and Morgenstern, O. (1953): Theory of Games and Economic Behavior. 3rd Edition. Princeton, N.J.: Princeton University Press, 1953

Zagare, F.C. (1981): Non-myopic equilibria and the Middle East crisis of 1967. Conflict Management and Peace Science, 1981, Vol. 5, pp. 139-162

Zagare, F.C. (1984): Limited move equilibria in 2x2 games. Theory and Decision, 1984, Vol. 16, pp. 1-19

Zagare, F.C. (1985): The pathology of unilateral deterrence. Dynamic Models of International Conflict, M.D. Ward and U. Luterbacher, ed. Boulder, Colorado: Lynne Reinner Press, 1985

BUILDING A US-SOVIET WORKING RELATIONSHIP:

IDEAS ON PROCESS

Scott Brown and Roger Fisher
Harvard Negotiation Project
Harvard Law School
Cambridge, MA 02138/USA

INTRODUCTION

The process of negotiating international agreements is often more crucial to the resolution of differences than the relative negotiating positions of the parties. The working relationship between the parties and the procedures for resolving disputes can determine whether a negotiation will deteriorate into accusations and recriminations or create a solution which serves the interests of both parties and strengthens the procedures for dealing with future disputes.

Negotiating with a stranger is different from negotiating with a friend; negotiating with an enemy is different from negotiating with an ally. Yet the objective status of the parties does not always determine the ease of reaching agreement. A businessman may find it easier to negotiate with some competitors than with others, and the United States may find it easier to negotiate with Canada than with Mexico. What are the operating determinants of an effective negotiating relationship? What relationship would help facilitate a particular negotiation? How do we create such a relationship when the two parties bear deep differences on substantive issues?

Contradictions in preparations for summit talks in November 1985 between the United States and the Soviet Union were symptomatic of uncertainty about how to pursue better relations in the face of deep substantive differences. Each government felt that a concession on a matter of substance would reward intransigence and accede to the other's strength; failure to make concession would condemn both sides to endless hostility and the disfavor of world public opinion.

After the summit talks in November, both Reagan and Gorbachev were able to paint the summit as a partial success. Each leader felt he had told the other what was wrong with the other's behavior (although neither indicated he had listened to the other). The leaders did not reach substantive agreement on security issues but they did sign a number of minor agreements and, perhaps most important, the leaders agreed to meet again.

NATO ASI Series, Vol. F 26
Modelling and Analysis in Arms Control
Edited by R. Avenhaus et al.

Since the summit talks, many officials and observers have indicated that while the first summit was fine, the two leaders will have to reach more substantive agreements on arms control at future talks to continue the process of improving relations. But this belief may be as false now as it was before the past summit. There is little reason to believe that an arms control agreement by itself will improve the relationship or the security of the two countries. What kind of relationship should the two countries want and how can they hope to achieve it?

Neither party expects to eliminate the differences between the two nations, nor do they expect to become allies or major trading partners. But they may hope to find a stable relationship in which the two governments can negotiate their differences amicably and efficiently without the threat of force. Such a relationship can be characterized as a "working relationship."

DIAGNOSIS OF OBSTACLES TO A WORKING RELATIONSHIP

Three factors prevent the United States and the Soviet Union from improving the way they deal with each other: confusion of process with substance, lack of a clear objective, and the tendency to make relationship-building behavior contingent on reciprocal action.

Confusion of process with substance.

Many people confuse a good working relationship with agreement on matters of substance. Both governments have, at different times, insisted that a good relationship depends upon the other government agreeing with a particular substantive demand. Gorbachev has suggested that good relations depend upon the U.S. abandoning the Strategic Defense Initiative (SDI). Reagan has suggested that good relations will depend upon the Soviet Union accepting SDI and changing its policy towards human rights, towards Afghanistan, or both.

Confusion between process and substance has led many to believe that since the United States does not agree with Soviet behavior in Afghanistan and elsewhere, and the Soviet Union objects to U.S. behavior in Nicaraugua for example, the two countries should not have good relations.

Yet it is a fundamental mistake to require agreement as a condition of establishing a good working relationship. Improving the relationship -- improving the process for dealing with superpower differences -- is not a favor either side is doing the other. It is action taken in the interest of each party. The more serious U.S.-Soviet differences, the more important it is that the two countries have a good working relationship to deal with them. If the Soviet Union and the United States refuse to improve their relationship until they agree on Afghanistan,

SDI, or any other issue, they limit their ability to influence each other on those very issues.

Many Americans, West Europeans and Soviets, hawks and doves alike, assume that the root of the problems between the superpowers is nuclear hardware. Arms control opponents and proponents focus their attention on finding better hardware solutions, through more weapons or less. In fact, massive cuts in weapons systems and radical shifts in weapons configuration would have relatively little effect on the balance of deterrence or perceived level of security. Neither Americans nor Soviets feel appreciably more or less secure than they did in 1970, although both have spent billions to improve their security. Without a change in the underlying relationship, one could assume that neither would feel appreciably more or less secure if both now spent billions to reduce armaments to the levels of 1970.

It often requires a fundamental shift in thinking to recognize that the relationship between two countries -- the process of interaction to solve differences -- is more important than any particular substantive issue. France has enough nuclear missiles to destroy most of the United States, but that substantive issue does not concern us. The relationship between our two countries is such that we solve our differences without the threat of force -- the relative number of nuclear weapons is irrelevant. Once we separate relationship issues from substantive differences, and improve the negotiating relationship, substantive differences become less devisive.

Certainly, there is a strong correlation between good relations and ease of agreement. We would find it easier to maintain good relations with the Soviets if we always agreed with them, and we would find it easier to agree if we had a history of good relations. But, although we desire both outcomes, neither is necessarily dependent on the other, and linking the two is usually more counterproductive than helpful.

Lack of a clear objective.

What is a "good working relationship?" There is substantial confusion in the media and elsewhere over the goal. The kind of relationship envisioned is one that will permit both governments, where possible, to negotiate practical agreements that are in their mutual interest, and to do so efficiently and amicably. Such a relationship involves procedural elements that are able to survive serious disagreements even as they grapple with those disagreements.

Many American doves thought that detente meant that peace was so important that the U.S. should not talk with the Soviet Union about serious differences. Many hawks thought that the differences were so serious that the U.S. should not talk with the Soviet Union. The result was no serious discussion about serious differences. And it is hard to resolve differences peacefully without talking about them.

Since the summit talks in November, the United States and the Soviet Union have begun to talk about their differences. Many critics have denounced the outcome of the talks a mere rhetoric. These critics tend to suggest that substantive agreements are necessary to solidify the relationship in the future. But substantive agreements will no more than rhetoric build a relationship. Instead, the governments should agree upon norms of problem-solving behavior to guide them when they face differences.

Relationship-building behavior is contingent on reciprocity.

A further problem in the U.S.-Soviet relationship has been the tendency of both governments at various times to make relationship-building behavior contingent on reciprocity. Too often, each government has used reciprocity negatively: "Our poor behavior is justified by your worse conduct" and, "We won't be more constructive unless you are."

When relationship issues are confused with substantive issues, the two sides may try to bargain one off against the other. They may try to buy a better relationship by promising substantive concessions, or may try to coerce substantive concessions by threatening to break relations. From this perspective, good relations are seen as a favor by one side to the other.

Meanwhile, adversarial images of the other country create zero-sum assumptions about the relationship. Since the goal of an adversarial relationship is to defeat the other party, any move which injures one party is perceived as beneficial to the other. Furthermore, each party suspects that actions by one are intended to injure the other. Each party reads malice into the actions of the other.

As a result of this partisan bias, each government sees its own behavior in a more favorable light than the behavior of the other side. For each government to wait for the other side to improve the relationship through conduct that is seen to be equal or better than its own is to wait indefinitely -- while the relationship grows steadily worse.

The two parties may escape this negative cycle in the relationship if they agree on relationship procedures which remove or inhibit the influence of partisan bias. Or, one party may take a positive breakthrough action which hurdles even the adversary's benevolent image of his own actions, thereby evoking a positive response.

PRESCRIPTIVE SUGGESTIONS FOR IMPROVING THE RELATIONSHIP

If the two governments could focus on the process of settling differences rather than on divisive issues, set a clear objective for the bilateral relationship, and agree to pursue improvement in the relationship regardless of the behavior of the other party, the two governments might establish the basis of a working relationship.

Disentangle relationship issues from substantive ones.

Relationship issues are those involving the process of dealing with each other, such as communication, respect, trust, rhetoric, coercion, and persuasion. Substantive issues are those that might be incorporated in a substantive agreement, such as numbers of missiles, tons of wheat, or an agreed boundary between permitted scientific research and prohibited military activity.

Difficulties occur when a government tries to use one of those sets of issues as leverage on the other. Typically, a government either tries to buy a good relationship by making substantive concessions, or tries to extort a substantive concession by threatening the relationship. But good relationships cannot be bought or sold. If the other side is misbehaving, rewarding their behavior is likely to produce more of it. And threatening a relationship damages it seriously, whether or not it succeeds in exacting short term appeasement.

It is true that a good working relationship greatly facilitates reaching good substantive agreements. But using one set of issues as coercive leverage on the other is doomed to fail. Substantive issues should be disentangled from process issues and pursued, vigorously, on their respective merits. Governments should neither refrain from reaching an agreement that is in their interest in the hope of thereby extracting a better relationship, nor accept an unwise agreement in the hope of thereby buying better relations.

Clarify the relationship objectives.

Once the relationship question has been disentangled from current disagreements over matters of substance, it would be desirable for both governments to clarify to themselves, to the other side, and to public opinion both their long-term and short-term goals for the relationship. A good working relationship cannot be unilaterally defined or imposed. Like a good substantive outcome, it needs to be negotiated; it should benefit from the ideas of both parties. Both sides can greatly help that process by clarifying their objectives.

1. The long-term goal: constructive collaboration.

The best vision of the future relationship between the Soviet Union and the United States is not that of two permanent enemies, armed to the teeth with hair-triggered nuclear missiles, ready to destroy each other -- and most of the world -- at any second. That is an unattractive alternative.

For both countries, a preferred long-term goal might be to deal with the other the way it now deals with former adversaries -- by honest, firm, problem-solving negotiation. The United States has had a lot of adversaries in the past, starting in 1776, through the War of 1812, the Mexican War, the Spanish American War, World War I, World War II, and Korea. With all those former enemies, Britain, Canada, Mexico, Spain, Germany, Italy, Japan, and China, the United States has now developed a constructive working relationship to deal with differences no matter how serious. And the U.S. and China have improved the relationship without either side having to win or lose a war. Similarly, Russia and France were once mortal enemies, but now enjoy a constructive relationship. One long-term objective for the Soviet Union and the United States might be to develop the same sort of relationship.

2. The immediate objective: a working relationship.

Because of the many uses of the words "relations" and "relationship," it is important to make clear that the immediate goal is not affection, approval, friendship, agreement, cultural exchange, or trade, but rather an enhanced ability to deal with problems in a professional,constructive way. Both sides seek to build a pattern of interactive behavior that will facilitate negotiation on any subject. They want to be able to negotiate good agreements efficiently.

The normative basis for a good working relationship cannot be defined unilaterally. Some preliminary thought, however, suggests that the elements of a good working relationship include those discussed below.

Mutual acceptance. Soviets continue to feel that Americans treat them as inferiors and deny the legitimacy of the Soviet Union as a negotiating partner. Americans feel the ultimate Soviet goal is the overthrow of all capitalist systems. Each government believes the other rejects its views only because the other rejects it as a legitimate government. Accordingly, neither listens.

As vigorously as each may oppose the conduct of the other, each can accept the other as fellow human beings on this fragile planet. The more each party accepts the other, the more likely each is to listen to the other. Each country can hope to establish an effective problem-solving relationship only if it accepts the other as a legitimate partner in a working relationship.

It is clearly difficult for Israel and the Palestinian Liberation Organization to establish effective negotiating relations when neither accepts the right of the other to exist. It is equally difficult for the United States and the Soviet Union to establish a working relationship when elements in the government of each country reject the legitimacy of the government, economic and social structure of the other.

Acceptance of the other country as a party worthy of working relations does not mean approval of the other's conduct. We can accept the people without attacking their humanity and integrity while we vigorously condemn their conduct as violating international norms of behavior. On matters of domestic affairs, we can respect their right to differ even as we promote our own values. Morality is more powerful as a positive guide than as a negative club.

Reliance on non-coercive means. In a bad working relationship, each side tries to influence the other by playing "chicken" -- by making threats, by locking themselves in to rigid positions, and by insisting that the other side move first. In a good working relationship, each side tries to influence the other not by talking about what it will or won't do, but by jointly considering what objectively *ought* to be done in this situation.

If the United States and the Soviet Union hope to change the method of interaction between them from making threats to making reasoned arguments, it will not be enough to stand firm against threats. Each country needs also to show that it is open to reasoned persuasion.

A contest as to which government can be more stubborn over SDI is a process which damages the relationship and hurts both parties. Making a substantive concession without knowing the eventual outcome or response runs significant risks. The US and the Soviet Union can avoid both being rigid and making substantive concessions by being open to persuasion -- by listening to the arguments of the other and showing that they have been heard; by acknowledging good points and giving credit for positive steps; and, by making arguments privately to remove the appearance of coercion through public opinion.

Empathetic understanding of interests. The better able each party is to put itself in the other's shoes, the better the chance of being able to negotiate a good agreement. Looking at a situation through the eyes of the other side tends both to improve the relationship and to help both parties design proposals that can best accommodate the other's minimal needs while serving one's own interests. The better Soviets and Americans understand the other's interests and perceptions, the better equipped each is to deal with them.

Negotiation is often seen as trying to persuade people to do things they don't want to do. Negotiation may be better understood as inventing something that is in the interests of both sides, and then persuading the other side to do something that is in its own interests. Most people understand their own interests, and rarely turn down something that is good for them. The better we understand the other side's interests, the better able we are to do such inventing.

Reliability. The more that statements are honest and promises kept, the better the working relationship. If promises are the currency of negotiations, reliability is the bank that ensures its value. Reliability is not essential to a negotiated agreement, but it facilitates the process, removing the complicated issues of verification and mistrust which threaten to derail many negotiations.

Before entering into an agreement, each party will have to compare the risks of not having the agreement with the risks of having it, which include the possible harm of open or undetected non-compliance. Each country can do little to make the other more trustworthy. Whether or not the Soviet Union or the U.S. believes the other is trustworthy, it is wise for each to enhance its own trustworthiness in the eyes of the other. The more trusted a party is, the more powerful it is; the greater its capacity to influence the other with its statements and promises.

Being reliable does not mean keeping every promise. One's reputation for reliability is often as dependant on how he manages a situation in which a promise must be broken as it is on the number of promises kept. The United States does not keep all its promises with the United Kingdom, but when it becomes necessary to break a promise, we are likely to consult with that government and find a mutually acceptable way to settle the issue.

One way for each party to demonstrate its concern with its reliability is to discuss with the other party any upcoming or current situations that raise the question of whether or not it is complying with a prior commitment. It is much stronger and more persuasive to admit that a question has been raised, to listen to the other's concerns, and then to decide that the conduct is permitted, than it is to walk away from the problem with simple statements that we know we are right.

Consultation before deciding. Nothing improves a relationship as much as consulting before deciding on matters that affect the other. Nothing better demonstrates acceptance of another party, concern for their interests, and openness to their views, than consulting with them before making a decision. A rule of thumb for a good relationship, at home, in the office, or between nations, is "ACBD: Always Consult Before Deciding." Even if a decision is certainly correct, those who will be affected by it will feel better if they are given an opportunity for input before the decision is made.

The quality of the overall U.S.-Soviet working relationship may dramatically improve if each party were to ask for the other's advice on three or four upcoming and still undecided questions. Asking for advice can effectively communicate respect and acceptance. The questions can be on any topic, even issues that do not directly involve the other side. For example:

> The United States might ask, "If your anti-alcoholism program is successful, we would welcome any suggestions you might have. In the United States, several hundred people a week die in automobile accidents that involve drinking."
>
> And, the Soviets might ask, "Do you have any ideas about what we can do to prevent acid rain from developing in our industrial regions."
>
> Both might ask the other, "Do you have any thoughts about how our two governments might help stop the war between Iran and Iraq?"

A working relationship is improved not only through consultation but through modifying the working assumption that both side's must tackle problems unilaterally. Without abandoning any decision-making power, a great deal of work can be undertaken jointly, such as joint fact-finding, joint research, joint brainstorming of options, a joint search for relevant precedents and models, and so forth. In trying to change the working assumption from one of *my* interests, *my* goals, and *my* decisions to one of *our* interests, *our* goals, and *our* decisions, small things can make a difference: for example,

- Sitting side by side, rather than face to face;
- In larger meetings, having the two leaders sit on one side of a table, with their staffs sitting on the other;
- Both writing notes on a common pad or "flip chart" on the wall.
- Both people writing items on the same piece of paper.

Since consultation can be misread as a signal by the press, it may be useful to establish periodic off-the-record consultations. To guard against polemical haggling at these meetings, it may be useful to set groundrules limiting discussion to questions and answers -- no decisions.

Act unconditionally to build the relationship.

Neither government can directly alter the other's behavior. Nor should it be expected to act in ways contrary to its own interests in the hope that the other will follow the example.

Each government should work to improve the relationship by doing those things that will be good for it and for the relationship whether or not the other side reciprocates and independent of major disagreements on matters of substance. This does not mean that either side must be soft on substantive disagreements. Neither country can sit idly by while the other invades a third party territory or doubles its nuclear arsenal. Antagonistic action deserves a response, both to redress an injustice or imbalance and to discourage coercion. The response, however, should not undermine the working relationship. Especially in the face of violent substantive disagreement, it is important to maintain the procedures and relations necessary to resolve the dispute efficiently. It is *always* in each country's interest to maintain an effective working relationship, regardless of the actions of the other.

Each country should accept the other as a legitimate and equal negotiating partner. Each should act reliably to increase its own trustworthiness. Each should communicate openly to eliminate misperceptions. Each should listen and consult to understand the other's interests and to demonstrate respect for its views. It is in the interest of each country should pursue each of these principles regardless of the behavior of the other country.

If the United States and the Soviet Union were to pursue these principles, they might more easily reach agreement on arms control and ease the tension which has so far made such agreements, even when agreed, ineffective for the purpose of increasing our mutual security.

CONCLUSION

The crucial determinant of U.S. and Soviet security, and the security of the world, will not depend on technological developments, breakthroughs in deterrence theory, or even agreements the two superpowers might sign at summit talks. The future depends on whether the two governments are able to work together.

Both the United States and the Soviet Union have developed procedures for solving conflicts with other governments, even former enemies, without hostilities or threats of force. The essential difference between these relationships and the U.S.-Soviet relationship lies not in the degree of difference in cultural heritage or security interests, but in the way the two governments approach their problems -- through consultations and dispute resolution procedures, or through conflict and recrimination.

The process of interaction is the essence of a working relationship. It means the difference between hostile confrontation and constructive collaboration, between fear and security, between war and peace. The two superpowers should turn their attention to changing the nature of the relationship, changing the focus of U.S.-Soviet interaction from antagonistic bargaining over divisive issues to constructive collaboration on possible solutions and working procedures.

PROBLEMS OF FLEXIBILITY IN THE NUCLEAR ARMS RACE

David Collingridge
Aston University, Birmingham B4 7ET, U.K.

My route to the problem of arms control has been roundabout, from the philosophy of science to an interest in decision making under great uncertainty, and from there to a concern for the social effects of technology, including that employed by the military. In the philosophy of science it is more or less universally recognised that the claims of science are forever beyond justification; at best they may be criticised as being false, and yet the analogous analysis for decision making has only recently been started (see COLLINGRIDGE (1982)). It can be held that decision can be justified; that any choice, after it has been made, is threatened by the discovery of facts which may cause the chooser to reject his original decision, perhaps beginning a search for ways of revising it. If all decisions are open to error, it makes sense to favour options where error can be quickly detected and the original choice revised quickly and without great loss. Such options have the virtue of flexibility. The identification of obstacles to the maintenance of flexibility is an important programme of research, given this sceptical analysis; and the nuts and bolts of technology provide a very important and easily understood obstacle to flexibility (see COLLINGRIDGE (1980)). If an airport is built on the basis of traffic forecasts which turn out to be too high, the mistaken decision is hard to ameliorate - there is little point in digging up the concrete and knocking down the terminals. The option of building an airport is an inherently inflexible one. Civilian nuclear technology has been studied in some detail, revealing four factors which together make it (and presumably other technologies) very inflexible and therefore particularly 'brittle' and 'unforgiving'; (1) long lead time, (2) large unit size, (3) capital intensity and (4) the need for infrastructure such as uranium mines and enrichment plants (see COLLINGRIDGE (1984)). The combination of these four factors is doubly damning to civil nuclear technology; they ensure that there will be many errors in planning the technology and that these errors will be very expensive.

Applying these ideas to military technology requires the idea of a *hedging circle*, which itself may be introduced by the example of forest fires (see HOLLING (1984)). There are two approaches to forest fires-they may be

NATO ASI Series, Vol. F 26
Modelling and Analysis in Arms Control
Edited by R. Avenhaus et al.

prevented, or ways may be found for living with fires which sweep through the forest every few years. A decision at one time to prevent fires seems innocent enough, but is has profound consequences for future choices. Once the forest is protected against accidental ignition, there will be a build-up of combustible material. Worse still, people will adjust to the now safe forest, for example by building houses or farms on the outskirts, or perhaps a large paper mill whose economics demand a guaranteed supply of wood every year. Any fire which does occur will now be worse than before - or to put it more officially, the error cost of the fire prevention policy will be elevated. It is therefore even more important to prevent fires than before. The next choice when it comes, between prevention and living with occasional and unpredictable fires, is therefore biased towards the former; the first decision in favour of prevention makes any other approach increasingly unattractive as time goes on. A second effect works in the same direction, compounding the problem, for although much may be learned about how to prevent forest fires, nothing has been learned about ways of ameliorating their cost. But, of course, fire cannot be prevented completely. Eventually there will be a conflagration whose damage will have been greatly inflated by the build up of combustible materials and the optimistic use of the forest for farming or a steady timber supply. Such an inherently unstable pattern of decision-making is called a hedging circle (or better 'spiral'). The nuclear arms race betrays the same pattern.

For present purposes, all the ways of keeping the peace between rival powers can be grouped into two classes. The first of these is what may be termed diplomatic methods; such things as treaties between the powers themselves and third countries, trade agreements, minor wars and border skirmishes, real and threatened trade embargoes, threats of war, cultural exchanges, negotiations and matters of friction, hot line communications, diplomatic exchanges and so forth. The other group contains all those developments which amount to mutual deterrence, each side possessing sufficient military might to ensure that its rival can never hope to benefit from a war. In an unstable world peace has to be maintained by the use of a combination of these methods, different ones being appropriate for different times. The use of some of these methods, however, has a profound effect on what methods can be used in the future. If the peace is threatened at some time, suppose one of the powers were to opt for a poliy of deterrence, acquiring the necessary weapons to ensure that no attack from its opponent can ever hope for success. The difference between weapons of deterrence and of attack typically lies in the intention behind them, and the other side cannot afford to trust the good intentions of the first power, even if they are real at the moment, for intentions can change like the wind. The other side must see itself as threatened and must use one of the methods of avoiding war to restore the situation.

All the diplomatic methods of avoiding war involve both powers - for example, in negotiations or in issuing and interpreting threats. As such, they all involve a risk of failure. One side may, for example, break agreements banning some new weapon and win a war with its illicit technology, or threats may be misunderstood with all sorts of complicated consequences including even war. These risks must now appear much less attractive than previously, because the newly acquired arms of the other side mean that the cost of failure, that is the cost of war, is now much bigger than before. Thus the option of deterrence is favoured, because this does not suffer from the same dangers. The decision to acquire deterrent weapons involves only one power, not both, so there is no other party whose deviousness can introduce a risk of failure. Unlike the diplomatic methods, deterrence is under one's own control.

Both powers now have deterrent forces, but these are not static and it will eventually happen that the balance of terror will shift to favour one side. How can the weaker side ensure the avoidance of war? It is, of course, in exactly the position of the weaker power in the above paragraph. Diplomatic methods of maintaining peace, being inherently risky, must be even less attractive than before, because the cost of failure is now even higher, the other side having a greater advantage than previously. The option of deterrence is, therefore, more highly favoured than previously as it is the only way to avoid these great risks. In this way the first decision to maintain peace by deterrence biases the second decision to be made in the same way, so that a vicious circle exists. The next time deterrent forces come unbalanced the cost of war is even higher because more weapons exist, and so restoring deterrence is even more favoured than at earlier times. The diplomatic options open to the powers gradually close as their failure becomes more and more expensive, until the only way of maintaining peace is through mutual deterrence.

Decisions about how to keep the peace have to be taken under very great uncertainty, meaning that flexible options should be favoured. Options should be favoured which leave future decisions open so that some response can be made as these uncertainties are resolved with the passage of time. These are options which can be quickly corrected so that the cost of error is low and the system's performance insensitive to error. Once the path of deterrence is taken it is increasingly difficult to adopt these options. Error costs rise as more and more weaponry is deployed, options of using diplomatic methods to maintain peace in the future gradually disappear because they pose greater and greater risks since nothing is learned about them, and the performance of the peace-keeping systems becomes increasingly sensitive to error as the cost of war increases. The path of deterrence is rational only to the extent that it can be abandoned.

The hedging circle explains some of the key features of the nuclear arms race, the continuous growth of destructive power, the inability of diplomatic methods to influence the race in any significant way, the employment of worst case analysis, and the stability of deterrence policy once that path is embarked upon. It is also a very depressing story. Wars, like forest fires, probably cannot be prevented forever; some trivial event will one day trigger the nuclear arsenals, a war which the hedging circle has driven to a level of unimaginable terror. Diplomatic methods of preventing war are, of course, far from foolproof, but the wars resulting from their failure would be on an altogether more modest scale. It may be useful to look at the US decisions to develop and deploy MIRV in this context (see COLLINGRIDGE (1980), chapter 4). Faced with the great uncertainties typical in such cases, a flexible decision would appear to be rational, one which, if wrong, would be known to be in error quickly and which would be easy to revise. MIRV represented the complete opposite; when the project was reversible, there was no possibility of gaining information which might signal the need for revision, and by the time such information was available, the project had become irreversible. MIRV, as planned, was a project of infinite inflexibility; events could exercise no control over the development of the project.

MIRV was conceived around 1962, and deployment began in 1970, a fairly typical lead time for deterrent systems. The planners of the early 1960s had to look ahead, at least ten years, guessing at what Soviet developments might have arrived by then, a highly perilous exercise. The principal worries then were that Soviet land-based missiles would become more accurate and more numerous, and that Soviet ABM would be able to protect some of these missiles from attack. MIRV was, among other things, the answer to these fears. Increasing the number of warheads would be able to saturate any ABM defense, at the same time enhancing the United States' counterforce strength and her ability to mount a second strike because surviving missiles would be much more destructive once fitted with MIRV. Information on the assumptions about Soviet moves made by those planning MIRV came in steadily as the project proceeded, but there was never any hope of obtaining information of sufficient quality to abandon the project altogether, or even to slow it up significantly. For example, the intelligence community became very concerned about the Tallinn system, which looked like part of Soviet bomber defences, but which might have been able to have been upgraded into an ABM system. Here the logic of the hedging circle operated; if the United States developed MIRV in the mistaken belief that Soviet ABM systems would be developed, the cost might be a few billion dollars of taxpayers' money, but if they mistakenly abandon MIRV, thinking that Soviet ABMs will not appear, then the cost could be beyond computation. MIRV was therefore upheld as a hedge that the Tallinn system would prove to be part of a Soviet ABM system. Whatever facts might have appeared to US intelligence during this period were treated in the same way. Facts were therefore quite unable to control the MIRV project, even though it was still open to cancellation.

By the time MIRV was ready for deployment, however, the picture had changed in many respects. ABM was seen as a much more troublesome technology than previously thought; estimates of the hardness of Soviet silos were greatly increased, showing that MIRV was not an effective counterforce weapon; and the feared increase in the number and the accuracy of Soviet land based missiles did not materialize. But by the time these changes had sunk into the consciousness of American strategic planners, these new facts could no longer point to the abandonment of MIRV. Once deployed, the logic of the hedging circle determined that the Soviet Union take the most pessimistic view of the new technology, that it was a weapon of first strike. The Soviet response, of course, was to balance the deterrent by developing its own MIRV.

It follows that MIRV was never under the control of its creators. In one sense it was, because it was possible for a few years at least, to abandon the project, but this cannot be seen as amounting to genuine control. Genuine control calls for the decision makers to be able to revise their decisions in the light of the information which they receive. When MIRV was reversible, there could be no such information. In this period whether the project went ahead or was abandoned could not be decided on rational grounds - in response to information showing that the original decision did not, after all, further the objective of avoiding war. Those favouring the technology painted pictures of the future which called for the project to go ahead, such as the sudden upgrading of the Tallinn line. Those opposed to it painted other pictures, such as Soviet reaction leading to Soviet MIRV, which called for the abandonment of the project. But all this is so much fantasy. These are pictures and pictures only, and cannot offer serious guidance as to the future of MIRV. This can only come with the acquisition of firm information, by which time, of course, the project cannot be abandoned. The pattern is clear in the case of MIRV, but it also underlies many similar episodes in the sad history of deterrence.

In the whole MIRV story the realization of the need for genuine flexibility is recognized only once, and then by such a minor actor as to have no influence on the decision. Martin McGuire was in the Office of Systems Analysis in 1965 when decisions were being made to continue the development of the two MIRV systems and to include them in estimates of future force. McGuire observed that the lead time for the deployment of MIRV was certain to be considerably shorter than the time needed for the Soviet Union to develop and deploy an extensive ABM system. He also feared that a hasty deployment of MIRV would merely stimulate a Soviet response which might destabilize the deterrent. He argued, therefore, that the United States could safely delay its MIRV programme until there was clear evidence of a developing Soviet ABM system, and perhaps use the threat of deploying MIRV to induce the Soviet Union into serious arms control talks.

Nothing came of McGuire's argument, and it is not possible for me to judge its merits in the light of the technical problems facing MIRV and ABM. What can be said, however is that the argument illustrates the approach to handling uncertainty which is essential if decisions like MIRV are ever to be taken in a better, more rational way. If McGuire's approach had been practicable and eventually adopted, then the United States could have safely kept MIRV in readiness for any Soviet ABM which might appear. If none appeared, then MIRV deployment need never see the light of day. In this way some sort of genuine control could be exercised over the technology. It might still be the case that once deployed, MIRV was impossible to scrap, but McGuire's approach would at least ensure that MIRV is only adopted if it is needed. Herbert York has performed a similar analysis on the American decision to build the first fusion weapon, the Superbomb first tested in 1950 (see YORK (1976)). The development of the bomb was suggested as a hedge against the Soviet Union developing it first. York argues that there was no need to hedge in this way, because the United States could delay development until the first Soviet test of the new weapon, after which the United States, with is greater technological resources could swiftly catch up, with no fear of the deterrent breaking down.

The analysis offered here seems to run counter to many attempts to understand the nuclear arms race which have been made in the past, some seeing the arms race as a straightforward political failure, or the result of bureaucratic arrangements of the superpowers, or the servant of the industrial-military complex. In each case, it is wrongly assumed that the option of abandoning the arms race is a real one, one which has become blocked in some way which can be remedied given the political will (see COLLINGRIDGE (1984) on Technology in the Nuclear Arms Race). Once mutual deterrence was established, the political and bureaucratic system became trapped in the way I have tried to explain. The arms race is now inescapable, but this is not to say that there are good and bad ways to compete in it. The history of MIRV shows how arms race decisions can be made of the very poorest quality, but the candle of hope burns dimly in the form of the lowly Martin McGuire who suggested greater flexibility in planning the technology.

REFERENCES

Collingridge, D. (1980): The Social Control of Technology. Frances Pinter, London

Collingridge, D. (1982): Critical Decision Making. Frances Pinter, London

Collingridge, D. (1984): Technology in the Policy Process. Frances Pinter, London

Collingridge, D. (1984): The Real Lessons of Nuclear Power I and II. Energy Policy, 12, 1984

Collingridge, D. (1984): Technology in the Nuclear Arms Race. Science and Public Policy, 6, 1984

Holling, C. (1984): Resilience of Ecosystems, Local Surprise and Global Change. IIASA Working Paper, Vienna

York, H. (1976): The Adivsors: Teller, Oppenheimer and the Superbomb. Freeman, San Francisco.

SUPERPOWERS AND ARMS NEGOTIATIONS: POLITICAL CLIMATES AND OPTIMAL STRATEGY

Umberto Gori
University of Florence, Italy

1. OBJECTIVE ASYMMETRIES AND SUBJECTIVE SYMMETRIES

When one looks comparatively at the superpowers, it is easy to realize that they show *asymmetries*: in ideology, in politics, in power, and in capabilities.

These *objective* asymmetries are at the very root of deeply divergent interests that are not likely to be reconciled, whatever the mutual personal empathy, if any, of the two top leaders. Only other macroscopic factors (such as a common pending danger) would provide a bridge for an otherwise unsolvable gap. This systematic and obsessive struggle stems rather from the *symmetry* of two specific *subjective* situations - fear and the perception of the other's fear (*mirror image*).

And as negotiations are very difficult when fear and suspicion characterize the relationship between the actors, there is a need to manipulate the subjective situations. Trying to transform directly the objective ones would be impossible.

Mutual trust is, in fact, much more important than blind arms reduction. History shows that wars stem from ideological and political rivalries, as well as from psychological attitudes, rather than from the existence of huge stocks of weaponry.

2. POLITICAL CLIMATES

The manipulation of *political climate* is one - perhaps the most important - of the measures to create favourable preconditions for negotiating important and complex issues such as control, limitation and reduction of nuclear arms. Present negotiations are too technical, and characterized by the absence of a positive political context whereby technicalities could be given a real meaning. A political context (climate) should have priority vis-à-vis a technical context.

NATO ASI Series, Vol. F 26
Modelling and Analysis in Arms Control
Edited by R. Avenhaus et al.

But what is political climate? Is there a way to define this otherwise vague concept operationally in order to be effective in its manipulations? Without presuming to be exhaustive, I shall try to advance here some ideas on which one might elaborate further.

First of all, two general considerations are needed:

1) An operational definition should be valid for as many actors as possible, and should be accepted at least by the superpowers.

2) The indicators employed should be of operational relevance to direct measures. That means that they should measure all those conditions likely to be directly manipulated by them (see EBERWEIN (1981)).

3. COMPONENTS OF INTERNATIONAL POLITICAL CLIMATES

Now, the concept of *political climate* - as applied to international relations - seems to have at least two basic elements: one is *tension* and the other *détente*.

Tension, in its turn, has two meanings: 1) a *perceptual* meaning (in this case, tension is viewed "as a short-term phenomenon related to perceptions and associated behaviors that raise the expectations that violence will occur"), and 2) a *structural* meaning (in this case, tension is "related to the structural context of interaction among nations. This implies that some configurations within the international system are more likely to favor the outbreak of violence than others, even though they vary slowly over time") (see EBERWEIN (1981), p. 123). In any case, there is an "interrelationship between the psychological component of tension and its structural component" (see EBERWEIN (1981), p. 124).

Détente - on the other hand - comprises three elements: *intentions, a set of behaviors,* and *effects*.

According to EBERWEIN (1981), a content-analytical approach is needed for studying intentions, whereas behaviors should be measured on interactions among nations, and effects should be determined "on the assessment of the degree of tranquility in the international system or some of its parts at any specific point in time". More generally stated, dêtente is a process whereby tension in the international system tends to be reduced.

Another helpful distinction when we try to assess and measure "political climates" is between *local* and *systemic* political climate, or - as the GLOBUS world model puts it - *dyadic* and *superpower* climate. Though, superficially, we may believe that in our case dyadic and systematic climates are the same, this is not exactly true. To measure the climate between East and West, one needs to aggregate all the interregional dyadic flows in terms of indexes of hostility and to divide them by all the interregional dyadic flows expressed in terms of indexes of cooperation.

In GLOBUS formalized terminology (still subject to review), the climate between East and West (EWCLIM) is defined in terms of the quotient

$$\text{EWCLIM} = \frac{[\text{HSENT (West,East)} + \text{HSENT (East, West)}]}{[\text{CSENT (West,East)} + \text{CSENT (East, West)}]}$$

where

HSENT = Index of the hostility sent from one bloc to the other;

CSENT = Index of the cooperation sent from one bloc to the other.

It is evident that when we speak of the necessity of manipulating the political climate in order to improve the possibilities of a successful negotiation, we refer to both the dyadic climate (between the US and USSR) and the systemic one. The latter represents the context of the former, in which relevant contributions by the allies of the one or the other of the superpowers are implied.

4. INDICATORS

The degree of *conflict* can be an indicator for tension in the same way as the degree of *cooperation* could be an indicator for dêtente. But in no case are conflict and cooperation to be considered synonimous with tension and dêtente.

One should elaborate further on these concepts, as EBERWEIN (1981) does, when he suggests three types of indicators: *power* indicators, *safeguard* (alliance) indicators, and *geopolitical* indicators. These indicators are valid for prediction, as they refer to a theoretical body of knowledge based on evidence (findings). Accordingly, one of the most intriguing findings - which is relevant in our case - is that *power parity* is strictly correlated to the outbreak of military confrontations.

5. OPERATIONAL DEFINITIONS

The use of indicators to give an operational definition of "political climate" could be a first possibility, but - though they are important - indicators exhibit the disadvantage that they could not be agreed upon by everybody concerned as representing the real and perceived dimensions of political climate (observe, for example, recent diverging interpretations of dêtente).

And here is the critical point. An abstract, scholarly interpretation of the concept, and of its subsystemic dimensions would be of no use for our policy-oriented purposes. The real question is whether we may be able to define climate with reference to some kinds of *data*, objective or preceived as real by the actors.

Three categories of data seem to be promising at least for this purpose:

1) *event* data,

2) *perceptual* data,

3) *transaction flow* data (see FREY (1980)).

Briefly stated, data based on *events/interactions* could 'measure' political climate along a scale "cooperation - conflict" of the COPDAB type (or, even better, on a similar scale containing 27 steps, as the one we began with our group more than a decade ago at the University of Florence). A political climate would be positive (or negative) according to a given percentage of data of that kind monitored in a given space of time.

This approach, however, presents two problems which could be solved only partially. One is the difficulty of properly weighting *breakthrough events* on the scale. The other - at least as important - is the difficulty of finding unbiased sources, or sources agreed upon by both contending parties.

Perceptual data and *transactional* data seem to be much more useful as their sources are either relatively objective, as in the case of transactions, or absolutely subjective, as in the case of perceptions. In this case, in fact, the sources would be the declaratory statements of the different decision-makers concerned, which could easily be organized, elaborated, and even compared.

With the perceptual and transactional approaches longitudinal profiles could be established, measuring the shifting from one period to another in terms of percentage rates upwards or downwards on a given scale, and even fore-casted as, for instance, Urs Luterbacher plans to do with a computer simulation study (see FREY (1980), p. 211).

6. NEED OF A CLEAR AND PREDICTABLE STRATEGY

Once these preliminary, but absolutely indispensable steps have been made both in scholarly efforts and in operations, one is ready to approach the theme of negotiation in general, and of the negotiation between the super-powers in particular.

We refer here to that formal procedure that is called *explicit* negotiation. This negotiation takes place between two "enemy" parties, and therefore it can be conceptualized both as an instrument of *indirect strategy* and as a tool to *solve problems*.

It is assumed here, for simplicity, that the objectives of the two powers under study are *symmetric*, both of them trying to use negotiations in the two senses. Also the major incentive, i.e. *fear*, is symmetric in the structure of nuclear arms negotiations. Two other incentives - *economic difficulties* and *international public opinion* - contribute to establish a rough symmetry in the global structure, simply because each of them exhibits an asymmetric pattern. For example, the US have far less economic difficulties while the Soviet Union is generally more successful in manipulating international public opinion.

Negotiations are being held normally *under pressure* which reduces the probability of success. Pressure, in other words, increases fear, shortens time for effective decision-making, and escalates misperceptions.

The problem of *perceptions* is crucial. If we establish a *matrix* of the factors that should be taken into account and analyzed before or while sitting at the table of negotiations, we realize that the perceptual variable is one of the most, if not the most, important of all the factors playing a role and having a predictive power.

For both actors, the perceptual variable comprises several disaggregates which are related to the perception of the situation, the opponent's interests, capabilities and his interpretation of the other's interests, capabilities and interpretation of the situation.

Without going here through intricacies, we only want to add that the theory of *expected utility* seems to be relevant. As a very simple example, if the US believes that it is stronger, and Soviet perception of US capabilities agrees with US perceptions, a space for concessions is surely open. In other words, a high probability for Soviet concessions exists, and should be taken into account.

Another problem is how to improve *preconditions* likely to bring about a successful negotiation. Without reproducing what has been said by a vast literature, three issues are worth noting.

One is *secrecy*. Nuclear arms negotiations should be secret, otherwise their major role would be that of amplifying emotions and misperceptions, and performing - willy-nilly - the function of "indirect strategy" tools. Secrecy should be kept vis-à-vis third parties and public opinion, but some sort of information should flow between the players. For a solution to an otherwise unsolvable problem, I refer here to the idea of a *computerized third party* by John D. Kettelle.

The second issue is the use and abuse of *linkages*. In negotiations on dangerous problems such as nuclear arms control, linkage should be used only when it can "*create* a zone of possible agreement" (SEBENIUS (1984)), but not for *leverage* or when it *destroys* one or the other of those "zones".

The third issue is the *timing* of negotiation. If the political climate is bad, negotiations can be provocative and amplify distortions. Thus, a favourable political climate should be promptly exploited, or if necessary nurtured, as a background for constructive negotiations.

Human behavior is deeply influenced by the political context, and that is even more true if applied to behavior during negotiations. So the decision to negotiate at a given time must be preceded by independent, or sovereign, (non-negotiated) initiatives to create a better context, and must be contemporaneous with the choice of a given strategy (ZARTMAN and BERMAN (1982))

What we want to propose here, in particular, is that the strategy called '*Tit-for-Tat*' (see, e.g., AXELROD (1984)) implies both diplomacy and deterrence, i.e., the two instruments normally used to solve (or stabilize) conflicts. A policy for solving international conflicts should use redundant tools. 'Tit-for-Tat' can be conceptualized precisely as a *system in parallel* which is by definition more flexible than any of its constituent subsystems. 'Tit-for-Tat' uses diplomatic methods (*negotiation*) without sanctifying them, as well as concrete actions (*retaliation*).

Given this structure, this specific strategy is highly *predictable*, and contributes to a decrease in misperceptions. We come back here to the importance of images, and to the primary goal of negotiations which should be the progressive transformation of the adversary's perceptions. Simulations prove that this is statistically guaranteed if a transparent, persistent, and therefore predictable behavior is applied.

As it is well known, the statistically successful performance of this strategy depends on its basic features:

1) *fair play* (it never begins with a *hard* move);

2) *immediate retaliation*;

3) *short memory* (it 'forgives' non-cooperative behaviors of the opponent exhibited *before the last move*;

4) *extreme clarity*.

7. DESTABILIZATION, STABILITY, AND SECURITY: CONCLUDING REMARKS

It is doubtful whether the superpowers have had such a negotiating attitude in the past, but what is clear enough is that they should learn to apply the 'Tit-for-Tat' strategy. A decision of that kind is an independent one that does not need to be negotiated. Either side can begin, and the other will follow after a while.

Looking at the simulated effects of the strategy, one rather has to condemn consistently hard, 'hawkish' attitude *twice*: from the moral and the technical point of view.

Superpowers have to elaborate on the problem of security more deeply. Clearly, SDI and the transition period, if any, from Mutual Assured Destruction (MAD) to Mutual Assured Security (MAS) risk jeopardizing strategic equilibria. Yet, theoretically speaking, SDI could be a way, though risky, to overcome the phase of the equilibrium of terror, and to shift to another phase where security might increase through a decrease in mutual vulnerability. That phase would not be that of '*defensive defence*' defined by J. GALTUNG in his *transarmament theory*, but it would represent a good step toward a '*Swiss model*' of security.

Gorbachev must understand that the concept of '*star wars*' is misleading, but Reagan cannot ignore that the price to pay for making SDI a reality is absolute reciprocity. If SDI aims at redistributing power at the world level, its logical consequence will be a catastrophic destablization. But if - as President Reagan claims - it aims at increasing security, then its major concern should be that of maintaining stability.

It is highly debatable that this concept will be defined in the same way by the two superpowers, as interests are objectively different, and geostrategic conditions are not the same. Given this difficulty, it seems easier to structure a negotiation in such a way as to include the perceptions and preferences of the contending parties.

As François de Callières, a French political philosopher, writing in 1716, said, "there is no durable treaty which is not founded on reciprocal advantage, and indeed a treaty which does not satisfy this condition is no treaty at all, and is apt to contain the seeds of its own dissolution. Thus, the great secret of negotiation is to bring out prominently the common advantage to both sides and to link these advantages that they may appear equally balanced to both parties" (see SEBENIUS (1984), p. 183). And de Callières significantly added: "For this purpose when negotiations are on foot between two sovereigns, one the greater and the other the less, the more powerful of those should make the first advance, and even undertake a large outlay of money to bring about the union of interests with his lesser neighbors ...". It is astonishing - to my view - how these lines, written even before the United States or the Soviet Union came into existence, reflect a serious warning that should be kept in consideration.

Last but not least, more attention should be paid to scholarly results, as the ones which prove that replicating situations of the "prisoner's dilemma" type contribute to bring about non-paradoxial behaviors. The decision taken at the Geneva Summit in 1985 to reconvene after a while is a good step in the direction of *institutionalizing* negotiations between the superpowers. Like it or not, there is no alternative left. Common sense and sophisticated analysis point at the same strategy: communication, diplomacy, and determined behavior.

R e f e r e n c e s

Eberwein, W.D. (1981): Macroquantitative Indicators for Détente. In: Definitions and Measurements of Détente (Frey, D., Ed.). Cambridge, Mass., pp. 122-127

Frey, D. (1980): The Measurement of Détente in Europe. In: Indicator Systems for Political, Economic and Social Analysis (Oelgeschlager et al., Eds.). Cambridge, Mass.

Sebenius, J.K. (1984): Negotiating the Law of the Sea. Cambridge, Mass.

Zartman, I.W., Berman (1982): The Practical Negotiator, New Haven

Axelrod, R. (1984): The Evolution of Cooperation. New York

A COMPUTERIZED THIRD PARTY

John D. Kettelle
Ketron, Inc., Arlington, Virginia 22209

1. INTRODUCTION

This paper outlines a novel approach to conducting negotiations and shows how this approach can apply to the specific problems of arms control. It reviews in fairly general terms the logical goals of arms control talks and the way these goals relate to the specific dimensions normally encountered in a treaty. It deals with the unfortunate complication of secrecy - the desirability of shielding not only one's capabilities but even some of one's goals from one's "opponent". Such secrecy makes the search for a viable treaty doubly difficult. The paper describes a process that addresses this difficulty. The process centers around a "third party device", together with some protocols and strategies for using it.

2. THE PROBLEM

What is the goal of an arms control negotiation? Some reflection suggests that one may have already started with a derivative question too far from a real goal to make useful sense. One must presumably start with national goals that have political, social, and economic dimensions. In the present context a dominating "boundary condition" of such goals is that they be obtainable without a strategic, nuclear war. One *then* can look for optimal pairs of military postures for the two adversarial groups. Finally, this paper takes as the goal the determination of such postures, and in particular those that are unlikely to be achieved by unilateral activity.

In the context of the present era, it is normally assumed that a major objective of an arms control agreement is an improvement in stability - that this somehow translates into a decreased likelihood of a strategic war. It may well be that stability will be *decreased* by an arms reduction, that both

NATO ASI Series, Vol. F 26
Modelling and Analysis in Arms Control
Edited by R. Avenhaus et al.

nations should significantly *increase* their military forces to achieve a reduced likelihood of a major war. In fact, it might be argued that this increase and the resulting reduced likelihood is just what has developed in the years since World War II, albeit largely without real negotiations. This can be buttressed by the converse argument that a stronger "allied" military posture in the mid 1930's might have deterred Hitler's adventurism that initiated World War II. As opposed to our continuous first-order concern for deterrent postures since then, the allied attention to this in the inter-bellum '20's and '30's was so inadequate that the resulting inefficient postures (such as the Maginot Line) almost invited aggression. Unfortunately, it can also be argued that the post-World War II reduced likelihood has been more than paid for by a disproportionate increase in the consequences of a war. The point is that an arms control agreement essentially is a special case of a military treaty - it must reflect all the goals and motivations with which any such treaty has to deal. A partial list of the elements of an arms control treaty is displayed in Figure 1.

It must explicitly *address* the military components of posture - that is, the forces and systems each side will maintain, and their deployments. It must *recognize* the components of national policy, which characteristically contain secrets of the individual nation. These include military attitudes, such as one's own first strike proclivities, ways to blunt the opponent's first strike capabilities, and such details as military presence and hegemony in various regions. Finally, these policies blend into national goals; almost by definition military posture is only a means to such goals. In the 1950's a quick answer was "a just and durable peace". To be operationally relevant, one has to operate at least one level down and talk about component economic goals of direct benefit to one's own country, of direct benefit to other countries or groups, and perhaps of direct harm to adversary countries. Figure 1 contains other typical components of this whole set of considerations.

Closely related to these elements are various war-fighting calculations and assumptions, illustrated partially in Figure 2. A typical calculation might be the expected result of certain actions given that the two nations were furnished with specific initial sets of forces. Normally, such results are

SYSTEMS AND CAPABILITIES

- Numbers and Locations of Platforms and Silos
- More Generally, Numbers and Types of Offensive and Defensive Weaponry
- Agreements Regarding Surveillance
- Verification
- Testing
- Research and Development
- Communications Capabilities

MILITARY GOALS

- First Strike Capabilities
- Second Strike Capabilities
- Alliance Postures
- Secondary Military Presence

NATIONAL GOALS

- Avoidance of Thermonuclear War
- Survival if Avoidance Fails
- In the Absence of Total War, Support of the Free World by Providing a Benign Environment for:
  - Economic Development and Political and Social Progress
  - Avoiding the Spread of Communist Regimes and Influence; In Fact, Weakening or Turning Back Such Influence

Fig. 1: Elements of Arms Control Negotiations

not negotiated directly in an arms control dialogue; instead, each side computes the results privately and uses them to evaluate alternative pairs of military postures.

An essential characteristic of this whole arms control problem has become its complexity. One might think that at least the national goals of the two adversaries were reasonably clear both to themselves and to each other, but one has to assume that even this is not the case. Even within a single administration (in either country) there are differing and changing sets of goals and policies. Furthermore, even if the goals and policies were well defined, the knowledge of the military postures and the translation of that knowledge into hypothetical results of various engagements is extremely inaccurate - inaccurate on almost every basis. Knowledge of component system performance is difficult to determine, even for operational systems. Worse yet, arms control issues address systems five, ten or even twenty years in the future. Knowlegde of opposing systems is at least as difficult to establish. The results of hypothetical component battles ("tactical" results) between the two systems is even harder to predict - not only with respect to net hardware capabilities, but also with respect to assumed tactics used by the opposing forces. Finally, the results of conflicting strategic maneuvers are influenced by the same uncertainties, compounded still further.

- Tactical - Predicting the Results of Conflicts Between Component Units of the Two Countries; e.g., SAM's vs. Bombers, ABM's vs. ICBM's, Submarines vs. Aircraft Carriers
- Strategic or Campaign:
  - Calculation of Residual Second Strike Capabilities
  - Calculation of "Value" Destruction of Components Such as Command, Counterforces, or Value
  - Calculation of Land Warfare Results associated with European Scenarios

Fig. 2: Calculations and Assumptions in Support of Arms Control Negotiations

Theoretically, policymakers can deal with such uncertainties by computing systematic sets of probabilities that reflect the various possible results, and by aiming at agreements that will best control these calculated probabilities. Even with the best of intentions, such calculations are far from being predictable or reproducible in the scientific sense of the word. This means that neither side can be very sure of what the other side's real perceptions and goals are, in an arms control negotiation. In practice, most policymakers (and many respectable analysts) do not even try to deal with such probabilities. Instead, they take a few "likely" scenarios and calculate the results with a few simplified assumptions based partly on data and partly on intuition. This process is also certain to generate convictions and goals for the two sides which neither can deduce for the other. This makes secrecy a central element of arms control negotiations. More complicated than secrecy, this issue requires particular attention to the kind of information that is provided or denied to one's adversary.

There are two conflicting reactions to this need for information management. On the one hand, there is the ethical tendency to regard cooperation as a good thing and to regard withholding of information - or worse, that of providing misleading information - to be a bad thing. Some might feel it is just plain bad; others might think it is likely to be at least inefficient, given that the already complex process of trying to find a treaty may be further acerbated.

On the other hand, it has been clearly established and explored by RAIFFA and others that your opponent's knowledge of your own goal can give him a unilateral advantage during a negotiation. In the arms control context, we are indeed confronted with an information problem that is multilayered. Not only your goals, but also your capabilities, your perceptions and those of your opponent become information assets that must be carefully managed. They must be kept secret initially. At various points in the negotiation you may want to provide misinformation about them. At other points it may be appropriate to "invest" some correct information in order to move the process along to an efficient conclusion.

This paper describes a device, and some procedures for using it, which might make a major contribution to this process.

3. THE APPROACH

We have tried to sketch out the legitimate need for secrecy and information management in arms control negotiations. The question now is: how can one permit each side its legitimate control over information and still reap the efficiency which would result from the sharing of such information. An unfortunately naive solution is the use of a trustworthy third party. The reason it is naive is that, in the context of something as critical as arms control, it is just plain unrealistic for two adversaries to share their innermost secrets with a third party negotiator - no matter how honest, neutral and well intentioned he might seem to be.

To remedy this seemingly unavoidable impediment, we herewith postulate a *computerized third party* (*CTP*). For the purpose of this paper, try to assume that the CTP will have the following characteristics:

1) Sufficient secrecy so that inputs by either side will not be available directly to the other side;

2) Mutual control over outputs, so that no information will be furnished to either side without prior agreement of both sides regarding such information;

3) Sufficient computational capacity to deal with the desirable calculations.

Let us explore how a device can address a few relatively simple problems.

3.1 Number of Silos

We want to begin with a "simple" one-dimensional case. Suppose that one is trying to negotiate number of silos allowed to the Soviets, in a context where all other issues are presumed fixed. Assume that the US prefers a low limit, and the Soviets a higher limit and furthermore that this direction, at least, is evident to both sides. As a first case, suppose that the US is secretly prepared to allow $x_1 = 200$ silos; any greater number would require some US action external to this specific negotiation. Following RAIFFA, x_1 is the "reserve" numbers for the US. Similarly, assume the reserve number x_2 for the Soviets is only 150; that they correspondingly fear the US will demand fewer but just might permit more.

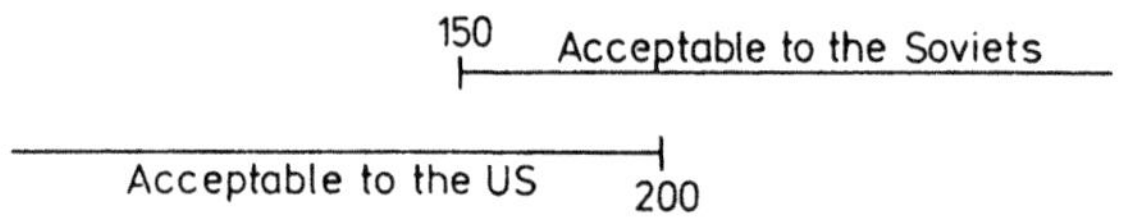

In this first case there is an overlap, or "excess", of 50 silos. Neither side knows it - for all it knows there may instead be a gap, with no room for negotiation (without perhaps reexamining other components of the posture). It is clearly a mistake for the Soviet Union to reveal that x_2 is 150; if it does, the US will quickly agree, thereby getting full benefit of the excess. The US has the identical inhibition against revealing x_1.

Without a CTP, the parties typically start the bargaining process by announcing numbers x_1' and x_2' more favourable than their actual reserves:

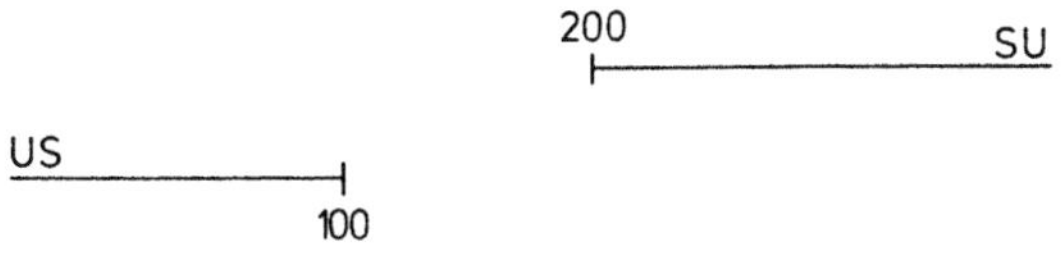

Because of this natural inflation of requirements, there is likely to be an apparent gap even when in reality an excess exists. Both sides have to guess. One side may easily believe that the difference is irreconcilable, and unnecessarily terminate negotiations. There are several other difficulties familiar to anyone participating in such negotiations. One is the anticipation that you will be invited to "split the difference" - a proposal that can be quite unfair, but one whose rejection can make one seem intransigent. This provides an added motivation to inflate the initial position, which may have been accompanied by statements such as "These are already more silos than we can prudently tolerate - allowing you any more would be irresponsible".

Although it does not inexorably arrive at a settlement even when there is an excess, the CTP seems to alleviate or eliminate these difficulties. Here are some ways it can work:

<u>Step 1:</u> Initial statements x_1' and x_2' are put into the computer.

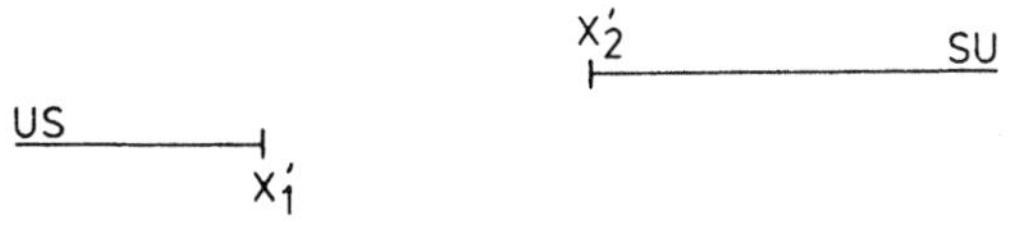

The two sides agree to ask whether there is any excess - whether there is room for a deal. In the illustration, the answer will be "No".

<u>Step 2:</u> The two sides recognize that if they really meant x_1' and x_2' that there really is no deal. (Note that neither one has learned the other's

input - just that it was on the wrong side of his own.) They therefore agree to try just once more - presumably to put in the most generous terms they can, to avoid losing a chance to make a desirable settlement. This can be a strong motivation. If the answer is still "no", no further time is wasted to look for an agreement on this one issue. (One still has two options: to wait until conditions change, or to reopen negotiations on other parameters that might make the present one less difficult.) Suppose now the answer is "yes":

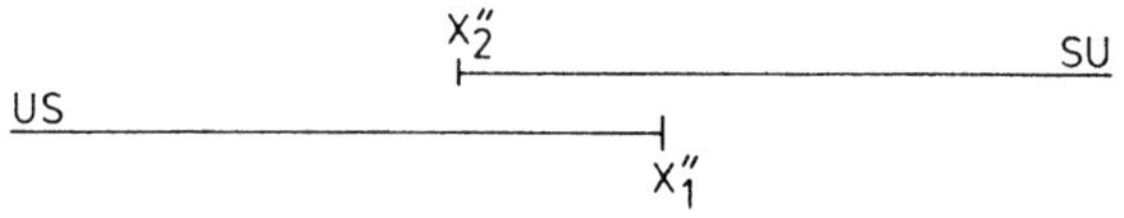

Without having revealed their reserve position to the other side, both sides now have reason to believe there is indeed an excess.

Step 3: To confirm that belief, the CTP can now invite the two sides to commit to what we shall call a "conservative" contract C_0. If both sides push the contract button, the CTP will announce to both sides contract C_0; otherwise it will say "no C_0". If the output is C_0, either side will henceforth have the unilateral right to conclude the negotiation by conceding to the opponent the reserve value he had entered at this previous step. For example, if x_1' had been 200 silos, and x_2' had been 150 silos, and if the C_0 condition has been registered, than the SU would be required to accept the value of 200 any time the US demanded the negotiations stop on the basis of step 3. The SU will not know this number unless or until the US invokes its option - only that it is larger than the SU secret "requirement" of 150. The US, of course, will have put forth in exchange a symmetric obligation to accept whatever number x_2 was, knowing only that it was less than 200. We call this the "conservative" contract because it confers on either side the rather mild right to concede to the other side all the (unknown) excess at that stage - in the interest of quickly concluding the negotiations.

Step 4: Suppose that Step 3 has been completed with "C_0" (exploration of "no C_0" is left as an exercise for the reader). Then one thing the principals can do is put forth another pair of offers x_1'' and x_2'', perhaps (but not necessarily) less generous than x_1' and x_2':

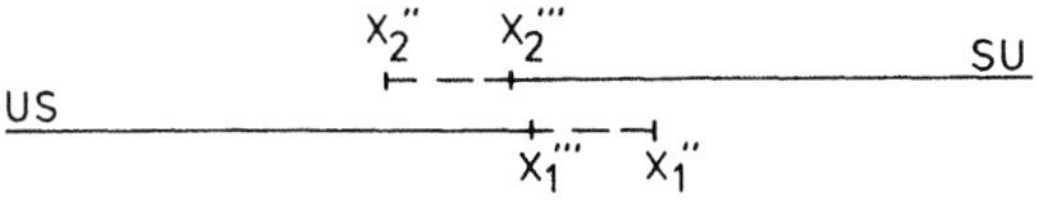

If they are both less generous (as in the illustration), if the answer about excess is still "yes", and if this step gets ratified with a "C", then each side will have a preferred (and acceptable) fallback position. The players can obviously iterate this "free-play" procedure at their mutual pleasure.

Step 5: *Proportional Compromise*. Suppose that "free-play" seems no longer to be promising, and that there is at least one ratified position. Suppose further that the players are able to select one such position as a basis for "compromise". We have already mentioned a typical compromise proposal in the absence of a CTP, namely "split the difference". The CTP offers some more flexible alternatives. One is proportional compromise. Here each player, knowing there is an excess E, but not knowing its size, tells the CTP what fraction of E he will give to his opponent. The two fractions f_1 and f_2 are entered into the CTP. The computer then gives a "yes" or "no" as to whether

$$f_1 + f_2 > 1$$

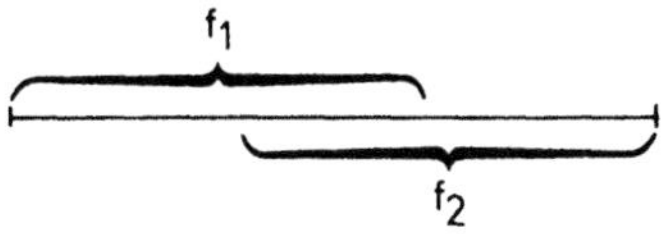

In the illustrated case the answer would have been "yes". They would then both know that their combined willingness to compromise is more than sufficient. This would presumably be good news; we can perhaps leave it to their imagination how they would share this excess flexibility. Even if the answer were "no", one might still pursue this branch - for example by asking if the absolute value of the remaining difference is less than some small number (like 10). In any event, this leads to the alternative (or supplemental) compromise process of Step 6.

Step 6: *Investigation of Acceptable Differences.* Once the existence of an excess E has been established, both sides will have a natural desire to know what it is, tempered by the desire not to let the opponent know one's own position. A suitably cautious approach can be to agree on some suitably small difference D (in this context D might be 20), and ask the computer whether the difference at any stage is less than D. The definition of "suitably small" might in fact be a willingness to split any difference less than D.

Step 7: *Conclusion of a Treaty.* Admittedly without being exhaustive, we have described a number of steps that might well result in a settlement, or conclusion. The whole set of negotiation will have been conducted in secrecy. In fact, it may well be that the CTP can be so "simple" to operate that it can be operated directly by the two heads of state with no intermediaries whatever. (The staff would at least have the jobs of helping structure the negotiation, and giving solicited information and advice. We do not mean to imply that intermediaries should not be trusted, nor that heads of state should be expected to do anything complicated; but we do want to emphasize the extreme security that a CTP can permit.) Once a deal appears to have been struck, the principals can of course think it over - either privately or by sharing it with some of their staffs. Only after it has survived that kind of review by both sides need it be announced. If one side really doesn't like it after all, he can be free to state privately that a deal does not in fact exist. The resulting deal must therefore end up being attractive (or at least acceptable) to both sides before it is formalized and announced.

3.2 Comments on the One-Dimensional Case

Compared with direct negotiation, perhaps the most striking aspect of CTP negotiation can be seen to be what can be called "reverse bargaining" -

a process that starts (at least theoretically) with the most *generous* position either side is willing to entertain (rather than the most *greedy* position either side can hope for). Once you establish that a pair of these "most-generous" positions overlap, you then iterate the bargaining process with respect to the excess. Effectively, once each side establishes there is a deal consistent with its initial "most-generous" position, it finds itself establishing successively better positions as the "excess" gets shared. This is of course the reverse of direct bargaining in which neither side is assured of a deal until it is struck (by which time the negotiation is of course completed), and in which each side typically puts forth successively less attractive (to itself) positions in the process.

The feature that reverse bargaining shares with direct bargaining is that it does not assuredly lead up to a deal even if a mutually acceptable one seems to exist. Oddly enough, this seems to be more of a strength than a weakness. Any process which *ab initio* commits adversaries to a coercive process necessarily forces them to surrender certain freedoms of decision, very possibly prematurely. Naturally, one *can* prescribe procedures that will guarantee a deal if a mutually acceptable one exists - a trivial one would be to flip a coin for the excess. The obvious problem with this is that now one has to get the adversaries to commit themselves to this procedure - to agree to a deal before they know what it is - to buy a pig in a poke. Furthermore, this problem is not just a reflection of annoying recalcitrance, greed, or timidity on the part of the adversaries. Each side has its inherent bargaining strength, based on its knowledge of the other side, and on its own alternatives; it is entitled to a deal that reflects that bargaining strength.

It is because of the virtue of minimizing the incremental commitments that are required of both sides (to proceed from one step to the next) that we have tried to provide reverse bargaining with a "starter set" of extremely gentle steps - steps that *permit* extreme caution in sharing information or extreme gradualness in approaching a commitment. This does not preclude large "quantum" steps which may suggest themselves because of pressure or improvements in "climate".

3.3 Two-Dimensional Negotiation

We have already emphasized the complexity typical of arms control negotiations. A central aspect of this complexity is that one does *not* negotiate only one issue at a time. Even on each of the elements, such as number of silos, one is looking for an acceptable (or desirable) pair of numbers - one number for the US and the other for the SU. It appears that the CTP is particularly effective in this multi-dimensional context. To illustrate its operation, we propose to discuss a simple two-dimensional problem regarding the sharing of a pizza.

Suppose two people A and B have jointly and equally purchased a pizza, without knowing its ingredients ahead of time. Suppose in fact that the left side of the pizza is mushrooms, and the right side is pepperoni. Finally, suppose A greatly prefers pepperoni, and B middly prefers mushrooms.

Perceived Value of Pizza Components

	A	B
Pepperoni	.9	.4
Mushrooms	.1	.6

Specifically, by A's reckoning, 90% of the value of the pizza is in the pepperoni, whereas it is only 40% for B.

If A and B each truthfully report their values to the CTP, the CTP can divide the pizza so that they each get the same fraction of their personal perceived value, and furthermore that fraction is maximized. Simple arithmetic gives the following result:

"Optimal Allocation" of Pizza Components

	Allocation	Unit Value	Net Value	Allocation	Unit Value	Net Value
Pepperoni	.77	.9	.69	.23	.4	.09
Mushroom			0	1.00	.6	.60
Total Value			.69			.69

The process therefore gives each side 69% of its perceived value - a result that could not have been achieved without knowledge of both sides values. The example also suggests a built-in incentive for both sides to give accurate inputs to the CTP. It is nevertheless instructive to investigate some strategies for lying. Suppose, for example, that A has learned B's values, and furthermore knows that B will enter them. Then A's best inputs will be:

Best Lies for A	
Pepperoni	$.4+\varepsilon$
Mushrooms	$.6-\varepsilon$

where ε is a very small number. The CTP will then believe that the two adversaries have almost identical value functions, but will conscientiously give both sides the benefit of the difference. The resulting allocation will be almost exactly:

Allocation if A Lies, and B is Accurate		
Pepperoni	1.0	0
Mushrooms	1/6	5/6
Total Value	.92	.50

The CTP will think each side has gotten almost exactly 1/2 of its perceived value (a little more, because of the ε's); whereas in fact A will have gotten 92%, and B will have gotten 50%. The general principle is clear: if you know your opponent's values, act as if yours are almost the same, with only the slightest preference for your own interest. Poetically just observation: if *both* opponents lie by putting in the values of the other side, the CTP will of course give each side the wrong part of the pizza. They will get the *minimum* equal values. In the example, their slices would be 31% (which is the wrong end of the 69% they would have gotten being accurate). Related point: the truth is a conservative strategy, in that it guarantees you at least half, no matter what your opponent puts in.

Given the admitted complications of lying, one can structure various steps for the two-dimensional problem, vaguely similar to those in the one-dimensional problem. Two examples:

(a) Simultaneous Alternatives: Each side puts in, for example, 3 sets of values. The computer makes "optimal" allocations for all nine (3 times 3) possible pairs. It then tells both sides which of their inputs corresponds with the most favorable allocation. If they both believe this also to be sufficiently accurate, they can both elect to be told what the payoff actually is. If it seems desirable, they may ratify it - that is, agree to accept it unless a better one for both sides can be found.

(b) Clean-up: Suppose an allocation, detected by any procedure, has been ratified. Then it may be attractive to have a "clean-up" round, in which each side will particularly want to be accurate. The agreement might be that the computer would announce the result *only* if the new solution was better for *both* sides than the one already ratified.

3.4 Comments on the Multi-Dimensional Case

As a computational remark, the optimal allocation for a given set of inputs, (if the value fractions are linear and additive) is neatly found by linear programming. In fact this device can also solve the problem if there are more than two parties to the negotiation.

On the minus side, the multi-dimensional case illustrates the need not only for secrecy but also for some amount of misrepresentation. Although this may seem a complication, precisely the same complication is present in direct bargaining *without* benefit of a CTP. On the plus side, the CTP at least *permits* determination of candidate treaties which are efficient and therefore more likely than others to be acceptable to both sides.

3.5 Some Generalized Structure

If each side can define a value function for itself on various pairs of postures, then conceptually there would be a pair of payoff functions as outlined in Figure 3. If these were to be put into the CTP, then we discover certain tantalizingly useful results that would reside within the computer. One is the subset of what might be called efficient deals, sketched in Figure 4 as the curve [x(t),y(t)]. These are characterized by the statement that for any other deal one can find an "efficient deal" that is at least as good for both parties - that in general any other deal will be less desirable for at least one party than one of the efficient deals.

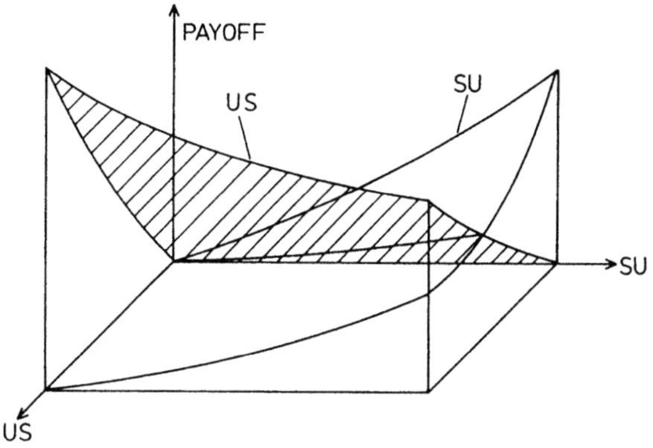

Fig. 3: Illustrative Arms Control Value Functions

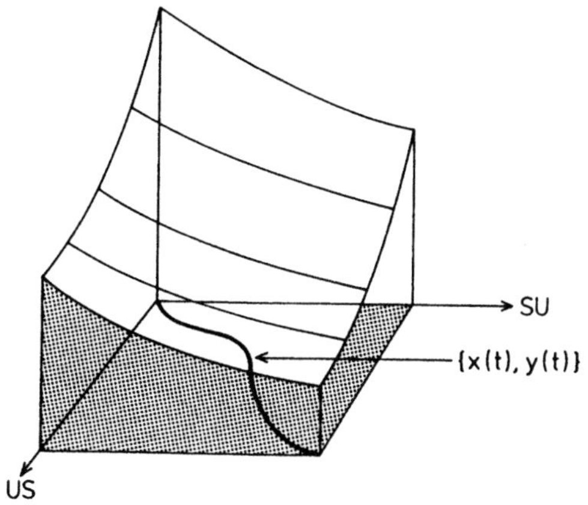

Fig. 4: Illustrative Set of Efficient Deals

Another curve of interest is displayed in Figure 5. This presents what is called the Pareto frontier of the various possible deals; it shows, for a given value to one side, what is the most the other side can get. A particular deal (there may be more than one) which provides this pair of values will be one of the "efficient deals" of the previous figure. The two sides could conceivably request the computer to provide both of them with one or another of these two curves. The reason the results are tantalizing, instead of compelling, is that one can easily show that such outputs might convey more information to one side than the other might feel was appropriate. We are left with the problem of just what the two sides might in fact be able to share. Given the apparent payoff of the process, one wants to try hard to find such protocols.

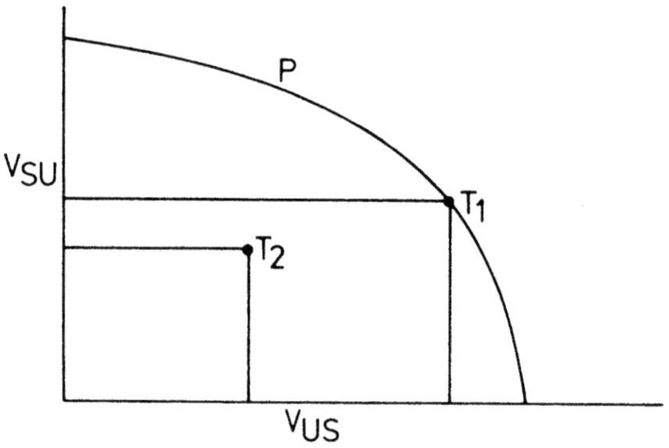

Fig. 5: The Pareto Frontier

4. ON THE IMPLEMENTATION

So far, we have made a theoretical case for the value of a CTP in arms control negotiations. Suppose this case looks attractive - what are some of the "practical" issues that would have to be addressed before it could be exploited?

When we first defined the CTP, we asked that certain stipulations are accepted - that it could be secure, and that it have appropriate computational capability. It is now time to discuss not only these stipulations, but also some other preparations that seem at least desirable if the CTP is to be comfortably used in arms control negotiations.

From a practical point of view, a secure system is by definition one that both countries believe to be secure. In this discussion it is not prudent to speculate on exactly how this might eventually be accomplished. Nevertheless, an example of how it might be done can at least help describe the problem:

1) Agreement is reached on the structure of the input and output variables, and the kinds of comparisons and computations (such as linear programs) that should be available.

2) In compliance with this, a computer program is written and entered into the computer, which is temporarily locked into a "read-only" mode.

3) Both sides convince themselves the program is as advertised.

4) Physically separate input devices are provided for each nation. Each nation inserts a decryption box in front of its input device.

5) In the simplest case, all outputs will be shared. This might require a *shared* encryption scheme for the outputs, for secure transmission to the negotiators.

The computer itself could be in a mutually guarded room or conceivably even in a satellite. In any case there could be provision for unilateral destruction of its contents by either side, in case it perceived a threatened compromise.

It may prove worthwhile for later generations of a CTP to be quite elaborate, and to be capable of complex calculations regarding the effect of various combinations of offensive and defensive systems. Nevertheless, the quite modest procedure outlined in this paper could be set up quite easily, and on a modest computer. Preliminary versions have already been explored on micro computers.

There are of course two sets of skills that would need to be developed if the implementation of a CTP became imminent - procedures for effective progress in negotiations, and strategies for each nation to use on its own behalf when following these procedures. Even the rather simple procedures that have been outlined here present an immediate promise for negotiations much more effective than those presently feasible with the "direct" approach. The likelihood that some sophisticated procedures can do even more should not delay the near-term payoffs that may be attainable.

Strategies for using the CTP are already hinted at by earlier parts of this discussion. Both sides will want to study these assiduously - first to find ways they can bargain to their own advantage, and second to strengthen the program and protocols for using the CTP, so that both sides can be better assured of a safe and effective bargaining process.

REFERENCE

Raiffa, H. (1982): The Art and Science of Negotiation. The Belknap Press of Harvard University Press, Cambridge, Mass.

PART IV

VERIFICATION AND POST-AGREEMENTS ASSESSMENTS

WORKING GROUP MEMBERS:

GILMAN, Ernest (Chairman)

AVENHAUS, Rudolf

BRAMS, Steven J.

CLEMINSON, Frank R.

DIN, Allan M.

FICHTNER, John

JONES, Derry W.

KILGOUR, D. Marc

MARKIN, Jack T.

SAUDER, Alphonse

VERIFICATION AND POST-AGREEMENT ASSESSMENT

Ernest Gilman
Operational Research and Analysis Establishment
Department of National Defence, Ottawa

and

Derry W. Jones
School of Studies in Chemistry and Chemical Technology
University of Bradford, England

1. INTRODUCTION

The overall purpose of this volume, like that of the Workshop from which it derives, is not only to present an interchange of experience and views between analysts with differing backgrounds, but also to identify research gaps and to suggest future research activities on arms-control problems. For the Verification and Post-Agreement Assessment Working Group, the focus would be expected to be on the practicabilities of arms control for the fairly near future.

Accordingly, in the first section of this chapter we outline briefly the nature of, and need for, verification in arms control. Successive sections then attempt to provide some links between the subsequent chapters dealing with individual verification topics in more detail and to convey at least the flavour of the discussion within the Working Group.

Verification has always been an essential component of arms control, even before the nuclear era, but it has been defined in several ways. In its general sense, verification, according to Webster (3rd International Edition, 1966),

NATO ASI Series, Vol. F 26
Modelling and Analysis in Arms Control
Edited by R. Avenhaus et al.

involves "the authentification of truth or accuracy by such means as facts, statements, measurements", while The Oxford Universal Dictionary (3rd Edition, 1955) defines it as "the action of establishing or testing the truth or corrections of a fact, theory, statement, etc., by means of special investigation or comparison of data." In the context of arms control in the post-World War II period it was agreed that the definition put forward by the US Arms Control and Disarmament Agency (ACDA) would be used in SALT I (Strategic Arms Limitation Treaty): "the process of determining the degree to which parties to an agreement are complying with the provisions of the agreement."

Essentially, the need for verification arises because violations of a treaty may not be obvious. In fact, the very existence of verification, especially if coupled with secrecy about its exact capability, can act as a powerful deterrent to violations. Should these occur, and be detected, the dangers can be realized by other parties; conversely, soundly-based conviction that substantial violations are not occurring can nurture mutual confidence between the parties.

It must be recognized at the outset that total certainty about the verification of an arms control agreement is never likely to be realized. In the past, inadequate verification has sometimes been at least the nominal excuse for lack of progress in arms control. As applied to arms control in the post-war period, verification involves both technical complexity - that is, sophisticated so-called National Technical Means (NTMs) - and political issues. Political issues may be less evident when there is a commonality of interest, as for example, occurred in the 1960s and 1970s. Today, however, the capabilities of NTMs are being challenged in the US just at the time when more stringent demands are being made for verification. From the standpoint of security the US now wants "effective" (instead of "adequate") verification of arms-control agreements. This change has come about primarily because of the altered superpower relationship, and because of the non-compliance issue.

2. STRATEGIC DEFENCE

In his paper on "Arms Control and Strategic Defence," Allan M. Din points out that the issue of non-compliance with the Anti-Ballistic Missile (ABM) Treaty of 1972 has come to the fore with President Reagan's Strategic Defense Initiative (SDI) speech of March 1983. Din believes that the long-term possibility of transition from offence domination to defence domination could create crisis instability through violations of the ABM Treaty.

He concentrates on the fact that research per se is not specified in the ABM treaty (since at the time it did not appear verifiable), but new physical principles for ABM systems are mentioned, albeit not in the main text. Another area of uncertainty, according to Din, is the extent to which field (as distinct from large-scale laboratory) testing of, for example, space-based systems, is excluded. While there is evidently some current debate within the highest levels of the US Administration, there does seem to be a movement towards change in the American interpretation of the ABM Treaty to permit development and testing of new strategic defence systems, short of actual deployment. As a consequence, more stringent means of verification of the amended ABM Treaty were advocated.

In addition Din claims that detection of the existence of research activities by NTM is feasible for laboratory complexes because of their size and the high energies involved (including X-rays). Developments in remote sensing (high resolution X-ray cameras for incoming rays of 2-60 kiloelectronvolts (keV)) should be able to cope with future reduction in the size of accelerators and lasers of directed energy components.

Within the Working Group, the ensuing discussion emphasised the problems of monitoring dual-purpose systems. In some cases, Global Positioning Systems (GPS), for instance, restriction to peace-time use could be achieved by limiting the numbers of equipment permitted to be operational at any one time. The problem of dual-purpose systems is particularly evident in space. Activities in space relevant to verification may be classified on a scale embracing military activity/"militaristic" activity/active weapon systems. These ranged from surveillance satellites, through target-locating indirect weapon satellites, to direct weapons, both conventional and advanced (such as SDI).

In his paper on "Space-based Remote-sensing Technology for Verification in Outer Space," F.R. Cleminson looks forward to the feasibility of monitoring a treaty which bans an arms race in outer space. Since both the orbital domains and external forms (closely related to function) of potential weapons for space-to-space operation are fairly predictable, he thinks that detection and evaluation need not present insuperable problems. Consequently an appropriate treaty may be agreed upon, perhaps within a decade or two.

This technical study is based on the "perfect world" assumption that the political issues required to obtain wide agreement for a treaty have been first dealt with, particularly those of concern to the superpowers. It is expected, therefore, that a verification organization tied to such a treaty would take into account not only technical but also political considerations. These would include political control, special interests of certain states, and avoidance of a veto, possibly by use of weighted voting by interested parties and by partially rotating the composition of governing bodies. Moreover, the organizational structure and outline of the decision-making process must be an integral part of the treaty. For such an agreement to be successful it is expected that some cooperative measures would be necessary, the most desirable being on-site inspections (OSI).

During the ensuing discussion it became clearer that verification of space weapons could, in principle, be carried out not only in space, but also through OSI - inspection at the launch pad, and OSI at the production line. The Working Group acknowledged that as a particularly difficult issue primarily because of the Soviet view that NTMs could handle the monitoring of any agreement. Some discussants noted that, while the Soviets remain convinced that OSI was just an excuse for espionage, they appear to recognize that it may be necessary in some situations. They have actually accepted the principle of OSI, at least for destruction of chemical weapons (although not for declaration of stocks), and for the monitoring of the Non-Proliferation Treaty.

3. THIRD-PARTY INVOLVEMENT

In a joint presentation on the use of "Third-Party Space-To-Ground Surveillance Satellites," Alphonse Sauder explains France's concept of an International Satellite Monitoring Agency (ISMA), and Allan Din concentrates on the related proposals put forward by the neutral states (Sweden, Switzerland and Austria) at the Conference on Confidence and Security-Building Measures and Disarmament in Europe (CCSBMDE), which has been taking place in Stockholm. The aims of ISMA, as proposed in 1978, would be to aid both monitoring compliance with arms-control agreements and international crisis management. In its early stages, the agency would hope to process data supplied by states and to acquire some information by itself. Later it would become fully independent, through means of its own satellites.

It was primarily because of the lukewarm reception of the ISMA concept by the superpowers that the European neutrals tentatively put forward their own proposal in 1985. Instead of using the UN the neutrals called for a less ambitious consortium of several neutral nations that would be responsible for monitoring a specific agreement in Europe. The overall costs of the project would depend on whether the object of surveillance was, for example, large army movements (whether long-term, over months, or short-term, over hours), or the fine detail of research establishments working on strategic defence projects. A third-party satellite even with limited capabilities could have both practical and politically symbolic implications.

The Working Group acknowledged the possibility of a third-party system supplementing the superpowers' NTMs in the verification of an arms control agreement. There were, however, obstacles which would have to be overcome. One obvious problem was the expected lack of skilled photographic interpreters among the third-party nations. In addition, it would be difficult to acquire an extensive data base. Cost estimates for such activities as launches and annual maintenance of satellites indicate that those participating in such a scheme would have to be affluent. Costs would be reduced in relation to the number of nations involved and, in fact, the whole financial question may not be as important if the primary justification for supporting such a system becomes more politically acceptable.

4. THE IAEA EXPERIENCE

Aspects of the organization of the Vienna-based International Atomic Energy Agency (IAEA) which may be relevant to the verification of arms control treaties are presented in a paper, "International Atomic Energy Agency Safeguards", by Rudolf Avenhaus and Jack T. Markin. The co-authors emphasize how important it was to detect diversions of significant amounts of nuclear material as soon as possible. Some of the safeguard procedures followed by the IAEA to verify the Non-Proliferation Treaty (NPT) could be used elsewhere although each issue is unique. The NPT signatories possess 500 nuclear facilities, including enrichment plants, reactors and reprocessing plants, which are inspected by only 150 IAEA representatives.

The officials make 2000 inspections per year. The IAEA has established specific tolerance levels for its monitoring and meets the potential problem of removal of material by considering its desirability and complexity as well as likely methods of concealment. During their inspections the IAEA representatives employ differing technologies, including neutrons, X-rays and isotope enrichment energies. Such tools could be used to enhance the on-site inspections of arms control treaties.

Avenhaus and Markin also offer a more quantitative approach to the IAEA safeguards issue. This behind-the-scenes look at the rationale for the safeguards reveals some obvious flaws in the NPT approach.

From its beginning the treaty was seen by some nations as "unfair" in at least two respects. Firstly, the rules apply only to those states which have ratified the Treaty and not, of course, to non-signatories; consequently, it is arguable that restrictions should not be too severe. Secondly, the Treaty discriminates between non-weapons states, for which controls are mandatory, and weapons states, for which they are optional. For these reasons it was crucial in the design stage that the safeguards measures to be implemented by the IAEA, as envisaged in the Treaty, were planned and carried through in a clear, rational, objective, and formalized manner.

IAEA safeguards are based on the principle of nuclear material accountancy, which follows the receipts into, and shipments out of, the Material Balance Area (MBA), and deduces the Material Unaccounted For (MUF), if any, over a given period of time. Although the plant operator reports to the IAEA all the data needed to establish the material balance via his national authority, the IAEA verifies these data by making independent measurements on a random sampling basis. Again, by means of a statistical test, it is decided whether or not the difference, between reported and independently generated data, can be explained by measurement errors.

Inspectors might be misled by direct diversion of material and/or falsification of records. By application of non-constant-sum game theory (neither side presumably favours a false alarm, therefore the sum cannot be zero), the capability of the system, defined as the guaranteed probability of detecting a diversion of nuclear materials, can be determined. The extension of these considerations to sequences of material balance areas and inventory periods is straightforward. If, however, the timely detection of diversion becomes an additional criterion for the applicability of the system, there are considerable statistical complexities; although some progress has been made, convincing solutions are still lacking.

The Working Group members agreed that the IAEA experience, including the reliance on mathematics, must not be ignored in the search for appropriate verification schemes for future arms control agreements. The IAEA safeguards were seen to be quite suitable as standards to be followed in specific cases. Nonetheless it was acknowledged that the success of the IAEA was primarily due to the close cooperation of the superpowers in seeking to arrest nuclear proliferation. Indeed, verification's primary goal is to deter violations rather than to detect them. The political consequences of reported violations was touched upon in the context of the possibility of proliferation having a stabilizing effect, but the disadvantages of such a possibility were considered to outweigh the advantages.

5. GAME THEORETICAL ANALYSES OF VERIFICATION

In their paper "Notes on Arms Control Verification: a Game-theoretic Analysis," Steven J. Brams and D. Marc Kilgour build on earlier work. They consider two-person non-constant-sum games of verification with an inspected party as one player and an inspector as the other; these have, respectively, options of compliance/non-compliance (that is, with a treaty) and acceptance/non-acceptance (including challenging but without the aid of a detector). They studied Nash equilibrium and also analysed cases in which (as in real life) the detector was imperfect.

While none of the games developed is ideal for the problems of verification, together they yield some interesting results. Thus, it appears that greater compliance (with the Treaty) might be induced if the inspector announced occasionally to the world (and hence to the inspected) different results from those indicated by the imperfect detector. The modellers indicated that, with some models, a detector has to be near perfect to overcome the strong strategic incentive for both players to revert to a stable situation which is not especially desirable for either party. Such apparently paradoxical (or "perverse") features prompted the authors to be cautious with practical conclusions, acknowledging that improvements were required in the models.

Following a similar approach, John Fichtner reviews " Concepts for Solving Two-person Games which Model the Verification Problem in Arms Control." He emphasizes the deterrence of the inspectee to violate an agreement as a consequence of the inspector announcing his strategy. Whereas the Nash equilibrium may lead to a probability for non-compliance which is greater than zero, one desires a solution in which the inspectee is induced to comply with the treaty. This is effected with the "Stackelberg" or "Price-leadership" concept, whereby maximum payoff is achieved by the inspector announcing his detection probability and the inspectee is assumed to act rationally.

This game-theoretical model may serve as the basis for statistical analysis of verification problems where stochastical errors (whether due to measurement and/or random sampling errors) cannot be avoided. This programme has been worked out for the case of the IAEA safeguards in partial fulfillment of the Non-Proliferation Treaty.

In view of the basic objectives of the Workshop, a general discussion was held on the applicability of these and related models for use by researchers and decision-makers in arms control. At their present state, some of the models were considered too theoretical but it was felt that further attempts should be made to deal with specific verification problems. Thus, it should be possible to explain the change of outcomes which can occur as a result of different assumptions.

The application of game modelling to arms control research, particularly relating to verification, is still in its infancy. There is clearly room for development, particularly in relation to specific agreements. It was acknowledged that such theoretical modelling in a refined form may become a valuable tool for arms control policy formulations, maybe even leading to unexpected but attractive options.

6. THE PRESENT STATE OF VERIFICATION

Ernest Gilman takes a broad approach to the issues being discussed in "Verification At The Crossroads." Although he agrees that NTM capabilities are being pressed by the challenges presented by new weapon systems, he believes that the problem lies elsewhere. To him the major issue is the political challenge to the concept of arms control itself, and only indirectly, to verification.

There appears to be a divergence between the capabilities of surveillance technology for military purposes and those for arms control. Until recently adequate verification was acceptable to the US as a prerequisite to signing a treaty. Now it appears that the system must be effective, something which has not been defined. Consequently treaties, such as that for a Comprehensive Test Ban (CTB), which appeared to be close to becoming a reality just a few years ago, remain unsigned.

NTMs will, no doubt, be called upon to meet serious challenges in the future but verification technology is making significant advances. Indeed many of the technical issues challenging NTMs may be overcome if as much attention is paid to surveillance systems for verification purposes as for other areas (such as SDI). Nevertheless OSI will have to be increased in order to complement NTM capability to monitor future agreements. Maybe of more importance is the political and psychological role that OSI could play in arms control.

7. POST AGREEMENT ASSESSMENT

Procedures for reviewing compliance with arms control treaties in the nuclear era are quite unique. For example, the NPT has a 5-yearly formal review procedure while SALT I relied principally on the Standing Consultative Commission (SCC) for clarification. Although the concept of technical consultations remains intact there is, however, concern about non-compliance of treaties and the seeming lack of appropriate means to respond to violations.

The compliance issue has recently generated a great deal of interest, although it has been around for a while. As early as two decades ago, Dr. Fred Iklé, a respected expert who is presently serving as a senior aide to the US Secretary of Defense, dealt with the subject in terms of the post-World War II period in the influential journal, Foreign Affairs

(January 1961). In the article "After Detection - What?" the possibilities of Soviet non-compliance of arms control treaties were examined, as were the consequences.

In spite of concerns about compliance, the Presidents who preceded Mr. Reagan seemed to have believed that the issue should not be an impediment to the signing of a treaty. Kennedy, for instance, overwhelmed opponents of the Limited Test Ban Treaty (LTBT) by making the point that, if the Soviets were not deterred from violating the agreement because of cost or fear of detection, he could always abrogate the treaty. Compliance mechanisms were therefore unnecessary. During the administrations of Nixon, Ford, and Carter the SCC was used extensively to clarify contentious technical points brought up by both superpowers, including those which may have gone beyond legal bounds. Overall the possibility that non-compliance at the margins might occur was accepted by previous US governments, because it was decided that national security would be weakened significantly more without a treaty.

The Working Group, recognizing that the growing American demands for increased security would have to be met as a prerequisite to agreement, proposed various options. One obvious approach might be to seek less complex agreements covering very specific subjects, consequently making verification and compliance less important. President Reagan's "Zero Option" is an example of this approach. A cautious loosening of the secrecy surrounding the SCC discussions might, at least, prevent potentially damaging surprises such as occurred as a consequence of the recent charges concerning the ABM Treaty. It was suggested that, as compliance was such a politically sensitive issue, concerns over violations should be dealt with at the highest official levels instead of by experts. From the game-theory perspective the idea was presented that deterrence against violations may best be achieved, not by graduated tit-for-tat responses, but by massive retaliation for small violations and moderate responses to major violations.

8. FUTURE RESEARCH POSSIBILITIES

In many fields interdisciplinary collaboration is a necessary pre-condition for setting out the problem, let alone solving it, and this is as true for arms control, and particularly for verification, as for anything else. In the past, verification relied primarily on science, with additional input from other disciplines and the military. Indeed, part of the present challenge to verification may be a consequence of this unbalanced approach. The nature of the issue, nevertheless, requires that science and technology continue to lead in the research and development of verification methodology. Furthermore, as research advances in other areas of security it is only logical that verification technology will benefit, particularly from work being carried out on surveillance within the context of SDI and C^3 (Command, Control and Communications). Clearly maximum gains can be obtained if serious funding is directed specifically towards verification research.

The appropriation of such funds is, however, a political decision. It is at this particular stage that assistance can be obtained from those outside the scientific community. Before systems are developed decision-makers must initiate the process by returning to first principles. As early as possible they, and their advisers, have to decide on what is wanted from arms control and - particularly where verification is concerned - how much uncertainty is acceptable in an agreement.

Besides the more traditional approach to this problem by political scientists, historians, strategists, officials, and so on, the game-theorist may also have a role to play, at least in the research stages. Game theory may not solve or even accurately model, real-world arms control issues, but it seems possible that its application may reveal valuable insights. Unexpected conclusions are not uncommon in this field. Such inputs can only contribute to the inter-disciplinary search required to advance verification at a time when verification has become so important to arms control and international security.

SUGGESTED READINGS

Alford, J. "Confidence-Building Measures and Verification," Survival, 6:3 (May/June 1984).

Bellany, I. and Blacker, C.D. (eds). The Verification of Arms Control Agreements (London: Frank Cass and Co. Ltd., 1983).

Buchan, Glenn C. "The Verification Spectrum," Bulletin of Atomic Scientists, 39:9 (November 1983).

Buchheim, R.W. and Caldwell, D. The U.S.-U.S.S.R. Standing Consultative Commission: Description and Appraisal (Providence, Rhode Island: Brown University, Center for Foreign Policy Development, Working Paper 2, May 1983).

Caldwell, D. "The Standing Consultative Commission - What Is It and What It Isn't," Arms Control Today, 14: 3 (March/April 1984).

Crawford A., et. al. Compendium of Arms Control Verification Proposals, 2nd ed., (Ottawa: Department of National Defence, ORAE Report No. R81, March 1982).

Crawford, A. and Gilman, E. A Quantitative Overview Of The Second Edition Of The Compendium Of Arms Control Verification Proposals (Ottawa: Department of National Defence, ORAE Report No. R89, April 1983).

Freer, Fredric S. "The Verification Problem: What It Is and What Could Be Done About It," Journal of Strategic Studies, 8:2 (June 1985).

Goldblat, Josef. Agreements for Arms Control: A Critical Survey (London: SIPRI, Taylor and Francis Ltd., 1982).

Graybeal, Sidney N., and Krepon, Micheal. "Making Better Use of The Standing Consultative Commission," International Security, 10:2 (Fall 1985).

Jasani, B., and Barnaby, F. Verification Technologies - The Case for Surveillance by Consent (London: SIPRI, Berg Publishers Ltd., 1984).

Krass, A.S. The Technology and Politics of Verification (London: SIPRI, Taylor and Francis, 1985).

O'Manique, John (ed.). A Proxy for Trust. Views on the Verification Issue in Arms Control and Disarmament Negotiations (Ottawa: Carleton University, Norman Paterson School of International Affairs, 1985).

President Reagan, Ronald. "Compliance With Weekly Arms Control Agreements," Weekly Compilation of Presidential Documents, 21 (17 June 1985).

Schear, James A. Arms Control Treaty Compliance: Buildup to a Breakdown?" International Security, 10:2 (Fall 1985).

Scott, William F. "Asymmetries in Arms Control Verification," Armed Forces Journal International (February 1985).

Scribner, Richard A., and Luongo, Kenneth N. Strategic Nuclear Arms Control Verification: Terms and Concepts (Washington, D.C.: The American Association for the Advancement of Science, January 1985).

Swedish National Defence Research Institute (FOA). Symposium on Verification of Disarmament in Europe (Stockholm: FOA, December 1985).

Towle, Philip. Arms Control and East-West Relations (London and Canberra: Croom Helm, 1983).

Trimble, Phillip R. Soviet Violations of Arms Control Agreements: A Legal Perspective (UCLA: Center for International and Strategic Affairs Working Paper No. 53, November 1985).

ARMS CONTROL AND STRATEGIC DEFENCE

Allan M. Din
Stockholm International Peace Research Institute
SIPRI, Bergshamra
S-171 73 Solna, SWEDEN

1. Introduction

Strategic defence activities have been pursued by both the superpowers since the late fifties. The effort involved has changed somewhat during the years reaching a relative maximum at the end of the sixties in association with the arms control process which led to the conclusion in 1972 of the ABM treaty. More than anything else, this treaty symbolized the current state of inadequasy concerning strategic defence options using other means than missiles which, in turn, were not found to be relevant to more than a rather limited point defence. Nevertheless, the ABM treaty has come to be considered, and rightfully so, as one of the most specific and valuable pieces of arms control of the past few decades.

The possible use of advanced technologies, involving for example directed energy weapons, for the purpose of strategic defence had been looked into extensively before 1972 and also continued after this time in the form of dedicated research projects. On the US side the level of funding, until the beginning of the eighties, might be characterized as a modest hedge against technological surprise breakthroughs of the adversary. Not much is known about the magnitude of the corresponding Soviet effort, but even if it may have been somewhat more substantial than the US one during the seventies, there has been no clear indication that it was running counter to neither the general sense nor to specific limitations of the ABM treaty.

NATO ASI Series, Vol. F 26
Modelling and Analysis in Arms Control
Edited by R. Avenhaus et al.

However, the launching of the Strategic Defence Initiative, SDI, by President Reagan in 1983 has raised numerous questions concerning present and future compliance with the ABM treaty, related to specific 'grey' areas of interpretation as well as to its basic *raison d'être*. With the SDI activities moving ahead as scheduled, a continual careful assessment of their legal and technical relevance for ABM treaty compliance is of the greatest importance.

In a longer perspective the problem of control and verification of strategic defence activities may, however, be seen as going beyond the ABM treaty concerns. In fact, if a serious international, or even just bilateral effort, is to be initiated with the declared purpose of realizing an orderly transition from the present offence dominated world to a defence dominated one, it will be overoptimistic to think that this could be accomplished by an uncontrolled introduction of strategic defence technologies. A change away from traditional nuclear deterrence doctrines can clearly not be allowed to take place at the expense of sacrificing crisis stability during the transition period and to assure this stability it will be paramount to dispose of appropriate technical means for a detailed monitoring of strategic defence activities, including certain types of research and development. This need is, in fact, already imposing itself at the present time with respect to the more limited scope of ABM treaty compliance.

2. Terminology and interpretation of the ABM treaty

There are (at least) two important points in the ABM treaty provisions open to contention with respect to the question of compliance: The first concerns the precise definition of which strategic defence systems are actually covered and the second, an explicit classification of what is meant by development, testing and deployment of the systems and their (sub)components.

The treaty defines ABM systems as 'currently' consisting of missiles, launchers and radars and from the main text it is *a priori* unclear whether more advanced systems are covered. During the years it has, however, always been maintained by the negotiators themselves, as well as officially in US arms control impact statements, that strategic defence systems based, for example, on directed energy technologies are in fact also covered to the same extent as the 'currently' defined systems.

This would in particular imply that article V stating that "each party undertakes not to develop, test or deploy ABM sytems or components which are sea-based, air-based, space-based or mobile land-based" applies to advanced systems as well. The preceding interpretation could in no way be superseded by agreed interpretation D which states that "in order to insure fulfillment of the obligation not to deploy ABM systems and their components except as provided in Article III of the Treaty, the Parties agree that in the event ABM systems based on other physical principles and including components capable of substituting for interceptor missiles, ABM launchers, or ABM radars are created in the future, specific limitations on such systems and their components would be subject to discussion in accordance with Article XIII and agreement in accordance with Article XIV of the Treaty".

As explained above, the main text of the treaty does, however, not explicitly affirm that advanced strategic defence systems (based on other physical principles) are covered. It now appears that this legal loophole is in the process of being exploited by the US administration in a major change of policy *vis à vis* the ABM treaty. In fact, on October 4, Arms Control advisor P. Nitze emphasized agreed interpretation D as permitting development of systems based on other physical principles, and just stopping short of actual deployment. On October 6, National Security Advisor R. McFarlane expressed the view that the treaty "authorized and approved" the development and testing of strategic defence systems as scheduled under the SDI program, and two days later a senior White House official confirmed that this interpretation of the treaty is indeed now the fixed position of the administration.

Bluntly stated, this new policy signifies changing the rules in the middle of the game and redefines the whole issue of ABM treaty compliance. According to treaty negotiator G.C. Smith, the new interpretation "makes a dead letter" of the treaty. Some US officials have more recently questioned the timeliness and the precise manner of expressing an altered interpretation, but the legal loophole option has not been excluded *per se*.

The second 'grey' area of the treaty is the definition of the key words 'development', 'testing' and 'deployment'. It must be emphasized that the word 'research' does not appear in the treaty but when it is claimed that research is permitted, the problem nevertheless arises of defining the borderline between research and development. Essentially only one authoritative statement offers some clarification of the issue. It is taken from a 1972 Senate testimony of G.C. Smith and states that "the obligation not to develop such systems, devices or warheads would be applicable only to that stage of development which follows laboratory development and testing. The prohibitions on development contained in the ABM treaty would start at that part of the development process where field testing is initiated on either a prototype or breadboard model".

This definition is far from sufficient in clarifyng the terminological uncertainties. It is an example of a guideline which endeavours to define verifiable limits beyond which strategic defence activities would be prohibited, but as such it does of course not represent more than the conventional wisdom of the seventies. If, in fact, the desire is to make the verifiable limits as stringent as possible, there is a possibility that new methods of verication may go as far as controlling certain research activities.

3. The prospects for detection, monitoring and verification

That some strategic defence research could be limited in a verifiable way using national technical means has been hinted in recent months by Soviet arms control negotiator Y.Kvitsinsky. This claim is corroborated indirectly by the launching earlier this year of a crash effort within the Verification and Control Technology program at the US Department of Energy.

Before going into the technical details of what might be possible in this respect it appropriate to make clear that the word 'verification' should properly speaking be reserved for the highest level of assessment of treaty compliance. However, verification is often used interchangedly with the words 'detection' and 'monitoring'; they belong, in fact, to a slightly less ambitious level with detection signifying the discovery of a general class of activity and with monitoring showing a capacity of a more detailed intelligence gathering. Verification implies that a detection and monitoring capacity is available to the extent that an activity can be assesed to conform - or not conform - to agreed limits or criteria in an undisputable manner.

The national technical means of verification relevant for strategic defence activities are mainly space-based and involve various types of photographic, infrared, nuclear radiation and electronic signal sensors. In the late seventies, US photographic reconnaissance satellites identified with some confidence a Soviet facility at Sary Shagan as being a novel design of an electron accelerator using special explosive generators to create the accelerating gradients. The facility may thus be characterized as a laboratory research complex, dedicated to directed energy weapon activities, permitting detection and some monitoring of the activities by standard intelligence gathering methods.

Correspondingly, the Soviet Union has certainly been able to gather useful information from satellite observation regarding the research activities around the Advanced Test Accelerator at the Lawrence Livermore Laboratory in California. The abovementioned research and development facilities concerned with strategic defence systems are of course given away partly by their big size. It is, however, a premise of directed energy weapon proponents that the accelerators and the lasers must eventually become smaller and associated herewith arises the possibility of conceiling the weapon research. New detection methods might nevertheless in the near future be able to circumvent this conceilment problem, as well as making possible a detailed physical monitoring of the development activities.

In fact, under the DOE program alluded to above, one of the purposes is to develop sensors to remotely detect, identify and characterize Soviet directed energy experiments and devices. At the Los Alamos Laboratory a high resolution X-ray camera has already been reported to be developed which is capable of providing images using incoming rays corresponding to a 2-60 kiloelectronvolt energy range. The range of view is defined by using 20 perfectly aligned metal plates, each having 26 000 drilled holes and the source image can presumably be reconstructed by applying advanced image processing algorithms to analyse the X-ray diffraction pattern.

A somewhat more practical and refined approach to X-ray imaging might be to make a computer aided analysis of the wavefront using sensors coupled directly to a large cross section of fibre optics cables. Apart from the source picture, the X-ray camera may of course also provide for detail about several physical parameters of the source by measuring the X-ray energy spectrum. This effort thus has much in common with other SDI projects concerned with developing methods for mass and materials discrimination of for example midcourse decoys of ICBM warheads.

Because of the atmosphere, a monitoring of ground-based directed energy weapon experiments from satellite platforms puts high requirements, and even some inherent limitations, on the capacity of the envisaged X-ray sensors. Discrimination from space of objects moving in space or in the upper atmosphere may be somewhat easier, but there an additional problem is the necessary illumination of the unidentified object by a neutral particle accelerator for generating the X-ray signature. It is, however, possible that this kind of neutron illumination methods are also being investigated for use with even more ambitious verification and control projects.

4. Conclusions

Arms control can only proceed if there is a political will to do so and this truism in particular applies to strategic defence activities. The ABM treaty, which is the only existing framework for discussing control of strategic defence, is at present in a rather bad shape. On one hand, there are alleged Soviet violations which have not been satisfactorily clarified and on the other hand, the SDI program seems to proceed with a momentum of its own accompagnied by a reinterpretation of the the ABM which suits the present state of the defence efforts.

The ABM treaty is flawed because of an unclear terminology and ambiguous interpretations. Whatever problems and uncertainties may exist, there is, however, a Standing Consultative Commission (SCC) which has the competence and duty to settle all outstanding issues. But, so far, the SCC has neglected to deal effectively with 'gray' area research, development and testing activities which are in the process of eroding the treaty completely because they appear to be part of a strive for a near-term deployment capacity of advanced strategic defence systems. At worst this would be a prelude to an abrogation of the treaty and a subsequent deployment phase.

If the political will to enforce arms control on strategic defence exists it would appear to be perfectly possible to device verification procedures for ensuring that the activities remain at an appropriate low key level. National technical means of verification already exist which go rather far in the monitoring of development and testing, and new means are quickly emerging which may allow for the monitoring of certain experimental laboratory research.

The ABM treaty was conceived, and must still be considered, on the background of an offence dominated world where nuclear deterrence is a key element unlikely to be done away with simply by initiating a massive defensive build up. It might, however, appear to be possible to supersede simultaneously the ABM treaty and the doctrine of nuclear deterrence through a concerted effort to realize a stable transition period towards a defence dominated world, the precise definition of which still remains to be spelled out. If political agreement about the desirability of this goal can be reached, there would be a great role for advanced verification technologies in assuring crisis stability during the difficult transition time.

THE PROSPECTS FOR A SATELLITE MONITORING AGENCY

Allan M. Din
Stockholm International Peace Research Institute
SIPRI, Bergshamra
S-171 73 Solna, SWEDEN
and
Aphonse Sauder
Centre d'Etudes de Défense de l'Université de Strasbourg III
1, Sentier du Goujon
F-67000 Strasbourg, FRANCE

1. The political framework

During 1985, the old idea about breaking the superpower monopoly on satellite monitoring for arms control purposes gained some new attention. First, the Swiss Secretary of State at the Department of Foreign Affairs, E.Brunner, stated that neutral countries like Sweden, Austria and Switzerland might be possible partners in establishing a satellite monitoring agency (SMA). There was, however, no direct follow-up to this statement, which apparently had not been preceded by any higher level contacts between the above countries.

Later, the Swedish Minister of Energy, B.Dahl, addressed the question more in detail at a conference in Stockholm[1]: "A number of neutral and non-aligned nations together with other countries with a well developed space technology should take the initiative to launch an independent satellite arms control

1) Opening address at the SIPRI conference on Space Weapons and International Security, 5 July 1985.

NATO ASI Series, Vol. F 26
Modelling and Analysis in Arms Control
Edited by R. Avenhaus et al.

observation system. The mission of this system should be not only to monitor arms control arrangements but also to collect information and data particularly on the crisis sensitive areas in order to make it possible to avert the crisis developing into a major conflict. The Swedish Government considers this proposal interesting and definitely worth studying. For a small country, Sweden is well equipped to support such an initiative." So far, no concrete steps have been taken in the direction alluded to, but it is likely that the different political and technical options are currently under scrutiny.

The proposal for an international satellite monitoring agency (ISMA) was put forward already some years ago, in 1978, by France at the UN Special Session on Disarmament[2]. Although the international response to this proposal was quite positive, also, for example, when the UN General Assembly in 1982 voted to produce a special report on the practicability of an ISMA, no specific UN action in the matter was ever on the horizon. It is unlikely that this situation will change in a foreseeable future because of the lukewarm to negative attitude of the superpowers towards anything which might threaten their exclusive capabilities in the satellite-based remote sensing field.

In the arms control context these capabilities have been codified in the so-called National Technical Means (NTM) of verification; for example, they are instrumental in a number of bilateral treaties like, the nuclear test ban treaties, the ABM Treaty and the SALT II Treaty. The precise technical capabilities of the superpower NTMs are of course closely guarded secrets, but it is commonly known that the state-of-the-art gives the possibility for space-based detection of ground-features down to a few tens of centimeters, which is more than sufficient for the vast majority of arms control issues. It is, however, important to emphasize that satellite monitoring which is even much below the state-of-the-art still is able to give very substantial arms control information.

With the dim prospects for a broad UN sponsoring of a SMA, it is only natural that attention has focussed on alternative possibilities, like the Regional Satellite Monitoring Agency (RSMA)[3]. Europe, for example, might be a possible

2) See the appendix for a summary of the French and UN proposals on ISMA.
3) B.Jasani, Environmental conservation, vol 10, No 3, 1983, p.255.

region where a RSMA could play a very important rôle, in particular if the Stockholm Conference on security and confidence building measures should turn out to lead to concrete arms control agreements and verification procedures. These might imply a need for a detailed monitoring of conventional force deployments, military manœuvres etc, which would most naturally require use of remote sensing platforms in space.

In a multilateral framework on the European scene, it would of course in principle be possible to let the satellite monitoring be taken care of by the USA and the USSR (being parties to the Stockholm Conference) or, alternatively, by the NATO and the Warsaw Pact; but since neutral and non-aligned countries are also involved, other monitoring alternatives seem more appropriate. A number of facts may lend encouragement and support to such alternatives. Thus, for example, the capacity to launch satellites might be expected to be acquired by several new countries, and other countries like France, China and Japan are continuously developing their space exploration technologies.

In February 1986, France launched the SPOT satellite which with a resolution of about 10 meters will be able to detect a certain number of military targets, like airfield, roads, railways, surface ships and possibly missiles sites. In fact, the pictures from the Nice and Po Plain areas shown on television were detailed enough to see clearly roads, railways and isolated houses. This event is a firm indication that the US-Soviet monopoly on "military quality" data is coming to an end and further progress in earth observation techniques are likely to exacerbate this trend.

How a RSMA could be set up practically still remains to be seen. The superpowers will certainly be reluctant to participate, but if the multilateral pressure for arriving at appropriately verifiable accords is strong, then the third party solution, which a RSMA would effectively constitute, might turn out to have a chance in the end. The acceptance of this solution might of course be facilitated if a small number of countries, neutral, non-aligned and others, on their own and as a matter of principle would take concrete steps to establish a space-based platform of even a quite limited scope. A framework for such a collaboration exists in ESA, the European Space Agency, and the Intercosmos

Agency, but there might be very severe problems, internally as well as externally, to arrive at any agreement on the matter within these organizations.

A possible stumbling block in setting up a SMA is obviously the cost of such an enterprise. The US and Soviet military satellite monitoring efforts have a price tag of several tens of billion $ due to the large number of launches and the thousands of analysts required to process the data. Civilian remote sensing systems are also quite expensive; for example, the LANDSAT 5 satellite cost about 600 million $ and the SPOT satellite about 200 million $. To these figures must be added the launch cost which may be in the range 25 - 170 million $, as well as the operating cost which for a LANDSAT type satellite is of the order of 50 million $ per year.

The mere economic aspect of a SMA is therefore something which makes the largest possible international collaboration a necessary condition for success of the idea. The cost for construction, launching and operation of a remote sensing platform evidently depends on the level of ambition for the kind of data to be collected. However, with decreasing launch costs (due to competition) and lower construction and operating costs due to technical progress (see the following section), it may not be unreasonable to estimate that a 'minimal' satellite monitoring system (i.e. one which may fulfil an arms control mission with a small, but acceptable margin) could carry a total price tag of around 300 million $ for an expected 5 year operating time.

Precisely what the level of ambition for an SMA should be is both an economic-technical and a political question. The nature of the data to be collected obviously depends on the arms control applications one has in mind, but it is unavoidable that satellite data relating to a number of military and civilian areas will be acquired in the process. A further problem is therefore how (i.e. under which control and according to which criteria) the dissemination of the remote sensing information is going to be carried out.

2. The technical possibilities

The sensors currently used on-board satellites are of a great variety. With photographic detection the film capsules can be returned to the ground at certain intervals or, more conveniently, the images relayed to ground stations in digital form. Radars, in particular synthetic aperture radars, may produce astonishingly detailed pictures under most weather conditions, but they require relatively high power requirements. Standard infra-red and nuclear radiation detectors are very significant arms control complements to the above imaging sensors and a great number of electronic detection methods are also available.

Some of the basic requirements on image producing sensors may assessed in terms of the resolution in meters needed for the interpretation tasks of the following list of objects[4].

Object	Detection	Identification	Analysis
Ports and harbors	30.5	6	0.3
Surfaced submarines	30.5	1.5	0.03
Roads	9	1.8	0.15
Surface ships	7.6	0.6	0.08
Bridge	6	1.5	0.3
Airfield facilities	6	3	0.15
Troop units	6	1.2	0.08
Aircraft	4.6	0.9	0.03
Vehicles	1.5	0.3	0.03
Rockets and artillery	0.9	0.15	0.01

By detection is here meant the location of a class of units, objects or activity of military interest, and identification requires discrimination within object types of known types. The table illustrates that a moderately powerful, space-based photographic sensor would be able to perform most of the detection tasks relevant for arms control purposes. There could be some practical limits

4) Reconnaissance Handy Book, McDonnell-Douglas Corporation, USA.

concerning identification and analysis tasks which may, however, represent less of an arms control problem than an insufficient military intelligence capability.

For the interpretation of satellite pictures a number of very powerful computerized techniques have emerged in recent years. In fact, these techniques could turn out be nothing but a special example of what may be called Computer-Aided Arms Control (CAAC), the arms control use of advanced computing and electronics, which promises wholly new perspectives in verification technologies[5].

Both technical limitations and atmospheric disturbances may adversely affect the quality of satellite pictures. Degraded pictures may nevertheless be enhanced using computer algorithms to process the (digital) data and features may appear which at first seemed too fuzzy to interpret. These methods require advanced concepts in pattern recognition which find a natural framework within the artificial intelligence (AI) techniques currently emerging on a large scale. As such techniques mature and the microchips become smaller and more powerful, it is perfectly reasonable to expect on-board processors to perform substantial, real-time interpretation tasks (as expressed recently by the US Defense Mapping Agency)[6].

The advent of CAAC, as well as of other technological progress, holds the promise of making a future SMA much more economically and technically viable than previously thought, both in terms of construction and operation. The hardware cost for complicated imaging and transmission systems may be expected to drop sharply in the coming years and, concomitantly, artificial intelligence techniques could contribute in an essential way to produce highly effective software for the image processing tasks, thus bypassing the need for time and money consuming analysis.

5) A.M.Din, Strategic computing, in SIPRI Yearbook 1986, Oxford University Press.

6) DMA stresses LANDSAT, AI, real-time ops, Military Space, April 29, 1985.

APPENDIX: Summary of ISMA proposals

The French 1978 proposal.
Third states which have no own satellite observation capabilities cannot rely absolutely on data supplied by the superpowers; international observation is therefore preferable to national observation. The proposal objective was twofold:
1. Reducing difficulties in monitoring compliance with the provisions of multilateral arms control agreements.
2. Contributing to effective international crisis management.

The 1982 UN Special Report.
The UN expert group designated to report on the feasability, organisation, cost and utility of an ISMA recalled that satellite monitoring is only a step, albeit an important and sometimes decisive one, in the process of monitoring compliance and the data collected should therefore be used in connection with other information souces.
The expert group proposed a gradual build-up in 3 stages of ISMA:
1. The agency would process data supplied by states already operating obsevation satellites.
2. As an interim step those states will continue to cooperate with the agency, but it would acquire direct access to some raw data received through its own ground stations.
3. The agency will establish a space observation system and operate its own satellites.

THE FEASIBILITY OF SPACE-BASED REMOTE SENSING IN THE VERIFICATION OF A TREATY TO PREVENT AN ARMS RACE IN OUTER SPACE

F. Ronald Cleminson
Arms Control and Disarmament Division
Department of External Affairs
Ottawa, Canada

INTRODUCTION

There are at least a dozen existing treaties and conventions which are of relevance to the arms control and outer space issue. These are discussed in a Canadian working paper (CD/618) submitted to the Conference on Disarmament (CD) in Geneva during its 1985 summer session.(1) From the multilateral aspect two treaties are of particular importance. The first one is the 1963 Partial Test Ban Treaty which specifically prohibited nuclear weapon test explosions in space. The second, the 1967 Outer Space Treaty, generally regarded as the corner stone of international space law, established a basic legal framework for general space exploration and utilization. While not an arms control treaty per se, it does, in Article IV, specifically address military activities. Article IV prohibits the emplacement of nuclear weapons or other weapons of mass destruction in earth orbit. It also bans the establishment of military bases, installations and fortifications, the testing of any type of weapons and the conduct of military manoeuvres on celestial bodies.

On the bilateral side, the most significant agreement is the 1972 ABM Treaty. Following the signing of the ABM Treaty, the arms race entered a period of relative stability as was indicated in its first review. Partly because of improvements to existing systems and partly as a result of new technologies, that stability was slowly eroded. The announcement of the Strategic Defense Initiative (SDI) in March 1983 and the subsequent, sometimes strident, discourse since then are the most visible symbols of this erosion.

On June 18, 1982, at the second United Nations Special Session on Disarmament (UNSSOD II) the (then) Canadian Prime Minister Pierre Trudeau called

NATO ASI Series, Vol. F 26
Modelling and Analysis in Arms Control
Edited by R. Avenhaus et al.

for the development of an arms control treaty which would ban the development, testing and deployment of all weapons for use in outer space.[(2)] In the same speech he focussed on the problems associated with verification of ACD agreements. While the Soviet Union has continued to use the outer space issue symbolically in terms of a number of proposals and resolutions, the issue has become one with both bilateral and multilateral dimensions.

PURPOSE

The purpose of this paper is to discuss the application of space-based remote sensing technology as one method of verification of a treaty to prevent an arms race in outer space.

TARGET CONFIGURATION

A weapon in space can have as its objective the destruction of, or the damage to another orbiting object, or the destruction of, or damage to targets situated on the earth. The former weapon's objective is accomplished in the space environment while the latter weapon's objective may be accomplished either directly from space or subsequent to a re-entry through the earth's atmosphere. The current debate over the Strategic Defense Initiative (SDI), a space-based ballistic missile defense concept more widely known as the 'Star Wars' concept, marks a third function for a space weapon: namely the destruction of sub-orbital ballistic missiles during flight.

The first step in a review of the technical problems associated with verifying conformity with or violation of arms control agreements is to prepare an accurate list of the various ways an anti-satellite weapon can be configured as a threat. Preparation of this list is a straightforward exercise in identifying the basic forms or genre of the weapons themselves and the choice of platforms on which they can be based, or from which they can be launched. This list then becomes the foundation upon which is built the analysis of what is distinctive about each threat configuration so that effective surveillance and detection methods can be identified. While it is beyond the scope of this paper to identify in detail the possible targets and systems, platforms on which anti-satellite weapons could be sited are shown graphically in Figure 1. For the purposes of this paper it is the space-based platforms which are being assessed.

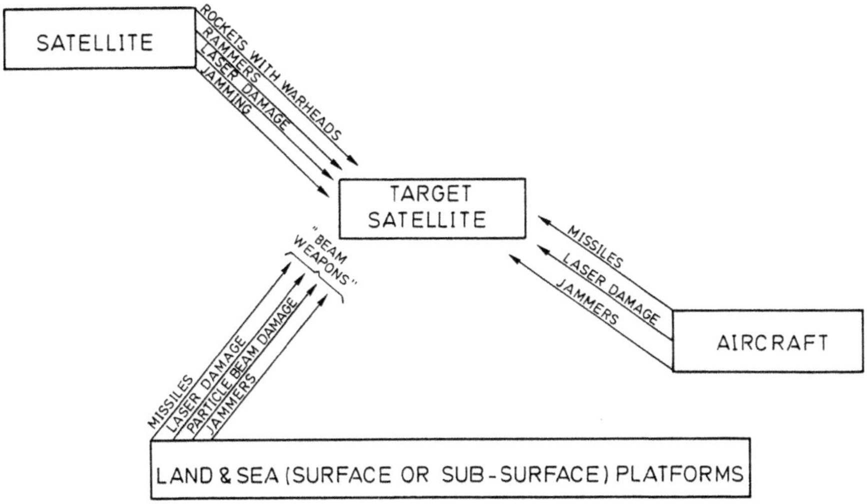

Figure 1. Platforms on which anti-satellite weapons can be sited

POTENTIAL WEAPONS IN SPACE

No known operational space-based weapon system for space-to-space operation has yet been deployed in space. Thus, there is still a considerable amount of uncertainty as to how these systems would be configured for optimal performance. What is known about the situation in space, however, is the location and distribution of potential targets in space.

Space as a location for weapons or portions of weapon systems provides a view of a large portion of the earth from a given position in orbit, or a revisit of a specific volume of space at frequent intervals. These characteristics make space highly significant from a military point of view. However, the energy required and thus the cost of placing spacecraft in orbit is such that the spacecraft design and its orbit must be highly optimized in terms of its required function. The result of this constraint is that all spacecraft whether scientific, remote-sensing, experimental applications, commercial, or of military application are found in several specific volumes of space defined by orbital parameters.

Typical distribution of military satellites
deployed by USA and USSR

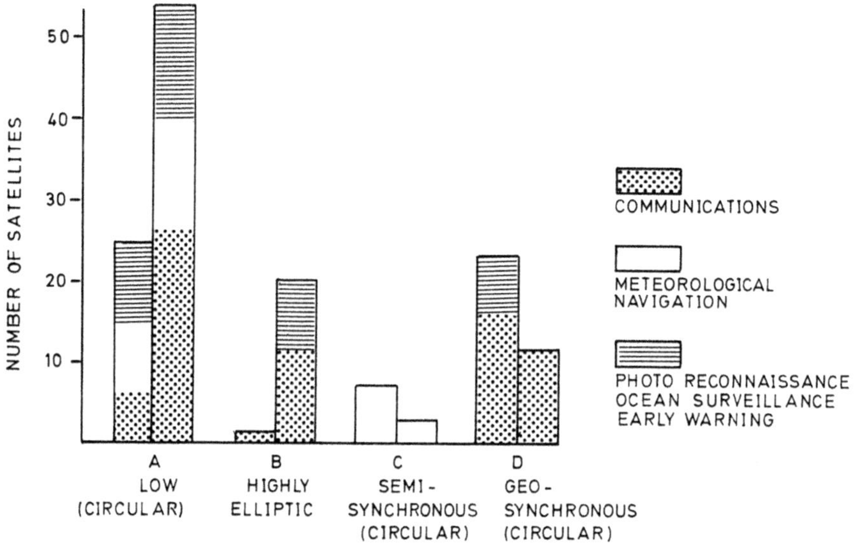

Altitude	150 - 2000 km	Apogee 40000 km Perigee 600 km	20000 km	36000 km
Inclination to Equator	65 - 115	63	63	0 - 6
Period	1,5 - 2 Hrs	12 Hrs	12 Hrs	24 Hrs

Figure 2. USA/USSR military satellite deployments

Figures 2, 3 and 4 show the location of all recorded military satellites launched by the United States and Russia over the past four years, their general orbit parameters, and their function---communication, navigation, meteorology, early warning, electronic intelligence, ocean surveillance, or photo-reconnaissance. Satellites in a low orbit, identified as "A" in figure 2, 3 and 4, have the most detailed view of the earth's surface and can also detect weak electronic signals from sources on the ground, at sea or in the air. In a near polar orbit by virtue of high orbit inclination relative to the equator, such satellites sense the entire earth at least once a day as it turns. Accordingly, photo-reconnaissance, ocean surveillance and most electronic intelligence satellites are in a low orbit. When the military mission is to continuously survey large areas, to communicate with large areas or to communicate with a fixed ground station, a geosynchronous orbit ("D") is preferred.

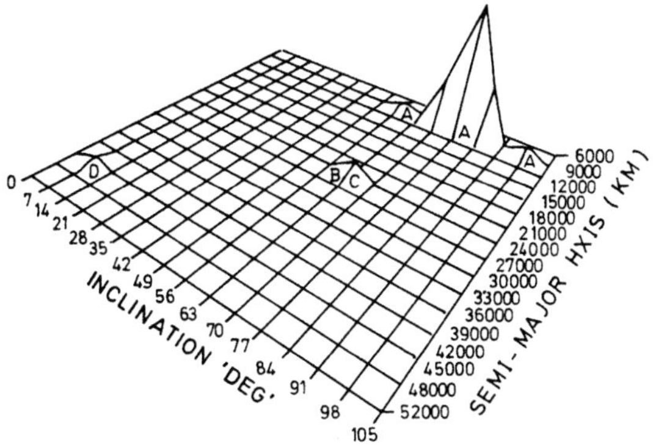

Figure 3. Orbital distribution of satellites

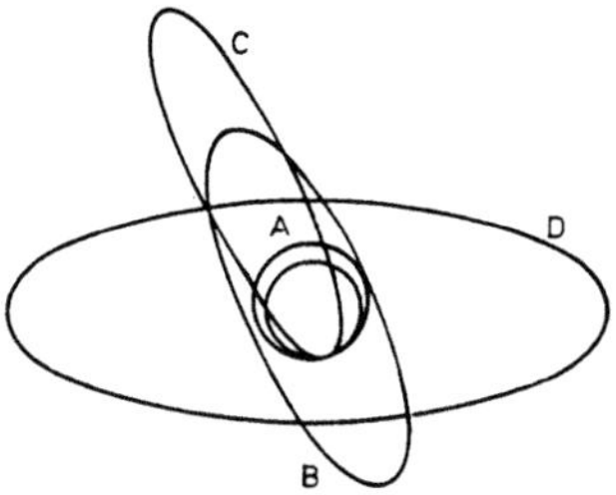

Figure 4. Four most utilized orbital domains

The geosynchronous orbit, however, does not provide clear line of sight of installations in high Arctic regions. This can be provided by a spacecraft in a highly elliptic orbit ("C") with its apogee over the Northern Hemisphere, for eight or more hours per day of the twelve hour orbit period of the satellite.

Any anti-satellite weapons stationed in orbit would likely be located in the same volumes of space as their potential targets. These would be the orbits of interest in a space-to-space verification mission.

TARGET DISCRIMINATION

One might expect that the determination of the exact function of an unknown spacecraft injected into space would be exceedingly difficult. However, the high degree of optimization inherent in the design of all spacecraft and in their orbital parameters, together with the nature of signals to and from the spacecraft, provide highly significant data as to function.

Clearly to the extent that form follows function, visual images of the spacecraft are highly determinate of its function and its purpose in space. From high resolution data, particularly in respect to appendages and apertures on the spacecraft, a skilled interpreter can provide assessments regarding the presence and magnitude of onboard propulsion capabilities for optical and/or infrared imaging as well as data regarding the generation of electrical power. Next generation weapon systems employing plasma or laser beams are likely to be even more distinctive in configuration. If the images can be acquired in the thermal-infrared region, then important data can be derived regarding the energy balance and energy utilization of the unknown spacecraft.

The operation of almost any type of spacecraft involves substantial communications to and generally from the spacecraft. The nature of these transmissions, particularly the data rate, frequency band of operation, radiated power and the operational cycle are of extremely high diagnostic value. These data when combined with the visual image data in respect to antenna apertures and power available are deterministic of communications and remote sensing missions.

Radar, of course, would provide additional investigative capabilities particularly in respect to target manoeuvering or thrusting operations from which the approximate mass of the spacecraft may be deduced.

Other sensors would likely be useful, such as gas analyzers to detect materials of chemically powered lasers, and radiation detectors to infer the materials associated with power sources or weapons.

POLITICAL CONSIDERATIONS

The outer space issue is being dealt with in two separate sets of negotiations in Geneva. The first set is the bilateral negotiations between the United States and the Soviet Union which met for their third round on September 19, 1985. These talks on space are part of the larger framework of discussions on strategic issues. These negotiations are fraught with superpower antagonisms and propaganda objectives beyond the negotiating table itself. As Henry Kissinger has pointed out recently:

> "Mikhail Gorbachev in recent interviews is clearly seeking to exploit the anxiety among the democracies by equating success at Geneva with abandonment of SDI - the Reagan administration plan to provide a defense against ballistic missiles."(3)

Meanwhile, in the multilateral context, an ad hoc committee on the prevention of an arms race in outer space was established by the Conference on Disarmament, also in Geneva, under a mandate "to examine, as a first step at this stage, through substantive and general considerations, issues relevant to the prevention of an arms race in outer space". The Committee on Disarmament concluded its latest session in an unspectacular manner on August 30, 1985.

A central question in constructing a plausible multilateral verification model is the issue of whether or not an outer space arms control agreement itself can be expected to be bilateral or multilateral in nature. If outer space arms control negotiations and the resulting agreement were to be a purely intramural superpower exercise, the task of defining a credible verification role for multilateral mechanisms would be entirely different from that present in the case of a multilateral treaty containing provisions for multilateral treaty administration and verification. Put somewhat starkly, the former case of a bilateral agreement would imply that the multilateral verification process operate outside the treaty context, relying essentially on self-contained technical resources, and doing so possibly even against the wishes of the superpowers. In the latter case, a more benign scenario can be envisioned, with US and Soviet acquiescence in and support of third party involvement in the mechanisms of treaty verification. Verification in this case might constitute a more cooperative multi-tiered activity, with far less onerous technical requirements in the context of a carefully constructed multilateral verification framework.

Although it is beyond the scope of this paper to identify the precise organizational structure of a multilateral treaty administration and verification body, or to spell out in detail the decision-making process, the following may serve as relevant guidelines in these areas:

(a) The organizational structure and decision-making process would recognize the political nature of the arms control agreement and associated verification provisions. Decisions to conduct various verification activities must be subject to political control by the signatory states.

(b) The special interests and prerogatives of the superpowers and to a lesser extent other space powers should be recognized in the decision-making process.

(c) Voting procedures for the initiation of verification activities should avoid a veto on the one hand and abuse of the investigatory process on the other through excessive use by individual states or group of states.

(d) In relation to the point just made, the governing body should reflect the political complexion of the signatory states.

(e) A technical secretariat would likely be required to conduct investigations and evaluate data derived from the verification process or given by signatory states.

(f) In order to secure agreement on the requirement for a multilateral treaty administration and verification body and to ensure its proper configuration, the essential organizational structure and decision-making process must be outlined in the treaty itself.

COOPERATIVE VERIFICATION MEASURES

Even in this short working paper, it is readily apparent that cooperative measures and certain collateral constraints would be necessary to increase the level of verification necessary to establish confidence in compliance.

In a workshop on arms control in space organized by the US Congress' Office of Technology Assessment in May 1984 difficulties associated with "on-orbit" inspection were identified. The workshop recognized that "some of the verification techniques discussed would require or would at least greatly benefit from cooperative verification procedures".[4]

CONCLUSION

This working paper has addressed the supposition that a properly configured set of observations in space can determine the function of an unknown satellite to an acceptably high degree of confidence such that it can contribute to the determination and control of the presence of weapons in space.

It specifically addressed two principle questions:

(a) "Can space observations determine the role or function of an object in space?"

(b) "Are there one or more political/international agreement or treaty contexts in which these observations could be effected?"

The tentative answer in each case is "yes".

REFERENCES

(1) Canada. "Working Papers: Survey of International Law Relevant to Arms Control and Outer Space" CD/618

(2) Canada. Department of External Affairs Statements and Speeches No. 82/10. "Technology Momentum The Fuel That Feeds The Nuclear Arms Race, an address by the Rt. Hon. P.E. Trudeau to UNSSOD II, New York, June 18, 1982"

(3) Kissinger, Henry. "Why The U.S. Must Stand Firm on Star Wars at Geneva Talks" Toronto Sunday Star, 8 September, 1985, page F.5

(4) U.S. Congress, Office of Technology Assessment. Arms Control in Space: Workshop Proceedings (Washington DC: OTA-BP-15C-28, May 1984)

NOTES ON ARMS-CONTROL VERIFICATION: A GAME-THEORETIC ANALYSIS

Steven J. Brams*
Department of Politics
New York University
New York, NY 10003

and

D. Marc Kilgour**
Department of Mathematics
Wilfrid Laurier University
Waterloo, Ontario
Canada N2L 3C5

Introduction

Arms control between the superpowers seems at a dead end unless the provisions of any treaty they negotiate can be verified. Indeed, in a recent assessment, one expert argued that "verification has become the most important standard against which arms control agreements -- both past and prospective -- are measured" (Potter, 1985, p. 1). Another expert echoed that viewpoint, calling verification "a fundamental requirement for establishing that a treaty is in the interests of the United States" (Richelson, 1985, p. 202).

The formal analysis of verification, based on strategic models of rational choice, has a curious history. Twenty years ago, such analysts as Maschler (1966, 1967) and Rapoport (1966) developed rather elaborate game-theoretic models to analyze the strategic implications of different inspection procedures. Then, except for some scattered and mostly unpublished reports, game theory and other formal tools of rational strategic analysis were not again applied to arms-control issues until recently.

In these notes, we shall illustrate a model of verification based on the two-person, nonzero-sum Truth Game, first analyzed in Brams and Davis (1985) and Brams (1985, ch. 4). However, we shall make some significant emendations in this model, from which apparently paradoxical features follow, that we shall illustrate with a particular example. The relationship of the Truth Game to other games that have been studied, and its relevance to superpower conflict, will also be discussed.

*Steven J. Brams gratefully acknowledges the financial support of the National Science Foundation under Grant No. SES85-20154.

**D. Marc Kilgour gratefully acknowledges the financial support of the Natural Sciences and Engineering Research Council of Canada under Grant No. A8974.

NATO ASI Series, Vol. F 26
Modelling and Analysis in Arms Control
Edited by R. Avenhaus et al.

The Truth Game

Define the Truth Game (TG) as a game between Row, who as an "inspectee" may either comply (C) or not comply ($\bar{C}$) with a treaty, and Column, who as an "inspector" may accept (A) or not accept ($\bar{A}$) Row's actions. (We assume Row will always claim that he complied.) Suppose that Column's choice, which follows and is a response to Row's, may be governed in part by Column's ability to detect whether or not Row complied. More specifically, assume that two parameters, x and y, characterize the reliability of Column's detector:

$$x = \Pr\{\text{detector signals violation} \mid \text{Row chose } \bar{C}\}$$

$$y = \Pr\{\text{detector signals no violation} \mid \text{Row chose } C\}$$

Note that $0 \le x, y \le 1$. The detector is perfect when $x = y = 1$ and would seem worthless when x and/or y are near or at 0. The probabilities of error are $1 - x$ and $1 - y$; in statistics, an error of the latter kind (incorrectly signalling a violation) is a type 1 error, whereas an error of the former kind (incorrectly signalling compliance) is a type 2 error.

TG, with cardinal utility payoffs r_i to Row and c_j to Column, is shown in Figure 1. Short verbal descriptions of each

FIGURE 1. OUTCOMES OF THE TRUTH GAME

		Column	
		Accept (A)	Don't accept ($\bar{A}$)
Row	Comply (C)	$(r_2, 1)$ Compliance accepted: strong verification	(r_3, c_2) Compliance challenged: weak falsification
	Don't comply ($\bar{C}$)	$(1, 0)$ Violation accepted: strong falsification	$(0, c_3)$ Violation challenged: weak verification

Normalization: $0 = r_1 < r_2 < r_3 < r_4 = 1$; $0 = c_1 < c_2 < c_3 < c_4 = 1$.

outcome are given in the matrix, which reflects the following primary goals of the players:

Row: Most wants his violations accepted (or overlooked) and his compliance challenged, so that the truth of his actions is hidden -- two best outcomes ("falsification") off main diagonal.

Column: Most wants to accept Row's compliance and challenge his violations, so that the truth of Row's actions is discovered -- two best outcomes ("verification") on main diagonal.

TG enables one not only to distinguish "verification" (main-diagonal outcomes) from "falsification" (off-diagonal outcomes) but also suggests a "strong" and "weak" distinction in each of these categories (see Figure 1). Thus, we consider verification stronger when compliance is accepted then when a violation is challenged, because the exact nature or extent of the violation may not be entirely clear. Similarly, falsification seems stronger when a violation is accepted than when compliance is challenged, because challenging compliance is less damaging for Column than when he is deceived into accepting a falsehood.

The primary goals separate the two best from the two worst outcomes for each player. To give a complete ordering of the four outcomes for each player, we postulate as secondary goals that Row prefers to be accepted (thus, he prefers the lower-left outcome to the upper right and the upper left to the lower right), and Column prefers that Row comply (thus, Column prefers the upper-left outcome to the lower right and the upper right to the lower left).

This is by no means the only plausible ranking of outcomes in a verification model. Rapoport (1966, pp. 169-185) applied a number of different solution concepts to a game between an inspector and evader, which reverses the priority of the primary and secondary goals of Column but assumes the same goals of Row. We shall say something more about the effects of this reversal on our conclusions about TG later.

Maschler (1966, 1967) proposed some rather elaborate inspection games, involving chance and an inspector who could decide whether or not to investigate a suspicious event. In his model, Maschler assumed that the inspector could announce and commit himself to a mixed strategy, against which the potential violator would maximize his expected payoff.

Brams and Davis (1985) and Brams (1985, ch. 4) used this

idea of inducement, which was originally proposed by Stackelberg (1934) to study price leadership, to investigate both "inducement" and "guarantee" strategies in TG. More specifically, they analyzed the benefits that not only Column but also Row could realize by inducing the other player to respond to him, comparing these with the payoffs that the players could guarantee for themselves whatever the opponent's choice (analogous to minimax/maximin strategies in two-person constant-sum games). More recently, Brams and Kilgour (1986) studied both inducement and Nash-equilibrium strategies in a game they called the Verification Game (VG), in which an inspector (Column) has the same goals as in Rapoport's inspector-evader game but the inspectee (Row) primarily wants his claimed compliance accepted, and secondarily prefers to violate the agreement.

Fichtner (1986) compared various game-theoretic approaches to inspection and verification of arms-control agreements; as well, he applied similar solution concepts to auditing, consumer protection, and nuclear safeguards. Avenhaus's (1986) treatment of the latter issue, in particular, makes significant use of game theory. Among other things, he finds optimal strategies for an inspector, with goals the same as Column's in VG, to induce compliance by an inspectee, whose primary but not secondary goal is the same as in VG.

There is probably no "best" game to model all aspects of verification. We analyze TG mainly to illustrate how one player's detector may play a central role in the strategy choices of both players.

It is worth noting that there is no pure-strategy Nash (1951) equilibrium in TG, as shown in Figure 1. Yet, because the players' payoffs are cardinal utilities and the game is likely to be repeated, the players have a meaningful opportunity to use mixed strategies.

Since Row has only two pure strategies, Comply (C) or Violate ($\bar{C}$), in TG, Row's mixed strategy can be represented by a single probability s such that

$$\Pr\{\text{Row complies}\} = s.$$

On the other hand, Column has three pure strategies, Accept (A) unconditionally, Challenge ($\bar{A}$) unconditionally, or consult his detector (D), choosing $\bar{A}$ if it signals a violation and A otherwise. We therefore represent Column's mixed strategy by two probabilities, t and u, such that

$$\Pr\{\text{Column consults detector}\} = t$$

$$\Pr\{\text{Column accepts unconditionally}\} = u.$$

Of course, Pr{Column challenges unconditionally} = $1 - t - u$, just as Pr{Row violates} = $1 - s$.

Given these probabilities, the four possible outcomes of the game (see Figure 1) will occur with the indicated probabilities:

CA: $s(u + ty)$

$C\bar{A}$: $s(1 - u - ty)$

$\bar{C}A$: $(1 - s)(t + u - tx)$

$\bar{C}\bar{A}$: $(1 - s)(1 - t - u + tx)$.

For example, CA results when Row chooses C (with probability s) and Column either chooses A (with probability u) or consults his detector (with probability t) and, detecting no violation (with probability y), chooses A.

The outcome probabilities may now be combined with the payoffs that the players obtain at the outcomes (see Figure 1) to give the players' expected payoffs (E's) in TG. To simplify notation, we shall henceforth distinguish the E's by subscripts R (for Row) and C (for Column):

$$E_R(s;\, t,u) = s(u + ty)r_2 + s(1 - u - ty)r_3 + (1 - s)(t + u - tx)$$

$$E_C(t,u;\, s) = s(u + ty) + s(1 - u - ty)c_2 + (1 - s)(1 - t - u + tx)c_3$$

<u>Example</u>

Assume for illustration that Column's ability to detect treaty violations when they occur -- the choice of $\bar{C}$ by Row -- and his ability to detect compliance when it occurs -- the choice of C by Row -- are the same, so $x = y$. Thus, the reliability of Column's detector is assumed to be independent of Row's strategy choice.

This simplifying assumption helps us avoid unnecessary computational detail in the numerical example to be described. Nonetheless, it enables us to illustrate the esential features of the players' strategic behavior as Column's detection ability changes.

Assume $r_2 = 1/4$, $r_3 = 1/2$, $c_2 = 1/3$, and $c_3 = 2/3$. In Figure 2a we indicate three zones through which the point (x, y) passes as it

FIGURE 2. NASH-EQUILIBRIUM STRATEGIES AND EXPECTED PAYOFFS OF TRUTH-GAME EXAMPLE

2a. Partition of Path from (0, 0) to (1, 1) into Zones

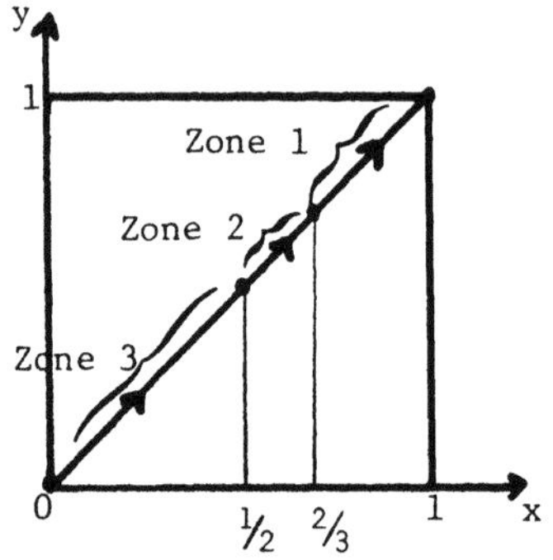

2b. Nash-Equilibrium Strategies of Row (s) and Column (t, u)

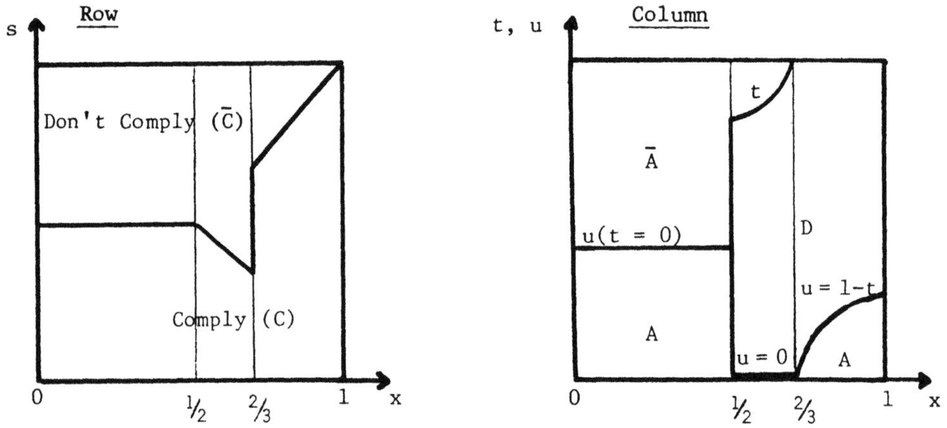

2c. Expected Payoffs of Row (E_R) and Column (E_C)

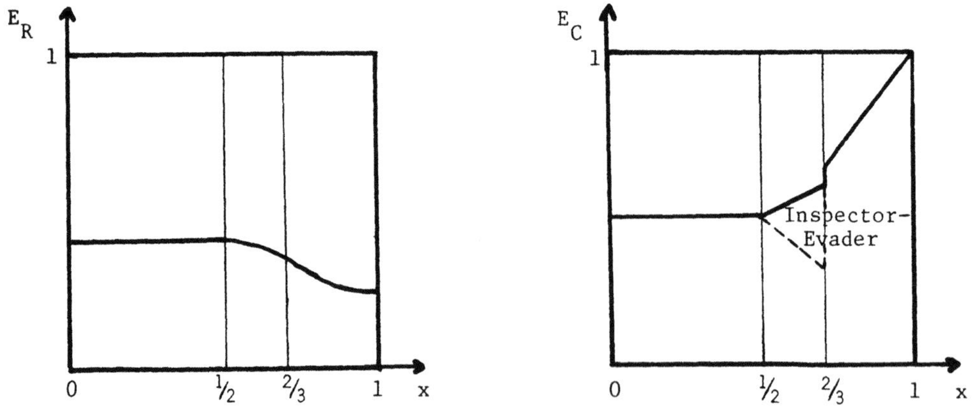

moves from (0, 0) to (1, 1) along $y = x$. In Figure 2b, we have graphed the dependence of Row's and Column's Nash-equilibrium strategies, s, t, and u, in each zone as Column's detector reliability x (= y) increases from 0 to 1. Finally, in Figure 2c we show the dependence of the expected payoffs of Row and Column on these equilibrium strategies as a function of x.

The following aspects of equilibrium behavior in each of the three zones are worth noting:

1. Zone 1 (detection good). For Column, $t + u = 1$, so he never challenges unconditionally; significantly, as x approaches 1, he consults his detector less frequently, even as it becomes more reliable. (When its reliability is 1, however, he still consults his detector with probability $t = 3/4$.) This apparently paradoxical tendency of Column to rely less on his detector is explained by Row's increasing choice of compliance as x increases -- approaching $s = 1$ as x approaches 1 -- that makes it less pressing for Column to check Row's compliance. As expected, Column's expected payoff increases in this zone as x increases, becoming 1 when $x = 1$ [total compliance by Row, total acceptance by Column, though sometimes ascertained only after Column consults his (perfect) detector]. Row's expected payoff, on the other hand, falls as x approaches 1, though at a decreasing rate. (In the general case when x and y are independent parameters, E_R actually increases as y increases but decreases with increasing x, as here.)

2. Zone 2 (detection moderate). Unlike zone 1, Column occasionally challenges unconditionally, but less so as x increases. The big surprise here is that Row complies less frequently as x increases, casting doubt on the commonsensical notion that greater detector reliability will always induce greater compliance. In this zone, given that Column has not challenged Row unconditionally (which he does with probability $1 - t$), he will always consult his detector since $u = 0$; but because Column's detector is only moderately reliable, Row still does better by complying less and less often up to the border of zones 1 and 2, where there is a discontinuous increase in compliance. As in zone 1, Column's expected payoff

increases with increasing x and Row's expected payoff declines, so better intelligence still "pays" for Column.

3. Zone 3 (detection low). In this zone, where $0 \leq x \leq \frac{1}{2}$, better intelligence does not pay: both Column's and Row's expected payoffs are constant as x increases; similarly, the players' equilibrium strategies are constant in this zone. Given that Column does not challenge Row unconditionally, Column always accepts Row's choice ($t = 0$) since his detector is so poor -- at best it has only a 50-50 chance of being correct. Hence, it is never optimal for Column to consult his detector. However, since this zone is probably not one in which most real world players operate -- at least if they take the trouble to try to gather intelligence and are not subject to crippling deception -- we will not consider it further.

In Rapoport's (1966, pp. 166-185) Inspector-Evader (IE) game, the priority of Column's primary and secondary goals is reversed as discussed earlier, which results in the interchange of c_2 and c_3 in Figure 1. However, the previous results for TG are unaltered, except in zone 2; there, the only change is that Column's expected payoff decreases as x increases (see Figure 2c). This phenomenon occurs because Row's Nash-equilibrium strategy is to violate more often, and Column detects what Row is doing more often as well. This hurts Column in addition to Row, who is motivated to be less compliant because, when Column challenges ($\bar{A}$), Row prefers violating ($\bar{C}$) to complying (C).

Conclusions

In general, better detection helps Column and hurts Row, but only beyond a certain point. Before this point of "good" detector is reached, Column may actually be hurt when verification is modeled by Inspector-Evader, but not the Truth Game.

Anomalously in both the Truth Game and Inspector-Evader, there is a strategic incentive for Row to violate the treaty more often as Column's detection reliability increases in the moderate zone. This is so even though Column in this zone will never accept unconditionally; he will always rely on his detector if he does not challenge unconditionally. Of course, when "moderate" changes to "good," which is a boundary that depends on Row's payoffs, Row will become increasingly more compliant; Column will never challenge unconditionally and will also be more willing to accept unconditionally, as would be expected.

The discontinous change at the moderate/good boundary indicates the importance to Column of achieving a level of detection reliability above this threshold. Otherwise, better intelligence may have a perverse effect, if not on Column's expected payoff then on his influence on Row's behavior, making Row more likely to violate the treaty. This discontinous jump is also found in the Verification Game (Brams and Kilgour, 1986) not only for Nash-equilibrium strategies but also for Column's inducement of compliance by Row.

It is difficult to say whether the verification equipment of the superpowers is sufficiently reliable to place them in the good zone. Nevertheless, the nuclear arms-control agreements reached since the Limited Nuclear Test Ban Treaty in 1963, though limited in scope, argue against unbridled pessimism.

We perhaps cannot be so sanguine about new and future weapons systems, including those, like cruise missiles, that are highly mobile or those, like anti-satellite weapons, that are hard to detect for other reasons. Yet, because it is in both sides' interest -- at least in the role of inspector -- to be in the good zone, our analysis suggests that each side's apparent obsession to conceal as much as possible is probably ill-founded.

We believe that, insofar as the Truth Game and Inspector-Evader capture the strategic interaction of the superpowers on the verification issue, the threshold effect that we have identified cannot be ignored. In fact, it may be in Row's ultimate -- though not immediate -- interest to allow Column sufficient intelligence so that both players are in the good zone, whereby more, not less, compliance to treaties is induced.

By contrast, if each side, as Row, can gain an advantage through more violations (in the moderate zone), then compliance with treaties is likely to be undermined. Although gaining immediately for violations as Row, neither player reaps the benefits, as Column, of the probably larger gains from compliance.

Because the superpowers play the roles of both Row and

Column, it is probably to their net benefit to encourage compliance, especially because of the discontinuous increase in Column's expected payoff as the game moves into the good zone. The best means to achieve this threshold effect, we believe, is to abet the gathering of intelligence that improves each side's detection capabilities.

REFERENCES

Avenhaus, Rudolf (1986). Safeguard Systems Analysis. New York: Plenum (forthcoming).

Brams, Steven J. (1985). Superpower Games: Applying Game Theory to Superpower Conflict. New Haven, CT: Yale University Press.

Brams, Steven J., and Morton D. Davis (1985). "The Verification Problem in Arms Control: A Game-Theoretic Analysis." In Interaction and Communication in Global Politics, ed. Claudio Cioffi-Revilla, Richard L. Merritt, and Dina A. Zinnes. London: Sage, pp. 133-154.

Brams, Steven J., and D. Marc Kilgour (1986). "Verification and Stability: A Game-Theoretic Analysis." Mimeographed.

Fichtner, John (1986). "Solution Concepts for Two Person Games Which Model the Verification Problem in Arms Control." In Modeling and Analysis of Arms Control Problems, ed. Rudolf Avenhaus and Reiner K. Huber. Berlin: Springer-Verlag (forthcoming).

Maschler, Michael (1967). "The Inspector's Non-Constant-Sum Game: Its Dependence on a System of Detectors." Naval Research Logistics Quarterly 14: 275-290.

Maschler, Michael (1966). "A Price Leadership Method for Solving the Inspector's Non-Constant-Sum Game." Naval Research Logistics Quarterly 13: 11-33.

Nash, John (1951). "Non-cooperative Games." Annals of Mathematics 54: 286-295.

Potter, William C. (1985). "Introduction." In Verification and Arms Control, ed. William C. Potter. Lexington, MA: Lexington, pp. 1-5.

Rapoport, Anatol (1966). Two-Person Game Theory: The Essential Ideas. Ann Arbor, MI: University of Michigan Press.

Richelson, Jeffrey (1985). "Technical Collection and Arms Control." In Verification and Arms Control, ed. William C. Potter. Lexington, MA: Lexington, pp. 169-216.

von Stackelberg, H. (1934). Marktform and Gleichgewicht. Berlin: Julius Springer.

ON CONCEPTS FOR SOLVING TWO-PERSON GAMES WHICH MODEL THE VERIFICATION PROBLEM IN ARMS CONTROL

J. Fichtner
Federal Armed Forces University Munich
Federal Republic of Germany

1. Introduction

Arms control agreements which include non-trivial verification procedures whose details are accessible to the general public are of special interest to the mathematically oriented analyst. This is typically the case with multilateral treaties under which verification is often performed by an international agency or by supranational commissions or institutions. Bilateral agreements often rely on national technical means or intelligence services. It is therefore extremely difficult to get sufficiently detailed information on these treaties as inputs to mathematical modelling.

The most important multilateral arms control treaties signed since World War II are undoubtedly the Partial Test Ban Treaty (PTBT, 1963) and the Non-Proliferation Treaty (NPT, 1968). Thus it is not surprising that most mathematical modelling effort in the field of verification has been with these treaties in mind.

Since there are at least two parties to a verification process - the inspectee and the inspector, both of whom have a number of strategies, it is evident that the mathematical theory of games could be an adequate modelling tool.

It seems that the first research work on this topic was done by Dresher (1962) and Kuhn (1963), shortly before the PTBT was signed. These authors used zero-sum games. While these games may well be the most developed and successful branch of game theory, they do not provide the best model for verification problems: It is evident that only in the event of a violation are the interests of inspectee and inspector diametrically opposed.

NATO ASI Series, Vol. F 26
Modelling and Analysis in Arms Control
Edited by R. Avenhaus et al.

The inspector wants to detect the violation, and the inspectee wants to evade detection. However, in case of compliance both parties are interested in avoiding **false alarms**.

Maschler (1966,1967) discarded zero-sum games for a slightly different reason. He argued that in a zero-sum verification model the inspector would get positive payoff for detecting a violation and would therefore be tempted to try and **trap** the inspectee. Since there are no generally accepted solution concepts for non-zero-sum games, Maschler had to find an apposite solution concept for this situation. He proposed - and was probably the first to do so - deterring the inspectee from a violation by announcing a suitable inspection strategy and he called his method the Price-Leadership method because of the links to the theory of prices where Stackelberg (1934) had already examined the consequences which follow when one of two firms announces its prices and the second firm responds in an appropriate way (see for example Shubik, 1980 or Friedman, 1977).

Maschler only applied this type of solution to special, relatively complex models, which will be discussed later. It is perhaps this complexity which explains why Maschler's ideas have not had a greater influence on subsequent efforts to design adequate models of the verification problem in arms control. This is particularly true of modelling efforts during and following the NPT negotiations and the establishment of the International Atomic Energy Agency (IAEA) in Vienna. An impressive array of mathematical and statistical methods has been specially developed for NPT safeguards. Further details can be found in the chapter by Avenhaus and Markin in the present volume and in Avenhaus (1986). Interestingly enough these models, where they are game-theoretical, have almost exclusively relied on the traditional concept of equilibrium in non-zero-sum games and have not made use of Maschler's Price-Leadership method.

But in the specific situations considered so far, where the exact values of the payoffs are unknown, and where only one generic type of compliance exists, both concepts lead to the same conclusions with regard to optimal decision procedures and optimal allocation of the resources available for inspection. It is however precisely in this area that the exceptional importance of false alarms (Avenhaus and Frick, 1977) and the close links with mathematical statistics (Avenhaus and Frick, 1979) were first recognized.

There are few references to Maschler's work in the handful of articles using the basic idea of the Price-Leadership method. Only Borch (1982), who is interested in auditing problems refers explicitly to Maschler. Goldman and Pearl (1976) are concerned with achieving "best protection of consumers against loss due to malfunctioning weighing and measuring devices." Brams (1985) is interested in a fairly general model of arms control verification. Both have developed what is in essence a version of Maschler's Price-Leadership method, but obviously without knowledge of Maschler's work and the nomenclature he used.

In the next chapter the idea behind this important solution concept will be explained and illustrated using a simple example comprising a 2 x 2 bi-matrix game. This game models a situation where a violation can be detected with certainty by verification, but where such verification is so expensive for both sides that only partial verification is feasible. Generalizations of this simple game are then discussed. Sequential games (Maschler, 1966,1967) and imperfect detection equipment (Maschler, 1967, Brams, 1985, Fichtner, 1985) will be introduced, inter alia. The concluding chapter briefly discusses the relevance of these simple game theoretic ideas to such a complex topic as arms control verification.

2. A Simple Verification Game

In order to grasp the solution concept we shall consider a very simple model of a verification procedure. One player - the **inspector** - has to verify whether the other player - the **inspectee** - is complying with a treaty he has concluded. The inspectee can either observe the treaty or violate it; we shall not consider different types of violation. We further assume that the inspector can either carry out thorough inspections, which are expensive for both sides, or not carry out any serious inspections. We shall use the term **alarm** for such an inspection. In the first case a violation will be detected; in the second it will escape detection. This situation can be described by a 2 x 2 matrix game (see Table 1), the payoffs of which will be discussed next.

Inspector \ Inspectee	Violation	Compliance
Alarm	(-a,-b)	(-e,-f)
No alarm	(-c,d)	(0,0)

Table 1: Payoffs to (inspector, inspectee) of the simple verification game considered in Chapter 2. According to the reasoning presented in the text, the inequalities

$$-c < -a < -e < 0 \quad \text{and} \quad -b < -f < 0 < d \qquad (2-1)$$

are satisfied.

If the inspectee complies, the inspector will certainly prefer **no alarm** to **alarm** owing to the high costs of an alarm, if for no other reason. Therefore $-e < 0$. If the inspectee commits a violation, the inspector will certainly prefer **alarm** to **no alarm**, since otherwise the game is trivial: There will never be an alarm and the inspectee can do as he likes without any danger of inspection. So we have $-c < -a$.

The question of whether the inspector prefers detection of a violation to a false alarm (i.e. an alarm in case of compliance) is more difficult to answer. In the case of an important treaty, however, the consequences of a violation might be so severe that the loss due to such a violation outweighs the costs of a false alarm. We therefore assume the following inequalities:

$$-c < -a < -e < 0 \,. \qquad (2-2)$$

Let us now consider the inspectee's viewpoint. In case of compliance he will certainly prefer **no alarm** because of the high costs of an alarm ($-f < 0$). Furthermore we must assume that an undetected violation offers some advantage to the inspectee since otherwise the situation would be trivial: The inspectee would always comply, whatever the inspector does. We accordingly have $0 < d$. The situation would be trivial for the opposite reason if detection of a violation were not worse for the inspectee than a false alarm because then he would violate the treaty, whatever the inspector does. We conclude $-b < -f$. We can summarize the above arguments by:

$$-b < -f < 0 < d. \tag{2-3}$$

We have now defined our model sufficiently to seek solutions. How should both sides behave in such a situation? There is no simple answer because pure strategies are unstable in the following sense: In case of **no alarm** the inspectee will prefer violation. This means that the inspector should verify, i.e. play **alarm.** In case of **alarm,** however, compliance is the inspectee's best strategy, while in case of compliance the inspector's best strategy is **no alarm.**

3. The Usual Nash Equilibrium for 2 x 2 Matrix Games

We have shown that our game has no equilibrium points in pure strategies. However, Nash's theorem guarantees that the mixed extension has an equilibrium point. Let us therefore assume that an inspection is carried out with probability α and that the inspectee violates the treaty with probability p. We must find α^*, p^* so that, if the inspector plays α^*, p^* is an optimal strategy for the inspectee, and if the inspectee plays p^*, α^* is an optimal strategy for the inspector.

The payoffs for the inspector and the inspectee are given by

$$Ir(\alpha,p) = -cp + [(c + e - a)p - e]\,\alpha \tag{3-1}$$

$$Ie(\alpha,p) = -f\alpha + [(f - d - b)\alpha + d]\,p \tag{3-2}$$

respectively. The impossibility of $\alpha=0$, $\alpha=1$, $p=0$ or $p=1$ being equilibrium strategies can be easily verified. Therefore for a given equilibrium point the terms inside the brackets must be 0. We conclude that

$$\alpha^* = \frac{d}{d + b - f} \tag{3-3}$$

$$p^* = \frac{e}{c + e - a} \tag{3-4}$$

Because of $f < b$ and $a < c$ these numbers do indeed lie within the interval (0;1). The equilibrium payoffs are:

$$Ir\ (\alpha^*,p^*) = -cp^* = \frac{-ec}{c+e-a} \qquad (3\text{-}5)$$

$$Ie\ (\alpha^*,p^*) = -f\alpha^* = \frac{-df}{d+b-f} \qquad (3\text{-}6)$$

We note several weaknesses in this solution, which raise doubts as to whether these formulae accurately portray reality: Firstly, the inspectee will always violate the treaty with a positive probability p. Secondly, this probability depends entirely on the inspector's (!) payoff parameters. The inspectee's payoffs for the various cases do not affect p. Thirdly, this model (i.e. this solution concept) does not allow for communication between the two protagonists.

4. One-sided Announcement of a Mixed Strategy and the Principle of Deterrence

In reality the inspector cannot keep his mixed strategy a secret. After a few inspections at the latest the inspectee will be able to estimate α. Moreover the inspector may opt to announce α so as to establish his credibility, e.g. by tossing a coin in front of the inspectee. The inspectee has no such option because by signing the treaty he has committed himself to compliance and cannot therefore announce an intention to violate the treaty with a probability $p > 0$ and still retain his credibility. Furthermore, if the inspectee's pronouncements were totally credible, a verification procedure would be unnecessary.

It follows that the inspector will announce his mixed strategy if his expected payoff is better than the one calculated above. Let us therefore see what happens if the inspector announces his α in a credible manner. Knowing α, the inspectee can easily calculate his best counter-strategy from (3-2). He obtains his best payoff

by complying ($p=0$) for $[(f-b-d)\alpha+d] < 0$ i.e. for $\alpha > \alpha^*$

by violating ($p=1$) for $[(f-d-b)\alpha+d] > 0$ i.e. for $\alpha < \alpha^*$ (4-1)

and by all $p\in[0;1]$ for $[(f-d-b)\alpha+d] = 0$ i.e. for $\alpha = \alpha^*$.

Now the inspector knows for $\alpha \neq \alpha^*$ the resulting p and from (3-1) he can therefore calculate his expected payoffs as a function of $\alpha \neq \alpha^*$. He obtains

$$Ir(\alpha) = \begin{cases} -c + (c-a)\alpha & \text{for} \quad \alpha < \alpha^* \\ \\ -e\,\alpha & \text{for} \quad \alpha > \alpha^* \end{cases} \tag{4-2}$$

From $e < a < c$ we conclude that the inspector should announce an $\alpha > \alpha^*$, and from $e > 0$ we see that in this boundary condition α should be as small as possible (see also Figure 1).

Before discussing the purely mathematical problem which arises because the interval $(\alpha^*,1] = \{\alpha|\alpha^* < \alpha \leq 1\}$ has no smallest element, we mention a problem which could occur if we allowed $e > a$, which is often proposed and means that the inspector prefers a detected violation to a false alarm. Figure 2 shows that for a greater α^* (which depends solely on the inspectee's payoff parameters), the inspector's best strategy could be to play an α which is slightly smaller than α^*, thereby inducing the inspectee to commit a violation in order to "trap" him. Maschler has termed this a "trap the inspectee" strategy. We have excluded this type of perverse verification modelling by assuming $e < a$.

W. Güth has noted that the "new" solution concept is basically also an equilibrium concept. He argues that in this chapter and the previous one it is not the solution concepts but the games which differ. This can easily be seen by taking a look at the extensive forms of these games. Whereas in the game considered in Chapter 3 both players have to choose their strategies independently of each other, in Chapter 4 the inspector chooses first, and then the inspectee who, knowing α, has to choose p.

There remains the problem that at the moment our game has no mathematically precise solution, because $(\alpha^*, 1]$ has no smallest element. This however reflects one important element of reality. As the inspector stands to lose so much, if a violation fails to be detected, he will not approach too closely the boundary where violation and compliance yield the same payoff to the inspectee. Instead, the inspector keeps a security distance from this boundary α^*.

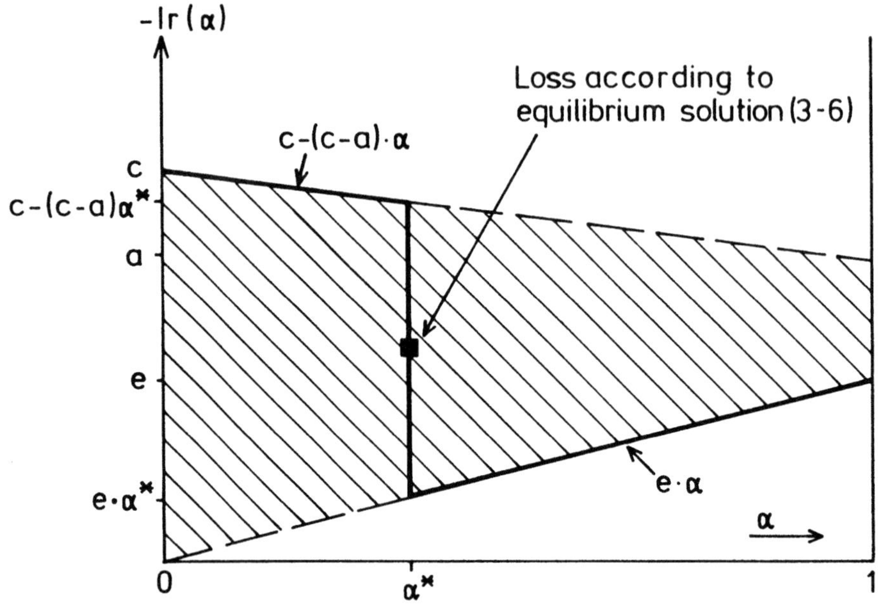

Figure 1: The loss to the inspector as a function of the inspection probability α. We have assumed $e < a$. The inspector's best strategy is obviously to play an $\alpha \in (\alpha^*, 1]$ which is "as small as possible." The solid line gives the loss for α announced to the inspectee and for rational behaviour by the inspectee. Losses in the shaded area can occur in case of irrational behaviour by the inspectee (i.e. if the inspectee does not correctly optimize his payoff).

A mathematically precise treatment of this problem (Fichtner, 1985) sets out from the assumption that the inspector wishes to award the inspectee a positive premium of at least ε for compliance, thereby strengthening deterrence. In this boundary condition

$$Ie\ (\alpha;0) - Ie\ (\alpha;1) \geq \varepsilon > 0 \qquad (4\text{-}3)$$

the inspector's payoff in case of compliance is minimized.

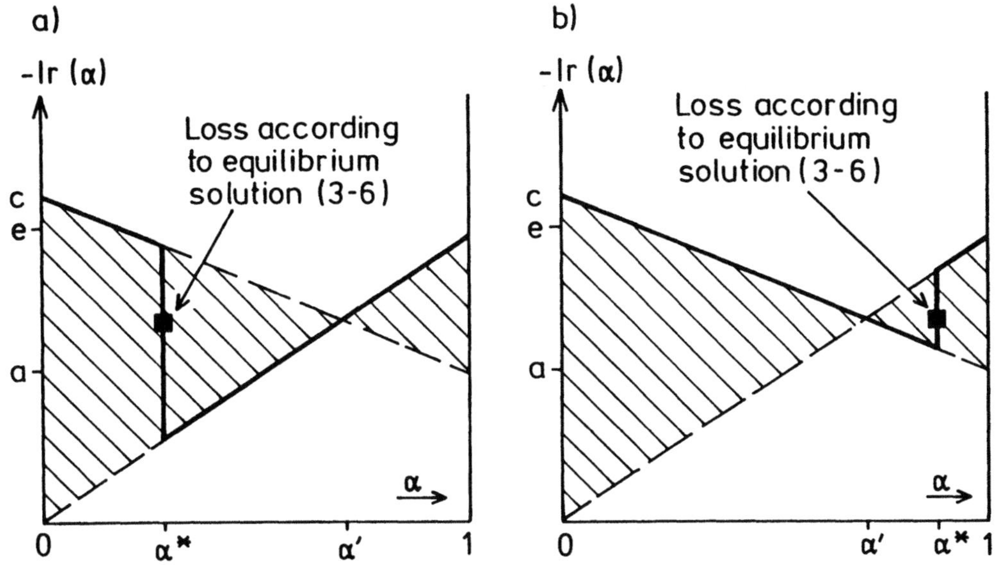

Figure 2: The loss to the inspector as a function of α for two typical cases and $e > a$. If α^* (depending solely on the inspectee's payoff parameters) is relatively small ($\alpha^* < \alpha'$) we have basically the same situation as in Figure 1. The inspector announces a small $\alpha \in (\alpha^*, 1]$, thereby deterring the inspectee from violating the treaty (Figure 2a). If however α^* is relatively large ($\alpha^* > \alpha'$), the inspector's best strategy is to announce a large $\alpha \in [0, \alpha^*)$, thereby inducing the inspectee to commit a violation in order to "trap" him. The inspector traps the inspectee. We exclude this "pathological" case.

By analogy with our previous calculation we obtain the solution

$$\alpha_\varepsilon = \frac{d + \varepsilon}{d + b - f} \tag{4-4}$$

We have $\alpha_\varepsilon \to \alpha^*$ for $\varepsilon \to 0$.

The payoffs for this solution are

$$Ir(\alpha_\varepsilon, 0) = -e\alpha_\varepsilon = -\frac{e(d+\varepsilon)}{d + b - f} \tag{4-5}$$

and

$$Ie(\alpha_\varepsilon, 0) = -f\alpha_\varepsilon = -\frac{f\,(d+\varepsilon)}{d+b-f} \qquad (4\text{-}6)$$

For the inspectee this means that compared with (3-6) he loses an additional amount of the order of ε. But he can do nothing about this. It is more useful to consider the inspector's payoff because he could opt to refrain from announcing his strategy.

From (3-5) and $e < a < c$ we can conclude that without such an announcement the inspector's loss is greater than e. From (4-5) and $f < b$ we can see that for $\varepsilon < b-f$ the inspector's loss, if he announces his strategy, is smaller than e. Therefore the best thing the inspector can do is to announce his strategy.

The result can be summarized as the

Principle of Deterring a Violation

The inspector's optimum strategy is verification with a probability α high enough to provide the inspectee in case of compliance with a payoff which is greater by a positive amount ε than his payoff in case of violation. ε cannot be determined by our model, the reason being that ε is a "factor of security" accounting for the inaccuracies of the model.

In order to deter from violation this strategy has to be announced in a manner conducive to credibility. In the interests of both sides α should - given the above boundary condition - be as small as possible.

This solution concept will be called the "deterrence" or "inducement" concept (Brams, 1985). Generalizations to deterrence from other kinds of action are evident; they will not be discussed here.

5. Applying this Model to more General Situations

In order to make the deterrence concept as clear as possible, which appears to be the best approach to modelling verification procedures, we have hitherto considered only the simplest case. Now we shall briefly discuss how we can model more complex situations with this solution concept.

Except for Borch (1982), who considers a three person game, the generalizations have been to sequential games or to systems with detectors. Maschler (1966) looks at a sequence of games similar to, but simpler than the game we analysed above and assumes that there is an upper limit to the number of inspections. His basic conclusion is that the inspector should announce his strategy, which is verification at each step with a probability just large enough to deter a violation at that step. In this model, however, it may happen that the inspector has used up the inspections available to him; then the inspectee can violate the treaty without fear of detection. Bierlein (1969, 1970, 1983) and Höpfinger (1974) investigate similar, but more general problems. However, they do not explicitly refer to the question of whether an inspector should announce his strategy. Instead they look for "reliable inspection schemes". A shortcoming of these models is that they do not allow for possible false alarms.

These can occur where the inspector has to rely on imperfect detection equipment. Maschler (1967) studied a situation with detection equipment capable of a finite number of discrete states. He was even able to investigate a sequential game with such detection equipment. Brams (1985) investigated detection equipment which can exist in two states.

The most extensive research into verification with the help of imperfect detection equipment (or sophisticated measurement with stochastic errors) was evoked by the NPT (Avenhaus, 1986). It is in this area that the importance of false alarms has been stressed (Avenhaus and Frick, 1977). The author of this paper has extended the solution concept described in Chapter 3 to fairly general non-sequential games which allow for arbitrary detectors and for an infinite number of different kinds of both compliance and violation (Fichtner, 1985). This can be done with partially non-standard methods of mathematical statistics. This paper will not go into the details of the method, but some of its features can be briefly described as follows.

Let us first assume that the inspector uses a detection mechanism for which he can determine α, the **false alarm probability.** Where there is compliance, α has the same meaning as above, namely the probability of an alarm. However, if the inspectee violates, the detection mechanism will in general more often result in an alarm. We call this probability $1-\beta$ and assume that β is a known function of α. An ideal detector would be characterized by $\beta(\alpha)=0$, an ineffectual detector by $\alpha=1-\beta(\alpha)$, i.e. the situation described above. Realistic detectors will have a function $\beta(\alpha)$ somewhere between these two extremes. From Table 1 we can now see that the expected payoffs for (inspector, inspectee) are given by

$$\begin{matrix} (-e\alpha, -f\alpha) & & \text{compliance} \\ & \text{in case of} & \\ (-a+(a-c)\beta(\alpha), -b+(b+d)\beta(\alpha)) & & \text{violation} \end{matrix} \qquad (5\text{-}1)$$

Assuming rational behaviour, the inspectee will comply if his gain in this case is larger than in case of violation, i.e. if

$$-b+(b+d)\beta(\alpha) < -f\alpha \ . \qquad (5\text{-}2)$$

Since the inspector's gain from compliance is $-e\alpha$, according to the inducement concept the inspector will minimize α, subject to the condition (5-2), and announce this strategy to the inspectee.

If both players have more strategies than simply compliance/violation or determining α, we first have to determine the function $\beta(\alpha)$. For example if the inspectee has a strategy set Y_M for violation and only one strategy for compliance, and if the inspector has for each α a set of strategies X_α leading to probability of a false alarm α, then $\beta(\alpha)$ can be determined by solving the optimization problem

$$\underset{x\in X_\alpha}{\text{minimize}} \quad \underset{y\in Y_M}{\max} \quad \beta(x,y) =: \beta(\alpha) \ .$$

Then one can proceed as above.

This procedure may serve as the basis for statistical analyses of verification problems where random errors - whether due to inaccurate measurement and/or random sampling - cannot be avoided. This chapter will not give details of the method. However, in order to illustrate it and simultaneously to compare the inducement concept with the equilibrium concept we shall examine one example. The reader is further referred to the chapter by Avenhaus and Markin.

6. Analysis of Brams' and Kilgour's Truth Game with the Inducement Solution Concept

In the foregoing chapter Brams and Kilgour defined a game called Truth Game between Column (= inspector) and Row (= inspectee). Whereas they investigated the consequences of employing the equilibrium concept, here we shall use and discuss the inducement concept. In order to compare the results numerically, first the payoff parameters have to be calculated, using our notation which to some extent has become standard (Avenhaus, 1986). Comparing Figure 1 of Brams and Kilgour and our Table 1 we obtain by noting that the payoffs are shown on two different but linearly related scales:

$$\begin{aligned} -b &= -r_2 & c &= 1 \\ -f &= r_3-r_2 & -e &= c_2-1 \\ d &= 1-r_2 & -a &= c_3-1 \end{aligned} \qquad (6\text{-}1)$$

From $r_2 = 1/4$, $r_3 = 1/2$, $c_2 = 1/3$ and $c_3 = 2/3$ we get

$$\begin{aligned} a &= 1/3 & d &= 3/4 \\ b &= 1/4 & e &= 2/3 \\ c &= 1 & f &= -1/4 \end{aligned} \qquad (6\text{-}2)$$

Let us assume that we know the inspector's strategy and therefore the probabilities of his making a false statement both in case of compliance and in case of violation. As usual in statistics we set

α = probability of first kind error = probability of accusing the inspectee in case of compliance

β = probability of second kind error = probability of not accusing the inspectee in case of violation.

Thus the inspectee's payoff is

$$Ie = \begin{cases} -f\alpha = 1/4\,\alpha & \text{for compliance} \\ d\beta-b(1-\beta) = -1/4+\beta & \text{for violation} \end{cases} \qquad (6\text{-}3)$$

The inspectee will therefore comply, if

$$1/4\,\alpha \; > \; -\,1/4 + \beta \tag{6-4}$$

holds good, and violate, if the opposite inequality holds good. In Figure 3 the points (α,β) in the shaded area guarantee compliance, those outside guarantee violation and for those on the borderline the inspectee has no incentive to violate, nor to comply.

Now that the inspectee's response to a given announced strategy is known, we can look for a "best" strategy for the inspector, whose payoff is shown by

$$Ir = \begin{cases} -e\alpha = -2/3\alpha & \text{for compliance} \\ -c\beta - a(1-\beta) = -1/3 - 2/3\beta & \text{for violation} \end{cases} \tag{6-5}$$

We observe that Ir decreases monotonically in α and β. From this it follows that the inspector will minimize β for a given α. We shall first look at this minimization and then optimize α.

At this stage we have to look more closely at the detection equipment, which is central to Truth Game. It is assumed that there is a detector signalling violation, e.g. a flashing red lamp, with probability

$1-y$	in case of compliance, and
x	in case of violation.

Without loss of generality we can assume $x+y > 1$; otherwise we would consider $1-y$ and x the probability of the red lamp <u>not</u> flashing.

With the help of this detector the inspector has to decide whether to accuse the inspectee of a violation or not. The observation of the detector can be considered a Bernoulli experiment with parameter $\theta = 1-y$ in case of compliance (hypothesis H_o) and with parameter $\theta = x$ in case of violation (hypothesis H_1). The decision problem is now a testing problem of H_o against H_1.

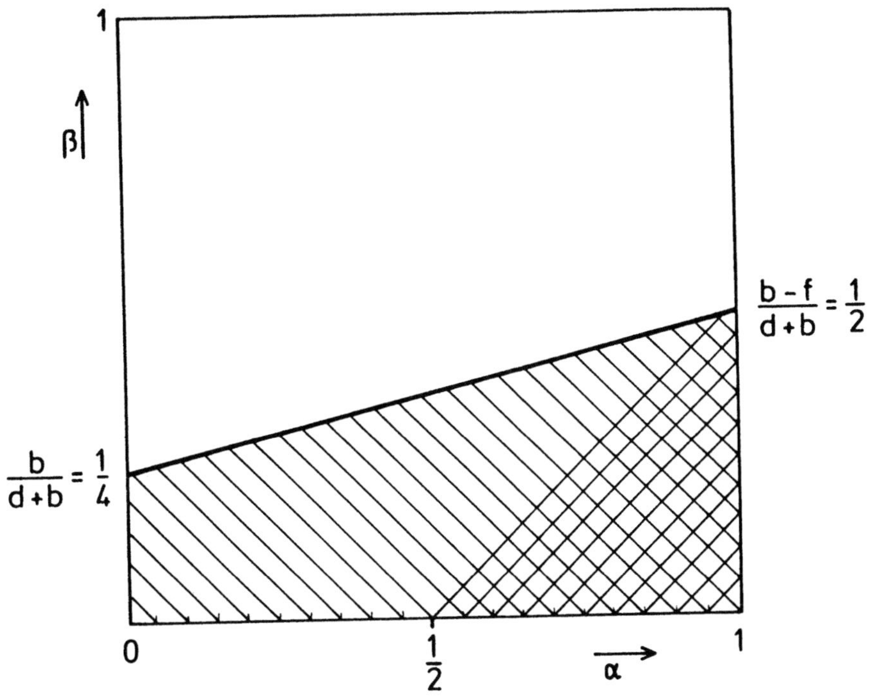

Figure 3: The values (α,β) for which a violation is deterred, i.e. for which (6-4) holds good (shaded area). Anywhere above the thick line the inspectee has an incentive to violate, on the line the expected payoffs are the same for both violation and compliance. In the bottom right-hand corner (double shaded) we find the values (α,β) for which the inspector would prefer a violation, i.e. to "trap" the inspectee. However, because (6-4) holds good for this area, a violation will not occur, so that the inspector cannot benefit from violations.

The inspector's strategy can be described by two real numbers, viz.

p = probability of accusing, if the red lamp flashes

q = probability of accusing, if the red lamp does not flash.

We have

$$\alpha = y\,q + (1-y)p \qquad p,\, q \in [0;1] \qquad (6\text{-}6)$$
$$1-\beta = (1-x)\,q + xp\,.$$

It is useful to examine Figure 4 to understand these equations and the minimization of β for a given α. The corresponding numerical calculations will not be reproduced here. The result is that the inspector for a given α plays

$$p = \frac{\alpha}{1-y} \qquad q = 0 \qquad \text{for } 0 \le \alpha \le 1-y$$
$$(6\text{-}7)$$
$$p = 1 \qquad q = 1-\frac{1-\alpha}{y} \qquad \text{for } 1-y \le \alpha \le 1$$

and the best (i.e. minimal) β for a given α is

$$\tilde{\beta}(\alpha) = \begin{cases} 1 - x\dfrac{\alpha}{1-y} & \text{for } 0 \le \alpha \le 1-y \\ (1-x)\,\dfrac{1-\alpha}{y} & \text{for } 1-y \le \alpha \le 1. \end{cases} \qquad (6\text{-}8)$$

From now on the candidates for the inspector's best strategies will be described by α.

The only remaining problem is how to determine α.

From (6-3) it follows that the inspector prefers compliance for

$$-2/3\,\alpha > -\,1/3 - 2/3\beta$$

or $\qquad\qquad\qquad\qquad\qquad (6\text{-}9)$

$$\alpha < 1/2 + \beta$$

For $\alpha > 1/2 + \beta$ the inspector would prefer the inspectee to commit a violation. However, he cannot induce him to do so, because the inspectee complies for $\alpha > -1+4\beta$ (cf. Figure 3) and therefore <u>a fortiori</u> for $\alpha > 1/2+\beta$. We had to exclude the possibility that the inspector could benefit

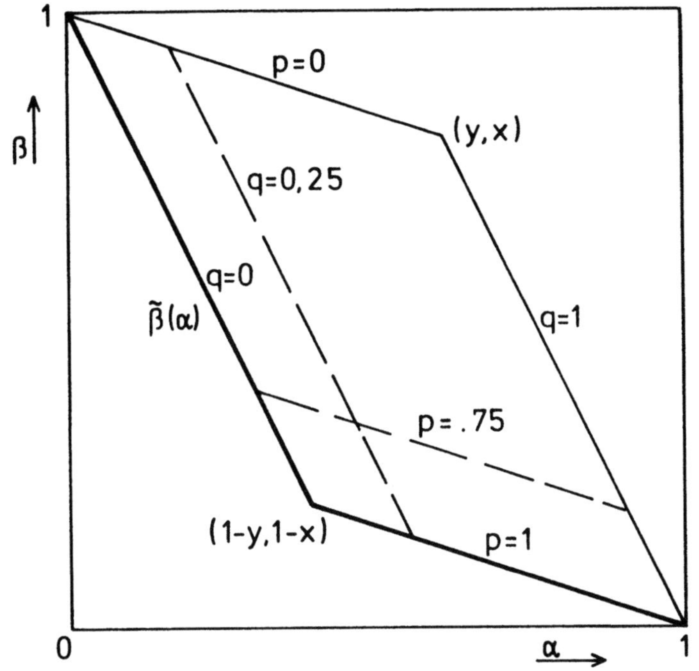

Figure 4: Illustration of (6-6) showing which values of (α, β) the inspector can achieve by choosing appropriate probabilities p and q. As the inspector minimizes β for a given α, he will only play strategies (p,q) for which (α, β) lies on the thick line, which can be considered the graph of a function $\tilde{\beta}(\alpha)$. Equations (6-7) and (6-8) can easily be derived from this figure.

from inducing the inspectee to commit a violation because in the Truth Game $e < b$ is not fulfilled, so that this situation could occur for other numerical values. The inspector could "trap" the inspectee.

Now we know that for the Truth Game the appropriately modified Principle of Deterring a Violation holds good. The inspector's payoff (6-3) is optimized if he announces a strategy α which:

- deters the inspectee from a violation
  (we have just shown that the inspector's payoff in relevant cases is better for compliance than for violation)

- maximizes the inspector's payoff for compliance, i.e. minimizes α in this boundary condition

Figure 5 shows this optimization for the special case x=y and some typical values of x.

We observe in contrast to the equilibrium solution, that according to the inducement concept

- the inspectee will always comply (i.e. probability of a violation = 0)

- the inspector's payoff is $Ir = -e\alpha_\varepsilon$ and therefore (for $x > 1/2$, which we may assume without loss of generality) decreases monotonically in x.

In our opinion, the inducement concept can faithfully model verification processes and does not conflict with what common sense leads one to expect. It shows that the better the detector, the more easily compliance can be induced. The inspector can deter a violation with fewer costs arising from false alarms.

7. Conclusions

Given the assumptions concerning the inspectee's payoff in Chapter 2, there is always a strategy for the inspector which leads to compliance by the inspectee. In order to deter from violation, the inspector may have to verify in a somewhat obtrusive way, thereby causing both sides considerable expense. This seems to be the position of the present United States administration, which fears that without **effective** verification a treaty will be violated, which is worse than having no treaty at all. We have excluded two cases merely because the results were trivial, not because the cases themselves were impossible. The first of these was $d > 0$, according to which the inspectee prefers compliance to violation, even where there is no alarm. Plainly, in this case the inspectee will always comply and obtrusive verification is unnecessary. This seems to be the view of the Soviet Union, which argues that by signing a treaty both parties evince their willingness to comply and that overly obtrusive

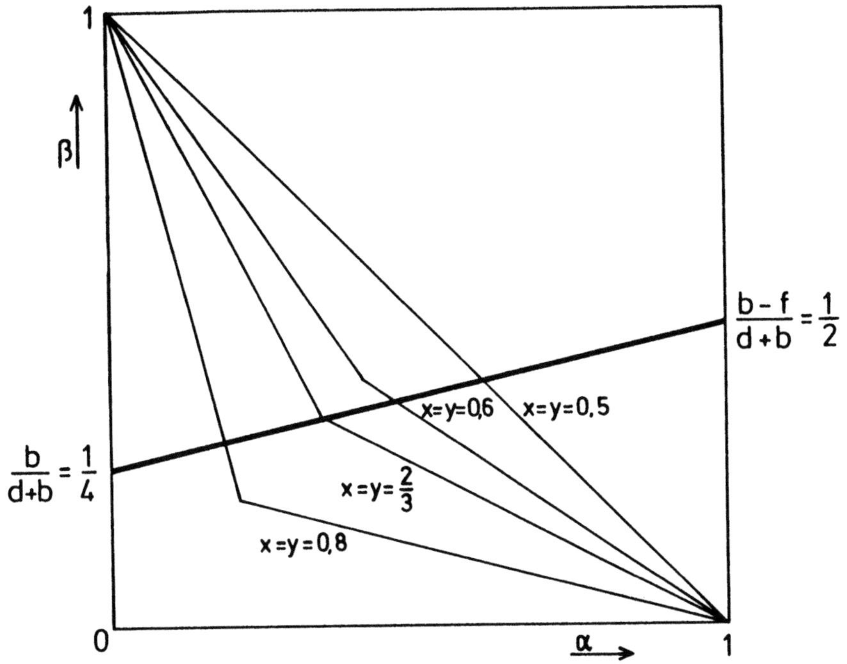

Figure 5: Determining the inspector's best α for some values of x=y. Four curves $\tilde{\beta}(\alpha)$ are drawn for x=y=0.5, 0.6, 2/3 and 0.8. We know that the inspector will announce a strategy which leads to $(\alpha, \tilde{\beta}(\alpha))$ i.e. to a point on this curve (Figure 4). His payoff is better if a violation can be prevented, i.e. if $(\alpha, \tilde{\beta}(\alpha))$ lies below the thick line (Figure 3). Under this boundary condition his loss is increasing with α. Therefore his best strategy is to choose α slightly to the right of the intersection of the thick line and $\tilde{\beta}(\alpha)$. It can be easily seen that for $x=y \geq 1/2$ the solution α decreases with the increasing reliability x of the detector and the inspector's loss with it.

inspections are merely costly and undermine mutual confidence.

Little need be said about the last case we excluded. For b < f the inspectee will always violate the agreement, so that the best the inspector can do is always to blame him for the violation. But verification has no chance of influencing the inspectee's behaviour.

It should also be remarked that game theoretic analyses of verification issues presume that verification has a significant effect on the inspectee's behaviour. If we do not set our sights too high with regard to verification, if we do not hope to deter violation nor reduce the probability of a violation by verification, then the goal of inspection can only be to ascertain the truth at reasonable cost by acceptable means. It is here that the notion of adequate verification is appropriate.

REFERENCES

Avenhaus, R. (1986): Safeguards Systems Analysis - with applications to nuclear material safeguards and other inspection problems. New York, London

Avenhaus, R., Frick, H. (1977): Analyse von Fehlalarmen in Überwachungssystemen mit Hilfe von Zweipersonen Nichtnullsummenspielen. (Analysis of False Alarms in Inspection Systems with the Help of Two-Person Non-Zero-Sum Games). Operations Research Verfahren XVI, pp. 629-639

Avenhaus, R., Frick, H. (1979): Vergleich zweier Verfahren der Materialbilanzierung. (Comparison of two Methods of Material Accountability). Operations Research Verfahren XXX, pp. 187-191

Bierlein, D. (1969): Direkte Überwachungssysteme. (Direct Inspection Systems). Operations Research Verfahren VI, pp. 57-68

Bierlein, D. (1970): Auf Bilanzen und Inventuren basierende Safeguards-Systeme. (Safeguards Systems Based on Material Balances and Inventories). Operations Research Verfahren VIII, pp. 36-43

Bierlein, D. (1983): Game Theoretical Models of Safeguarding Different Types of Illegal Activities. Proceedings of the 4th Formator-Symposium on Mathematical Methods of the Analysis of Large-Scale Systems, Czechosl. Acad. Sc.,Prague

Brams, S.J. (1985): Superpower Games. Yale University Press, New Haven, London

Dresher, M. (1962): A Sampling Inspection Problem in Arms Control Agreements: A Game Theoretic Analysis. Memorandum RM-2972-ARPA, The Rand Corporation

Fichtner, J. (1985): Statistische Tests zur Abschreckung von Fehlverhalten - Eine mathematische Analyse von Überwachungssystemen mit Anwendungen. (Statistical Tests for Deterrence from Illegal Behaviour - A Mathematical Analysis of Safeguards Systems with Applications). Dissertation, Universität der Bundeswehr München

Friedman, J.W. (1977): Oligopoly and the Theory of Games. Amsterdam

Goldman, A.J., Pearl, M.H. (1976): The Dependence of Inspector-System Performance on Levels of Penalties and Inspection Resources. Journal of Research of the National Bureau of Standards -B. 80 B, N. 2, pp. 189-236

Höpfinger, E. (1974): Zuverlässige Inspektionsstrategien. (Reliable Inspection Strategies). Z. Wahrscheinlichkeitstheorie verw. Gebiete 31, pp. 35-46

Kuhn, H.W. (1963): Recursive Inspection Games, Applications of Statistical Methology to Arms Control and Disarmament. A United States Arms Control and Disarmament Agency Report under Contract ADCA/ST-3, pp. 169-182

Maschler, M. (1966): A Price Leadership Method for Solving the Inspector's Non-Constant-Sum Game. Nav. Res. Logistics Quart. 13, pp. 11-33

Maschler, M. (1967): The Inspector's Non-Constant-Sum Game. Its Dependence on a System of Detectors. Nav. Res. Logistics Quart. 14, pp. 275-290

Shubik, M. (1980): Market Structure and Behaviour. Cambridge, MA, London

Stackelberg, H. von (1934): Marktform und Gleichgewicht. (Market Form and Equilibrium). Berlin

INTERNATIONAL ATOMIC ENERGY AGENCY SAFEGUARDS

Rudolf Avenhaus
Federal Armed Forces University Munich, FRG

Jack T. Markin
Los Alamos National Laboratory, USA

1. INTRODUCTION

The International Atomic Energy Agency (IAEA) is unique among international organizations in its use of on-site inspections to verify that states are in compliance with the terms of a negotiated agreement. These inspections are applied in 52 countries at nearly 500 facilities to assure that uses of nuclear materials and facilities are limited to peaceful purposes. The legal basis for the inspections is agreements between the IAEA and the state, concluded in the framework of the nuclear Non-Proliferation Treaty, for full scope safeguards on all nuclear materials. In addition, other more limited agreements for safeguards on a portion of a state's nuclear material are also concluded with states not party to the treaty. In either case, the role of the IAEA is to verify compliance with the terms of these agreements by auditing facility operating records and reports submitted to the IAEA by the state, by independent measurement of nuclear materials by IAEA inspectors, and by emplacement of surveillance devices to monitor facility operations in the inspector's absence.

Although IAEA safeguards are applied only to peaceful nuclear activities and do not attempt to control or reduce the numbers of nuclear weapons, there are aspects of the IAEA methods and technology that may be applicable to treaty verification for arms control. Among these aspects are

- the form of the IAEA's agreement with states;
- the IAEA approach to inspection planning; and
- the instrumentation employed by the IAEA for monitoring facility activities and for measuring nuclear material.

In the following, we will first describe the IAEA safeguards system in more detail, thereafter we sketch the quantitative analyses of the efficiency of this system and finally we discuss its applicability to further arms control agreements.

NATO ASI Series, Vol. F 26
Modelling and Analysis in Arms Control
Edited by R. Avenhaus et al.

2. GENERAL AGREEMENTS, FACILITY ATTACHMENTS, AND INSPECTION GOALS

General agreements between the IAEA and state describe in broad terms the obligations and privileges of the two parties with respect to implementation of safeguards. The general agreements are approved by the state's parliament and the IAEA Board of Governors.

Under agreements drawn up in accordance with IAEA Document Information Circular 66 (IAEA (1968)), materials, equipment, and facilities may be subject to safeguards to assure they are not used for a military purpose. In these cases, IAEA activities are applied only to specific items placed under safeguards. In contrast, agreements under IAEA Document Information Circular 153 (IAEA (1972)) emphasize that safeguards is on nuclear material, and the scope encompasses all nuclear material used by the state in its peaceful activities. Noncompliance with the terms of the agreements would be reported through the IAEA Board of Governors to the United Nations Security Council. Because the IAEA has no power to enforce compliance, it must rely on the political and economic sanctions that might be applied by other states in response to evidence of a violation of agreements with the IAEA.

For each facility under safeguards, the IAEA and the state negotiate a facility attachment describing the inspection activities permitted and the state's obligation for cooperation. A typical facility attachment includes

- facility design and process operating descriptions;
- safeguards measures that the IAEA is permitted to apply at the facility;
- records of facility operations to be maintained by the operator;
- a description of the state's systems of accounting to be maintained by the state; and
- materials accounting reports to be submitted by the state to the IAEA.

IAEA inspection procedures applied under these agreements include examination of facility records and state reports for completeness, correctness, and consistency; measurement of materials to confirm that the amounts are consistent with those declared by the state; and the use of containment and surveillance to confirm in the inspector's absence that material amounts remain unchanged and that there are no undeclared movements of material.

The general IAEA objective of the timely detection of the diversion of a significant quantity of material from peaceful purposes is quantified in the inspection goals. They specify

- a significant quantity as the amount of special nuclear material required for manufacture of a nuclear device (for example, 8 kg Pu, 25 kg of contained U-235 in uranium enriched to greater than or equal to 20 percent and 75 kg of contained U-235 in uranium enriched to less than 20 percent);
- the detection time, estimated as the time for conversion of the material to a weapon (1 month for direct use material such as plutonium or highly enriched uranium, 3 months for direct use material in irradiated fuel, and 1 year for indirect use material such as low-enriched uranium); and
- a probability of 0.9 to 0.95 for detecting the loss of a significant quantity of material within the detection time period.

In practice, these idealized goals are not strictly adhered to but may be modified according to the size of the facility inventory and throughput, the material type, whether the material is in item or bulk form, and the measurement uncertainty of the methods available to the IAEA for verifying material amounts.

3. SAFEGUARDS APPROACH, VERIFICATION METHODS, AND CONTAINMENT/SURVEILLANCE

A safeguards approach is a coordinated system of inspection activities consisting of materials accounting and containment/surveillance methods, which are designed to confirm a state's compliance with safeguards agreements. Factors considered in developing the approach are the inspection goals, design characteristics of the facility to be inspected, terms of the safeguards agreements with the state, effectiveness of the state's system of accounting, technical limitations of the IAEA measurement and surveillance technology, inspection manpower available to the IAEA, and technically credible scenarios for misuse of facility materials or equipment.

Although IAEA safeguards are applied in a collaborative spirit with the state cooperating in the implementation of inspections, the development of the safeguards approach is adversarial in its assumption that violations of safeguards agreements may occur. This assumption is essential in planning safeguards activities to assure other states that IAEA safeguards conclusions are valid.

For each facility type, IAEA systems studies have identified potential scenarios for undeclared removal of material from a facility or from its assigned location in the facility, undeclared introduction of material into a facility, and undeclared modification of material. These scenarios are specified in terms of the material types and amounts, physical paths for movement of the material, methods for modification of the material, and methods for concealing evidence of treaty violations.

The safeguards approach is designed to detect anomalies in facility operations that would be created by the postulated scenarios. Facets of an approach are identification of key points within a facility for application of safeguards measures; a set of inspection activities that includes examinations of facility records and state reports; verification of material inventories and transfers, and containment/surveillance measures; and the frequency and intensity of applying these activities.

Within the facilities inspected by the IAEA, which include light-water reactors (LWRS), research reactors, Candu reactors, conversion/fabrication facilities and reprocessing facilities, safeguarded material containing uranium and plutonium appears in a variety of forms. Among these forms are uranium and plutonium oxides in pellets, fuel rods, and fresh and irradiated fuel assemblies; UF_6 in cylinders; and nitrate solutions of uranium and plutonium in process vessels. These materials are independently verified by IAEA inspectors through analysis of samples sent to an analytical laboratory or through in-situ measurements with nondestructive assay (NDA) techniques (Rogers (1983)).

The IAEA maintains a laboratory where about 2000 samples per year are analyzed by destructive analytical methods to determine the chemical concentration and isotopic composition of uranium and plutonium. This laboratory is equipped for wet chemical analysis, mass spectrometric analysis, radiometric measurements, and emission spectrography.

The laboratory facility for analysis of material samples from inspected facilities is complemented by an IAEA capability for in-situ nondestructive analysis (NDA) of nuclear material (IAEA 1984). Development of these NDA techniques was motivated in part by difficulties in shipping samples of radioactive material and in destroying the integrity of valuable items such as fuel assemblies to obtain samples.

Applications of nondestructive assay instruments to measure the total amounts of uranium and plutonium or their isotopic composition are based on the unique characteristics of the radiations emitted by these materials. NDA devices may be characterized as passive methods based on the detection of radiation emitted by the material itself without external stimulation; and active methods based on the irradiation of the material with neutrons or photons to induce atomic or nuclear reactions and subsequent measurement of these induced radiations. In either case, these devices measure the intensity of gamma rays at specific energies, total neutrons, or coincident neutrons from fissions.

Among the measurements routinely performed by IAEA inspectors with NDA instruments are determinations of the enrichment of uranium in pellets, rods and fuel assemblies; concentration of plutonium and uranium in nitrate solutions; U-235 enrichment of UF_6 in cylinders; and total plutonium in oxide and metal forms.

Examples of the portable NDA devices developed specifically for IAEA use at facilities are a multichannel analyzer, which displays gamma-ray spectra from sodium iodide or germanium detectors for determining U-235 enrichment, total uranium, and plutonium isotopic composition, and a neutron coincidence counter with ^3He neutron detectors for determining U-235 and U-238 content in LWR fuel assemblies and plutonium content in oxides. Other more qualitative methods are the gross determination that a fuel assembly has been irradiated using Cerenkov glow night vision devices; and correlations between operators declarations of spent fuel burnup and cooling time with gross gamma and neutron measurements using ion and fission chambers.

Because continuous presence of inspectors at a safeguarded facility may not be practical, containment/surveillance measures were developed for assuring, in the inspector's absence, that materials previously measured remain intact, that there are no undeclared movements of material, and that there is no tampering with inspector equipment remaining at the facility (IAEA 1984). For example, a seal applied to a container ensures that the material has remained unchanged since the seal was applied and devices for recording optical images can provide evidence of undeclared movements of fuel assemblies in spent fuel ponds.

The IAEA currently employs about 9000 type-E metallic seals each year. These are applied to material containers such as UF_6 cylinders, containment penetrations such as reactor shields, and tamper indicating enclosures for agency equipment such as film cameras. Because the identity and integrity of these seals must be determined by detaching and returning them to IAEA headquarters for examination, other seals that are verifiable in-situ are under development.

Surveillance devices are primarily applied to detect undeclared material movements in the spent fuel storage areas of reactors and reprocessing plants. These devices are film cameras with automatic timers, a tamper-resistant sealable enclosure, and battery power; closed-circuit television (CCTV) systems are employed when continuous monitoring is required and when high radiation fields preclude the use of film. Surveillance film is reviewed at IAEA headquarters and CCTV may be reviewed in-situ or at headquarters.

Other surveillance devices in use by inspectors include radiation dosimeters to detect the passage of irradiated fuel, reactor power monitors to measure the power level from a reactor, and spent fuel bundle counters to monitor the flow of fuel bundles from a Candu reactor to the spent fuel area.

4. QUANTITATIVE ANALYSES

What does material accounting mean in quantitative terms? Let us consider one inventory period $[t_0,t_1]$. At time t_0 the initial physical inventory I_0 is taken; during $[t_0,t_1]$ receipts R and shipments S are measured which together with I_0 are added to the so-called book inventory B at time t_1, $B_0 = I_0 + R - S$, i.e. that amount of material which should be in the plant at t_1. This book inventory is compared to the physical inventory I_1 at t_1, which means that for the Material Unaccounted For,

$$MUF = I_0 + R - S - I_1 = B - I_1$$

a hypothesis test with the two hypotheses

$$H_0 : E_0(MUF) = 0, \quad H_1 : E_1(MUF) = \mu > 0,$$

is performed, where E_i is the expectation operator under H_i, $i = 0,1$, and μ the missing amount of material. For this purpose a significance threshold s is fixed, and H_0 is rejected if the observed MUF is greater than s, otherwise H_1 is rejected. If the measurement errors are normally distributed, then also MUF is normally distributed with variance σ^2, and the false alarm probability α, i.e. the probability of rejecting H_0 if it is in fact true, is given by

$$1 - \alpha = \Phi\left(\frac{s}{\sigma}\right),$$

where Φ is the normal distribution. Furthermore, the probability of detection $1 - \beta$, i.e. the probability of rejection H_0 if H_1 is true, is given by

$$\beta = \Phi\left(\frac{s - \mu}{\sigma}\right) = \Phi\left(U(1 - \alpha) - \frac{\mu}{\sigma}\right),$$

where U is the inverse of Φ. Thus we have established the relation $\beta(\alpha)$ which has been mentioned by Fichtner in his contribution to this book, and one can use his decision theoretical formalism in order to fix the value of α and therefore, of s.

If one considers a sequence of n inventory periods $[t_{i-1}, t_i]$, $i = 1 \ldots n$, then things get more complicated. As long as detection time does not play any role, one can formulate the inspector's decision problem as follows: Given then n observations $MUF_1 \ldots MUF_n$. Then a decision has to be made between the two hypotheses

$$H_0 : E_0(MUF_i) = 0 \quad \text{for} \quad i = 1 \ldots n$$

$$H_1 : E_1(MUF_i) = \mu_i \quad \text{for} \quad i = 1 \ldots n, \quad \sum_{i=1}^{n} \mu_i = \mu > 0.$$

Thus, if one defines the set of tests with false alarm probability α as X_α, the set $\{\mu_i, \ i = 1 \ldots n, \ \sum_i \mu_i = \mu > o\}$ as Y_μ, then one can again apply Fichtner's formalism, i.e. determine

$$\min_{X_\alpha} \quad \max_{Y_\mu} \quad \beta(x, y; \alpha).$$

The result of this analysis (Avenhaus and Jaech (1982)), which uses the wellknown *Neyman-Pearson Lemma* of Statistics (see e.g., Lehmann (1959)), is that the test statistic of operator is

$$MUF_1 + \ldots + MUF_n = I_0 + \sum_i R_i - \sum_i S_i - I_n,$$

i.e. that the overall material balance for the whole sequence of n inventory periods is taken, and that all intermediate inventories are ignored.

If, however, detection time does play a role, things get much more complicated. First, up to now there is no formalism which leads to such a simple optimization criterion as the one given above. Second, there is no equivalent to the Neyman-Pearson Lemma in sequential statistics. Therefore, one is just using well-known sequential test procedures and analyses their statistical properties, especially their run length distribution. So far, no very best procedure has been identified; here research is vitally going on.

Up to now, we have assumed that the data I_0, R_i, S_i, I_i, $i = 1 \ldots n$, reported by the operator to the safeguards authority are not falsified. Since, however, falsification of data cannot be excluded in general, inspectors verify these data with the help of independent measurements. Just in order to give an idea of the type of analyses to be performed here, we consider the case of inventory data verification.

Let us assume that the operator has reported the set of data x_{ij}, $i = 1 \ldots K$, $j = 1 \ldots N_i$ to the safeguards authority, and that the safeguards authority verifies these data with the help of independent measurements y_{ij}, $i = 1 \ldots K$, $j = 1 \ldots n_i$, $n_i \leq N_i$. Since the safeguards authority is not interested in the true values but only in the differences $z_{ij} = x_{ij} - y_{ij}$, $i = 1 \ldots K$, $j = 1 \ldots n_i$, a statistical test is performed for the two hypotheses

$$H_0 : E(Z_{ij}) = 0; \quad H_1 : E(Z_{ij}) = \mu_i, \quad i = 1 \ldots K, \; j = 1 \ldots n_i .$$

(For a more detailed discussion of these assumptions see Avenhaus (1986)).

According to the *Neyman-Pearson-Lemma,* the best test for this problem leads to the probability of detection

$$1 - \beta_{NP} = \Phi\left(\sqrt{\underline{\mu}' \cdot \underline{\underline{\Sigma}}^{-1} \cdot \underline{\mu}} - U(1-\alpha)\right),$$

where $\underline{\mu}' = (\mu_1 \ldots \mu_K)$, $\underline{\underline{\Sigma}}$ the covariance its matrix of the Z_{ij}, ϕ the normal distribution und U is inverse. If one now assumes that the inspectee will falsify all data by the total amount

$$\mu = \sum_{i=1}^{K} \mu_i \cdot N_i ,$$

and that the total inspection effort is

$$\varepsilon = \sum_{i=1}^{K} \varepsilon_i \cdot n_i ,$$

where ε_i is the effort to verify one datum in the i-th class, then the solution of the optimization problem given above leads to the guaranteed probability of detection

$$1-\beta_{NP}^{*} = \Phi\left(\frac{\mu}{\sigma} - U(1-\alpha)\right); \quad \sigma = \frac{1}{\sqrt{\varepsilon}} \cdot \sum_{i=1}^{K} N_i \cdot \sigma_i \cdot \sqrt{\varepsilon_i}; \quad \sigma_i^2 = \mathrm{var}(Z_{ij}),$$

and the optimal strategies of both players are

$$\mu_i^{*} = \frac{\mu}{\sigma^2} \cdot \frac{\sum_k N_k \sigma_k \sqrt{\varepsilon_k}}{\varepsilon} \cdot \sigma_i \cdot \sqrt{\varepsilon_i},$$

$$n_i^{*} = \frac{\varepsilon}{\sum_k N_k \sigma_k \sqrt{\varepsilon_k}} \cdot \frac{N_i \sigma_i}{\sqrt{\varepsilon_i}}, \quad i = 1 \ldots K.$$

Thus, one sees that the optimal class sample sizes n_i^{*}, $i = 1 \ldots K$, are the larger, the larger the number of data, the larger the measurement uncertainty and the smaller the verification effort for one datum of that class.

It should be mentioned that the test statistic which corresponds to the guaranteed probability of detection, is the so-called D-statistic

$$D = \sum_{i=1}^{K} \frac{N_i}{n_i^{*}} \cdot \sum_{j=1}^{n_i^{*}} Z_{ij},$$

which was proposed by K.B. Stewart (1970) who justified it at that time with heuristic arguments. In business accounting, it has been known already for a long time (Arkin (1974)).

Again, the sequential data verification problem is much more complicated than the non-sequential inventory verification problem considered here. In addition, there arise technical problems since some receipt data cannot be verified after the material has 'disappeared' in the production process.

Furthermore, the whole safeguards system, consisting of material accountancy and data verification, allows for combined 'diversion into MUF' and data falsification strategies which have to be taken into account if the overall efficiency of the system shall be evaluated (see, e.g., Avenhaus (1986)).

5. APPLICATION TO FURTHER ARMS CONTROL AGREEMENTS

Until today IAEA nuclear material safeguards is the only international system the purpose of which is to control the compliance of the partners with an arms control agreement. Therefore, it is but natural that it has been asked in which way this system could serve as a model for further safeguards systems. A partial answer to this question has been given some time ago by an IAEA official (Fischer (1982)); he emphasized, however, the organisational aspects of the whole problem. In the following, some technical aspects are considered.

Because the IAEA must account for large numbers of item and bulk quantities of nuclear material based on imprecise measurements of these quantities, it has developed procedures for making decisions with information containing statistical uncertainties. These procedures include methods for determining sample sizes and for setting decision thresholds on measured quantities so that anomalies in the observed population are detected with a specified probability. For arms control purposes, these methods could be applied to discriminate between members of the same weapons system having different performance characteristics, where these characteristics are imperfectly observed.

Verification of arms control agreements to reduce or ban the production of plutonium or highly enriched uranium could be supported by a full range of inspection procedures and technologies of the type employed by the IAEA. System analysis studies modeled on those that the IAEA uses to develop safeguards approaches could determine the inspection activities for detecting significant departures from agreed limits on production levels. Non-destructive assay measurements and containment/surveillance devices could provide a technical basis for verifying the correctness of a state's declared production of plutonium or highly enriched uranium.

Technology employed by the IAEA for non-destructive assay of nuclear material may also be applicable to monitoring of agreements that limit deployed nuclear warheads. Among the potential uses of this technology are distinguishing between nuclear and non-nuclear warheads on missiles, or monitoring for presence of nuclear weapons in nuclear-free zones. Further, tamper-protected containment/surveillance devices may be applied for monitoring weapons production and final assembly points.

Finally it shall be mentioned here that in the years 1973 to 1976 there were major studies carried through that analyse the basic means and procedures, the boundary conditions, and the effectiveness of a verification system for Mutual Balanced Force Reduction in Central Europe. These studies which have only been partially published (Häfele (1980)), (Wittekindt (1984)), represent a remarkable effort to apply the principles of accountancy and verification to non-nuclear arms control measures.

6. REFERENCES

Arkin, H. (1974): Handbook of Sampling for Auditing and Accounting McGraw Hill Book Company, 2nd Ed., p. 164, New York

Avenhaus, R. and Jaech, J. (1981): On Subdividing Material Balances in Time and/or Space J. Inst. Nucl. Management 4 (3), pp. 24-33

Avenhaus, R. (1986): Safeguards Systems Analysis. New York

Fichtner, J. (1985): Statistische Tests zur Abschreckung von Fehlverhalten - Eine mathematische Analyse von Überwachungssystemen mit Anwendungen. Dissertation, Universität der Bundeswehr München

Fischer, D.A.V. (1982): Safeguards - A Model for General Arms Control? IAEA Bulletin, Vol. 24, No. 2, pp. 45-49

Häfele, W. (1980): Verifikationssysteme bei einer ausgewogenen Verminderung von Streitkräften in Mitteleuropa. Europa Archiv, Folge 6, pp. 189-200

IAEA (1968): The Agency's Safeguards System (1965, as provisionally extended in 1966 and 1968). INF/CIRC/Rev. 2. Vienna

IAEA (1972): The Structure and Content of Agreements between the Agency and States Required in Connection with the Treaty on the Non-Proliferation of Nuclear Weapons. INF/CIRC/153 (Corrected), International Atomic Energy Agency. Wien

IAEA (1984): Safeguards Techniques and Equipment, INF/5. Wien

Lehmann, E.L. (1959): Testing Statistical Hypotheses. New York

Rogers, D.R., Ed. (1983): Handbook of Nuclear Safeguards Measurement Methods. Washington, D.C.

Stewart, K.B. (1970): A Cost-Effectiveness Approach to Inventory Verification. Proceedings of the IAEA Symposium Safeguards Techniques in Karlsruhe, Vol. II, Vienna, pp. 387-409

Wittekindt, R. (1984): Verification of MBRF-Agreements - A Systems Analysis. In: Quantitative Assessments in Arms Control (Avenhaus and Huber, Eds.). New York, pp. 383-411

VERIFICATION AT THE CROSSROAD

Ernest Gilman*

Operational Research and Analysis Establishment
Department of National Defence, Ottawa

At first glance the present lack of movement in arms control appears to be the result of the significantly differing positions of the West and the East on verification. This view, however, is superficial. A closer look at the issue may indicate that verification is being used to attack the concept of arms control itself.[1]

True, verification is coming under more pressure from new weapon systems with increased covert capabilities. The challenges are being met in many areas by surveillance technology but there will always be some uncertainties; agreements can not be air-tight. Where necessary other means of verification can be used to obtain mutually acceptable arms control agreements; the most obvious being on-site inspection (OSI). The primary goal remains the enhancement of verification so that the arms control process can help to prevent an all out arms race.[2]

---

* The views expressed by the author in this essay do not necessarily represent those of the Canadian Government.

1) For views questioning the concept of arms control see: Malcolm Walop, "Soviet Violations of Arms Control Agreements: So What?" Strategic Review, 11:3 (Summer 1983); Amron Katz, Verification and SALT: The State of the Art and the Art of the State (Washington, D.C.: Heritage Foundation, 1979); and Richard N. Perle, "What is Adequate Verification?" in Gordon Humphrey et al., SALT II and American Security (Cambridge, Mass.: Institute for Foreign Policy and Analysis, 1980).

2) For the most recent comprehensive look at verification, see: William C. Potter (ed.), Verification and Arms Control (Lexington, Mass.: Lexington Books/D.C. Heath and Company, 1985). The eleven chapters of this volume cover a wide range of topics with emphasis on the political and technical aspects of the issue.

NATO ASI Series, Vol. F 26
Modelling and Analysis in Arms Control
Edited by R. Avenhaus et al.

It is still political insecurity that has created the present mistrust so obvious in international relations. The problem is not technical issues related to arms control. History records that SALT II was abandoned principally because of the military behaviour of the USSR in the Third World (who remembers the Soviet brigade in Cuba?), particularly in Afghanistan. The loss of US monitoring facilities in Iran caused some serious worries, but alternatives were found within a very short time.

1. THE POLITICS OF VERIFICATION

Verification has come under attack in the US predominantly from those who believe that arms control restricts the development of technology required by the West to maintain its security responsibilities. The issue is, therefore, a political one. Past US administrations, liberal Democratic and conservative Republican, accepted the concept of 'adequate verification' because the monitoring equipment available was believed to be capable of detecting cheating of military significance.[3] The present government, however, has not accepted this view. It calls for 'effective verification', although never defined, appears to indicate a need for absolute confidence. Such a state of affairs in international relations has never been attained, even amongst the closest of allies, including Roosevelt's America and Churchill's Britain during the Second World War.

Those sceptical of the arms control process have been strengthened by Washington's accusations of Soviet cheating. Most of the serious charges were not new, but because of the poor state of relations between Washington and Moscow

---

3) Perle.

they were heard by a wider, more receptive audience. As a consequence the arms control debate has become increasingly politicized and the public's confidence in arms control has been eroded. Even more so, the public's view has been influenced by the linkage issue - the linking of arms control to both the dismal human rights record of the Soviet Union and its military activities in the Third World.

2. THE NEW TECHNOLOGICAL CHALLENGES

The future of traditional arms control has been placed in doubt by the view that the monitoring capabilities of National Technical Means (NTMs) to verify a treaty at an acceptable level are progressively deteriorating. Satellites, usually photographic and electronic reconnaissance and early warning, are the primary monitoring devices. These are supplemented by radar and optical equipped reconnaissance aircraft, such as the modified American U-2 and SR-71 which operate close to the Soviet borders. In addition there are remote sensing equipment and ground-based electronic listening posts. Besides those in the US and the USSR the Americans rely on sites in China, Turkey and Australia, and the giant over-the-horizon backscatter radars, such as the Cobra Dane facility in the Aleutians, about 700 km distant from the impact zone of the major Soviet ICBM test range. In the same region are also surface ships which collect telemetry signals and possess Cobra Jane radars for tracking.

The technology of arms control verification has been impressive and it continues to move forward. Nevertheless, satellites, which until now were the primary tools of verification, are coming under increasing scrutiny. No doubt fanned by growing political suspicions, questions are now being asked about the capability to survey the entire 5.7 million km^2 of the Soviet Union. Even with maximum coverage of only designated target areas, demands on American photo-analysts are thought to be unmanageable. Weather appears to be another inhibiting factor, as satellites are not entirely reliable for seeing through darkness or clouds which cover a large part of Europe for long periods of time.

NTMs have other possible weaknesses. These include equipment failure, possibly affecting the quality of image resolution or data recovery; the contour of the land, which may distort the distance of a potential target; the regularity of coverage and the likelihood of missing a conceivably important indicator which occurs only periodically. Furthermore, it appears that NTMs will have little success in monitoring those areas of civil technology which may be used for military purposes, such as advanced uranium enrichment technologies, and later, inertial confinement fusion which may breed fissile materials.

So far the verification of the major arms control agreements have been relatively easy because the delivery systems of nuclear weapons and their characteristics are quite distinct. Extensive ICBM silo complexes cannot be hidden. They not only include the conspicuous missiles but, amongst other related signs, are large numbers of security and technical personnel, railroads and access routes. Test sites are familiar. Furthermore, the development of a weapon has usually taken about ten years, time enough for it to be well documented by observers.[4]

In the future, however, nuclear and other arms control will be more difficult to obtain. In addition to the present limitations on verification, those anticipated for the future, particularly dealing with missiles, include versatility, concealment, mobility, diversity, quantity and

4) William C. Potter (ed.), Verification and SALT: The Challenge of Strategic Deception (Boulder, Colorado: Westview Press, 1980).

testing obscurity. As a consequence the traditional approach to monitoring agreements will have to be changed.

Weapons are becoming increasingly versatile. Some missiles, like the cruise, will have dual capabilities, delivering conventional or nuclear warheads. There will be weapons built for conversion from conventional to nuclear, and from one yield to another. It is also becoming easier to conceal weapons. The trend toward miniaturization and micro-miniaturization of weapon systems and the advances in stealth technology will make monitoring even more difficult. Weapons are likely to become so small that they will be able to be stored in undistinguishable depots which will not attract attention and surveillance.

Weapon systems, notably ICBMs and IRBMs, are expected to increasingly become mobile. This will occur not only because of miniaturization but as a result of advances in encapsulization, remote control navigation and the ability to separate components of a weapon system unit. As a consequence it will be more difficult to monitor such weapons and to judge whether they are operationally capable at any specific time.

The cruise missile is unique, and, therefore, a problem in terms of verifying an agreement to ban or limit the weapon. It is mobile and concealable. It can be launched from the air, land or sea. In time its range and speed will probably be increased.

The Submarine Launched Cruise Missile (SLCM) will be a primary obstacle to verification.[5] Both conventional and nuclear weapons can be mixed and they can be placed in

---

5) Milton Leitenberg, "The Genesis of the LRTNF Issue in NATO", in Bo Huldt and Atis Lejins (eds.), The Military Balance (Stockholm: Swedish Institute of International Affairs, 1982).

torpedo tubes of submarines or on modern warships. As a result of miniaturization for example, the sea-launched Tomahawk, which is 6.3 m long and 53.3 cm in diameter, is small enough to be produced in such large numbers as to have a significant reload capacity. Unlike ballistic missiles, the cruise does not require lengthy and elaborate testing which can be monitored for essential information. In addition, test ranges are relatively shorter, experiments can be done in piecemeal fashion and to some degree, in the laboratory.

3. VERIFICATION ADVANCES

In spite of serious problems the utility of NTMs to verify future arms control agreements may not be as bleak as some believe. Once opposed to the use of NTMs for verification purposes, Moscow now contends that this technology is not being fully utilized. Washington claims otherwise, and continues to press for increased on-site inspections. In this situation the Soviets may be exhibiting their traditional view on secrecy and, or, giving too much credit to American technology. The recent reports by Washington on non-compliance, on the deployment of SS-20s and the storing of chemicals in Eastern Europe could, however, be interpreted as evidence of the superior capabilities of the American NTMs.

Surveillance technology has indeed made significant gains in recent years.[6] For example, computer processing has led to the enhancement of visual images, while thermal-imaging sensors can penetrate through camouflage and

---

6) James Bamford, "America's Supersecret Eyes in Space," The New York Times Magazine, January 13, 1985; David Hafemeister, Joseph J. Roman and Kosta Tsipis, "The Verification of Compliance with Arms Control Agreements," Scientific American, 252:3 (March 1985); G.M. Steinberg, Satellite Reconnaissance: The Role of Informal Bargaining (New York: Praeger, 1983); and Potter.

darkness. Such technical progress, and the anticipated deployment of more photo-reconnaissance satellites to survey the Soviet Union should markedly increase the chances of detecting violations. This should strengthen at least the deterrent aspect of verification. It is inevitable that NTM technology will make even more significant advances in the future, possibly as a consequence of the space programme, but also if political decisions are made to put additional resources specifically into this area.

The monitoring of some arms control agreeements, for example, should become more manageable because of crucial improvements in seismic and acoustic detection.[7] Nevertheless American officials continue to claim that NTMs cannot properly verify a comprehensive test ban (CTB) treaty. It appears that the uncertainties held for twenty years remain: whether or not low yields can be detected and, more importantly, could decoupling (that is, the explosion of a nuclear device in a mined out cavity) be concealed? Nevertheless, since the superpowers acknowledged in principle the use of black boxes (tamper-proof remotely monitorable devices), and the establishment of national seismic stations, interest in using this technology has grown.

4. BEYOND NTMs

There is no doubt that on-site inspection (OSI) is a necessary mutual component to NTMs for proper verification.[8]

---

7) Swedish National Defence Research Institute (FOA), Seismology 1983, Nuclear Test Ban Verification, Earthquake and Earth Resource Investigation, 4th yearly report C-2537-T1, Stockholm, May 1984; W.J. Hannon, "Seismic Verification of a Comprehensive Test Ban", Science, 227:4684 (January 18, 1985); "Letters: Verification of Nuclear Testing", Science, 228:4701 (May 17, 1985); and L.R. Sykes and J.F. Evernden, "Verification of a Comprehensive Nuclear Test Ban", Scientific American, 247:47 (October 1982).

The issue, however, is to what degree and under what circumstances must it be applied. We are only in the early stages of the development of OSI because of the long-standing opposition to it coming primarily, but not solely, from the East. OSI has not been popular because it is seen as intrusive and, therefore, a threat to national sovereignty and security.

OSI will have to help in meeting the new technical challenges to arms control. Possibly of more importance, however, is the role it could play in breaking the vicious cycle of psychological insecurity. A recent experiment at the US Chemical Agency Destruction facility at Tooele, Utah, for example, successfully showed an international audience how OSI monitoring of a CW treaty could be achieved with little intrusiveness. Furthermore, the mutually arranged on-site inspections carried out by the IAEA to prevent nuclear proliferation have not eroded sovereignty. In fact, such practices should strengthen agreements which will move us further away from conflict, thereby increasing the security of nations.

Until recently cooperative measures were seen as unique and temporary arrangements, even though some were included in the SALT I Agreement. However, because of doubts about NTM capabilities, Moscow was asked shortly after President Reagan was elected to accept measures which would reduce the chances of either side successfully concealing weapons or supplying disinformation. In July 1981 the head of ACDA, Eugene V. Rostow, told the Senate Committee on Armed

---

8) James R. Blaker, "On-Site Inspections: The Military Significance of an Arms-Control Proposal", Survival, 26:3 (May/June 1984); Karl Pieragostini, "Cooperative Verification", Arms Control Today, 13:5 (June 1983); and Wolfgang K.H. Panofsky, "On-Site Inspection: Cliché or Reality", Loeb Lectures No. 3, Harvard University, March 1983.

Services that the Soviet attitude toward cooperative measures may be a good indication of how serious they took arms control. Rostow was somewhat optimistic as he believed that the Soviets had, in fact, already accepted in principle the idea of cooperative measures.[9]

It appears that both sides agreed in START to try to save those parts of SALT II (also incorporated in other treaties) which would assist NTMs in verifying future agreements. While this was a postive move, ratification of SALT II would have actually moved the Soviets close to recognizing cooperative measures in international legal terms. Most of what was accepted in SALT II was in the first strategic agreement, but changes were made because of experience in this and other areas of arms control, and in order to meet future challenges.

5. THE VIEW FROM MOSCOW

The Soviets consistently claimed that verification was just an excuse for spying until the signing of SALT I.[10] Since then Moscow has clearly altered its view on the usefulness of satellites for world peace. Recently there have been signs of some sort of begrudging acceptance of on-site inspection. Overall, however, the Soviets still exhibit a strong sense of suspicion of surveillance of any sort.

---

9) "An Interview with Eugene V. Rostow", National Defense, 66:377 (April 1982).

10) Stuart A. Cohen, "SALT Verification: The Evolution of Soviet Views and Their Meaning for the Future", Orbis, 24:3 (Fall, 1980); and R. Zheleznov, "Monitoring Arms Limitation Measures", International Affairs, Moscow, (July 1982).

Soviet attitudes toward verification of arms control in the nuclear era have been shaped to a large degree by the Open Skies proposal of 1955.[11] It has been revealed that President Eisenhower genuinely wanted to reduce the chances of surprise attack in Europe, contrary to Moscow's suspicions. Nevertheless, Soviet apprehensions were not entirely unfounded as the President's advisers did see this as a good way of spying on the Russians. Ironically, Moscow's refusal to be monitored led to an overestimation of the Soviet missile force by the Americans, who then began unprecedented peacetime military expenditures. The missile-gap claim of the Kennedy Administration was only proven false after the first US photo-reconnaissance satellite was able to give a more accurate view of the situation. It was, however, too late to stop the development of some major US weapons projects.

The Soviet penchant for military secrecy continues, but in the past few years there have been indications of change. Moscow has agreed to some form of OSI for a comprehensive test ban treaty and a peaceful nuclear explosion treaty. The latter, however, remains unratified and talks on both treaties have been suspended by Washington. Not too long ago the Soviets agreed to OSI of specific civilian nuclear facilities by the IAEA, something already agreed to by the UK, the US and France. In addition the Soviets acknowledged at the Geneva-based Conference on Disarmament (CD) in 1983, that some degree of OSI would be needed to verify a chemical weapons treaty. Recently the new Soviet leader, Mikhail Gorbachev, has referred to "reasonable verification!"

---

11) W.W. Rostow, <u>Open Skies: Eisenhower's Proposal of July 21, 1955</u> (Austin: University of Texas Press, 1983).

6. CONCLUDING REMARKS

The information released recently on Soviet arms control violations and the deployment of SS-20s and of chemical weapons in Eastern Europe appears to be at odds with the claims of decreasing NTM capabilities to monitor arms control agreements. If the technical problems are as large as some believe then, logically, the concept of deterrence may also be challenged.[12] Is it, in fact, becoming more difficult to evaluate the strength of opposing strategic forces? The weakening of these intelligence gathering sources could create instability and the serious erosion of deterrence. Furthermore a decline in NTM capabilities may weaken the effectiveness of any strategic defensive system, expected to rely so heavily on satellites.

The superpowers will need to create a close working relationship in the arms control field if the technical challenges of the future are to be properly confronted. If arms control is to be taken seriously it cannot continue to be used as a political tool. The process should be ongoing and the foundations strong enough to be built upon. Cooperative verification, including increased on-site inspection, is imperative to meet new technological challenges. Further research is also necessary, particularly in the area of surveillance technology.

There is no doubt that it will be more difficult in the future to verify arms control agreements. Nevertheless, the technical problems will be easier to confront if the political will is present and new approaches are contemplated. More attention in arms control must be paid first to the possibility of banning future categories of weapons, then to the development and production stages, rather than

---

12) D. Ball, "Targeting for Strategic Deterrence", Adelphi Paper No. 185 (London: IISS, 1983).

to testing and deployment. Overall, each problem should be dealt with individually, including the particular level of verification needed to support an arms control treaty which a nation would be more secure with, than without.

WORKSHOP PARTICIPANTS

Albers, W.	University Bielefeld, FRG
Avenhaus, R.	Federal Armed Forces University Munich, FRG
Bode, J.R.	Braddock, Dunn and McDonald (BDM), Albuquerque, NM, USA
Bracken, J.	Institute for Defense Analyses (IDA), Alexandria, VA, USA
Bracken, P.	Yale University, New Haven, CT, USA
Brams, S.J.	New York University, New York, NY, USA
Brown, S.	Harvard University, Cambridge, MA, USA
Buzacott, J.A.	University of Waterloo, Canada
Cleminson, F.R.	Department of External Affairs, Ottawa, Canada
Collingridge, D.	University of Aston, Birmingham, UK
Din, A.M.	Stockholm International Peace Research Institute (SIPRI), Solna, Sweden
Dompke, U.	Federal Armed Forces University Munich, FRG
Fichtner, J.	Federal Armed Forces University Munich, FRG
Fraser, N.	University of Waterloo, Canada
Gibson, J.W.	Sevenoaks, Kent, UK
Gilman, E.	Department of National Defence, Ottawa, Canada
Gold, S.P.	Department of Defense, Washington, D.C., USA
Gori, U.	University of Florence, Italy
Gündogdu, H.	Marmara Institute, Gebze, Turkey
Güth, W.	University of Cologne, FRG
Huber, R.K.	Federal Armed Forces University Munich, FRG
Jeanclos, Y.	University of Strasbourg III, France
Jenkins, F.	Science Applications International Corporation (SAIC), McLean, VA, USA
Jones, D.W.	University of Bradford, UK
Kettelle, J.D.	Ketron, Inc., Arlington, VA, USA
Kilgour, D.M.	Wilfried Laurier University, Waterloo, Canada
Lieberman, A.	United States Arms Control and Disarmament Agency (ACDA) Washington, D.C., USA
Machado-Jorge, H.	Junta Nacional de Investigação Científica e Technológica (JNICT), Lisbon, Portugal
Markin, J.T.	Los Alamos National Laboratory, Los Alamos, NM, USA
Paldy, L.G.	State University of New York at Stony Brook, USA

Pastijn, H.	Royal Military Academy, Brussels, Belgium
Prins, G.	Emmanuel College, University of Cambridge, UK
ReVelle, Ch.	Johns Hopkins University, Baltimore, MD, USA
Rudnianski, M.	University of Paris VII, France
Rühl, L.	Ministry of Defence, Bonn, FRG
Saaty, T.L.	University of Pittsburgh, PA, USA
Sauder, A.	University of Strasbourg III, France
Schmidt, Ch.	University of Paris IX, France
Struys, W.	Royal Military Academy, Brussels, Belgium

ABOUT THE AUTHORS

WULF ALBERS

is Professor of Economics at the Institute for Mathematical Economics of the University of Bielefeld, Germany. Prior to his academic appointment in 1978, he was Research Assistant at the Faculty of Economics and Social Sciences of the University of Augsburg, Germany. His fields of research are limited rational behavior in bargaining and economic decision making, mathematical game theory, experimental games, experimental economics and international negotiations.

Dr. Albers was born in 1943. He studied Mathematics and Physics at the University of Kiel, where he obtained his doctorate in 1972. In 1978 he got the Venia Legendi (Habilitation) in Mathematical Methods of Economic and Social Sciences from the University of Augsburg.

RUDOLF AVENHAUS

is Professor of Statistics and Operations Research at the German Armed Forces University Munich. Prior to his academic appointment in 1980, he was Research Assistant at Mathematics and Physics Institutes of the Universities of Karlsruhe, Germany, and Geneva, Switzerland, and he was Research Scholar at the Nuclear Research Center Karlsruhe. In between, from 1973 to 1975 and again in 1980, he worked at the International Institute for Applied Systems Analysis (IIASA), Laxenburg near Vienna, Austria. He is the author of numerous papers on mathematical problems in solid state physics, statistics and its application to nuclear problems, especially nuclear material safeguards; he is author of the books "Material Accountability - Theory, Verification, Applications" (Wiley 1977) and "Safeguards Systems Analysis" (Plenum 1986), and co-editor of the book "Mathematical and Statistical Methods in Nuclear Safeguards" (Harwood 1982). From 1982 to 1983, he was elected council member of the German Peace and Conflict Research Society (DGFK).

Dr. Avenhaus was born in Zwickau, Germany in 1938. He studied Mathematics and Physics at the University of Munich, where he was awarded his diploma in

1964. He obtained his doctorate in 1967 from the University of Karlsruhe and in 1975 his Venia Legendi (Habilitation) in Statistics from the University of Mannheim, Germany.

JOHN R. BODE

is the Vice President and General Manager, National Defense Architectures with The BDM Corporation. He has twenty-five years professional experience in military research, development, operations, and analysis spanning tactical and strategic forces. Currently, he leads a study group developing strategic force architecture concepts to integrate offensive force modernization programs, potential defensive options, and arms control initiatives. He has provided analyses in the strategic area for the National Security Council, Army Contracting and Development Agency, Defense Nuclear Agency, Lawrence Livermore National Laboratories, Under Secretary for Research, Development, and Engineering, and National Aeronautical Space Administration. He pioneered development of a new generation of combat simulations, which differ from classical models in their treatment of maneuvers, decision making, C^3I, weapons systems, tactics and doctrine at a level of realism meaningful to operational commanders. He directed Strategic Defense Initiative research efforts by BDM in the areas of directed energy weapons, optics, fire control, damage and vulnerability, and simulation.

JEROME BRACKEN

is a research staff member of the Institute for Defense Analyses in Alexandria, Virginia. Prior to joining IDA in 1967 he was with the Research Analysis Corporation and The George Washington University Logistics Research Project. He received the B.S. in Civil Engineering from Carnegie Institute of Technology, Master of Engineering Administration from The George Washington University, and Doctor of Business Administration from Harvard University.

Dr. Bracken is the Area Editor for Defense and International Security of the journal *Operations Research*. He is the author or co-author of three books and of 30 articles in *Operations Research, Naval Research Logistics Quarterly, Management Science* and other journals, and of technical reports on a wide variety of topics in defense analysis.

PAUL BRACKEN

is Professor of Public Policy at Yale University. Prior to his academic appointment in 1982, he was associated with the Hudson Institute for nine years working on problems of strategic policy, arms control, and non-defense areas of public policy. Before joining Hudson Institute he was employed at Ketron Inc, Arlington, Virginia where he worked in the field of military operations research and systems analysis.

Dr. Bracken was born in Philadelphia, Penn. He has a B.S. from Columbia University in Applied Mathematics and a Ph.D in Operations Research from Yale University.

STEVEN J. BRAMS

is Professor of Politics at New York University. He is a graduate of the Massachusetts Institute of Technology and received a Ph.D in political science from Northwestern University. He has taught at a number of institutions, including the University of Rochester, Syracuse University, the University of California, Irvine, and the Institute for Advanced Studies, Vienna. Prior to his academic career, he was a research associate at the Institute for Defense Analyses and worked in the Office of the Secretary of Defense.

Dr. Brams received a Guggenheim Fellowship in 1986-87 for research on game theory and national security, which is also supported by the National Science Foundation and the Sloan Foundation. He is the author or coauthor of eight books, the most recent of which are Rational Politics: Decisions, Games, and Strategy (1985), Superpower Games: Applying Game Theory to Superpower Conflict (1985), Superior Beings: If They Exist, How Would We Know? Game-Theoretic Implications of Omniscience, Omnipotence, Immortality, and Incomprehensibility (1983), and, with Peter C. Fishburn, Approval Voting (1983).

SCOTT BROWN

is Associate Director at the Harvard Negotiation Project of Harvard Law School, Harvard University, where he directs the project activities related to U.S.-Soviet relations. In particular, the Negotiation Project is conducting research to develop theory and mechanism for improving the efficiency of U.S.-Soviet negotiations.

Mr. Brown was born in Toledo, Ohio. He graduated from Dartmouth College in 1978 and Harvard Law School in 1982.

F. RONALD CLEMINSON

is an active Lieutenant Colonel in the Canadian Armed Forces currently serving in a research and advisory position with the Arms Control and Disarmament Division of the Department of External Affairs. He assumed his present position in 1979. Prior to that he served with the Royal Canadian Air Force and the Canadian Armed Forces in a variety of operational and staff appointments in Canada, the United States and Europe.

Col. Cleminson holds a BA (Geography) from the University of Western Ontario (1954) and a MA (Government and Politics) from the University of Maryland (1967). He is a graduate of the Canadian Forces College (PFSC 1967) and the NATO Defense College (NADC 1974).

ALLAN M. DIN

is a Danish citizen and graduated in physics and mathematics from the Niels Bohr Institute, University of Copenhagen in 1968. He is a docent of theoretical physics at the University of Gothenburg, Sweden and has held positions at the European Centre for Nuclear Research (CERN), Geneva and at the University of Lausanne.

He was scientific director of the Geneva International Peace Research Institute, 1982-83 and is presently a Senior Research Fellow at the Stockholm International Peace Research Institute (SIPRI).

JOHN FICHTNER

is Research Assistant at the Institute of Applied Systems and Operations Research of the Computer Science Department of the German Armed Forces University Munich.

Dr. Fichtner was born in Trostberg, Germany. In 1981 he graduated from the University of Munich with a degree in mathematics and physics and he obtained his doctorate at the German Armed Forces University in 1985. His research interests include applied mathematical statistics, decision making methods and the application of mathematical methods to arms control problems.

JOHN W. GIBSON

is a retired British and NATO civil servant engaged in occasional consultant activities. He is a mathematical statistician by discipline; he was commissional in the Royal Navy from 1942-46, following which he completed his studies at the University of Sheffield and University College London.

Mr. Gibson developed his early career in research, development and analysis in the British Ministry of Defence (MOD). He was Assistant Chief Scientific Advisor (Studies) in the MOD from 1969-74, Under-Secretary (Science and Technology) in the British Cabinet Office from 1974-77, and Chief Operations Research at the SHAPE Technical Centre from 1977-84.

ERNEST GILMAN

has been a strategic analyst at the Operational Research and Analysis Establishment of the Canadian Department of National Defence in Ottawa since 1973. Prior to taking this appointment he was a member of the history department at the Royal Military College of Canada. Amongst other academic institutions he has attended the NATO Defense College and the Department of War Studies, King's College at the University of London, where he successfully defended a doctoral thesis in international history.

SYDELL P. GOLD

is Deputy for Strategic Requirements, Office of the Assistant Secretary of the Air Force for Research, Development and Logistics. She is responsible for initiating, directing, evaluating and coordinating programs, policies and analyses in the research, development, acquisition and utilization of strategic systems and in the arms control arena.

Prior to accepting her current position in November 1982, Dr. Gold was a member of the professional staff of the National Security Council. While there she was responsible for formulating and implementing measures pertaining to our nuclear weapons program, in areas such as special nuclear materials, underground testing, the stockpile, safety and security. She also addressed strategic offensive and defensive system issues, non-proliferation matters, weapon-related technologies, and arms control issues.

Dr. Gold was an applied mathematican and systems analyst at Sandia Laboratories in Albuquerque, New Mexico and Livermore, California from 1962-1967, and at Lawrence Livermore National Laboratory, Livermore, California from 1974 to 1980. She analyzed options for strategic weapons research and development, ICBM effectiveness and warhead and basing options, ballistic missile defense, nuclear test ban treaty and strategic arms limitations issues.

She earned an A.B. from Barnard College, an M.S. from the University of New Mexico and a PhD from the University of California, Berkeley, all in mathematics. She has published or co-authored numerous articles on strategic issues, nuclear weapons and special nuclear materials.

UMBERTO GORI

is Professor of International Relations at the Department of Political Sciences "G. Alfieri" and Director of the Institute of Political Sciences of the University of Florence. Prior to his academic appointment he was Assistent Professor of International Law at the Universities of Rome and Mocerata, Deputy Director of the Italian Society for International Organization, and Lecturer at the Diplomatic Institute of Ministry of Foreign Affairs in Rome.

Born in 1932, Dr. Gori is an Italian citizen. He is author of many scientific papers and books (E.g. Relazioni Internationali: Metodi e Tecniche die Analisi (1973), Natura ed Orientamenti delle Ricerche sulla Pace (1978), Analisi dei Sistemi e Decisioni Politiche (1979), Tecniche Analitiche per le Decisioni Politiche ed Economiche (1980), Strategia e Scienze Sociali (1984), L'Analisi del Rischia Politica (1985)) and Editor of "Progretto Pace", a Quarterly on Peace Research.

WERNER GÜTH

is Professor of Economics at the University of Cologne since 1977. He graduated at the University of Münster (1970) where he also received his doctoral degree in 1972. He was a research scholar at Yale University (1974) and at the University of California, Berkeley (1975). In 1981 and 1982 he was with the International Institute for Applied Systems Analysis (IIASA) in Laxenburg, Austria. A sabbatical semester in 1983 he spent at the Hebrew University in Jerusalem and at Standford University. Since 1985 Güth is the German representative in the Board of IAREP (the International Association for Research in Economic Psychology).

Dr. Güth's main area of research is the theory of strategic games, its application to the social sciences and experimental studies of social decision problems. Most of his publications fall into this area.

REINER K. HUBER

is full Professor of Applied Systems Science at the German Armed Forces University Munich where he was elected Dean of the Computer Science department for the period 1981-1982.

Prior to his academic appointment in 1975, he spent 12 years with West Germany's principle defense research establishment IABG in Ottobrunn, eventually as Head of the Defense Systems Studies Division. He has been a Visiting Professor at the Naval Postgraduate School in Monterey, California (1979 and 1983) and a Visiting Lecturer at the Korea Institute for Defense Analyses (KIDA) in Seoul (1980). From 1971 to 1976 he was a member of the NATO Science Committee's Panel on Operations Research and the Special Programme Panel on Systems Science, from 1981-1982 a consulting member of the German Ministry of Defense Commission on Long-term Defense Planning. He is a charter member of the German Strategy Forum (DSF) and The Military Conflict Institute and author of numerous papers on military systems analysis and defense planning and editor of nine books. He chaired the scientific conferences on "Modelling Land Battle Systems for Military Planning" (Ottobrunn 1974), "Modelling and Analysis of Defense Processes" (Brussels 1982) and "Modelling and Analysis of Arms Control Problems" (Spitzingsee 1985). Current research interests include theory and modelling of military conflict, assessment of force equilibria and their stability, and command and control models and systems.

Dr. Huber was born in Weimar, Germany, 25 September 1935. From 1954 to 1960 he studied mechanical, aeronautical and industrial engineering at the Technical University Munich and the University of Texas. He obtained his doctorate in 1970 from the Technical University Munich. He served in the German Air Force from 1960-1963 and is currently in the GAF Reserve as a Colonel.

FRANK JENKINS

is Director of the Center for National Security Negotiations at Science Applications International Corporation in McLean, Virginia. He has been in his present position from 1982, concentrating on defense and strategic policy issues. Prior to joining SAIC, he was Chief of the International Negotiations

Division of the Joint Chiefs of Staff as a Colonel in the United States Air Force. Colonel Jenkins has been a member of numerous arms control delegations to Geneva and Moscow. He is the author of several scientific and technical papers and has lectured on such subjects as arms control, nuclear policy, and strategic defenses at, amongst others, universities, the International Institute for Strategic Studies, the Royal United Services Institute and the Military Operations Research Society.

Colonel Jenkins holds a BA from Syracuse University and an MSA from George Washington University. He is a graduate of the Air War College and the Industrial College of the Armed Forces.

DERRY W. JONES

is an honorary professorial fellow at Bradford University, where he has been a Lecturer, Reader and Professor of Applied Structural Chemistry. His researches have involved mainly X-ray and neutron diffraction (at Grenoble, Harwell, etc.) and NMR spectroscopy; they have led to over 150 papers covering mainly structure and spectroscopy of carcinogens, fuel extracts, polymers etc. During long service in the British Territorial (reserve) Army (TA), for which he was awarded ERD and TD, Professor Jones spent 10 years as Lieut. Col. in a section concerned with operational research.

Professor Jones was born in Hull, England, and holds the degrees of B.Sc. (Manchester) in Physics and Chemistry, Ph.D. (Leeds) in Chemical Crystallography and D.Sc. (Bradford) in Polymer Structure; he is both a Chartered Chemist and a Chartered Physicist.

JOHN D. KETTELLE

is President and founder of Ketron, Inc., a company primarily engaged in the application of quantitative analytical techniques to the problems of government and industry. He is a graduate of Harvard College (A.B. in Physics, 1945) and Brown University (Sc. M. in Mathematics, 1949). After working as a researcher for the Geophysics Department of Columbia University, Mr. Kettelle served as a submarine officer during the Korean war. In 1953 he joined Arthur D. Little, Inc. and in 1957 Borroughs Corporation as an operations research analyst. In 1958 he and Dr. D.H. Wagner formed a partnership providing services in military and industrial operations research. In

1963, this led to the formation of Kettelle Associates which has since become Kappa Systems, Inc.. In 1970, he founded Ketron, Inc., which now has a staff of 350 employees and 40 active consultants.

Mr. Kettelle's professional experience has been primarily in the area of operations research for industry, government, and the military. For the latter, his work has been in the areas of decision theory, surveillance and tactical analysis. Presently, his professional interests focus on the analysis and modelling of conflict termination and negotiations. He is the author of numerous professional papers and the editor of monographs published by the Military Applications Section of the Operations Research Society of America. For the latter, he has served as chairman of the Philadelphia Chapter and has been program chairman for one national meeting. He is presently chairman of the Committee for Ethics and Professional Practice, and chairman of the Military Applications Section. He has been a director and vice-president of the Military Operations Research Society. He is a Director of the Council of Professional Service Firms.

D. MARC KILGOUR

received three degrees from the University of Toronto: a B.A.Sc. in Engineering Physics in 1968, an M.Sc. in Applied Mathematics in 1969, and a Ph.D. in Mathematics in 1973. He is currently Professor and Chairman of Mathematics at Wilfrid Laurier University in Waterloo, Canada, as well as Adjunct Professor of Systems Design Engineering at the nearby University of Waterloo. His interests, in both research and consulting, center on game theory and the application of mathematics to conflict modeling, but also encompass many other problems involving mathematical models. His research is supported by both the Natural Sciences and Engineering Research Council of Canada and the Social Sciences and Humanities Research Council of Canada. He has published in journals covering a wide variety of disciplines, including engineering, mathematics, political science, economics, philosophy, and biology. He is co-author, with T. J. Levesque, of the paper which won the Duncan Black Award for the best paper in the 1984 volume of the journal Public Choice.

ALFRED LIEBERMAN

is Chief, Office of Operations Analysis, U.S. Arms Control and Disarmament Agency. In this position, he is the senior advisor to the Director of the

Arms Control Agency on issues involving quantitative analyses. His principal areas of work at ACDA have been the Strategic Arms Reduction Talks (START), the INF and SALT negotiations, and Nuclear Test Limitations. He has been with ACDA since 1963.

Previous positions include work on national defense issues as a Senior Analyst at the Institute for Defense Analyses (IDA) between 1958 and 1961. He was a Mathematical Statistician working on the design and analysis of naval tests for the Bureau of Ships from 1956 to 1958. He was associated with the development of the Titan missile system with the AVCO Corporation in 1955 and 1956. Prior to this Mr. Lieberman was involved in research on biological warfare at Ft. Dietrick from 1952 to 1955.

Mr. Lieberman graduated the City College of New York with a degree in mathematical statistics and obtained a master's degree at the University of Southern California and did further graduate work at American University. He served in the U.S. Army from 1944 to 1946.

JACK T. MARKIN

is Deputy Group Leader in the Safeguards Systems Group at Los Alamos National Laboratory. His recent interests have been in the applications of mathematics and statistics to improving the effectiveness of domestic and international safeguards.

Past experience includes system analysis studies of the employment of strategic nuclear weapons systems.

Dr. Markin holds a BS (mathematics) from Indiana University, and a Ph.D. (mathematics) from the University of Southern California.

GWYN PRINS

is a Fellow and the Director of Studies in History at Emmanuel College, University of Cambridge. He teaches Modern History and International Affairs in the University. He also directs the University's extra-mural teaching in these fields. This includes the University's collaboration with the British Armed Forces, in which he is active.

Dr. Prins is a graduate of the University of Cambridge, from which he also holds his doctorate. He is a Fellow of the Royal Historical Society. He has written, lectured and broadcast extensively on the dynamics of the nuclear arms race. He is also engaged in issues of the North/South divide. He is a British member of the Pugwash Conferences Workshop on Conventional Forces in Europe.

CHARLES REVELLE

is Professor at The Johns Hopkins University in Baltimore, Maryland. He teaches in the University's Program in Systems Analysis and Economics for Public Decision Making and is Coordinator of the Operations Research Group at the University. His special field is mathematical optimization with emphasis on the development of new public sector applications of optimization.

He is the author of more than 75 papers applying optimization to scientific and engineering topics. The topics of his research include arms control, facility location, network design, water resources, water quality management, epidemic and population management. With his wife Penelope, he is author of The Environment, Issues and Choices for Society (2nd Edition, The Willard Grant Press).

Dr. ReVelle hold bachelors and doctoral degrees from Cornell University.

HUGO PASTIJN

is Professor of Operations Research and Statistics at the Royal Military Academy, of Decision Support Methodology at the Staff College for Military Administrators in Brussels, and Director of the Centre for Computer Science at the Royal Military Academy. He has published several papers in Operations Research, Management Science and Applied Statistics and is a Lt. Colonel in the Belgian Engineers Reserve Forces.

LOTHAR RÜHL

As Secretary of State in the German Federal Ministry of Defense, Dr. Rühl is the senior advisor to the defense minister on all issues of security policy. He is author of several books (e.g. Machtpolitik und Friedensstrategie (1974), Rußlands Weg zur Weltmacht (1981), and of numerous contributions to collected works.

Born in 1927 in Cologne/Germany, Dr. Rühl studied law and political science in Bonn und Paris and obtained a doctorate in political science from Sorbonne University, Paris in 1971. In journalism from 1949 - 1981, he was, among others, a political correspondent in Bonn and Paris, deputy chief editor of the German daily "Die Welt", and special correspondent and head of the ZDF TV team in Brussels. He was appointed Deputy Spokesman of the German Federal Government in 1981 and to his present position in 1982. In 1986 he obtained the Venia Legendi (Habilitation) from the Department of Economic and Social Sciences of the University of Cologne, Germany.

STEPHEN E. SCHODERBEK

has performed defense analysis since 1960, when he was a member of the Air Force team which first brought avionics systems with production reliability requirements into the DOD inventory. During tours of duty at the USAF Academy and the Air War College, he conducted numerous economic analyses, among which were various officer accession programs, base functional realignments, and DOD recruiting policies and programs. He lectured extensively from 1965 until 1979 on national defense economic issues at the Defense Weapons Systems Management School, Armed Forces Staff College, and the Air War College. After completion of his Air Force career, he joined The BDM Corporation, where his principal interests turned to space weapon analysis. He contributed to, and directed, the development of operational concepts for space-based lasers, design of scenarios for applications of these weapons, evaluations of the effectiveness of directed energy weapons, X-ray lasers, and life-cycle-cost modeling and analysis for three major Air Force space weapon application studies. Presently, he works as a national security consultant for several corporations.

WALLY STRUYS

is Professor of Economics at the Royal Military Academy and the Staff College for Military Administrators in Brussels. He obtained his doctorate in 1977 with a treatise on Defense Economics and has published several papers in this field. He is founding member of the European Association of Defense Economists, and a Lt. Colonel of the Belgian Logistical Reserve Forces.

INDEX

NATO ASI Series F

NATO ASI Series F

Vol. 23: Designing Computer-Based Learning Materials. Edited by H. Weinstock and A. Bork. IX, 285 pages. 1986.

Vol. 24: Database Machines. Modern Trends and Applications. Edited by A.K. Sood and A.H. Qureshi. VIII, 570 pages. 1986.

Vol. 25: Pyramidal Systems for Computer Vision. Edited by V. Cantoni and S. Levialdi. VIII, 392 pages. 1986.

Vol. 26: Modelling and Analysis in Arms Control. Edited by R. Avenhaus, R.K. Huber, J.D. Kettelle. VIII, 488 pages. 1986.